IN THE SHADOWS
OF WAR

IN THE
SHADOWS
OF
WAR

*

AN AMERICAN PILOT'S ODYSSEY
THROUGH OCCUPIED FRANCE
AND THE CAMPS OF NAZI GERMANY

THOMAS CHILDERS

Henry Holt and Company · New York

Henry Holt and Company, LLC
Publishers since 1866
115 West 18th Street
New York, New York 10011

Henry Holt® is a registered trademark of
Henry Holt and Company, LLC.

Library of Congress Cataloging-in-Publication Data
Childers, Thomas, 1946–
    In the shadows of war : an American pilot's odyssey through occupied
France and the camps of Nazi Germany / Thomas Childers.—1. ed.
        p.   cm.
    Includes bibliographical references and index.
    ISBN 0-8050-5752-8 (hc.)
    1. World War, 1939–1945—Underground movements—France—
Biography.   2. Florin, Colette.   3. Mulsant, Pierre.   4. Allen, Roy.
5. World War, 1939–1945—Prisoners and prisons, German.   6. Prisoners
of war—Germany—Biography.   I. Title.

D802.F8 C476 2003
740.53'44'0922—dc21   2002032343
[B]

Henry Holt books are available for special
promotions and premiums.
For details contact:
Director, Special Markets.

First Edition 2003

Designed by Paula Russell Szafranski

Maps designed by James Sinclair

Printed in the United States of America

1   3   5   7   9   10   8   6   4   2

For Colette Florin Loze and May Allen,
women of courage

Let us now sing the praises of famous men, our ancestors in their generations. The Lord apportioned to them great glory, his majesty from the beginning. There were those who ruled in their kingdoms, and made a name for themselves by their valor; . . . those who spoke in prophetic oracles; those who led the people by their counsels and their knowledge of the people's lore. . . . All these were honored in their generations, and were the pride of their times.

But of others there is no memory; they have perished as though they had never existed, they and their children after them. But these also were good men, whose deeds have not been forgotten. Their offspring will continue forever, and their glory will never be blotted out. Their bodies are buried in peace, but their name lives on generation after generation.

ECCLESIASTICUS 44:1–15

CONTENTS

• Contents •

PROLOGUE

In the summer of 1944, the climactic year of the Second World War, three young people, unknown to one another and separated by back ground and nationality, were hurled together by fate. Like millions of their generation who did not make policy or formulate strategy, they found themselves caught in a world convulsed by war. Colette Florin was a schoolteacher in a village just east of Paris. In the fall of 1942, she had stumbled into a secret life of resistance and danger. Pierre Mulsant was the son of a wealthy family from the south of France, a university graduate, and a veteran of the *débâcle* of 1940. Since 1943 he had also been an agent of the British secret service, operating a resistance organization in occupied France. Roy Allen was a star athlete from the Olney section of Philadelphia, recently married, who, before the war, had never ventured far from home. In the spring of 1944 he was a bomber pilot in the American Eighth Air Force, flying missions against targets in German-occupied Europe. Their paths were about to converge in a small village in France and their lives, and those of countless others like them, would be forever changed. This is their story.

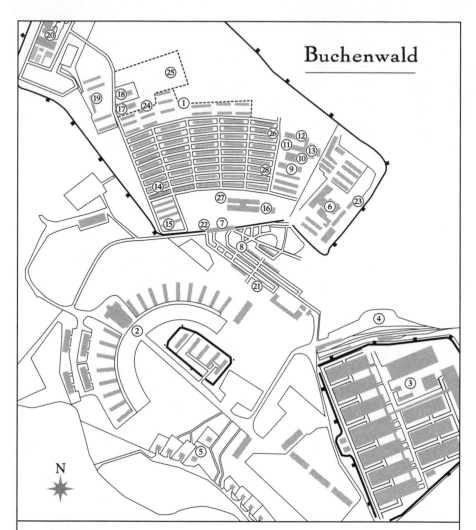

Buchenwald

1. Little Camp
2. SS Barracks
3. Gustloff Works
4. Train Depot
5. SS Leaders Settlement
6. German Munitions Works
7. Main Gate
8. Political Department
9. Kitchen
10. Coal Storage
11. Laundry and Bath
12. *Effektenkammer*
13. Disinfection Building
14. Compound for Soviet POWs
15. Prisoners' Canteen
16. Crematorium
17. Movie Theater
18. Prostitutes' Building
19. Infirmary
20. Animal Pens
21. Camp Headquarters
22. Bunker/Torture Chamber
23. Shooting Ranges Where Pierre and Charles Were Executed
24. Block 58
25. Tents
26. Block 45
27. *Appellplatz*
28. Block 17

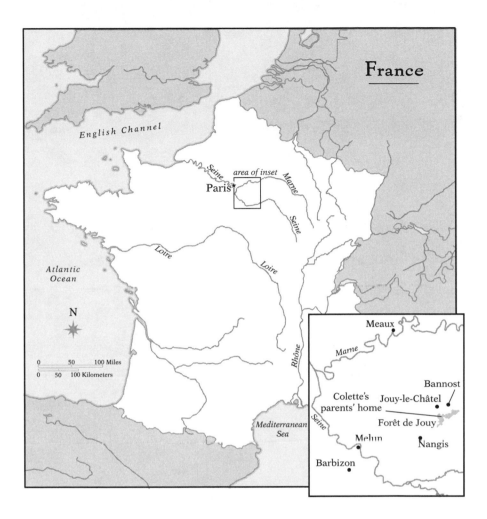

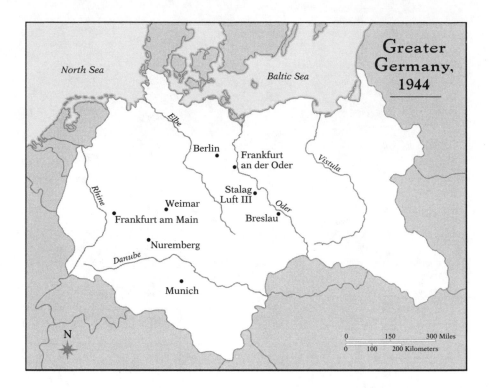

Greater Germany, 1944

North Sea

Baltic Sea

Elbe

Berlin

Frankfurt
an der Oder

Vistula

Rhine

Stalag
Luft III

Weimar

Oder

Frankfurt am Main

Breslau

Danube

Nuremberg

Munich

N

| 0 | 150 | 300 Miles |
| 0 | 100 | 200 Kilometers |

PART I

IN HARM'S WAY

CHAPTER 1

Operation *Amoureuse*

November 6–7, 1943

T he winter moon had risen beyond the woods that bordered the field to the east, bathing the frosty stubble with a sheen of brilliant light. Huddled in the shadows of the leafless trees, the reception committee waited in silence, straining to catch the first faint sound of the plane. Although she could not see him, Colette Florin knew that Monsieur Jonckheere was crouched beneath the giant poplar that towered above the others about one hundred meters in front of her. On beyond would be the others—Nenette Pivert, the daughter of the mayor, and Raymonde Lemaur, the girl from the farm, each spaced at 150-meter intervals along the tree line, waiting.

Her fingers were numb, but she clutched the flashlight tightly against her wool coat. She hoped that the flashlight, lashed to the end of a wooden garden stake, would work but she was not confident. The batteries were weak. It was impossible to get reliable batteries, and many times during the hours of waiting she had been tempted to test the light, shining it inside her coat, but she did not dare. Colette could not see her watch in the dark, but surely they had been in the field for two hours now, maybe three.

Everyone was nervous. For days, as the full moon approached, they had anticipated this operation, waiting anxiously for the word from London. Tonight it had come. *"Yvette est devenue amoureuse d'Henri."* Colette repeated the words soundlessly to herself, shifting her weight from one foot to the other, trying to coax some warmth into her legs. A chill breeze had sprung up, rattling the dark branches above her, and she wished she had some coffee, even the bitter acorn brew Madame Pivert had poured for them at the farm.

"Yvette est devenue amoureuse d'Henri." She could still hear the oddly formal, inflectionless voice, like a schoolmaster or a bored language instructor. Maybe the man who owned the voice was French Canadian or even English. She had stared, stupefied, at the small radio set beside the divan when she heard it. The volume was turned low and she had to strain, leaning forward from the edge of the divan, to hear above the rasping static. The Germans were jamming again, as they did every night during the BBC's broadcasts to France, but on this evening the cold November air was clear and dry and the interference was little more than a dull crackling. Above it she could hear the familiar opening notes of Beethoven's Fifth Symphony, notes that corresponded in Morse code to the letter "V"—V for Victory—and signaled the opening of the BBC's French language program. *"Ici Londres,"* intoned the faint French voice that spoke to them every night at 7:30 and 9:15. "Today is the one thousand two hundred forty-fifth day of the struggle of the French people for its liberation." She listened to the news and Pierre Dac's "Chronicles" of daily life and Jean Marin's commentary on events from the war, and each night she waited for the messages.

The messages came in the final moments of the broadcast, in a segment called *Les Français parlent aux Français.* *"Et maintenant voici quelques messages personnels,"* the announcer would begin, and dozens of personal communications for listeners in occupied France would follow. Sometimes these "personal messages" would be snatches of nursery rhymes, poetry, or well-known phrases from Molière, Balzac, or Jules Verne. Sometimes they consisted of apparently innocuous, nonsensical sentences: "Jacques needs a new pair of shoes"; "Uncle Octave is sending roses"; "The blue boat has sprung a leak." Some had no meaning whatsoever, intended only to confuse German counterintelligence, which would be listening as well, transcribing each message for further analysis at Abwehr headquarters in Paris. But others, she knew, were prearranged signals to specific resistance groups somewhere in occupied France, alerting them that some agreed-upon operation was under way—an arms drop, the arrival of a secret agent from Britain, the demolition of a railroad bridge. Most nights she found it difficult to wade through the steady stream of messages, but tonight was different.

In the jumble of monotonous messages, the one sentence with meaning for her—"Yvette has fallen in love with Henri"—rang out from the tiny set at the conclusion of the 7:30 broadcast. Amazed to hear the words she had long anticipated but never actually believed she would hear, she jumped to her feet. *"Je répète,"* the expressionless voice said, pausing for emphasis. Colette crouched again by the set, hardly daring to breathe. *"Yvette est devenue amoureuse d'Henri."* The message was for them, for the tiny group in Jouy. It alerted them to stand by. If it was repeated during the 9:15 program, they would know that the operation was under way, that a plane had already left its base somewhere in Britain, heading directly for them, for Jouy-le-Châtel. The "reception committee" would then spring into action, moving by bicycle or on foot through the fields and narrow country lanes to their rendezvous at Vimbré, Monsieur Pivert's farm four kilometers southwest of the village.

As she waited for the second broadcast, Colette found it hard to fathom that in the great sweep of a war raging all around the world, a message would be transmitted from London to a tiny group waiting sixty kilometers southeast of Paris. Jouy, after all, was an obscure village of barely one thousand inhabitants in the Département Seine-et-Marne, of no particular strategic importance, and the group, or *réseau*, led by the mayor, Robert Pivert, and Rémy Jonckheere, the captain of the local gendarmerie, was itself minuscule, consisting of no more than a dozen patriots. They had been active since the very beginning of the occupation, but until recently the group's activities had been confined to isolated acts of economic sabotage or hiding an occasional Allied aviator. They had little contact with other resistance organizations. That had all begun to change in June, when an agent of the Free French government in exile led by General Charles de Gaulle established contact with the group. Since then they had participated in several parachute drops at a farm in nearby St. Barthélemy, receiving weapons, radios, and even food. Tonight would be different, she thought. Tonight, if the second message came, a plane would actually land in the field at Vimbré.

So, when at the conclusion of the BBC's second French program, the radio voice repeated, "Yvette has fallen in love with Henri," Colette quickly closed up her apartment above the Ecole des Filles in Jouy and set out for Monsieur Pivert's farm. It was always dangerous to be out after the *couvre-feu,* the curfew. There were no longer Germans billeted in Jouy—the closest Wehrmacht units operated out of Provins, some twenty kilometers to the south—but the *Feldgendarmerie*, the German military police, might be out, enforcing the curfew, conducting spot-checks for papers, and as she hurried along the narrow road in the dark, she watched for any sign of their patrols.

She had seen them many times before, jumping from their trucks, fanning out across the fields, gray flecks against the yellow of the wheat. In the early days of the war, in the nightmare summer of 1940, the Germans had been everywhere, in the villages, on the roads, roaming across the fields in their gray-green tanks. The sky seemed filled with their planes, and no day passed without the sound of their boots echoing on the ancient stones of village squares. And so it remained for almost two years, years when it seemed that the war would never end and that the Germans were invincible.

On this night she saw no German patrols. The road to Vimbré was desolate, and the scattered farmhouses, huddled among the trees, stood shrouded in darkness. The high wispy clouds lifted, and the moon, a perfect silver orb, drifted high above the church in Jouy. The silent moonlit landscape was as bright as a pearl, clearly visible, she hoped, for the British pilot to follow.

They always came during the full moon, Monsieur Jonckheere told her. Flying low to avoid German radar, the pilot would navigate visually, following a trail of landmarks that would lead him to the field just outside Jouy. When Monsieur Jonckheere had first explained to them how the operation would work, that a small plane—he called it a Lysander—would touch down at Vimbré, Colette had been skeptical. She tried to visualize the English pilot in the cramped cockpit of a plane, a map spread out on his knees, searching the countryside for the one field where the reception committee waited. In the darkness the danger of a crash would be enormous, and even if a plane should land safely the sound of its engines would surely alert every German for miles. But Monsieur Jonckheere seemed confident. The Royal Air Force pilots had been putting Lysanders down in fields such as this since 1941. The landing site, he assured her, had been carefully selected by Monsieur Pivert and the Gaullist agent, and it met all the essential requirements for a clandestine landing strip. It was secluded, far from roads and railway lines, and the terrain was flat and firm, with no deep grass or gullies, no fences or hedges at the ends of the landing strip. The field would provide a clear L-shaped flare path for

Lysanders, which required a runway only six hundred meters long, with three hundred meters on the short tangent of the L. After Monsieur Pivert and the agent had selected the field, its location had been radioed to London, and an RAF plane had flown over to photograph it for analysis. Later the Gaullist agent reported that the landing site had been accepted and given the code name "Lulli."

Colette arrived at the farm within an hour of the broadcast. One by one the others trickled in, gathering in the large country kitchen of the house for Monsieur Pivert's briefing. To her surprise, Monsieur Pivert was not there. He had been called away on urgent business in the village, and Monsieur Jonckheere would assume leadership of the operation tonight. Colette, Monsieur Pivert's daughter Nenette, and Raymonde, one of the girls who worked at Vimbré, would join him to form the reception committee. Sitting beside them around the massive kitchen table were the three agents from the Gaullist underground organization who had been hidden at the farm for the past several days and who would be evacuated to England tonight.

Monsieur Jonckheere briefed them carefully. The *réseau* must expect the plane to arrive within the next two to three hours. He went over their jobs again, drew a diagram of the flare path they would form with their flashlights, where each would be stationed, and what to do once the plane landed. Each had a flashlight; each understood the signals. It was possible, even likely, that the Lysander would be delivering another agent, a wireless operator perhaps, but it was not clear. Colette agreed to hide him—or her, for it was not uncommon for the underground to employ women agents—in her rooms at the school. In October she had concealed two agents there for several days. They listened intently, studied the diagram, asked questions. Everyone was anxious to get to their stations in the field.

Standing now in the darkness at the edge of the glistening field, stamping her feet softly on the frozen ground, Colette was nervous, but she knew her job. When the plane approached, she would sprint out into the field to her designated spot. Then, at the signal from Monsieur Jonckheere, she would turn on the flashlight, beaming it directly into the sky above so that it could be seen by the plane but by no one on the ground. The others would do the same, rushing from the tree line to take up their positions in a straight line, 150 meters apart for a distance of approximately 700 meters. Two of the outgoing agents would stand at an angle 50 meters apart, the whole forming a gigantic flare path in the shape of the letter "L," the longer arm pointing downwind.

When the plane passed only two hundred meters above them, Monsieur Jonckheere, from his position at the base of the L, would flash the agreed-upon Morse signal up to the pilot, who would then beam down the prearranged response. The Lysander would bank sharply, landing into the wind. If all went smoothly, its wheels would bounce along the long arm to the angle, then turn and taxi back to the base of the L where Monsieur Jonckheere would be waiting. Its passengers, if it carried any, would scramble out and the three outbound agents, standing beside Monsieur Jonckheere, would scurry up the ladder into the cramped compartment just behind the pilot. The time on the ground would be less than four minutes.

Somewhere beyond the trees a dog barked, at first just an isolated yapping, then an insistent howl that hung in the air like distant thunder. She tried to determine the direction but it was impossible. Was it a German patrol? It was true that there were no Germans based in Jouy, no Milice—the Vichy paramilitary units—and the *Feldgendarmerie* only occasionally appeared in the village. But German patrols ranged over the entire region and you could never really predict where they might show up.

Or someone might have betrayed them. Some in the village were collaborators, enthusiastic supporters of Marshal Philippe Pétain and his pro-Nazi government in Vichy, others were merely opportunistic, seeking personal advantage from any situation, but most were merely inscrutable. In the larger towns and cities, the Germans hired informants—they called them *Vertrauensmänner* or *V-Männer*—and although she did not believe that there were such people in Jouy, denunciation, especially anonymous denunciation, was a constant threat.

The Germans had decreed that harboring or aiding Allied soldiers on the run—agents, downed aviators, or others seeking to evade the authorities—was a capital offense. If caught, men would be summarily executed; women would be deported to the camps in Germany, a fate that meant certain death. The Germans offered a reward of ten thousand francs for such denunciations, and posters to this effect had been plastered all over the village and run prominently in the regional press. Still, it had been a shock when it happened to her.

It was almost a year ago now, in December of 1942, when she hid the American aviator, and, to her own surprise, took her first step into the shadow world of resistance. Even now she could not fully explain why she had helped him, why she had stepped out of the crowd of farmers and tradesmen from the village who had surrounded the frightened American in the field where his chute had carried him. She had acted instinctively, had stepped forward on that blustery day when planes were falling all over the region, and said, "I will take care of him." No one had said a word. No one had come forward to join her, to offer help or advice. They had turned wordlessly away, people she had known all her life.

She had taken the aviator—his name was Bob Leasman and he was from a place called Atlanta, Georgia—to her parents' house in the Fôret de Jouy. It was not far away, and the American followed behind her as she pushed her bicycle along the winding forest path. Her parents, too, had watched the parachute fall beyond the trees, but they were startled when Colette led the airman into the garden. Of course she had done right, her father said, but they could not hide him at the house. Too many people had seen her with the aviator, and the Germans would come looking for him.

They considered hiding him in a cramped space under a rabbit hutch at the edge of the woods but decided that it was too exposed and too close to the house. A family of foreign workers—Yugoslavians—were cutting wood in the forest nearby, and Colette approached them, asking for their help. They were uneasy about the American, but the mother and father and their two children set to work, helping Colette arrange a stack of wood in a small clearing. With Bob Leasman looking on in bewilderment, they built a small hut, disguised to look like a simple woodpile. There was just enough space for him to climb inside. While the Yugoslavians finished up and Alice and Ange Florin stood lookout, Colette raced back to the house, returning with a blanket and an open bottle of champagne. She told Bob Leasman to wait there until the morning, when she would return with food. They would find another hiding place tomorrow. He seemed to understand. Then, working nervously, they closed the opening to the nest, adding a layer of chopped wood to the pile, and nothing could be seen of Bob Leasman.

During the late afternoon a German patrol swept through the area, just as her father had feared, searching the house and the outbuildings—and beneath the rabbit hutch. Then, taking up positions along the road, the soldiers fanned out, maybe one hundred of them, and disappeared into the woods. The Florins listened as the patrol moved through the underbrush until at last the sound of their tramping receded and the woods fell silent.

Early the next morning, Colette hurried along the trail to the wood-pile. From somewhere deeper in the woods, she could hear the saws and axes of the workers. As she approached the woodpile, everything seemed in order, untouched since the day before. But as she drew nearer, she could see that one side had toppled over, spilling out into the clearing. The opening had been uncovered, and Bob Leasman had vanished. Looking all around, she could find no trace of him. Had the Germans found him after all? Maybe he had not understood her. Maybe he did not trust her. Maybe he felt it was too dangerous there, that he had to move on and had set out on his own during the night. She hoped that he would turn up at the house later in the day.

But Bob Leasman did not return. Her father asked the Yugosla-vians what they knew, and, after much hesitation, they admitted that they had grown nervous after the Germans had searched the area and urged the aviator to leave. The soldiers had passed right by the wood-pile, hardly giving it a glance, but what if they came back with dogs? They would think that the workers had hidden the American. They had been lucky once, and they wanted to take no more chances. They told the aviator to leave.

A few days later Colette heard in the village that an American avia-tor had been caught by the Germans at a farm nearby. The American had hidden in a barn and gone to sleep, covering himself in the straw for warmth. But he had been unlucky. During the night one of the cows had gone into labor, lowing and bellowing so loudly that the farmer and his wife had come to the barn with their lanterns and dis-covered him. The farmer—Colette knew him well—had not known what to do. He did not want to turn the American over to the authori-ties but did not dare to shelter him either. It was simply too danger-ous. So while the family held the aviator at bay, someone—local rumor claimed it was a German-speaking Swiss who worked on the farm—had informed the Germans, and the American was arrested.

For days she thought about Bob Leasman, worried that he had been tortured, that he had talked, and that the trail would lead back to the forest house, to her parents, and to her. But in the days that fol-lowed, the Germans did not come. She was not questioned, and in time the incident apparently was forgotten. Then, three months later, in March, her father came to visit her. She lived in a small suite of rooms above the village school for girls, and although they saw each other regularly, his visit was a surprise.

10

Someone, he did not know who, had written an anonymous letter to the German authorities claiming that a certain Mademoiselle Fl . . . — the handwriting had been so poor that no one had been able to decipher the name—was hiding enemy aviators. The letter had been postmarked Maison Rouge, a village only a few kilometers to the south, and Gestapo agents, arriving there in a large black Citroën, had begun making inquiries with the local police. A secretary in the office of the mayor had alerted her father, and he had come to warn her. So far no one in Maison Rouge had been able to help the Gestapo, but if they expanded their investigation to Jouy, someone, he felt certain, would direct them to her.

Who had written such a letter? An angry neighbor? Her headmistress? She could not believe that of Mademoiselle Berthe. They had lived and worked alongside each other since they took up their posts at the École des Filles for the 1941 school year. They were both young women—Colette was barely twenty-one, Mademoiselle Berthe not much older—and together they constituted the entire faculty. They lived above the two classrooms of the little *école,* their respective apartments separated by a narrow corridor. At first they had been cordial—they took tea together in the headmistress's rooms and Colette was flattered when, shortly after their first meeting, the headmistress insisted on being called by her Christian name. But for reasons Colette did not understand, the relationship had cooled. They were still polite and professional in their interactions, but they were no longer close. Still, she did not believe that Mademoiselle Berthe had informed on her. Many people had seen her with the American on that day, others would have heard about it. It could have been anyone.

For days she dreaded every passing car, every knock at the door. Looking into the faces of the people in the *boulangerie* or at Mass, she would wonder: Could it be you? Each day brought new suspicions. She combed through her papers, hiding a diary she had kept in 1940 and letters she had written but had been unable to mail to an English family she had met during the last days before the German invasion. Monsieur Jonckheere tried to keep tabs on the investigation, but he could find out little. It was an agonizing time.

In the end, she had been lucky. The Gestapo had not pressed their investigation very far. They had not bothered to interrogate people in Jouy, and the incident faded. Still, she remained vigilant. The Vichy authorities, Monsieur Jonckheere warned her, tapped telephone lines and opened mail. You could never be too careful. In a village of almost a thousand inhabitants, only a handful were involved in resistance activities. She now found herself among them.

Colette thought of the others hidden beneath the trees at the edge of the field and wondered if they were as nervous as she was. She did not know the full extent of the group's activities or the names of others in the area who were involved or how the circle of patriots in Jouy was linked to groups—*réseaux*—beyond the village. Only Messieurs Pivert and Jonckheere knew these things, and they did not discuss them with her. They had been active in the resistance since the beginning, living with these dangers since the Germans arrived in 1940.

In the first confusing days of that dismal summer she was a student, boarding at the school in Melun, preparing for her exams. They were scheduled for the end of June, and all the girls were excited. Soon they would be qualified as teachers, ready to begin their careers, and few paid attention to the reports in the papers, stories speculating about a German attack in the west. When war had been declared the previous September and Poland had fallen in just a matter of weeks, she had been frightened, and everyone seemed to be preparing for an onslaught against France. But time passed, and the Germans did not come, and although there was constant talk of rationing and civil defense measures in the cities and sometimes even rumors of enemy parachutists and air raids, the war had no real meaning to her. She read the headlines and listened when she could to the news bulletins, but the war—the papers called it *drôle de guerre*, "the strange war"— seemed remote.

At the school no one seemed overly concerned when the radio brought the first news of the long anticipated German attack in the west. It was a bright, clear day in May, in a spring such as the poets write about, and the voice of Paul Reynaud, the premier of France, crackling through the radio in her tiny room sounded supremely confident. Hitler had waited too long. He had missed his chance to smash the west. Now all was prepared for the defense of France. The army was mobilized, Gen. Maurice-Gustave Gamelin, the commander of French forces, assured the public, and the allies of France stood ready. In those splendid spring days her father, too, spoke with confidence about the impending battle. He was a much-decorated veteran of the Great War, wounded at Verdun, and he understood these military matters. He knew how to interpret the daily communiqués from General Headquarters, and the situation, as he saw it, seemed well in hand.

Throughout the warm days of early May, while she hurried to class and studied for her exams, military vehicles rumbled through the streets of Melun, streaming north toward Paris, fifty kilometers away, and toward the frontier beyond. It was reassuring to see them, imposing staff cars with motorcycle escorts, trucks bulging with soldiers, motorized artillery pieces, and even an occasional tank, all being thrown into the coming battle. News was meager—the Germans had attacked in Holland on May 10, had seized Maastricht and Arnhem by the second day of the offensive, and German parachutists were reported over Rotterdam—but the communiqués from General Headquarters remained calm and the premier upbeat, positive in his evaluation of the situation. Havas, the official news agency, reported with confidence: "The French High Command in Belgium has built a wall which will stop the German steamroller." A fierce battle was raging in the Low Countries, but the news reports gave few details, and she was not worried. Her math exam loomed before her.

But just a few days later a cryptic bulletin from the front tersely acknowledged that enemy troops had reached the river Meuse from Liège to Namur to Sedan in northeastern France. That, she realized with a shock, meant that the Germans had already overrun almost all of Belgium! In his radio addresses, aired nightly at 11:30, Monsieur Reynaud maintained his soothing, confident tone. He had replaced Gamelin with Gen. Maxime Weygand and had brought Marshal Pétain, the ancient hero of Verdun, into the government. That boded well, her father believed, but the situation was nonetheless troubling.

Classmates returning from Paris brought more unsettling news. Wild rumors abounded in the restaurants and cafés—German paratroopers had landed in the suburbs, German planes had bombed the city, German spies were everywhere. Her friends confirmed that the police, now armed with machine pistols, were stopping pedestrians on the streets for identity checks, and some of the papers hinted that a communist uprising was imminent. By the end of May, the city's newspapers were reduced to a single sheet, printed on both sides, and hard news was increasingly difficult to come by. If the papers revealed little about the military situation, they did carry somber announcements that rationing on some items—sugar and bread, for a start—would go into effect at the beginning of June, and other stringent economic measures would follow. Almost every night air-raid sirens wailed over the darkened city. The children of Paris were being evacuated in convoys, accompanied by their teachers. Sandbags had appeared around government buildings and cultural monuments, and all around the outskirts of the city soldiers were digging trenches. Paris, it seemed clear, was preparing for an attack.

Most unsettling were the refugees. They began appearing in the streets of Melun in mid-May. At first they were almost all Belgians, but soon they were joined by others, French citizens from the *départements* of the northeast fleeing the advancing Germans. By early June the battle of France had begun, and the streets were choked with refugees. They poured through the town, mattresses strapped to the roofs of their motorcars, some in horse-drawn wagons, some on bicycle. Some trudged along the roadways pushing farm carts, wheelbarrows, and even baby carriages brimming with jumbled belongings.

The school authorities insisted that the exams would take place on schedule, but it was impossible for Colette to concentrate. Although Monsieur Reynaud tried to stem the mounting tide of panic, exhorting the nation to resistance, nothing could conceal the contagious unspoken fear that a catastrophe had occurred at the front. Like her classmates, Colette clung to the conviction that the army would rally, that another "miracle on Marne" would save France, just as in the Great War, but the flow of refugees outside her window grew with each passing day, and the swelling torrent of civilian conveyances now swept along with it the flotsam and jetsam of the disintegrating French army.

Her exams were set to begin on June 11, but when Colette awoke on that morning, a dense, foul-smelling haze hung over Melun. Soot collected in the windowsills and the air itself seemed greasy. A soldier passing through the congested streets told her that fires had been started to cover the evacuation of Paris, but others claimed the Germans had bombed the petroleum depots of Rouen. By 10:30, the streets were black with frantic soldiers and civilians streaming southward across the Seine. The school authorities abandoned any pretense of continuing and told the students to pack and get back to their families as quickly as possible.

Everyone at the school clamored for telephones and the circuits jammed and the lines in some areas were down. She was afraid she would never get through, but she reached her father, and late in the day a car arrived at the school for her, a military car arranged by her father. She still did not know how he managed to secure a motorcar that dreadful day or how the driver, a soldier from her village, fought through the chaos on the roads. Every artery from the *route nationale* to the small country lanes and byways was clogged with vehicles of every kind. Some forty kilometers east of Melun, soldiers swarmed through the usually peaceful streets of Jouy, and the ordinarily deserted dirt roads that led from the village through the woods to her parents' house were cluttered with military vehicles and equipment, much of it abandoned by the roadside. It was what the army called the *"train des équipages,"* the transportation units that ferry troops and supplies to the front. Today, her father remarked, the front had come to them.

For two days, while German planes roared overhead, firing occasionally into the woods nearby, they waited anxiously for word that the front had held. They exchanged rumors with the soldiers bivouacked all around them, and they listened to Monsieur Reynaud's broadcasts, telling of the government's evacuation of Paris, of his plea to the American president for immediate aid and his determination to continue the fight. She still believed that there would be a heroic stand, but when the soldiers began to withdraw toward Orléans, her father said that it was time to leave. Nothing now stood between them and the onrushing Germans.

Several retreating soldiers helped them pack the family's belongings into a cart, and on the morning of June 14, after a night of sporadic shelling, the Florins closed up the house and joined the ragged exodus. A family from a neighboring farm wanted to travel with them, and at dawn her older brother, André, and the farmer's two sons started with the heavily laden horse-drawn carts, while her father rode ahead on a motorcycle to scout the route. Colette, her mother, and her younger brother, René, climbed into the farmer's automobile—it was an immaculately polished Matford—with him and his wife, and they too set out.

As their little caravan emerged from the country lane that led through the woods toward the route south, they found themselves swept up in the vast retreat. The endless file of military vehicles inched along the crowded road, and soldiers, some riding bicycles, some hanging from the sides of trucks, some stumbling through the fields in no discernible formation, swarmed like gnats. Caught in the midst of the convoy, a ragtag collection of horse-drawn carts, piled high with lamps, tables, carpets, and crockery, straggled along. Automobiles bulging with battered luggage, radio consoles, and birdcages, were joined by taxis, fire engines, hearses, and a handful of county buses brimming with dazed, defeated people. Beside the endless column of vehicles, exhausted, dusty figures of every age and description toiled along on foot, straining under their misshapen bundles, tugging vendor's carts, perambulators, and children's wagons loaded with household items. Some farmers had even brought along their cows, which wandered through the adjacent fields, their tongues lolling in the oppressive heat. Abandoned steamer trunks spewing clothes, tattered mattresses, shards of shattered dishes, discarded toys, and broken bottles littered the roadside, and the stench of dung and diesel hung like a pall over the scene.

Dodging through the serpentine column on his motorcycle, Colette's father drove on ahead of them. He knew the back roads of the province and hoped to find a route across the rivers Seine and Yonne. Then together they would move to the southwest toward the Loire, where the army would regroup for a final stand. It was already mid-afternoon before he returned to find them. The soldiers were going to blow the bridges over the Seine at around four o'clock, he had learned, but the refugees could make it across at Bray. From there it was not far to the Yonne. Monsieur Florin would go on ahead, and if he did not return again with a change of plans, he would be waiting for them at the bridge over the Yonne in Courlon.

But progress during the long hot afternoon was agonizingly slow. Time and again they were forced to the side of the road to make way for military traffic, and the horses, straining to pull the heavily laden carts, needed to rest. Colette and her mother pleaded with the farmer not to stop before they were all safely across the bridges, but he would not listen. The horses would never make it in this heat, he insisted, and so, while the column ground slowly by, the farmer pulled their automobile and carts to the side of the road and they rested. When they resumed their journey, André and the farmer's sons stayed behind to secure the carts and tend to the animals. Colette and her mother were uneasy, but the farmer assured them that the boys and the carts would follow. The carts would catch up with them at Courlon, if not before. It took hours to reach Bray-sur-Seine, less than one hundred kilometers from Jouy, and they did not cross over the river until late in the afternoon. The carts were nowhere in sight.

When at last they arrived in Courlon, the town was jammed with refugees and they could not find Monsieur Florin. While the others stayed with the car on the outskirts of town, Colette pushed through the throng of exhausted, desperate people in the direction of the town square. There, in the lengthening shadow of the ancient stone church and the war memorial, she came upon the community bulletin board of the Hôtel de Ville. A crowd of anxious refugees jostled to read the dozens of handwritten notices affixed to the board, plaintive messages from family members separated in the exodus, notices of items lost—treasured heirlooms that had fallen from carts or the roofs of cars—and, most terrifying, the pleas of anguished parents: "Searching for Antoine Thébaud, age five, lost in the vicinity of Courlon, June 10. Write Mme. Thébaud, Post Office, La Rochelle." "M. Dupuy seeks news of his daughters, Hélène and Gabrielle, four and seven years old, lost near here, June 8." She could hardly bear to read them. As she scanned the messages, she saw the name Ange Florin and, grabbing the note, she quickly read the few scribbled lines of her father's writing. He was going on to Pont-sur-Yonne, just a few kilometers away, where a bridge over the river was still intact. They should follow as soon as possible. He would wait.

It was a relief to find the note, and they soon rejoined the column heading for Pont-sur-Yonne. But Colette was troubled. Squeezed between them in the stifling backseat, René kept peering out the rear window, asking about the carts, about his brother André. Her mother tried to reassure him, but they had been on the road for less than a day, and already they had lost contact not only with Monsieur Florin but with André as well.

It was early evening when the column reached Pont-sur-Yonne. As the long line of vehicles crept toward the town, Colette was relieved to see the bridge still standing. Her father would probably be waiting just on the other side or at the church square, where refugees congregated. Beyond the Yonne they would wait for André and the carts and then, perhaps in the morning, continue on.

From the back of the queue Colette watched the long column laboring across the bridge. Suddenly she saw dark figures amid the trucks and automobiles and carts stop and turn. They were pointing to the eastern horizon, to a spot high above her head. Then she heard the first deep droning of the engines, and the figures on the bridge scrambled frantically for cover. For an instant the purple silhouette of the bridge and the blacked-out town beyond seemed suspended in

17

time. Then a wild, ghastly whistling cut the air. Like a bolt of summer lightning, a flash of white-orange flame shot into the dusky sky above the town, and even before the rumble of the first concussion rolled across the river, she felt the force of a terrible tremor jolt the car.

Gaping through the dusty windshield, Colette caught a fleeting glimpse of planes knifing through the early evening sky, diving one after another over the town. Whirling clouds of black smoke billowed high above the burning buildings, and geysers of silver spray erupted from the river all around the bridge. The very ground seemed to shift in a series of bone-jarring shudders, and just ahead of her, an earsplitting shock, then another, and another hurled everything—carts, horses, furniture—into the air. Lurching violently, the car scudded across the road, almost flipping over. A hail of falling debris pounded the roof and hood, and the world seemed to go black all around them.

Then, as suddenly as it had begun, the attack was over. Muffled explosions still rocked the town, but the terrible screeching in the sky stopped. As she lay huddled against René and her mother, the only sounds Colette could hear were the crackling of flames and the wailing of children.

Miraculously, they had not been hit. They crawled from the car and stumbled into the drifting haze. All around them mangled vehicles were strewn across the narrow roadway, and bodies, singed the color of carbon, lay smoldering in the wreckage. A farmer's cart had taken a direct hit just as it turned onto the bridge, and splintered furniture, shredded clothing, stray shoes, and farm tools were scattered all across the road. A horse, a great muscular bay, lay twisted grotesquely on its back. It was ripped open from the neck to the haunches, its gaping underside heaving entrails onto the slippery stones of the bridge. A soldier, his soot-streaked face glistening with blood, wandered aimlessly among the carts, muttering, pleading for help. Across the shattered remains of a demolished cart, a stark white wedding dress hung forlornly, its satin sashes glimmering in the yellow light of the burning bridge.

Sidestepping the wounded and the wreckage all around them, Colette, René, and their mother raced across the bridge, but in the chaos on the other side of the river, they could find no trace of Colette's father. He was not at the church or the town square, filled now with a throng of terrified refugees, and in the gathering darkness it was useless to search the crowded streets. Unsure of what to do, they recrossed the bridge and returned to the car. The bridge had sustained only minor damage and refugees were still straggling across. It would be some time before it was cleared for vehicles of any sort. They decided to pull the car to the side of the road and wait for the carts. Maybe her father would find them in the morning. All through the night, as they tried to rest, refugees continued to file past, dark figures plodding through the gloom on the route south.

At dawn the planes returned, firing into the woods beyond the town, strafing the column of refugees somewhere ahead. Sporadic shelling continued as the sun rose higher, but André and the carts did not arrive. Someone in the passing crowd yelled out that German tanks had been spotted crossing the wheat fields behind them, closing in on the town. While they debated what to do, a terrific blast shook the road before them, showering the column with bits of plaster, brick, and stone. "It's the bridge," a voice wailed above the din. "They've blown up the bridge!" Rushing forward with the crowd, Colette saw through the drifting smoke the buttresses of the bridge crumble into the roiling waters below. She did not know whether the French soldiers had blown the bridge or German planes had hit it. It made no difference. There would be no crossing of the river here.

They had no choice now but to push on to Sens, twenty kilometers to the southeast, before the bridge there was destroyed. But the farmer did not want to go on. What was the use? Even if they made it across the Yonne, he argued, the boys would never catch up. The carts, the furniture, everything, would be lost. It was useless, his wife agreed. Colette and her mother pleaded, begging them to continue. Surely there could be no turning back now, not into the onrushing German panzers. With great reluctance, the farmer agreed to go as far as Sens.

But as the procession reached the entrance to the town, he balked again. Sens was a sizable town and the streets were hopelessly clogged with carts, stranded automobiles, and refugees. Smoke was rising from the direction of the bridge, and German planes circled ominously overhead. The farmer would go no farther. Colette, René, and Madame Florin climbed out of the car, and, clutching their small valises, started for the bridge. Everywhere the buildings bristled with soldiers, their guns protruding from the windows and doorways. Machine gun teams had placed their weapons on rooftops, ready for the advancing Germans. The soldiers tried to maintain order, to direct the stream of frantic refugees surging through the streets. But everyone knew that the soldiers were ready to blow the bridge, and in near panic the crowd rushed forward.

Swept along in the maelstrom, the Florins fought their way through the maze of carts, moving as fast as they could. Along the way, they had to abandon their bags, and when they crossed the bridge and were south of the river and could at last stop, a wave of despair washed over them. They had made it across the Seine and the Yonne, but they were now utterly alone. They had lost the cart with all their possessions, they had lost their bags, and, with the Loire still over a hundred kilometers away, they were now on foot. Worst of all, Colette thought, they were separated from her father and from André. Sitting at the side of the road, her mother dissolved in tears of exhaustion and strain.

The procession plodded on to the southwest, toward the Loire, and the Florins fell in with the column. They walked without stopping through the long afternoon and into the evening. There was heavy fighting behind them in Sens. The sky over the town flickered red from the explosions and the deep thumping of the detonations followed them for hours. Toward evening, wondering what they would eat and where they would pass the night, they stumbled across a family they knew from Chenoise, a small village near Jouy. The people were making their way to Montargis, in the west, where they had relatives, and they asked the Florins to join them. They shared their meager food, and together the two families walked on through the night.

Just after dawn the column came to a halt. All during the night, military vehicles had sped along the road in the direction of Sens, forcing the refugees to stop and move aside for them. As Colette stumbled on, half asleep on her feet, word passed along the line that the road to Montargis was closed. The Germans, someone said, were in front of them. They were trapped. The carts ahead of them began to edge to the side of the road, and a column of trucks spearheaded by motorcycles and armored cars roared toward them. She stood at the edge of an oat field as the column slowed to pass. The vehicles were gray and dusty and each of the motorcycles sported a small red pennant with a black swastika at the center. The column did not stop but rumbled on to the east, uninterested in these civilians. From the open trucks, smiling soldiers waved and tossed chocolates to the refugees. It was Sunday, June 16, 1940, and she had seen her first Germans.

For Colette the evacuation was over. Those who had not reached the Loire were turned back, ordered to return to their homes. The Germans were in control. With no news of her father or of André, with no cart or automobile or bicycle, with no food or additional clothing, the Florins began the long walk back to the forest house. They trudged along the road north for another five days, days of fear and hunger and surprising nighttime cold, scrounging for potatoes in the fields, sleeping in barns or abandoned houses or simply on the side of the road. Many of the villages along the way had been demolished, their houses burned, their streets littered with the scorched debris of battle. The larger towns were swamped with refugees, but the shops, the cafés, the *boulangeries* were closed, their shutters drawn tightly. Animal carcasses of all sorts—horses, cows, sheep, pigs—lay rotting on the side of the road, and the fields of trampled yellow wheat were dotted with makeshift crosses, many bearing simple inscriptions: "Here lie seven French soldiers" or "Unknown French soldier" or "*Mort pour la France*"—"Died for France."

Arriving home on June 21, exhausted and filthy, they found the forest house empty but untouched. All that remained of their possessions were a few plates and spoons, but it was good to see the old familiar rooms. Best of all, standing at the edge of the small ravaged garden in back, was André. After they became separated on the road, André told them, he and the farmer's sons had abandoned the cart in a village beyond the Yonne, hiding it in an empty barn. From there he and one of the boys had commandeered a motorcycle and gone as far as Vichy before they were turned back by the Germans. He had no word of his father.

It would be a month before they heard from him. Then in late July a letter arrived from Auch, in the south. He was safe, but sick with worry about them. He had searched for them on the road, in Sens and beyond, but finally had been forced on to the south by the German advance. Beyond the Loire he joined officers and men from a unit of the Paris National Guard who were trying to regroup for a final stand, but then, on June 26, the armistice had come and the Germans would allow no one to cross their lines. Since then he had worked on a farm near Bordeaux and would return home as soon as it was possible.

In spite of the rout they had witnessed on the road, the Florins were shocked by the armistice. They had no radio in the forest house and there were no newspapers, but they learned of France's surrender from the farmer with whom they had begun the evacuation. The Germans had seized his car, the much-cherished Matford, on the road outside Sens, and he and his wife had bicycled back to Jouy. He brought news of the armistice on that bicycle, and the report, no less stunning, that a German flag now flew from the church tower in the village.

Standing in the cold moonlight at the edge of Monsieur Pivert's field three years later, it still seemed incomprehensible to Colette. France, which had withstood four years of death and privation in the Great War and which in 1940 possessed, they had been assured, Europe's strongest army and bravest men, had fallen in just six weeks. It was, as everyone called it now, *le débâcle.* How had they allowed it to come to this, the Reynauds and Gamelins and Weygands? Her father, who returned to Jouy in August 1940, had pinned great hopes on Marshal Pétain, but he was soon enraged by the actions of his old commander. Pétain, the "Savior," the "Father of France," and the others in the new Vichy regime had soiled the honor of the country with their surrender and betrayed the people with their collaboration. Thinking back on those horrible humiliating days, as she had done so often in the bitter years of the occupation, she realized how naïve she had been, how full of trust. She had believed the words of the newspapers and the radio commentaries and the "great men." Now, as her father said to her, the time had come "for the French of the lowest classes to expiate the sins of the highest."

At first it was just a faint murmuring beyond the trees, so soft and indistinct Colette was not sure she had heard it. The wind had fallen and a deep hush had settled over the field. For hours she had strained to catch even the faintest hint of the plane's motor, but there had been nothing. Much earlier a train, probably the last eastbound Melun-Provins local, had chugged along the tracks to the south, but since then only the barking dog and the intermittent calling of two owls had broken the enveloping silence. She had almost given up, but now she could hear a distant droning, which grew steadily louder, dissolving into the distinct throbbing of an engine. With her heart pounding, Colette stepped through the frozen underbrush to the edge of the tree line and looked up, scanning the horizon.

The moon was high above the trees, arcing to the west, and against the bright, luminescent sky, the shape of a small black plane emerged. It flew low to the ground, no more than two hundred meters high she guessed, and the roar of its engine as it approached the field was almost deafening. Dark forms emerged from the tree line, racing into the field, and Colette, her legs stiff from the long standing in the bitter cold, bolted out into the moonlight. Pools of mist hung in patches over the low ground, and she stumbled, almost losing her flashlight, as she took up her position. Several hundred meters in front of her, a sliver of red light, from her vantage point no more than a dim crimson halo, beamed upward, and as the plane roared directly over them, it blinked a crisp response.

The plane disappeared beyond the trees in the direction of Jouy, but in a moment it banked and swung back toward them. Aligning herself with Monsieur Jonckheere's red light, Colette switched on her flashlight and held it high above her head. As the small plane dropped, coming in low over the trees, heading directly for them, its landing lights suddenly blazed in the dark, illuminating a swath of glittering frozen field. The whining of its engine was stunningly loud as the Lysander touched down, bounced along the flare path, then turned and taxied back toward the red light.

When the plane came to a halt, idling beside Monsieur Jonckheere, the pilot extinguished its landing lights, and in the sudden darkness, Colette could just make out the scurrying of figures under its wings. A single person, carrying, she thought, a small suitcase, had climbed over the side of the plane and others, the outbound Gaullists, scrambled quickly up the ladder and into the rear cockpit. Colette rushed toward the plane, joining Raymonde and Nenette to get a closer look. For an instant she could see the pilot with stunning clarity. A look of surprise shot across his face as he peered out into the field to find three women converging on the plane. He raised his hand to wave, and the women, as startled as he, waved back. Then, sliding the forward canopy shut, he opened up the throttle. Bits of debris blew wildly in the prop wash, and the thundering of the engine boomed across the field. Colette and the others stepped back, and the Lysander lurched forward, rumbling across the field in the darkness. Within seconds it lifted off, climbed steeply over Vimbré, and vanished into the night.

Colette stood for a moment in stunned silence, listening as the drone of the plane receded and the haunting stillness returned. The Lysander had been on the ground for only a matter of moments, just as Monsieur Pivert had predicted, but it had seemed impossibly long to her. Surely every German in the entire area had heard it and would be bearing down on them now. Colette switched off her light. For tonight her part of the mission was over. She began walking slowly back toward the tree line, the frozen stubble crunching beneath her feet. She had done her job. Now she was a *résistante*. There would be more jobs for her, she knew, more nights such as this.

As she approached the trees, an almost overpowering, primitive impulse to run, to flee, surged within her. It was essential to be careful now, to be alert for patrols and proceed cautiously. But in the darkness of the woods her resolve melted. Quickening her pace, she headed for the tractor path that would take her back to Jouy. In the open field again, she broke into a trot and finally, abandoning all restraint, she tore headlong down the path. It was almost dawn when Colette Florin reached her apartment over the school in the village. She had run all the way.

CHAPTER 2

"Specially Employed"

March 3–4, 1944

Pierre Mulsant pulled the straps of his parachute harness snugly around his legs, adjusting them as best he could. The flying suit, stretched tautly over his coat, was uncomfortably bulky, and he flexed his shoulders trying to find a comfortable position on the ribbed metal floor. In the darkness of the plane, he fingered a small package attached to his parachute rigging. It was bound up tightly so that it would not burst on impact, spewing the clothing, the money, the revolver onto the field.

A low wind whistled through the plane, seeping into the fuselage from the unsealed turrets and hatches, but their altitude was low—no more than one thousand feet—and the cold was bearable. Slumped on the floor just across the exit hatch from him, Charles, his wireless operator, appeared to be dozing. It was difficult to hear over the whining of the wind and the deep droning of the engines, and neither man felt inclined to talk much anyway. They had ridden in silence for almost three hours, glancing occasionally at each other in the murk. There were no windows in the fuselage, and when the plane left the English coast, the already dim interior lights were extinguished and they sat in utter darkness. From time to time Pierre could sense the plane shifting course and altitude as it made its way across the Channel, rumbling toward their destination in a farmer's field somewhere in occupied France.

At intervals, the dark form of the dispatcher, an RAF sergeant, jostled through the tangle of straps and packs, his way illuminated by a tiny pocket flashlight. Above the throbbing of the engines, he updated them on their progress, checked the equipment, and offered them biscuits and tea from a thermos. He examined the rubber-coated packages containing the all-important wireless sets, inspecting their rigging. "Won't be long now, mates," he shouted on his last check.

Pierre was anxious to get on with it. He had suffered through the long tense afternoon at the air station, waiting for the final weather report, for the "all clear" to proceed. The old hands called these ago-nizing hours of waiting "being crucified," and Pierre understood why. While they sipped tea in a hut near the flight line, F-Section's "con-ducting officer," who had delivered them to the field, went through the final checks of their clothing, making sure that their pockets con-tained no English coins, no London theater tickets, no laundry stubs bearing English addresses. He checked their false identity papers, labor cards, and various ration books they would need on the ground. Then finally, in the gathering twilight, the word had come—the weather would hold; everything was ready. They struggled into their parachute harnesses, said their good-byes, the conducting officer call-ing out, as was the custom, "Merde," and Pierre responding "Merde."

As they walked out to the waiting plane, he was disappointed to see that it was not a Whitley. In training he had jumped from a Whitley, and he was familiar with the aircraft. But on this night the aircraft waiting on the revetment was a silver four-engine Halifax. He had seen these planes at the aerodrome at Ringway during parachute training, but had never been inside one. The Halifax was originally designed as a heavy bomber but was being gradually phased out by Bomber Command, replaced by the gigantic Lancasters he had heard so often in the dark skies over France. Some Halifaxes had been modi-fied for covert operations, and SOE—the Special Operations Execu-tive—used them for delivering "bods," as the staff sardonically called the agents, to the Continent.

As he climbed awkwardly through the side hatch into the cramped fuselage, he was relieved to find that the interior structure bore a striking resemblance to the Whitley. A hole, covered over by retractable planking, had been cut in the floor just aft of the pilot's compartment. When the time came, the dispatcher would attach static lines to their parachutes to ensure automatic opening, remove the planking, and at his signal, they would drop, one after the other, through the hole. To minimize the danger of being seen by the Germans, the jump would be made from an altitude of no more than five hundred feet, and the chute would open quickly, deploying only seconds before they reached the ground. On a relatively still night, no more than fifteen seconds should elapse between slipping from the hatch and standing on the ground.

The jump would be only the beginning of his worries. He hoped that the pilot could locate the field in the blacked-out French landscape, that the reception committee was waiting there, that they had made the necessary preparations and maintained security. He did not know who was handling the reception, but he hoped it would be their SOE successors in the Troyes organization. He hoped it would not be the Free French, the Gaullists. They were great patriots and he respected them, but their security, he believed, was bad.

"Leveling off at six hundred feet," the dispatcher called out over his shoulder. In a matter of minutes he would fling himself out of a British aircraft into the cold moonlit sky and would arrive on the soil of France with a new identity, a new life. Before the war, he had studied law in Paris, served honorably as an officer in the French army in 1939–40, and been discharged after the armistice. Although his family owned a large textile factory in Lyon that employed fifteen hundred workers and produced upholstery and seats for Renault and Citroën, he had chosen not to return there or to the family chateau at Villefranche-sur-Saône. Instead he settled in Troyes and assumed the management of his father-in-law's prosperous timber and construction business. Like so many others, he had chafed under the German occupation, doing what he could to help friends in trouble with the authorities, and on several occasions he had helped find shelter for patriots on the run from the Germans or their Vichy collaborators. But he had done little in an organized way. Then everything changed. A surprising invitation came from his friend Octave Simon. They had done their military service together but had not been in touch for some time. Octave was twenty-nine, his own age, a talented sculptor with a budding reputation, and he was having a large dinner party in his Paris studio. He wanted Pierre to come.

The party was as festive as an evening could be in February 1943. The ornate lift in the lobby, deprived of electricity, no longer worked and the guests climbed the darkened stairs in the numbing cold. But the crowded, unheated rooms, lit by flickering candles and sparkling with more wine than Pierre had seen since before the war, bubbled with sophisticated talk about the Parisian art scene, the museums, the theater, anything but the war. Steering Pierre to an alcove at the edge of the loud, bustling room, Octave made the usual small talk, inquiring about his family, his contacts in Troyes, their old army friends. Smiling broadly and nodding pleasantly to other guests as they sauntered by, his manner was casual, confident, as if he were analyzing the races at Longchamp. He seemed gay and absorbed in his various sculpting projects, but something, Pierre could tell, was on his mind.

His art was coming along nicely, Octave said, but he was doing some other work these days, special work. He thought Pierre might be interested. Since the armistice he had been involved in underground activities of one sort or another. Now he worked for friends across the Channel—"specially employed," they called it—and they needed someone they could trust in Troyes, someone well connected, who knew the town and the area. He wanted to suggest his old army comrade Pierre Mulsant. It was important work, Octave said, and dangerous. He could not say more on this evening, but wondered if his old comrade was interested. Pierre had known in an instant that he would do it. He did not know what would be required of him, but he did not hesitate. They could count on him, he replied, and Octave, smiling, told him that someone, a friend, would be in touch.

Shortly thereafter, in the bleak days of early March, Octave arrived in Troyes with a man he introduced as Émile Garry. At that meeting, he explained that they worked for a British underground organization. He was vague about the name, sometimes referring to it as the Intelligence Service, sometimes simply as the War Office. The name was not important. This organization operated a network of groups, circuits, in occupied France. They were not spies, Garry emphasized, gathering intelligence and passing it on to the Allies. No, theirs was a *"mission de combat"*: to recruit patriots and train them for operations behind German lines, to conduct sabotage, and to aid in any way possible the coming Allied invasion of northern Europe. The groups communicated directly with headquarters in England via wireless and received weapons, explosives, and other necessary supplies by airdrops to carefully selected landing grounds. Garry ran a small circuit south of Paris, code-named **CINEMA**, and he needed to find a secure landing ground near Troyes and someone to arrange a reception committee. Pierre agreed to help, and they set to work at once. Within days, both a secure landing ground and a handful of reliable friends had been found.

Then in April, as the rain-soaked spring began and the BBC broadcast news of Allied advances in Sicily and a mounting German catastrophe on the eastern front, Garry brought a British agent to Pierre in Troyes. The agent's operational name was Germain and he had just been dropped into the area along with his wireless/transmitter (W/T) operator, Honoré. Germain was a savvy, experienced agent on his third mission to France, and he exuded a quiet confidence in his ability. Pierre liked him at once. His mission was to establish a new circuit around Troyes and to conduct a campaign of sabotage against selected targets in the area. He needed a lieutenant, someone he could trust. Pierre Mulsant, he understood, was the man for the job.

Pierre began by securing a small flat for Honoré on the outskirts of Troyes and a vacant house in another suburb for Germain's arms depot. He also found a room in the city where Germain could live and several safe houses where they could go in an emergency and from which Honoré could make his wireless transmissions. Germain impressed upon him the need for tight security. He had seen too many agents fall into the hands of the Gestapo, too many circuits blown through failure to observe the basic rules of security.

Pierre's father-in-law's timber firm was an ideal cover for the circuit's activities. Most agents, Germain pointed out, were forced to move about by bicycle, but because of the business, Pierre had a number of lorries at his disposal and possessed the necessary papers to travel from town to town. He could maintain contacts with farmers and tradesmen throughout the region and could circulate freely on the roads, making deliveries of lumber and construction supplies. He could even arrange for a lorry and a reliable driver, the mechanic Frascati who worked for the business, to make runs into Paris.

Proceeding with great caution, they recruited others—drivers, mechanics, farmers, schoolteachers, restaurateurs, bakers—in Troyes and the surrounding villages. These recruits would serve as "letter boxes" and form the reception committees, provide barns, garages, and abandoned cottages where the circuit's munitions could be concealed. Using the telephone or the mail to communicate was out of the question. The *boîte aux lettres* were individuals willing to receive messages, either written or verbal, and pass them on from one agent to another. For security reasons, it was not uncommon for groups to employ intermediaries, *agents-de-liaison*, in passing messages through the letter boxes, one who knew only the sender, the other knowing only the recipient. The circuit would also need a courier, someone who could deliver messages without attracting attention. Since women were not required to have demobilization papers or a work card, they found it easier to move about without being harassed by the police, and whenever possible the resistance preferred to use them as couriers.

In his first days in Troyes, Germain made contact with a Dr. Mahée, the leader of a local Gaullist group, who suggested a young woman he thought would be ideal for the courier's job. Dr. Mahée had known Yvonne Fontaine all her life and vouched for both her character and her anti-German convictions. At thirty, she was twice married, once divorced, and her second husband, an Italian, had vanished. She was not unhappy about his disappearance. Vivacious and smart and worldly, Madame Fontaine was an independent woman with no strings, no family obligations, and at present she was working as the manager of a local dye and dry cleaning firm in the city.

Dr. Mahée arranged a rendezvous, and Germain was instantly impressed. Yvonne had not been involved in any resistance work before, although she did have contacts with the local Gaullist underground. She respected their courage and their goals, but their members, she complained, were "too politically minded" and, more importantly, "the majority of them talked too much, endangering both themselves and their organization." Germain tried to reassure her on both scores. His mission, as he explained it to all the recruits in Troyes, was to contribute to the Allied war effort by wreaking havoc with the Germans, pure and simple. He was not interested in French domestic politics and would cooperate with anyone committed to Germany's defeat. As for security, there was something in Germain's confident professional manner, in his crisp description of the circuit's operational procedures and the role she would play, that seemed to reassure her. She was quickly recruited for the group.

They decided to call her "Nenette," her *nom de guerre*, and she proved to be both reliable and fearless, carrying messages to the circuit's operatives in the town and in the outlying villages. She also put her flat at the group's disposal. Since it possessed both a front and back entrance, it was ideal as a meeting place. Whenever he wanted to arrange a rendezvous there, Germain contacted her and she left the flat. She would stroll down to a café along the Seine canal or visit the cinema near the Église St. Pantaleon, returning only when she was sure the meeting was concluded. If Germain left one window open, it was safe to go inside.

Although he did not keep a wireless set in Nenette's flat, Honoré could also make occasional transmissions there. He had arrived with two sets, both compact Mark II's, which could be hidden in a small suitcase. Later he would acquire another wirelsss from Dr. Mahée's group, exchanging ten grenades for it. One of the sets remained in his rooms in St. André-les-Vergers, a suburb of Troyes where Pierre had found a safe house for him. In time Pierre located two additional sites where he could hide the other sets, one in a barn near the hamlet of Derriery-St.-Julien, about fourteen kilometers west of the town, and another in Tonnerre, a village thirty-five kilometers to the south. Honoré did most of his transmitting from his flat in St. André, though he sometimes operated from other safe houses within the town.

He communicated with London headquarters on a prearranged schedule, or "sked" as he called it, and would bike from one house to another when he was ready to transmit. Limiting transmission time and changing the site from transmission to transmission were extremely important precautions since the Germans prowled the streets with radio detection equipment, trying to pinpoint the source of the signals. Day and night, they played an unremitting game of cat and mouse, and the pressure on Honoré was enormous. More circuits had been broken due to breaches of wireless security, Germain cautioned them, than any other cause.

Germain and Pierre also scoured the region for additional landing grounds, and within a month, the new circuit, code-named **TINKER**, received its first airdrop. The reception work was carried out by Germain, Pierre, Frascati, and two local farmers, one named Tenace, who had found the landing ground, and his neighbor Buridan, who agreed to hide the weapons in his barn. Their two sons also pitched in. The containers of weapons were parachuted into a tree-lined field near Buridan's farm during the full moon, and the men, working frantically in the darkness, emptied their contents—weapons, explosives, ammunition—into sacks on the landing ground, and then buried the containers and parachutes. They would hurry away on bicycle, leaving Pierre or Germain to stand guard on the landing ground with a gun until daylight. For Pierre, these were always the worst hours of the mission, waiting at the edge of the field through the last lonely hours of night for Buridan to return with his horse and cart. When at last the farmer and his son appeared on the trail, their figures indistinct in the gray morning light, Pierre would step into the field and signal, and they would load the cart and smuggle the sacks to their farm, four kilometers away. The sacks were concealed there until Frascati could arrive in a truck to pick them up. The truck was outfitted with a special false bottom where the sacks could be hidden, and Frascati would drive them into Troyes for distribution. Only Germain, Pierre, Frascati, and Buridan knew where the demolitions and weapons were taken.

In the weeks of April and May 1943, Germain, Pierre, Honoré, and Nenette developed into a first-rate team. Germain instructed Pierre in security procedures, in reception committee organization, and demolitions, and more airdrops brought the weapons and explosives needed to conduct a campaign of terror against the Germans in Troyes. By July they were ready for their most ambitious operation, one they had been planning for weeks.

Troyes was an important rail center where five trunk lines converged on the main Paris-Belfort line. Massive marshaling yards sprawled away from the station and in their midst was an enormous engine depot that caught Germain's eye. The depot consisted of two cavernous roundhouses, where locomotives were serviced and repaired. A locomotive would be driven along a spur of track into the roundhouse and onto a great turntable that was surrounded by a ring of stalls. Then the turntable swung around and the engine would be backed into one of the empty stalls. In late June the roundhouses were filled with locomotives, and among them were several of the powerful express engines, brand new and ready for service. It was an inviting target, and although the depot was heavily guarded, Germain believed that a small team of saboteurs could gain access to the building, plant explosives on the locomotives, and escape.

Through contacts at the marshaling yards, Germain learned the layout of the depot's interior and the number and routine of the sentries. He observed the area day and night, planning routes of access and escape. He selected six men for the job, then coached them in handling the plastic explosives, the time fuses, and everything they would need to know about placing the charges.

Then, just as they were ready to put the plan into action, Pierre learned from sources he cultivated in the police that the Germans had somehow gotten wind of a plot to sabotage the depot and were ready to pounce. For days Germain and Pierre waited anxiously for the Gestapo to swoop down upon them, wondering how they had found out, wondering if someone in the circuit was a traitor. But when the Germans did finally spring their trap, they seized several leaders of the local Gaullist underground. Dr. Mahée, Nenette's old friend, was among them.

Pierre worried about Dr. Mahée and the others. Would they talk? Would they implicate Germain or Nenette or himself? Each of them had contacts in Free French circles, but the two groups were not connected and did not coordinate their activities. Now their caution seemed more than justified. Days passed and the Gestapo did not come. Their investigation seemed to sputter. Though still wary of an attack on the depot, the Germans were apparently convinced that they had broken the local resistance, and, thinking the would-be saboteurs safely behind bars, they seemed to relax. Now, Germain and Pierre agreed, was the time to act.

Just after 0100 on July 3, after weeks of surveillance, meticulous planning, and rehearsal, Germain, Pierre, and six of the circuit's men crept across the crowded marshaling yards and into the depot. It was a warm moonless night, and they slipped soundlessly past the German sentries, sliding beneath the gigantic locomotives smelling of steel and soot and oil. Operating in teams of two, they began the nerve-wracking work of placing the explosives. It was dark and hot, and in the vast open spaces of the vaulted building, every footfall on the concrete floor, every tap of metal against metal, seemed to ring out, tolling like the cathedral bells of Troyes. The sentries made their rounds, pacing back and forth like metronomes through the cluster of locomotives, their flashlights raking the darkness. Occasionally they called out to one another, stopped to chat briefly, then went on.

Working feverishly in the dark, pausing only as the sentries lumbered by, the teams labored for over an hour. Germain had coached them well. They knew just where to place the plastic explosives on the engines to ensure that they were destroyed, and they used timed charges set to go off at varying intervals.

Their work done, the men regrouped in the shadows where they had entered, and again dodging past the sentries, they escaped through a maze of boxcars that stood, dark and immobile, on the sidings. They were just beyond the canal that separated the tracks from a line of stunted, soot-stained poplars when the first explosion ripped through the depot. A booming shock wave rumbled through the silent rail yard and a blossom of incandescent flame burst into the moonless night. Then, as sirens wailed and German troops rushed to the depot, one locomotive after another erupted in fire.

By the next morning all Troyes was buzzing with rumors, and German soldiers seemed to be everywhere. Throughout the day Pierre heard many stories about the attack. Six locomotives had been destroyed in the roundhouse and another six were badly damaged. According to one story, British agents had been dropped into the town. Another had it from a reliable source that a team of Gaullist *résistants* was at work in the area. The Germans were certain it was the work of Bolsheviks. To Pierre's amusement, at least two of his business acquaintances intimated that they themselves had been involved.

Pierre was closing up his desk at the office when his chief clerk tapped at the door.

"Monsieur," he said, grim faced, "a German officer is waiting in the outer office. He demands to see you."

Pierre was stunned. It seemed incredible that the Germans had discovered him, and so soon. His mind racing, Pierre quickly went over the cover story he had worked out with Germain and the *réseau*. Then he composed himself and nodded to the clerk.

The officer was dressed in the field gray of the German army and not the dark suit of a Gestapo official. Pierre motioned for his guest to sit, and the officer wasted no time with preliminaries. "Monsieur Mulsant, you have heard about the incident at the rail yard last evening." He stared across the desk at Pierre, speaking French with the stiff politeness of educated foreigners. His manner was cordial, unnervingly so. "Unfortunate," he muttered, "most unfortunate."

"Yes," Pierre agreed, "it is shocking that such things could happen in Troyes, of all places." The officer snapped open a silver cigarette case, offered a cigarette to Pierre, and took one himself. They were Gauloises—real tobacco—and despite his nerves, Pierre's hand was steady as he accepted the light. "*Ah, oui*," the officer said, shaking his head wearily. His eyes were watery blue and above them his thick colorless eyebrows arched into a deeply furrowed forehead. "There are still terrorists in Troyes . . . and," he added ominously, "an Englishman must certainly be among them. Germany's French friends would not be guilty of such an act. The whole business is regrettable, bad for France's relations with the Reich. Very bad."

The officer scrutinized Pierre for a moment, drawing deeply on his Gauloise. "Something must be done," he continued. "And that," he said, his voice brimming with meaning, "brings me to my visit to you today. It has been suggested from sources in the town that a Monsieur Mulsant might be able to help." Pierre's heart sank. He kept a pistol in his desk drawer, a small-caliber revolver he had carried since his military days, but it would do no good. He could not escape. His house was probably being watched even now. His wife, Raymonde, might already be in custody. Germain's instructions about interrogation, about holding out for forty-eight hours to give the others a chance to destroy incriminating materials, to flee, rattled through his head. He would do his best.

"*Wir brauchen Holz, Herr Mulsant*," the officer coughed, slipping into German for the first time. Pierre almost jumped. The officer stared at him across the table. "*Holz*," he repeated after a pause, "lumber, for barriers. The Kommandant has ordered wooden barriers to be erected in front of all German installations in the city, as a measure against terrorism. And you, Monsieur Mulsant, have been highly recommended as a source for lumber." Dumbfounded, Pierre could only stare. "We will need a great quantity," the officer concluded, "and, of course, we will pay. We will pay handsomely."

The visit to the lumber office in July was only the first of many such encounters. After working through a stormy night at Buridan's farm, unpacking several large containers of weapons from a recent airdrop, dispersing the guns and ammunition to the men, hiding others on the farm, Pierre was on his way back into town. He rode a small motorcycle with a suitcase containing a few items of clothing strapped onto the luggage rack over the rear wheel and, tucked up under the seat, hidden by his long legs and loose raincoat, was a package holding an assortment of plastic explosives. The package was carefully sealed to prevent the powerful odor of the plastics from seeping out, but whenever he stopped he thought he could detect a faint whiff of their distinctive almond smell. Perhaps this was merely an illusion, he told himself, a sort of memory from the process of packing the puttylike explosives. Surely no one else would notice anything.

The German *Feldgendarmerie* liked to conduct spot-checks on the roads. Sometimes they would establish roadblocks at key intersections, stopping all passersby, checking papers and baggage. Sometimes they would position a lookout with binoculars to observe the road and then, hidden in the bushes beyond a turn or over a hill, a small squad would wait to intercept any suspicious traveler.

As Pierre rounded a bend, slowing to hold the curve on the rain-slick road, a group of German soldiers stepped out from the roadside, motioning for him to halt. They surrounded the motorcycle, demanding to see his identification. *"Ausweis, bitte,"* the ranking soldier barked, *"Ihre Papiere."* Reaching carefully into his raincoat, Pierre produced his wallet with the small bundle of papers all Frenchmen were required to carry, his *carte d'identité* with his name, nationality, profession, date and place of birth, home address, physical appearance, distinguishing marks, and photograph; his *fiche de démobilisation,* establishing that he was a veteran and not a deserter; and finally an additional document certifying that he was exempt from the STO, the hated Service du Travail Obligatoire and its forced labor service in Germany. While one soldier carefully examined his papers, another turned to the suitcase, slipped it from the rack, and began rifling through it. The other two stood by, their small carbines at the ready. Pierre remained seated, his legs still straddling the motorcycle. He was sure that he could smell the plastics. He could hear one of the soldiers behind him, fumbling with the suitcase, with the rack. As he usually did on these trips, he carried his revolver in his raincoat pocket, but, surrounded by four soldiers, he did not loosen his grip on the handlebars.

Snapping Pierre's wallet closed, the German looked out at him from beneath his gray helmet for a moment and then, with a flip of the wrist, handed the papers back to him. *"Weiter fahren,"* he said, and, stepping back from the motorcycle, waved him on his way. It was a miracle. Relating the incident later to Germain, Pierre realized that he had placed the explosives under his seat on a whim, without thinking. He had not intended it as a hiding place. It had been merely a matter of chance.

On another occasion a curious neighbor informed the police that there were suspicious goings-on at the house used by Germain as his arms depot. Men on bicycle came and went at odd hours, carts and trucks made deliveries, the man reported, and yet no one appeared to live in the house. The informer gave the police the license number of a car he had seen parked frequently in front of the house, but a sympathetic official in the Préfecture de Police intercepted the denunciation before it reached the Germans or the Sûreté, the Vichy security police. Looking up the license number, he found that the vehicle belonged to Pierre and alerted him.

But the hiding place was no longer safe. During one frantic day, Germain and Pierre emptied out the house, packing the explosives and weapons and then ferrying them by bicycle as quickly as possible to a nearby workshop owned by a friend of Pierre's. Early the next morning the police raided the house. The premises were permeated with a curious almond smell, but otherwise empty.

In the late summer Octave Simon appeared in Troyes, warning them that the Gestapo had made arrests of several members of the **PROSPER** circuit in Paris and was, he feared, closing in on him. So far his own circuit, **SATIRIST**, operating in Sarthe, remained intact, but a number of his friends had been shadowed, and he had sent his wife and child into hiding. A wireless operator from another circuit, a young man Pierre had sheltered in the spring, was also arrested, as were other friends with War Office connections.

At the same time the Gestapo began to close in on Germain. The sabotage of the depot had put the Germans on the alert in Troyes, and they redoubled their efforts to root out "terrorism" in the city. From his sources in the Préfecture de Police, Pierre learned that one of the Gaullists captured in July had admitted under torture that an Englishman was operating in Troyes and had offered to lead the Gestapo to him in exchange for his own release. The Gestapo had obtained a description of Germain and were on the lookout for him. London ordered him to leave. He was not eager to go, but delay was unwise and the circuit, he believed, was in good hands. Leaving Pierre to run **TINKER**'s operations until a new agent arrived from London, he made his way to Paris and from there to Angers, where on the night of September 17–18 a Lysander scooped him up from a farmer's field and returned him to England.

Honoré stayed on in Troyes, as did Nenette, and the circuit continued its work. They received another airdrop, distributed weapons, and continued to study a target that had occupied the group for weeks: the electrical station at Creney, just east of Troyes. The station consisted of six large transformers carrying the electrical current to Paris, and Pierre and Germain had reconnoitered it many times. It was an imposing target. The station was surrounded by a high wall through which there was only one door with one key. When the door opened, it set off a system of alarm bells. Two German sentries, armed with machine guns, were posted on each side of the transformers, and another set of armed guards manned a watchtower with a searchlight system that operated at random intervals. Mobile patrols with police dogs roamed the station grounds and fifty soldiers slept in a guardhouse on the premises. It was just the sort of challenge Germain thrived on, but even he had come to the conclusion that an attack on the station would be suicidal.

The only hope for sabotage was to find an accomplice on the inside. Shortly after Germain's departure, Pierre thought he had found their man. For some time he had been cultivating an Alsatian workman employed at the station. The man's job was to check the temperature of the transformers, which he did every morning at 0500. It would not be difficult for him to smuggle the explosives into the station and, once inside, to plant the plastics on the transformers—Pierre would show him how it was done. The man's shift ended at 0515 and a train left for Paris at 0630. The explosives would be time-fused, and he would be safely in Paris when they detonated at 1100. Pierre had worked it all out and was ready to offer him anything—money, escape to England, whatever he wanted—but the man was scared. Pierre would have to work on him, but the target, London agreed, was worth it.

While Pierre continued to explore an attack on the transformer station, the *réseau* channeled a number of Allied aviators, Americans mostly, to circuits that managed the evasion lines. These circuits specialized in helping downed aviators evade capture, funneling them to Paris or to the south for escape over the Pyrenees. Working with evasion lines for Allied aviators was not a high priority for British agents in France, but they helped whenever they could and people were always showing up.

Pierre was always surprised by these ordinary people who harbored the aviators. Concealing an enemy soldier was punishable by death, and informers were everywhere. Even after an Allied bombing raid on Troyes in September 1942 when the Germans paraded the captured aviators through the streets, hoping for a display of public rage against the "terror fliers," the meager crowd cheered the bedraggled Americans. In the following days, much to the chagrin of the German authorities, flowers appeared on the graves of the Americans killed in the raid.

In early September Nenette was involved in the evacuation of no fewer than twenty American aviators hidden in the area around Troyes, and not long thereafter Pierre's police sources informed him that her name had surfaced in their investigations of underground activity in the city. They might arrest her themselves or turn her over to the Germans. Pierre also learned that the Gestapo had information linking him to Germain. He was not surprised. By this time he was operating with several aliases—André, as he was known to London,

Pedro, and Henri-Paul—but as the weeks passed and his contacts multiplied, he ran greater and greater risks. Troyes, after all, was not a large city—only fifty thousand inhabitants—and he was a well-known figure about town. It was only a matter of time before the Gestapo once again picked up the scent. Circuits, Germain had told him, had a limited life expectancy—five, maybe six months—and **TINKER** was running out of time.

With his situation in the city growing precarious, Pierre wanted to find a secure hiding place somewhere in the country. On weekends Germain and Honoré sometimes slipped away to a country inn at Précy-Notre-Dame, a picture-postcard hamlet about twenty kilometers east of Troyes, whose proprietress was well known throughout the area for her cooking. She was also sympathetic to the resistance and had been very helpful to the circuit. Madame Mielle knew that they were English and engaged in subversive actvities, and although her *auberge* attracted many German patrons, she allowed members of the organization to stay there and eat without the necessary papers. Through a contact in the mayor's office in Troyes, she had even helped to procure ration books for them. Madame Mielle indicated that she knew of a deserted bungalow near her inn, one that might be useful for wireless transmissions or as a *planque*, a safe house. One night, after the kitchen was closed down and only a handful of patrons lingered at the tables, she offered to drive Honoré out to inspect it.

It was pitch black in the courtyard behind the inn as they climbed into her car for the short trip. They were not alone. In the backseat, to Honoré's astonishment, sat an enormous black-faced sheep that, Madame Mielle explained in passing, was to be dropped off at a farm nearby for slaughter. She pulled into a narrow tree-lined lane, driving through the shadowy darkness without headlamps. The road was deserted, the occasional farms shuttered and quiet. But as they slowed at a crossroads, a German patrol seemed to materialize out of the surrounding hedges. The soldiers stepped into the road and blocked the car's path. With their rifles trained on the car, the Germans surrounded it, and one soldier, a sergeant, stepped forward. He leaned down and peered into the car. His broad face beneath the steel helmet was so close Honoré could smell the sausage on his breath. "*Papiere, bitte,*" he said. The soldier examined Honoré's documents with little interest, giving them only a cursory glance, but he recognized Madame Mielle from the inn. He and his comrades had eaten there many times. *Magnifique,* he said, kissing his fingertips in appreciation, *très magnifique.* He handed the papers back. But why was *la Propriétaire* driving without lights, he wanted to know, and what was she doing with a sheep in the car?

She drove without lights because her battery was low, she replied calmly, and she was taking the sheep to be slaughtered because the prefect was coming to dine at her restaurant. Barreling along through the night in this manner was dangerous and looked suspicious, he warned, and slaughtering livestock on the side was illegal, black market business. She must know this. He leaned menacingly into the car and stared for a moment at Madame Mielle. Then, without missing a beat, he glanced into the backseat, lowered his voice, and whispered, "How much for the sheep?" Of course, Honoré thought with relief, of course. And a small price to pay, under the circumstances. *"Ce n'est pas à vendre,"* she said firmly. How could she sell the sheep with the prefect coming? The prefect's love of *navarin d'agneau*—lamb stew—was well known throughout the district. She had her kitchen's reputation to consider. It was imperative to make an impression on the prefect, who could, if he wished, order the restaurant closed. Surely the sergeant must understand her position. He did not speak for some time, his eyes darting from the impassive sheep to Madame Mielle. Finally, he let out a deep sigh and, stepping back, motioned them on their way. *"Wir sehen uns wieder,"* he called out, *"beim Abendessen."* He even waved.

Throughout the incident, Madame Mielle remained supremely cool, striking just the right chords. She had played it to perfection, and Honoré was very impressed. But afterward, the innkeeper became so rattled by the experience that she consulted her doctor. She needed something for her jangled nerves, and she told him the whole story. He was not discreet. Within days the entire village was whispering about Madame Mielle and "her Englishman" and it was only a matter of time before the Germans would be on their trail.

In late August, Pierre learned that the Gestapo had arrested a Gaullist W/T operator in the area and were now zeroing in on another enemy agent transmitting from Troyes. Honoré was shaken but hardly surprised. During one week early in the month, Home Station had been unable to hear his signals, and for four nights running he sent messages every half hour for five minutes on alternative frequencies from midnight to 0300. Now radio detection teams were on his track, and German operators were posted all over Troyes to listen for him.

Nenette reported seeing a car containing a German detection unit patrolling the streets of the city, and on another occasion, cycling home to St. André, Honoré passed a parked detection van where five Germans, four of them in uniform, were wearing earphones.

Still, communication with London was essential for the circuit, and so for a month Honoré used his main set in St. André only for listening and transmitted from his country sets in Dierry and Tonnerre, cycling by side roads to avoid the German patrols. It was only in late September, when he learned that the German detection teams had left the city, that he resumed his transmissions from Troyes. Within days they were back and there were new signs that his transmissions had been compromised. It was time to leave.

During the October moon Germain's successor, Maurice Dupont, code-named **ABELARD**, parachuted into the region, bringing with him two additional wireless sets. Pierre organized the reception committee and led the new man back to a safe house on the outskirts of Troyes. In the days that followed, Pierre briefed him on the situation in the area, especially the ongoing plans to sabotage the transformer station at Creney, introduced him to the members of the circuit, and showed him the landing grounds, drop zones, arms depots, and safe houses. Germain had identified nine targets for D-Day, the anticipated Allied invasion of France, and had chosen the men to attack them. With Pierre's help, **ABELARD** began recruiting new men for other tasks.

Then in early November London sent word for Pierre, Honoré, and Nenette to stand by for evacuation. They would be airlifted out of France. Pierre put his affairs in order and made arrangements for his wife, Raymonde, to slip away from Troyes. The War Office could not evacuate family—that was policy and Pierre understood—but leaving Raymonde was hard. Her brother Robert would accompany her to the south, to the Mulsant chateau in Villefranche, but despite her unflagging courage, her health was not good. She had always been delicate, and this separation would be hard on her. He hoped that they could arrange a coded message to her on the BBC, confirming that he had arrived safely in England.

The group dispersed, each traveling to safe houses in Paris where they would wait for the final confirming message from the BBC before moving to the landing ground. Then, on the night of November 15–16, they were alerted, and a two-engine Hudson, the largest plane used by London for these nocturnal airlifts, landed in a frozen wheat field near Angers, to the southwest of Paris. It delivered a new set of agents to the area, and Pierre, Honoré, Nenette, and a handful of other *résistants* raced out into the frosty meadow, clambering aboard for the return trip to England.

No one spoke during the long flight across France. The ten passengers sat, shoulder to shoulder, along the curved floor of the plane. Some carried briefcases or valises, which they checked from time to time. Others were empty-handed. They hardly glanced at each other. Pierre sat in the blackness of the plane, numb with cold and lost in thought, as the engines droned and everything he loved slid away beneath him. It was his first time to fly, and he had never felt more alone in his life.

When the Hudson landed at an aerodrome north of London and the passengers stepped out into a blustery wind and light drizzle, they were led to a low-lying structure where several officials, some in military uniform, others in civilian dress, were waiting for them. A group of uniformed young women offered them tea and sandwiches and made small talk, while the new arrivals thawed and the officials checked their papers. During the processing that followed, Pierre was separated from Honoré and Nenette, and after his identity had been verified, he was escorted to a waiting automobile for the short trip to London.

In the first pale light of dawn they left the sleeping countryside behind them and drove, virtually alone on the silent roadway, through endless tracts of drab industrial suburbs, through mile after mile of dull brick row houses and grim colorless factories stained with the soot and grime of decades. After a time the stunted houses gave way to commercial buildings and then to busy thoroughfares and finally to verdant parks and winding city streets, pulsing already with hurrying pedestrians, red double-decker buses, and brown military vehicles of all sorts.

He was being taken, his "conducting officer" explained to him, to a "safe flat" in Bayswater near Paddington Station, where he would spend a few days at the Crown's expense. During that time he would be investigated by Scotland Yard and Military Intelligence's security branch, MI-5. "Put through the cards" was the way the conducting officer expressed it, and when that security check was complete and he had been cleared, he would be thoroughly debriefed—interrogated. In the meantime he was free to walk about, to see the sights, visit the cinema, go dancing, whatever, but he would be escorted everywhere by security personnel.

While he waited for his clearance, Pierre wandered the streets like a tourist, never out of sight of his conducting officer. After years of somber occupied France, he was awed by London's bristling energy. The streets and undergrounds swarmed with men and women in uniform. Soldiers and sailors of every Allied nation sauntered through the parks, sang in the pubs, and bantered with the prostitutes. In the crowded dancehalls and markets, fragments of French, Czech, Polish, Dutch, even Hindi—almost every language, he was delighted to realize, but German—could be heard amid the perpetual hum of British and American voices.

He read the papers and listened to the radio. He watched the newsreels at the cinema, absorbing every detail he could glean about the war. Hawked at every street corner and tube entrance, London's newspapers poured forth a stunning stream of war news that for years he had struggled to filter through the sieve of Vichy censorship and the static of the BBC's meager French broadcasts. Everyone in this bustling blacked-out city seemed primed, poised for the long-awaited invasion of Hitler's Europe, which, they seemed to expect, would surely come in the spring.

It was exhilarating to be out of occupied France, to be free of the Germans for the first time in years, but through the interminable days and nights of waiting for his clearance, Pierre agonized about leaving Raymonde. She was capable and could manage any situation—of that he was certain. From the outset she had supported his activities, helping in any way she could. Although it was dangerous, Germain and Honoré had occasionally spent evenings in their house in the rue Colonel-de-Bange, resting, relaxing. Raymonde loved to play the piano, and, they discovered, so did Honoré. That was particularly fitting, Raymonde laughed, since wireless operators were referred to as "pianists." He could see her still, seated on the piano bench, her blond hair just brushing her shoulders. He had no picture of her with him, a terrible oversight that he regretted now.

On November 24, his security clearance at last complete, Pierre was ready for his interrogation. That morning at another flat nearby, a team of men in civilian dress who spoke flawless French quizzed him about his connections, the activities of the circuit, the quality of the weapons dropped, possible targets for future operations, the effectiveness of the BBC broadcasts, the morale of the French population. They asked about rationing cards and train schedules, about supplies of heating fuel and electricity, about the availability of alcohol in restaurants in Troyes. He was impressed by their relentless thoroughness. He inquired about Germain and about getting a message to Raymonde. He asked for news of Octave Simon and Emile Garry and other agents he knew. All in good time, the interrogator told him.

Several days later, his conducting officer accompanied him to an elegant apartment house at Orchard Court, Portman Square. He led Pierre through an archway into an inner courtyard, toward a doorway to the left. They entered a lobby beneath an ornate crystal chandelier. "The lift is just here," the man said, and they stepped inside. Creaking to a halt at the third floor, the *ascenseur* deposited them in a carpeted hallway. The conducting officer led him to an unmarked door and, after ringing the bell, suddenly vanished. When the door opened, an erect tallish man, the very essence of a British butler, peered out. He smiled faintly. "Welcome, Monsieur Mulsant," he said, "please do come in."

Pierre followed the man through what clearly had been an elegant residence in those remote days before the war. The flat was spacious, with many rooms, and as they proceeded down a marble-floored hallway, he thought he heard someone behind them, but when he looked back, no one was there. His host stopped suddenly, held open a door for him, and motioned him inside. When the door closed behind him, Pierre found himself alone in an ornate bathroom. The bathtub and basin and bidet were of smooth black marble, highlighted by sparkling chrome fixtures, and the inlaid black tiles of the walls shone in the bright gleam of the overhead light like a vein of coal.

He could hear the murmur of voices beyond the walls and footsteps clattered in the hallway. Doors opened and closed. He was standing between the tub and bidet, not knowing what to do with himself, when a young woman entered. "Monsieur Mulsant," she said, extending her hand. "I see that Park has taken good care of you. He directs traffic here—wouldn't do to have agents running into one another here in the flat, would it?" She smiled. "I'm Vera Atkins. You will be meeting the chief in just a moment, but first please come with me." She led him into an office just down the hallway and, opening a file, said, "Let's see. We have a hotel booked for you. I think you'll like it. It's in the name of Pierre Mazenod. That will be your name while here in England. I hope that meets with your approval." Before Pierre could reply, she handed him an envelope filled with British currency. The woman was attractive, he thought, in the English way, crisp in her speech and precise in her movements. Everything about her exuded competence, intelligence, confidence. "You will be needing this. An advance on your pay. Now," she said, "you are to see Colonel Buckmaster."

Pierre knew the name. He had heard Germain and others in the field use it often. Maurice Buckmaster was the chief of British agents operating in France. When Pierre entered the room, a tall, lean man, rather round shouldered, with bright intelligent eyes, rose from his desk and stepped forward to shake hands. *"Bonjour, bonjour,"* he said, speaking French pleasantly and with only a trace of an accent. "I'm delighted to meet you. We've heard a good deal about you. You come to us highly recommended. Your friend Ben Cowburn—Germain, to you—thinks very highly of you, indeed."

Settling back in their chairs, the two men exchanged pleasantries for a time. Pierre asked about the possibility of seeing Germain and sending a signal to the *réseau* in Troyes, a message to Raymonde that he had arrived safely. He asked about Honoré and Nenette and whether he would meet them again. The colonel, indicating that these things would be attended to, at last turned to the business at hand.

"Let me explain a bit about our organization," he began, his eyes settling on a large wall map of western Europe behind Pierre. "For the past several months you have been working for SOE. SOE—Special Operations Executive—was created at the order of the prime minister in 1940 and charged with conducting subversive activities and sabotage throughout occupied Europe. It is to recruit patriots, anti-Nazis, in every country under German domination, to organize resistance cells, to train teams to wage guerrilla warfare before and after the Allied landing, and to carry out airdrops of arms and equipment to resistance groups throughout Europe. Its mission, as Mr. Churchill put it, is nothing less than 'to set Europe ablaze.'

"SOE is organized into sections. Each country in occupied Europe has its own section with its own staff, its own organization, and its own operations. Since the beginning of the war F-Section has established some forty operational resistance circuits in France, landed approximately three hundred officers, and carried out six hundred airdrops of materiel. As you no doubt know, SOE agents are often referred to in France as *'agents de l'Intelligence Service.'* Technically this is not true. Sometimes you have heard us referred to as agents of the 'War Office,' and although this, too, is not quite correct—we are technically a branch of the Ministry of Economic Warfare—it has become a practical way to distinguish F-Section operatives from Gaullist agents, who are controlled by the Free French government in exile.

"In the early years of the war, the organization relied on British subjects such as Ben Cowburn or your W/T man Honoré—oh yes, *his* real name is Denis Barrett, also a British subject—whose command of French made them at least credible for undercover assignments on the Continent. We reached an agreement with General de Gaulle and his chaps that we would not recruit French nationals for our operations in France, but earlier this year the situation changed. Now if a French national such as yourself has worked with an SOE circuit in France, has served an apprenticeship in the field, so to speak, he may be smuggled out of France, trained in England, and then returned to establish a new circuit. This is exactly what we would like to propose to you, Monsieur Mulsant."

Pierre knew that relations between the underground organization of de Gaulle's Free French (the Bureau Central de Renseignements et d'Action, BCRA) and the British organization—F-Section of SOE— were strained, but it was of little import to him. From his experiences with the Gaullists in Troyes, he understood that the British delivered weapons, radios, and other equipment to the BCRA and maintained wireless reception facilities for the Free French in England. The British did not, however, interfere with their operations, and the two organizations ran on parallel tracks, rarely intersecting.

"It says here," Buckmaster continued, reading from Pierre's open file, "that you are a 'very keen young Frenchman, intelligent, observant and reliable.'" He looked up at Pierre. "Our evaluators believe that you would be ideally suited to run your own circuit. It might be possible to arrange it so that you would work again with Honoré and Nenette." He paused, gauging the effect of these words on Pierre. "Teamwork and trust are essential in these operations, as you well know, and from all accounts the three of you performed quite well together.

"Although you obviously have invaluable operational experience in the field—Germain, that is, Cowburn, has vouched enthusiastically for you—we think that, should you decide to accept our offer, you would benefit from some additional SOE training. We think, for example, that your knowledge of sabotage material should be brought up to date, together with whatever additional specialized instruction the commandant at Special Training School 42, the first phase of your training, considers you should be given."

Pierre did not need to consider this proposition. "How long," he asked, "will the training last? When can I expect to be back in France?"

"Soon," the colonel responded. "We anticipate that you will be ready for the January moon."

It was exactly the answer Pierre wanted to hear.

For several days, Pierre remained in London awaiting orders. He was issued a British military uniform with the rank of lieutenant. "Less conspicuous out in public," Vera Atkins explained. "It is unusual to see a young man, obviously fit and in good health, wandering about in civilian dress. You will attract less attention this way." He was on the payroll, assigned to the General List, with the notation in his army file that he was to be "specially employed."

In mid-December, after a short stay in a secluded country estate used by SOE to house its agents between assignments, Pierre at last received his orders. From his handlers he understood that most prospective SOE agents were subjected to five grueling weeks of para-military training in the barren wilderness of Scotland, but because of his experience in the field, he would be spared this initial phase of training. Instead, Pierre was dispatched directly to Special Training School (STS) 42 at Howbury Hall, Watersend, in Bedfordshire.

Howbury Hall, he discovered upon arrival, was one of several stately country houses scattered across the country requisitioned by the government at the outbreak of the war and turned over to SOE. At STS 42 recruits were instructed in the basics of covert operations, intelligence gathering, and security. They studied coding, ciphering, and German counterintelligence practices. They learned how to dress, how to look natural, how to spot someone following them, how, as Colonel Buckmaster put it, to pick out individuals in a crowd from an oral description, how to pass messages in a crowded place without being seen or overheard. They studied French and German security formations, how they were organized, how they operated. The Vichy government alone commanded fourteen different security organizations, and their uniforms, weapons, and methods had to be mastered. Among the most important—and realistic—exercises of the course was the lesson on how to handle an interrogation. At the outset of their training, each student was given an elaborate cover story to remember, just as he or she would have in the field. Then after a long day of classes, they would be dragged out of bed in the middle of the night and taken to the cellar for *Verhör,* interrogation, where experienced staff portrayed Gestapo interrogators.

But the main focus of the course at Howbury Hall was on "reception work." The trainees learned how to recruit, organize, and lead a reception committee, how to operate the new S-Phone and Eureka devices, radio sets that Pierre had never seen and that could be employed by reception committees to communicate directly with aircraft overhead. Pierre was impressed with the technology. Although he had considerable experience with reception committee operations, he found the training surprisingly realistic and thorough.

In late January, as the weather deteriorated and a wet chill settled over the landscape, Pierre moved on to STS 40, SOE's training course in weaponry and demolitions at Brickendonbury in Hertfordshire. Through short raw days of bitter frosts and sodden thaws the trainees learned the basics of commando fighting—hand-to-hand combat, the techniques of "silent killing," as the instructors put it, how to use a knife, rope, pistol, and automatic weapons. They were given a crash course in how to operate British and German small arms, especially the Sten submachine guns favored by SOE for resistance work. They learned demolitions—how and where to place charges on locomotives, bridges, rail lines, and other structures. There was work with the special timed fuses—"time pencils"—and the new plastic explosives, both of which Pierre had used in the engine depot attack in July. The plastic explosives had the consistency and color of butter and possessed the distinctive almond smell that he recognized instantly from Germain's arms depot outside Troyes.

As the culmination of this phase of training, the students were put through a demanding exercise that extended over several days. Assigned a target and ordered to develop a "scheme" to destroy it, they had to conduct a reconnaissance, to rendezvous with other agents by prearranged password, and in some cases to smuggle dummy explosives to the targets, where they would actually place them on trains or ships in port. Throughout the exercise, the trainees were closely watched by undercover agents of SOE, some of whom tried to trip them up, get them drunk, even seduce them. In fact, Pierre discovered, the staff kept the students under constant surveillance throughout all the arduous phases of their training. Were prospective agents overly fond of drink, of women—or men—or did they have other habits that might prove disastrous in the field?

When the demolitions training concluded, the staff pronounced Pierre "a first-rate man," skillful and enthusiastic. He was physically fit, a good shot, and, the instructors noted, he displayed a particular aptitude for demolitions of transportation targets. In the important final exercise, he had "carried out a good scheme, of which he was the leader," and was, in the school's view, "fit for leadership and organization." Pierre, the commander concluded, was "the best student on the course."

Those who survived this round of training—and at each phase many washed out—moved on to parachute training. Although F-Section smuggled some operatives onto the Continent by sea, the vast majority were delivered by air. Since 1941 two RAF "special duty" units, 161 and 138 Squadrons, stationed at specially camouflaged bases at Tangmere and Tempsford, had been ferrying agents and materiel to the Continent for SOE. Operating at night and only during the full moon, these "moon squadrons" flew the dangerous missions to France. While 138 Squadron handled the parachute operations, 161 Squadron actually touched down in farmers' fields to deliver agents to the reception committees and take waiting operatives back to Britain.

Although 138 Squadron sometimes employed twin-engine Hudsons for this sort of mission, the plane most often used was the Lysander, a small but sturdy aircraft capable of landing and taking off in very close quarters. The Lysander, Pierre learned, had proven highly vulnerable to enemy fighters during daylight operations, but because it was designed for short landings on rough ground and was very maneuverable at slow speeds, it was ideal for the sort of nighttime mission SOE planners had in mind.

Pierre had seen the plane several times in the field. Mottled with splotches of gray-green camouflage paint, it was a stubby, single-engine, high-winged aircraft, not very impressive to look at. The pilot rode in a cockpit just behind the engine and the passengers—the Lysander could carry only three, two in seats and one on the floor—were squeezed into a rear cockpit under the wing. When the plane touched down in a field in France, the incoming passengers would slide back the rear canopy and scramble out, while the outgoing agents would climb up a ladder affixed to the port side of the plane. Pierre had flown out of France in a Hudson, which could accommodate more passengers, but nothing he had seen in the war struck him as more dramatic, more improbable, and more dangerous than the Lysander landings he had witnessed in the area around Troyes.

Most agents, though, did not arrive in France by Hudson or by Lysander. Most, Pierre knew, were dropped by parachute; 138 Squadron handled this duty, flying Whitleys and Halifaxes. No one jumped from a Hudson or a Lysander. As a consequence, almost all agents bound for the field were given instruction in parachute jumping. Ordinarily each agent made three to five jumps in training, the last, and certainly most terrifying, at night. Pierre made his three jumps from Dunham House in Cheshire. Two were from aircraft, one from a balloon. Since agents bound for France were always dropped at night, his final training jump into the black sky somewhere over the English Midlands was a preview of things to come. He completed the parachute course in late January and the staff rated his jumps "first class."

In early February, having successfully completed his training, he was officially commissioned a captain in the British army and summoned back to Orchard Court. After meeting briefly with Vera Atkins, he was ushered into one of the apartment's briefing rooms, its walls and tables cluttered with aerial photographs, lunar tables, and maps of France, and waited for Colonel Buckmaster to spell out his mission. The colonel was congenial but brisk, congratulating him on his splendid record during the phases of training and on his commission, but wasting few words of praise.

Then, turning to a large topographical map of northern France, Buckmaster said, "You will be returned to the field very shortly. You will lead your own team and form a new circuit. Your mission is to marshal resistance forces in the area between Meaux and Nangis in the Département Seine-et-Marne," the colonel continued, his finger tracing a triangle on the map east-southeast of Paris. "You will mold an effective organization, train it, equip it, and execute sabotage on selected communications and transportation targets in connection with D-Day. The invasion," Buckmaster went on, "can be expected in the near future, in late spring or early summer. There is precious little time. I'm afraid it's too late to deliver you this month but you should be ready for the next moon period in early March."

Pierre felt a surge of excitement. He knew the terrain—Meaux, Melun, Nangis. The area was just northwest of Troyes, and he had traveled there often on business. It would be too dangerous to visit his old town, but he would contact his brother-in-law and somehow reach Raymonde. He did not want to put her at risk, but he longed to see her, hear her voice, to know that she was safe.

"Your team," Buckmaster continued, "will consist of yourself as leader, a wireless man, and a courier. A demolitions specialist will be assigned to the team later and will rendezvous with you in the field. The wireless chap is an experienced operator, first rate, and will return to the field with you. His name is Denis Barrett. You know him by his nom de guerre in Troyes—Honoré—but for this mission we've rechristened him Charles Meunier."

Leaning back in his chair, Pierre beamed. He had hoped to have Honoré with him. He trusted Honoré's judgment and skill with the radio. He had seen him operate under tremendous pressure in Troyes, dodging the detection vans, spending days and nights alone in various safe houses, his entire existence dominated by the transmission schedules. Honoré knew the procedures and equipment, and, most important, he understood security. He did not make mistakes or take unnecessary chances.

While waiting for the arrival of the moon period, Pierre was sent to a country estate near Cambridge where agents relaxed between training or field assignments. He had been there only a short time when Honoré arrived. The men were delighted to see each other again. The strain of those last frantic days in Troyes no longer showed in Honoré's face. He looked fit and relaxed and ready for a new assignment. But he was, as he reminded Pierre, no longer Honoré. For this mission SOE had given him a new identity, a new past, and a new name. He was now Charles Meunier, and his operational name for radio transmissions was **INNKEEPER**.

In the days that followed, Pierre and Honoré—Charles—saw a lot of each other. Pierre learned that his friend had been born in France, in Colombes on the Seine, in 1919. His parents were English but he had been raised and educated in Paris, where his father made a successful career as a tailor. For F-Section's purposes he was ideal. He spoke French like a native, knew French customs and manners, and he had joined the RAF as a volunteer reserve in Paris in 1939. At first he worked as an interpreter, but back in England he was recruited by SOE. He had completed his training course, excelling in communications, and had been sent for advanced instruction as a "pianist."

During the gloomy weeks of February the two men studied maps of the area, listened to briefings about conditions there, read reports about enemy strengths and activities. They learned the disposition of the existing *réseaux*, possible new contacts, and potential targets. Over and over again they rehearsed the details of their new identities. F-Section constructed these cover stories with meticulous care, devising fictitious grandparents, aunts, uncles, occupational backgrounds, addresses. French postal guides and telephone directories were used, and an elaborate set of identity papers generated. Pierre Mulsant had left Troyes in November, had been re-created for his stay in Britain as Pierre Mazenod, and now, on the eve of his return to France, he had become Paul Guérin.

As they worked through the short, windswept days of March, they waited for the moon period with mounting anticipation. Then on March 3, Buckmaster summoned them to attend a final briefing at Orchard Court. With Pierre and Charles seated before him in the cluttered office, Colonel Buckmaster handed them their operational orders and talked them through the neatly typed pages, paragraph by paragraph. They went over their cover stories, their maps and codes and procedures one last time.

"You will proceed to France by air—a Halifax, I should think," the colonel began, "to a point near Troyes." He gave the coordinates. "I think you know the drill. You will be met by a reception committee, who will give you any assistance you may require during the first few hours after your arrival and will see you to your destination. After leaving the reception committee, you will have no further contact with them whatsoever."

He proceeded to outline again the specific communications and transportation targets—railroad lines, canal systems, telephone networks throughout the area—and the BBC messages that would alert the circuit to launch its attacks on each. He paused, leaned forward over the desk, and handed each man a sheet of paper. "Here are the coded messages for your circuit. The first is the signal to strike the designated railway targets, the second is for telephone targets." Pierre and Charles scanned the nonsense lines they would commit to memory. They handed back the paper and Buckmaster resumed. **MINISTER** was to arm and train groups that would attack these targets but, as always, the colonel emphasized security. "It is never our policy," he reminded them, "to assemble large groups of men since in our opinion the only basis for effective action is the small self-contained group."

The briefing concluded, Vera Atkins scrutinized their clothing, checking their pockets, even their trouser cuffs, for any minute vestige of their stay in England, and Pierre checked the money belt he would be carrying. Then in the early afternoon, the conducting officer arrived and the colonel wished them luck. As Park escorted the men toward the lift, Buckmaster pressed a small lighter into Pierre's hand. It was of French manufacture, Pierre noticed. "A custom of mine," the colonel explained a bit sheepishly. "I like to give departing agents a little gift, a memento." He smiled. *"Au revoir et bonne chance."*

In the courtyard, the men climbed into an enormous Ford station wagon that idled noisily beneath the porte cochere. A young woman clad in a blue Women's Auxiliary Air Force uniform sat behind the wheel. "It's called the hearse," the driver laughed jauntily, as Pierre and Honoré, surrounded by their gear, settled into the back. The driver, supplied for these trips by the WAAF, released the brake and eased the station wagon down the drive and through the archway. It was already late afternoon and blue blackout lights winked on in the gathering dusk as they weaved through the sparse London traffic into the Great Northern Road. Their destination was the air station at Tempsford, west of Cambridge.

Seven hours later, the pitch of the engines suddenly shifted lower and the Halifax began easing down. In just a few moments Pierre would be back in France. Ahead of him, the form of the dispatcher stirred in the darkness. "The signal has been sighted," he called out. "Best get ready."

Pierre felt the plane begin a long descending turn, then level off. Pierre and Honoré—now Paul and Charles—shifted into position on either side of the exit hatch. The dispatcher leaned over and attached the static lines to their parachutes. He gave each line a tug to reassure them that they were properly secured. Then he lifted the lid of the circular hatch. A blast of frigid air swept into the fuselage, and Pierre slid forward in the dark body of the plane. Below them the moonlit landscape slid dreamily by. Suddenly a muted red light flickered on above them, bathing the equipment, the men, the riveted skin of the plane in an unearthly crimson glow. The two men edged toward the gaping hole. The dispatcher peered steadily at the red light. He raised his right arm, and Charles swung his legs out over the darkness. The light flashed suddenly green and the dispatcher's arm dropped and Charles vanished into the night. The static lines snapped taut, then flapped loosely against the edge of the hatch. Pierre extended his legs over the rim. He felt a rush of wind and, looking down into the howling darkness, he jumped.

CHAPTER 3

Milk Run

June 14, 1944

Nangis was a crosshatched mark on the map eighty kilometers southeast of Paris. It appeared to be a small town, not much more than a village, surrounded by open country, and it straddled a railroad line. From the air it would be easy for the lead navigator to spot. Roy Allen, sitting in the pilot's seat, ran his finger along the thin red line that marked the briefed course to the target. The formation would cross the French coast near Caen, bear south toward Le Mans, then pivot sharply to the northeast at Orléans. Twenty thousand feet above Nangis, thirty-six B-17s from the 457th Bomb Group would turn again, swinging suddenly back toward the target on the outskirts of Paris. Nangis was the IP, the "initial point" at which the planes would uncover and the Group would begin the long approach toward the target, the Luftwaffe aerodrome at Melun.

They would have plenty of company this morning. The Eighth Air Force was putting three hundred heavies, all B-17s from the First Air Division, into the air around Paris, hitting airfields at Villaroche, Le Bourget, and Melun. It would be a major effort. A week after D-Day, the Allied invasion of France, the troops were still bogged down in Normandy, only a few miles inland from the invasion beaches, and the Germans were rushing fighter units to the west as fast as they could.

Roy adjusted his goggles against the glare, glancing down at the folded chart in his lap. He checked the times and distances. From the IP to the target, the bomb run would be five minutes. An eternity. During that time, they would fly at a set speed, at a set altitude, straight as an arrow toward their objective. They could not break formation or take evasive action. The operations officer who conducted the main briefing at 0300 was upbeat. Intelligence annexes to the field order that had clattered into the Group's Teletype machines during the wee hours of the morning indicated they could expect little flak at the target, though enemy fighters were a distinct possibility. It would be a nice, neat surgical operation, the operations officer said, tapping his pointer to the map for emphasis. Three hours in, bombs away, three and a half hours out. Back in time for the Liberty Run into Peterborough.

Just the day before yesterday, they had attacked an aerodrome in the vicinity of Le Havre. All had gone just as the operations officer had predicted—no flak, no fighters. "A day at the office," someone joked at the interrogation after the mission. Roy wasn't convinced. The Germans liked to ring their airfields with mobile flak batteries, sneaking them into position overnight. Fighters were always somewhere in the vicinity—you could bet the German FW190s and Me109s would be there. Still, he wasn't going to complain. A target in France was a target in France, and the boys were relieved. They weren't going to Germany today. They had not been back over the Third Reich in three weeks, and that was fine by them. They had flown five missions in June, each one to a target in western France—transportation choke points, airfields, defensive positions near the Normandy beaches. No flak damage, no enemy aircraft, no casualties. Milk runs all.

"Ten thousand feet," Verne's voice crackled over the interphone. "Going on oxygen." Roy adjusted his mask, checked the vents, drew on the rich oxygen. It smelled strongly of rubber and sweat. Beside him, his copilot Verne Lewis was making the oxygen check, and the men were calling in. He listened absently: bombardier, navigator, radio, top turret, ball turret, right waist, left waist, tail gunner. All were on oxygen. Verne would make checks every five minutes. They would be on oxygen for almost four hours. If something went wrong, if a mask froze over, if the oxygen at one of the crew stations failed, anoxia would set in. Within two minutes a man would lose consciousness, within ten he would die.

Two voices sounded strange. Left waist, tail gunner.

"Who's back there today," he asked Verne.

"Spares. Don't know them. One's from Kentucky, somebody said."

This morning's mission was the crew's eleventh. Less than halfway through their tour of duty, they had lost two of the original gunners, Grimes and Duvall, to wounds and illness and now flew with fillers, spares, on each mission.

They were climbing steadily. Twelve, thirteen, fourteen thousand feet. Beads of ice formed on the Plexiglas, and wind whistled through the turrets and the open windows in the waist. The first cold began to brush against his face. Later it would seep into his bones. At twenty thousand feet, operational altitude, the temperature inside the unheated plane would drop to twenty below. He was bundled in layer upon layer of flying clothes. He wore thick gloves.

They had taken off at 0415, as the first hint of dawn tinted the field, flying the briefed course, forming into three combat boxes of twelve planes each. They rendezvoused on schedule with the 351st and 401st, the two Bomb Groups that together with the 457th comprised the Ninety-fourth Combat Wing. Then, with over one hundred Fortresses stacked and spread across the bright sky, the formation turned south. The sun had climbed high over the morning haze when they passed to the west of London, heading for the radio beacon near Brighton. Other Combat Wings would be joining them; in all, a thousand aircraft were heading for targets in France.

"0654. Departing the English coast," Joe Brusse reported laconically over the interphone. "On course, on time." The navigator's slow south Texas drawl always seemed reassuring when they were in the air. Roy could visualize him down in the ship's Plexiglas nose, hunched over his crude navigator's table, the protractors and maps spread before him. All business. From the very beginning, when the crew formed back at Ardmore in February, he had been Roy's favorite. He could get you home from anywhere. He had proven it on the Dessau mission.

They were still climbing. The first contrails appeared, long white spears of vapor spreading from the wings of every plane in the vast formation. Above them he could make out other vapor trails, each in the form of an "S." Friendly fighters—Mustangs and Thunderbolts— escorting the formation, flying S curves to stay with the slower bombers. The "little friends" were a comforting sight. In approximately twenty minutes the lead elements of the formation would cross the enemy coast at twenty-one thousand feet. Below, through the wispy clouds, Roy could see sunlight glinting off the silver-green blankness of the Channel. Within minutes they would be appearing on German radar.

Not long ago Roy had been a freshman in college, struggling with calculus, playing football and baseball at Duke. He had never flown in a plane, never even set foot in one. He hadn't had much of an opportunity growing up in the Olney section of Philadelphia—Lower Olney, the locals called it scornfully, a rough-and-tumble section of relentless two-story row houses, shallow porches, beer-and-a-chaser taverns, trolley tracks. His whole world was Olney, Fisher Park, the Fernrock Movie Theater, the street corners and stoops, the house on Champlost Avenue where his wife, May, lived when they first met. Downtown Philadelphia, where his mother worked as a legal secretary, might as well have been Zanzibar for all he saw of it.

No one in the family had any military connections—in fact, connections of any kind. His father had died when Roy was just over a year old, and his mother did her best to raise him. They lived in a succession of cramped apartments in the neighborhood, mostly second-floor, two-room flats with thin walls and cracked bay windows that overlooked the street. Money was always tight. He helped out, working part-time jobs, full time in the summers. He learned to look out for himself, to improvise. Sometimes he brought home slightly spoiled vegetables from Beck's Produce at Third and Cayuga, where he hung out in his spare time. When things were really tough, he slipped a few milk bottles from the porches down the street.

Sports provided his ticket out. He played everything—football, basketball, baseball, track. He was a natural. At thirteen he was over six feet tall, weighed almost 180, and wore a size thirteen shoe. His name was always in the paper. A columnist from the *Daily News* called him the best high school quarterback in Pennsylvania. Connie Mack, the owner and manager of the Philadelphia Athletics baseball club, invited him over to Shibe Park to work out with the team when he was only fifteen. Mr. Mack was impressed but thought the kid needed some seasoning and urged him to attend college. Roy spent a year at Franklin and Marshall Academy in Lancaster, waiting on tables, getting his grades in order, and then, with Mr. Mack's help, entered Duke, in Durham, North Carolina. He went to class, he made the teams, but whether it was the small-town setting, the heat, or the well-heeled southern boys who strolled the campus, he always felt out of place.

In early 1941, just before his sophomore year, he was drafted out of college, his papers stamped "Army Air Corps." He went through basic training, spent several weeks at radio school in Illinois, and was shipped out to Pearl Harbor. It was there that he learned about the aviation cadets, an elite program to train pilots. He had over a year of college, his aptitude scores were high, and his eyesight and coordination were excellent. He applied and, to his astonishment, was accepted.

He entered the program at the Army Air Force Training Command at Santa Ana, California, where, among other wonders, he was issued six pairs of pants, six shirts, six pairs of shorts, undershirts, a dozen pairs of socks, two ties, two pairs of shoes, a raincoat, four garrison caps, one service cap with visor, and an assortment of toiletries. It was more clothes than he had owned at any time in his life. For as long as he could remember he had washed out his shirt every night and worn his only other one the next day. At school he borrowed coats, ties, shirts, sometimes even shoes, for any sort of formal occasion—proms, graduation, even his induction into the Philadelphia Schoolboy Sports Hall of Fame.

He survived the cuts at Santa Ana and Preflight at Santa Maria, marching through courses in navigation, aerodynamics, meteorology, and aircraft identification, and proceeded on to Primary Pilot School at Lemoore Field near Hanford, California. There he flew for the first time in his life, logging sixty-five hours in the sturdy old Spearman PT-13Bs. In the nine-week course he flew solo, mastered takeoff and landing, and learned all the standard maneuvers—spins, stalls, rolls, loops, and chandelles—while managing to avoid the disastrous ground loops and noseovers that spelled doom for so many others. At each stage along the way, cadets fell by the wayside. Many washed out, failing in the classroom or in the cockpit, and some were killed, perishing in the accidents that attended every training base. But in May 1943 Roy was ready to move on to Advanced Pilot at Stockton, California. If he passed there, he would win his wings; he would be an officer and a pilot.

At Lemoore he wrote a letter home to May. She was living with her parents on Seventy-seventh Avenue, working in her father's heating oil business. They had been sweethearts since early high school, since she was fifteen. They walked to school together, sat for hours on the front porch of her house, then on Champlost Avenue, and went to his senior prom together. In the summer he worked for her father, installing furnaces, making oil deliveries. He practically lived at their house. When he went away to college, they wrote. They stayed in touch, but they had not seen each other since he entered service, almost two years ago. And so he wrote from the 43-H, Squadron A barracks, inviting her to join him in California. It amounted to a proposal, though not a very romantic one, he worried, and he did not know if she would come.

She had never traveled very far—to New York, the Jersey shore, and to Marblehead in Massachusetts—but when his letter arrived, she did not hesitate. She packed a small suitcase and boarded a train at Thirtieth Street Station bound for California. She made the exhausting three-day journey across the continent alone, changing trains in cavernous dusty stations, sitting, standing, sleeping in the crowded smoke-filled cars. Her train was late arriving in Los Angeles and she missed a connection. When she reached the station at Hanford, Roy had been called back to the field. He could not see her until the weekend—another six days—but he had arranged a room for her nearby.

Two weeks later, on May 29, 1943, they were married in the garden of the residence where she was staying. The house was a large rambling villa, with a lavish, well-tended garden, though the family's Japanese gardener had been sent to one of the internment camps for Japanese-Americans a year before. May's father came all the way from Philadelphia to attend the ceremony. Roy was only able to get away from the field for an afternoon, arriving by bus just in time. After the vows and photographs and toasts, May changed out of her dress, and the two of them rushed down to the bus stop at the corner. Roy had to hurry back to the field. It was, they laughed, the shortest honeymoon on record.

On August 30, Roy graduated from Advanced at Stockton; he was no longer an aviation cadet. May pinned his wings on his shoulders, and together Lieutenant and Mrs. Allen traveled to his next station at Roswell, New Mexico. Every town near a base was awash with wives, fiancées, and girlfriends. They lived in boardinghouses or hotels or tiny cabins in motor courts. Families rented out rooms in private homes, and while Roy reported to the field, May found a room they could share on weekends. For Roy, it was the happiest time of his life.

At Roswell, he transitioned from piloting twin-engine planes to the giant four-engine B-17 Flying Fortress. With a reputation for toughness—it could take tremendous punishment and still get you home—the Fortress was the mainstay and glamour plane of the Army Air Forces. It was a monster. Weighing forty thousand pounds, with a wingspan of 103 feet, and powered by four Wright Cyclone engines, it took muscle and coordination to handle. It could fly at 325 miles per hour, had a ceiling of thirty-eight thousand feet, and could haul a bomb load of eight thousand pounds. A Fortress carried a crew of ten, four officers—pilot, copilot, navigator, and bombardier—and six enlisted men—a radio operator, flight engineer, and four additional gunners. Roy would not be simply a pilot but an aircraft commander. After forty-five weeks of intensive training, he was eager to have his own crew.

"Gunners," Verne said over the interphone, "you're clear to test fire your weapons." From all over the aircraft short thunderous bursts of machine-gun fire erupted. Everything shuddered, rattled. The acrid scent of cordite filled the plane. All around the formation Roy could see silent jets of smoke spewing from the other planes as other crews fired off a few test rounds.

They were flying in the lead element this morning, just off the left wing of Colonel Cobb, the command pilot for the mission. Roy was pleased with their position in the formation. It meant he wouldn't be fighting the prop wash of one hundred other aircraft, struggling for hours to hold the plane in position in the relentless turbulence. Still, even at fifteen below zero he was sweating. He had been since the Group formed up.

Ordinarily, the copilot would fly the aircraft in this position in formation, with a plane just off the right wing, but Roy was at the controls this morning. He always was when they were in formation. Verne was fine with takeoff and landing. He assisted ably on the flight deck, monitoring the instruments, conducting the oxygen checks, and in the flak over the target he was calm. He always knew what to do. But in formation he was not the same man, not since the accident.

In training at Ardmore, Verne had been a first pilot with his own crew. On one of his first exercises in formation flying, the instructor, riding in the tail gunner's cone of the lead plane, kept screaming for the pilots to close it up, close it up, tighter, tighter. None of them had ever flown in this sort of large formation—two elements, two or three planes in an element, but not this. The instructor did not let up. This was preparation for the big time, the real thing, he barked over the command set. Close it up! B-17s were bobbing in the prop wash all around them, just above and below them, just off their left wing. For all new pilots it was a nerve-jangling experience.

Then, as the formation began a sweeping turn, Verne's plane seemed to buck, to drift upward. In a split second it knifed into the ship above it, slicing off the tail just at the waist gunners' position. The giant tail fluttered crazily through the air, spilling oxygen bottles, bits of equipment, and men into the sky, while the truncated fuselage, its engines screaming wildly, went cartwheeling into a sickening dive. Twenty thousand feet below, a fireball erupted on the prairie floor. There were no survivors.

The inquiry never established who was responsible. Was the high aircraft out of position? Did it slide down into Verne's? Did he ride up into it? Accidents occurred with terrifying regularity in every phase of training—fiery crashes, black smoke billowing from the edge of runways, sirens screaming, fire crews swarming, charred unrecognizable bodies borne quietly away. You couldn't think about it. Verne was removed as aircraft commander, and there was talk of a court-martial, but it came to nothing. Instead, the training commander asked Roy if he would take Lieutenant Lewis on as copilot. Roy agreed, and Verne was assigned to the crew.

He fit in right away. He got along with everyone, and on the flight deck Verne and Roy seemed to work well as a team. But during their early training flights he was reluctant to take the controls when they were in formation. At first Roy did not recognize a pattern, and he let it slide. Then he thought it would pass, that it was the accident, and the shock would wear off. But weeks passed and it did not. Verne would not fly the plane in formation, and by then Roy was reluctant to disrupt the crew's delicate chemistry. He mentioned it to no one, not even Joe. Now he had to live with that decision. It meant that he flew formation for six, seven, eight hours without relief, and he returned from every mission drenched in sweat. It soaked through layers of flying clothes, leaving crusty white arcs beneath the arms of his leather flight jacket.

Still, it was a good crew. They had formed in late January, spending eight grueling weeks of Phase III crew training at Ardmore, Oklahoma. The navigator, Joe Brusse, was a quiet, gentlemanly character from Brenham, Texas, whose easygoing manner cloaked an engineer's keen mathematical sense. On the long cross-country exercises, many of them at night, he always knew where they were and how to get them to their destination. Larry Anderson, the bombardier who rode in the nose with Joe, was from Pittsburgh and showed extraordinary skill with the demanding Norden bombsight. On their practice missions his hand was steady, his aim accurate. He put the bombs, as the instructors liked to say, "in the pickle barrel."

The crew's six enlisted men, all sergeants, worked well together. Ray Plum, a tough guy from southern California, was the flight engineer and top-turret gunner. His job was to know the plane inside out, its systems, its operations, its limitations. In the air he would be the crew's troubleshooter. Ernest Smith—Smittie—was the radio operator, an unhurried competent man from Oklahoma who knew his Morse and his radio procedures and whose cowboy twang over the interphone sounded as if he had just stopped by from the rodeo. Roy could count on him. Leonard Henson, a country boy from southern Illinois, and Joe Duvall manned the fifty calibers in the waist. Bob Grimes rode in the isolated tail-gunner's cone, facing backward, and Bill Goldsborough, from Baltimore—the smallest man on the crew—climbed down into the cramped ball turret that extended beneath the belly of the ship. All had come out of gunnery school with high ratings.

At twenty-five, Roy was the oldest guy on the crew. At some point, Henson started calling him "Pappy." The name stuck.

Through the cold clear days of January and February 1944 the crew flew practice missions of every kind, dropping bombs on target ranges in the Texas desert—finding and hitting the chalky white circles that were painted like bull's eyes on the bare red earth. They flew long cross-country navigational exercises to Canada and California and the Gulf of Mexico, and day after day they practiced the tight box formations they would need to survive in combat. When they were not in the air, they attended ground classes, everything from aircraft maintenance to first aid to American strategic air doctrine. They had all heard about high-altitude daylight precision bombing. Now they trained for it.

In March, they moved to Salt Lake City for a week, and then on to Grand Island, Nebraska, where replacement crews were finally dispatched to their new units. It was to be their last station before moving overseas. They were on alert, their gear packed, and each morning they reported to the squadron dayroom, ready for immediate departure. For two weeks they waited and watched as other crews roared off the runways, bound for the war. It was a frustrating, agonizing time.

Roy was not required to live on the base, and May found them a room in a hotel in town. The Command discouraged wives from coming to Grand Island. Verne's wife, Helen, was not there, and Joe's wife, Frances, had driven their '38 Oldsmobile back to Texas. They had gotten to know one another in Ardmore, especially May and Frances, offering moral support and company while they waited for the weekends and their husbands to arrive from the field. But May was determined to come to Grand Island. In Ardmore they discovered she was pregnant, the baby due in September, and she wanted to be with Roy.

Each morning in Grand Island, they got up before dawn, dressed in the small room, and had breakfast in the coffee shop off the lobby. Each morning they said good-bye. They did not know whether his orders would arrive that day, whether he would be coming back that night, and so each kiss, each farewell could be their last. Finally, the daily dosage of torment became too much, and after a week they agreed that she should leave. She would go home to her parents' house in Olney, on Seventy-seventh Avenue, not far from the old neighborhood. They would say only one more good-bye.

Several days later, on March 21, 1944, the word came. The crew was not to leave the base. They could make no phone calls. Be prepared for immediate departure. Their orders were sealed, not to be opened until the aircraft was in flight. When they found the plane they would fly, a sparkling new B-17, the wheels of the landing gear were frozen to the concrete hardstand. They worked in the drizzling cold to free them. They ran up the engines, tested the systems, and then—just like that—they were airborne. While Verne took the controls, Roy tore open the sealed orders and read them over the interphone. They were on their way to Grenier Field in Manchester, New Hampshire. From there they would depart the United States, proceeding via the Northern Atlantic Route to the European Theater of Operations (ETO). They were to report to Commander, Eighth Air Force Service Command, Air Transports Command Terminals of Arrival, British Isles, for further assignment and duty with the Eighth Air Force. The biggest and most glamorous of all Army Air Force commands, the Eighth was also the most dangerous.

From New Hampshire they flew alone across the vast emptiness of the North Atlantic, hopping from Goose Bay to Gander Lake, Newfoundland, to Reykjavik in Iceland, arriving finally in Northern Ireland. They reported to a crew replacement center, completed an in-country orientation course, and were at last assigned to the 749th Squadron, 457th Bomb Group on April 12.

A truck deposited them at Air Station 130, some seventy miles north of London, just off the Great North Road. The closest city of any size was Peterborough, only a few miles away, but the base itself, with over three thousand men, was a small town in its own right. Its elongated triangle of runways, hardstands, hangars, barracks, mess halls, firing ranges, and bomb dump seemed to have been dropped into the midst of an unsuspecting English countryside. Farmers' fields bordered the runways—Rose Court farm actually operated in the center of the base—and just beyond the perimeter track, hidden by a copse of trees, lay Conington, a picturesque village whose soaring church tower and ancient castle were welcome landmarks from the air.

The weather was cool and wet—it seemed to rain off and on every day—and the crew settled in, learning the ropes. The enlisted men moved into their quarters in the 749th area, and the officers took up residence in a gloomy half-moon tin hut already occupied by the officers of another crew. They flew several practice missions, dropping bombs in the North Sea, acclimating themselves to formation flying in the ETO, learning the Group's procedures.

They were as ready as they were ever going to be, Roy thought, when they were alerted for their first mission on May 11. It was a short jump to Luxembourg, easy in and easy out. They had taken off and formed up in the bright sunlight of late afternoon and were back at the field in the early evening. Less than six hours in the air. The crew performed with calm and precision, just like training at Ardmore. At the hardstand after the mission, their flight bags at their feet, they were jubilant with relief. They could do this. It was almost enough to make them forget that the number of missions required to complete a tour had just been raised from twenty-five to thirty.

Then came the missions to Germany.

A day after the Luxembourg raid, the 457th attacked synthetic oil refineries at Lützkendorf, near Merseburg in central Germany. It marked the beginning of a renewed Allied assault on German oil production, the operations officer explained at briefing. The trip in was uneventful. They saw no enemy fighters and no sooty smudges of flak appeared in the sky as they approached the target. The first ominous puffs did not materialize until the formation was almost directly over the city. Then the guns, the terrible .88s, opened up and the sky went suddenly dark. The barrage lasted less than a minute. It seemed like an hour. The 457th suffered no casualties in the raid, but their ship suffered minor battle damage—flak hits in the nacelles of three engines. They had been lucky. Back at the field, they learned that German fighters had ambushed planes from the Third Air Division, trailing their own formation. Thirty-two Fortresses had been shot down.

They did not fly a mission again for a week. They flew practices, and they waited. Roy went to the movie theater at the base with Joe; he wrote letters; he listened to the radio, the BBC and the Armed Forces Network (AFN). He liked the musical broadcasts—the Hit Parade, the Glenn Miller Program. He knew all the tunes, the lyrics, the singers, the bands, even the British ones—Vera Lynn, Ray Noble, Al Boley. He sang along. He sang in the plane, in the hut on the hardstand. His mother had been in the road company of Broadway shows before he was born, and she always sang in the apartment. There was a Group glee club. He thought about it, but there was no time. He did the crosswords in *Stars and Stripes* and the British papers he found in the Officer's Club. They seemed to soothe his nerves.

They flew their next mission on May 19. Briefing was at 0330 and when the S2, the operations officer, unveiled the enormous target map and the men saw the long black string extending from the coast of England to a large red splotch deep in eastern Germany, silence fell over the hut. Feet shuffled on the concrete floor. Men shifted in their chairs. The target was Berlin. After only two missions, this. The 457th had been to Berlin on May 7 and 8, the S2 reminded them, and the flak had been both intense and accurate. Enemy aircraft had been everywhere along the route. This time would be no different.

On the way in, fighters tore into the formation. Dozens of them. They cued up on the horizon, black dots no bigger than pencil points. Then, as the formation approached the city, they came in waves. Brilliant flashes lit the sky as they roared past, and the interphone erupted. "Bandit at seven o'clock low; one coming in at eleven o'clock high; three of 'em at five o'clock high!" For twenty-five frantic minutes the gunners called out attacking fighters, and the plane shivered as its fifties blazed away. The fighters—Me109s, FW 190s, thirty, forty of them—seemed to be everywhere, above them, below them, boring in. Then, as suddenly as they appeared, they peeled away, and the formation plowed into the field of flak over the target.

Five miles below them fires raged mutely, and towering sulfurous clouds billowed from the gray-brown city. Grainy black puffs, each hurling hundreds of metal shards around the sky, sprouted all around them, and shrapnel clattered against the thin skin of the plane like hail. The plane shuddered and lurched around the darkened sky, rocked by the muffled blasts. Grimes screamed out from the tail. A chunk of flak had torn a hole as big as a grapefruit just behind him. He was bleeding. The bomb bay door took a direct hit. A jagged gash appeared in the left wing, just beyond the number-one engine. Power was failing in the number three. It was smoking.

The plane stayed aloft, and somehow they limped home. They were in the air, in formation, for over nine hours. The aircraft sustained major battle damage, and Grimes was wounded. Five days later they went back to Berlin for more of the same.

On the twenty-seventh, the Group flew a mission to Ludwigshaven. The Roy Allen crew was not alerted. They were scheduled to fly a practice mission later in the morning, but their hut mates, the officers of the Bill Dee crew, were roused long before daybreak. Roy could hear them dressing in the semidark—Dee and his copilot Bob Cotterell, Larry Oberstein the navigator, and Don Jay the bombardier. Roy rolled over. This morning he could sleep in.

That afternoon, when the planes returned, everyone lined the field as they always did, counting. They could see that it had been a rough mission. Planes were missing, others, badly damaged, landed with dead and wounded on board. One sputtered in with a prop missing and power in only one engine. Three planes did not return. Bill Dee's was one of them. The formation had been attacked on the way in, a horde of 109s swooping out of the sun in a massive frontal assault. Dee's plane was hit, dropped out of the formation, and turned back toward the Channel. When last seen, it was under control but losing altitude. No one had seen chutes. No one had seen a crash. Maybe they had made it. Maybe they would show up at another field.

The next morning, just after chow, a sergeant from Personal Effects came into the hut. He was an older man with thinning hair. He wore glasses. He took a long look at the four empty bunks and the long rack of clothing and equipment hanging behind them. Working quietly, he sorted through the duffel bags and footlockers, placing the toiletries, the letters, and the photographs neatly into small, labeled bags. He folded the uniforms carefully. He stripped the beds, folded back the mattresses. He did not speak to Roy or the others, and they studiously avoided looking at him. As he left, Roy could see that the rims of the sergeant's eyes were red.

It was at this time, in the days before the Dessau mission, that Larry Anderson's nightmares began. He seemed fine at the Officer's Club and in the mess hall, in the Liberty Run trucks into Peterborough. He wrote regularly to his wife. He was a good bombardier, and he did his job in the plane. He was a little quiet, but everyone was jumpy. At night, in the hut, was another story. Long after lights-out Roy could hear him thrashing around in his bunk, sobbing, muttering to himself. Other times his voice was clear and firm, as if he were wide awake, making a deposit at the bank: he was at the bombardiers' briefing and couldn't get the calculations right or he was in the nose, hunched over the bombsight, flak shattering the Plexiglas, bandits coming in. He called them out. Roy or Joe would shake him, and he would sit bolt upright, his eyes wide, starring at them in the darkness, sweating. "We're not going to make it," he said quietly, like a judge handing down a sentence, "we're not going to make it." Next morning he would remember nothing.

Then came Dessau. On May 28, the Group was briefed for a mission against an aircraft factory at Dessau. As the formation approached the city, they found it socked in, buried beneath a ten-tenths cloud cover, and the command pilot chose to move on to the secondary at Leipzig. It was close by, just forty kilometers to the south, but Roy, flying in the low box, never made it to the IP. As the formation wheeled into a turn, 109s suddenly swarmed all around them, screaming past the formation. On their first pass, the aircraft seemed to stagger. White smoke shot from the number-two and -three engines at the same moment. They were gone, out completely, starting to windmill crazily. Fire streaked from the nacelle of the number four. Vern instantly reached forward. He closed the shutoff valves and turned the booster pumps off, shutting off fuel to the shattered engines. Roy feathered them.

The windmilling stopped, but the aircraft was fully loaded—six one-thousand pounders were riding in the bomb bay—and with the sudden loss of power, the aircraft sputtered. At twenty thousand feet, it stalled. For an instant the plane seemed to have stopped dead in midair, suspended by invisible wires. The nose lifted slightly, then tucked under, and they started down. A high piercing shriek filled the plane. They were in a steep dive, picking up speed. A fierce pressure pushed against Roy's face, shoving his head back against the bulkhead. He strained at the control column, Verne helping, both pulling back as hard as they could. Bursting suddenly through a layer of cloud he could see a swirling patchwork of yellow-green countryside rushing toward them. Instruments, papers, charts, flew around the flight deck. Over the interphone he could hear screaming.

Finally, the nose began to rise, to pull up. Vibrating wildly, the plane leveled out. Roy was gasping for breath. Sweat coursed over his face, streaming into his eyes. He couldn't talk. His mouth was dry as cotton. Verne gathered himself. He glanced out the right window. The fire in number four, he said, was out. The dive must have extinguished it. Roy closed the cowl, trimmed the plane. One by one the crew checked in.

They had dropped to 5,500 feet. Roy gave the order and Larry toggled the bombs and the plane heaved upward. High above them the formation was droning on toward the target. German fighters were all around, looking for stragglers, ready to swoop in for the kill. But there were "little friends" in the area, too, Mustangs who might escort them home.

"Get on that radio, Smittie," Roy spoke into the interphone. "Fighter frequency. See if we can't get some help here."

Roy waited. The radio crackled with fighter pilots calling back and forth to one another. The Mustangs were scattering away in dogfights.

"No soap," Smittie said. "Nobody's home. I can't get a response. Nothing."

They were alone, but for the moment they were still in the air. Two engines were finished; a third might go at any second. Plum was working feverishly to transfer fuel to the two good ones. In the nose Joe was doing some quick figuring. He had recorded their position in his log every five minutes on the route in, plotting their course and verifying it by the terrain below. Pilotage navigation, it was called. Now he calculated airspeeds and times from his last pilotage read, their last known position. They were pretty far north. On one engine they might reach neutral Sweden. If two engines held, they might even make it home, to a field in Scotland. He informed Roy.

Sitting out the war interned in Sweden didn't seem very attractive to Roy, not if there was a chance to make it home. Verne agreed; so did Joe. Roy decided to put it to a vote. Speaking on the interphone, he explained the choices, and one by one the boys called in. No one hesitated. They would try to make it home. Somehow they had to make it to the coast and out of German airspace. Alone and underpowered, they were sitting ducks.

"Navigator to pilot, there's a weather front building up north of the briefed route. Meteorological report said it should extend all the way to the coast." Roy recalled it from briefing, and he could see a high bank of stratocumulus off in that direction.

"Roger," he said. "If we can get into the clouds, we might shake the fighters."

"We'll have to hurry, Pappy." It was Henson's voice on the interphone. "Bandits are lining up for a pass at three o'clock level."

"I see them," Verne confirmed.

Roy coaxed the wounded plane upward, sliding into the clouds just as the fighters swept by. Machine-gun fire sprayed the ship. The engines coughed and whined from the strain, and suddenly the plane was enveloped in white.

"Bandits breaking off," Goldsborough called in from the ball. "They're not coming in after us." But they would be out there waiting, Roy knew, skimming the fringes of the cloud bank. Okay, he would stay in the clouds as long as he could. It meant flying blind, on instruments. He hoped that no one else was lumbering along in the clouds with them.

Joe gave him a north-northwest heading, and he swung onto the new course. The ship wallowed through waves of turbulence, surging upward, then, with gut-wrenching suddenness, dropping like a stone. The men slammed into the walls like sailors caught in a storm at sea. "Can we go back and pick up my stomach," Henson called in. The strain on the engines was intense. Trying to escape the terrible buffeting, Roy prodded the plane into a steady climb, but when he broke into the clear, the Messerschmidts were waiting for them, hiding in the sun.

Unable to see the ground, Joe was navigating by dead reckoning. "I put us northwest of Hannover," he calculated. He read out a set of coordinates. "We're on course to cross the coast just west of Wilhelmshaven." Verne held a mission map in a waterproof pouch in his lap. Roy glanced over at it. They would have to avoid the flak concentrations at Oldenburg and Bremen, and that would mean periodic adjustments in the heading.

For what seemed an eternity they pitched and yawed through the clouds, bouncing in the choppy air. From time to time the whiteness would brighten and they would burst suddenly into a vast pool of light and calm, only to be swallowed up again by a sea of cloud. The interphone was silent, each man alone with his thoughts.

"Can we drop down, see if I can get a fix on our position?" Joe asked at last.

"We'll give it a try," Roy said. Just below the ceiling, a sprinkling of villages, railroad tracks, a canal swam into view. A volley of flak appeared off to the right and below them. Three quick bursts, then nothing. Only one battery. Joe got a quick look, and up they went again, back into the clouds. No one reported any fighters, but it was too dangerous out of the clouds.

"Are we gonna make it, Pappy?" Goldsborough's voice crackled over his headset.

"Home for dinner," Roy answered calmly. He had no idea.

Roy glanced at the altimeter, the fuel gauges. The fuel was holding. They were maintaining altitude.

"We're over the North Sea now," Joe called in at last. He sounded confident, and Roy eased the ship down. Breaking through the clouds into the clear, they found themselves directly over a wide bay teeming with ships. A harbor and docks with giant hoisting cranes appeared off to the left. "Christ awmighty," someone groaned. In a flash ack-ack opened up, tracers arcing toward them from all over the bay. "Wilhelmshaven," Joe yelled. "It's Wilhelmshaven!"

There weren't many choices. With the two engines gone, Roy couldn't climb back up to the ceiling fast enough. With no place to go, he pushed the control column down, dropping the giant plane almost to the wave tops. His heart was in his mouth. They were skimming the whitecaps, spray slamming against the windows. The plane shook and pitched, as the gunners fired off burst after burst. They roared right over the ships, low enough to see frantic sailors racing around the decks below them. If the bastards fire at us now, he figured, they'll be shooting at themselves.

They thundered out of the bay, leaving the ships behind them. Miraculously, no fighters appeared. Shaking, Roy climbed slowly over the North Sea, swinging at last to the west-southwest toward Britain. They had made it out of Germany, but the plane was losing power. They couldn't maintain altitude, and they were too far away from Scotland to ditch. Air-sea rescue would never find them. At fifteen hundred feet Roy gave the order to jettison everything they could— guns, ammo, flak jackets, helmets, even their heavy clothing, anything not tied down.

Laboring across the waves toward the Scottish coast, they were utterly defenseless now. "Bogeys at one o'clock high," Plum called out.

He was back in the top turret. The machine guns were still there—he couldn't get them out of the turret—but he had no ammunition.

"They're asking for a call sign," Smittie said from the radio compartment. "They're British."

"Mosquitoes," Henson added. "Two of 'em."

Smittie transmitted the coded call sign, and the Mosquitoes acknowledged. They offered to lead them to the nearest base, an RAF emergency landing field.

Plum dropped down from the top turret and checked the fuel gauges. They looked good. Joe confirmed their position, off the coast of Scotland. Unless something else went wrong, he thought, they could make it home. Roy agreed. They would try for AS 130.

The engines grumbled but held. Within minutes the familiar snout of East Anglia appeared off their left wing and they slipped down the Wash, crossing the English coast at Kings Lynn. Beyond Peterborough the spire of Conington Chapel slipped into view. They had made it. Roy began his approach to the field, and Verne leaned forward, flipping the switch to extend the landing gear. Roy glanced out his side window. He could not see the left landing gear.

"Down, right," Verne reported. The right gear was extended. "Try it again," Roy said. Verne flipped the switch to the up position, then pressed down again. The left gear still was not visible. Plum climbed back from the flight deck to get a better view.

"It doesn't look too good," he said over the interphone. "The left landing gear's been hit."

"Get on the manual crank," Roy responded. The crank was stowed on the aft bulkhead of the radio compartment. He radioed the tower. He was going around again. As he swung onto the downwind leg, Plum was on the interphone again. Henson and Goldsborough were taking turns with the crank, working as fast as they could. "But the son of a bitch won't extend," he said. "Looks like the retracting screw is bent."

Already in the landing pattern, Roy radioed the control tower. He was low on fuel, but he would go around again, make a new approach. He warned the crew to prepare for a crash landing. Larry and Joe crawled out of the nose, joining Smittie in the radio compartment. The other gunners would take up their emergency positions there too. There wasn't time to drop the ball turret—it would take twenty minutes and the fuel wouldn't last. With the ball still in place, a belly landing was out. It meant coming in on one wheel. Roy had seen ships land this way, skidding across the runway, dragging a fuel-laden wing across the tarmac in a blizzard of sparks until the tanks blew and the plane was engulfed in flame.

He was sweating. Suddenly a familiar voice blared over the command set. "Lieutenant," it said, "this is Colonel Luper." Roy shot a quick glance at Verne. It was the Group commander, speaking from the tower. "Lieutenant, that's my plane you're flying up there," he said. "It's named for my wife—*Renee III*—so I want you to be very careful with her." He asked about their fuel, about the landing gear, the hand crank, the ball turret. He went over emergency-landing procedures.

"I'm on intimate terms with that aircraft, Lieutenant. Logged lots of hours in her. So pay attention. I'm going to talk you down." Roy banked into another turn, flying the long upwind leg of the landing pattern. Luper kept up a steady stream of instructions, "Trim it here, ease back, ease back!" In a deep command voice he talked on and on, giving directions, asking questions, demanding answers. Roy was going over the procedures in his head, trying to recall from pilot training. "Bring it in on a normal power approach," he murmured to himself, "directly into the wind, with speed slightly above normal. Put down only three-quarter flaps. Make what would be a normal three-point landing. Use plenty of runway, use the throttles to keep the ship straight. Don't use brakes." Roy swung into a tight turn. He was going to land. "No, no," the colonel barked, "what are you doing? Go around again, is that clear!"

Roy had had enough. "The hell with him," he grunted, ripping off the headset. "We're going in," he said, alerting the crew. "Brace yourselves." The interphone was silent.

The runway rushed up at them like a freight train. Roy held the plane steady, the left wing as high as he dared. Holding, holding until the right landing gear bounced, bounced again. The plane screamed down the tarmac. Emergency vehicles, the black-and-white control truck, tents, parked aircraft shot past in a blur. The left wing dipped. Sliding to the left, the plane swung off the runway into the grass. He held as tight as he could. The plane didn't slough or loop. It scraped and bounced until at last the props plowed into the soft earth, and the plane skidded to a thudding halt in the short grass beside the runway.

Roy slumped in the pilot's seat, unable to move. His fingers, still gripping the controls, ached. His head throbbed. Verne shook him. They had to get out. The ship still might blow. Ambulances and fire trucks were converging on them as the crew scrambled out. They staggered away as fast as they could, keeping their distance while the fire crews secured the plane. The aircraft hugged the ground, the props on the left wing bent backward at the tip. The vertical stabilizer, the dorsal fin and both wings were riddled with ragged holes. The radio room window was shattered, the tail gunner's side windows broken. The two and three engines were scorched black.

Colonel Luper, his pipe clinched tightly in his fist, was out of the control tower and down on the runway before Roy could collect himself. The Group commander was not happy. Hadn't the lieutenant heard his command? Lieutenant Allen had endangered the lives of his crew and risked the aircraft. Stunned, Roy glared at Luper. He didn't trust himself to speak. While the two men faced each other, the Group public relations officer and his photographer arrived on the scene, snapping pictures of the plane, talking with the crew. Ground personnel and other fliers crowded around. They had seen it all. Everyone agreed that it was a remarkable landing. Colonel Luper posed with the crew.

Dessau didn't do Larry's nerves any good. His night terrors continued. Hell, all of them were shaken, Roy thought. He could see it in their haggard faces in the photograph taken by the PR man that day—his, too. But at least they had not been back to Germany. On May 31 they hit a target in western France, easy in, easy out. "A dream mission," Roy said at interrogation. They flew on June 3 and 4, again easy targets in France. No flak, no fighters.

Through the first rainy days of June, the base was supercharged with excitement. The invasion was imminent, and everyone knew it. The men had been expecting it for weeks, searching for signs that the big day was at hand. They listened to the news bulletins on AFN and followed the reports in *Stars and Stripes*. The base buzzed with rumors. Everybody on the crew, everybody in the hut, everybody on the flight line had a buddy who knew somebody who had gotten it from a clerk in another squadron, another group. Tomorrow was the day. Then the next day. On and on, through the last weeks of May, the beginning of June.

Then, on June 4, returning from a target just south of Paris, bad weather over the Channel forced the formation to drop down to the deck, and a stunning sight greeted them. In the failing light of late afternoon a vast armada of ships, hundreds of vessels of every size and shape, was scattered across the Thames estuary. This had to be it, Roy believed. But that night rain hammered on their hut like gravel, and the CQ, the duty officer who would wake them if they were to fly a mission, did not come. All day on the fifth rain raked across the field in great gusting squalls, and low clouds, as heavy as sandbags, piled up from horizon to horizon. Late in the day, the sky, still dismal and low, began to clear, but even with the marginal improvement, it was terrible weather for a major operation.

Still, something was up. In the early afternoon, while rain still pelted down, the base was sealed. All leaves were canceled. All combat crews were put on alert. An air of expectancy hovered over the Officer's Club, the hangars, the barracks. By the time the weak evening sun set at about 2200, the showers had stopped. Roy had barely climbed into the sack when the CQ poked his head inside the hut. It was 2300. "Better get up, boys," he sang out. "Breakfast at 2345, briefing at 0100. You don't want to miss this one."

They dressed quickly in the clammy midnight darkness, fumbling with their clothes, stuffing their gear in their flight bags. No one groused or joked. At breakfast no one could eat. They pawed at the powdered eggs, sipped the fruit cocktail, the bitter coffee. The crowded officer's mess was buzzing. This was it at last. The only question was where. They were in their seats waiting when Colonel Luper strode into the main briefing hut. He marched to the front, stopping before the giant wall map of Europe. As the Group commander turned to face them, the smoke-filled hut was so still Roy thought he could hear his watch ticking.

"Gentlemen," Luper said. "This is it. This is what we've been waiting for. I need not tell you how much depends on today's operation. Every resource in our possession must be put to use to make this mission successful. It must be successful." The target was Arromanches, on the beach in Normandy. The Group was to strike a defensive position consisting of three pillboxes and three bunkers on the beach just north of Creully, just behind the British landing zones.

They took off in the pitch black at 0430. The IP was not even on the Continent, but Brighton, on the south coast of England. Two hours later, as the sun rose hesitantly over the eastern horizon, the formation turned over the Channel, heading directly toward Normandy. They bombed through the clouds at 0700, using radar, and were back at AS 130 in the early morning. They stood by, ready to fly a second mission if necessary, but the call never came. No one had observed what happened, though later Colonel Luper pronounced the results excellent. Yet, for all the excitement, all the anticipation, the day was,

Roy had to admit, a disappointment. He had seen virtually nothing, not the landing beaches, the ships at sea, the German positions. He had seen a veil of cloud, shadowy black slivers in the sea and nothing more. It was just one more mission, their ninth.

For the next six days they did not fly combat. They flew several practices. They took the Liberty Run into Peterborough. They were planning a trip into London, a prize they could claim after completing their tenth mission. While they stood down, word came through channels at Squadron HQ that Colonel Luper had recommended Roy and Joe for the Distinguished Flying Cross. The recommendation was lavish in its praise—a remarkable job of piloting, an excellent piece of navigation under extremely adverse circumstances. They were both surprised. Word also reached them that the Group commander had selected them for lead crew training. The paperwork would arrive at Squadron HQ in a day or so.

Roy and Joe talked it over. Their tour of duty had already been extended from twenty-five to thirty missions, and nobody was happy about that. Flying lead would mean time away from combat missions to train, maybe three weeks to a month, and then they would fly an additional five missions—thirty-five. And lead crews did not fly with the same frequency as regular combat crews, so that would further extend their tour. May was expecting in September, and Frances had an infant son, Joe Jr., at home. If things went smoothly now, they had a very good chance of getting in their thirty missions and rotating back to the States by late summer or early fall. They wanted no part of the promotion.

Just before they were alerted for their tenth mission on June 12, Roy was summoned to the colonel's office at Group headquarters. It was not a comfortable conversation. They would obviously do what they were ordered to do, but, Roy tried to explain, both he and his navigator strongly preferred to stay with the crew they had trained and flown combat with. A third of their tour was almost behind them, and they did not want to change now. They did not want to fly lead. The colonel was irate. He hadn't expected this, he said. He hoped Lieutenant Allen would reconsider.

Then, yesterday, June 13, an officer from Public Relations burst into the hut. He was furious. The colonel had rescinded his recommendation of them for the DFC, he said. He had submitted a recommendation, all right, claiming that because of his previous knowledge of the flight characteristics of the plane, he had talked the pilot down, enabling him to land the aircraft safely. Luper had, the officer exploded, recommended *himself* for the Silver Star. Roy had no idea if the story was true; he had not had time to check with his sources at Squadron HQ. But relations with Luper were strained already, and he was glad the Group commander was not leading the mission today.

"0728. Crossing the French coast on time, on course," Joe called out. Far below and off their left wing, Roy could see fires burning. "Caen," Joe said, "that's Caen down there." The Germans still held the city, blocking the Allied advance. The American positions were to the west, only a few miles inland from the invasion beaches. Their course would take the formation directly over them, at the base of the Cotentin Peninsula.

The giant formation rumbled along, following a southeasterly course. Just north of Le Mans, it began a slow turn to the east, toward Orléans. After several minutes, the planes dipped south, then veered sharply to the north-northwest. Roy checked the time. The IP—Nangis—would be coming up in just a few minutes. So far so good. They had encountered no fighter opposition; they had seen no flak.

"We're south of the IP," Joe said from the nose.

Roy strained to glance down into the low overcast. Far below wispy patches of cloud glided across the terrain. He could make out nothing. The formation was turning again, this time to the west, toward the target at Melun. This was the bomb run.

"We are off course, south of the briefed route," Joe insisted. Verne consulted the map. He nodded.

Smittie's voice broke through the static. Ahead of them, the lead plane was swinging into another turn. This was not in the briefing. Listening in on the command frequency, Smittie heard the order. "We're going around again," he said. Roy's eyes widened. He switched his headset to listen. Smittie was right. Verne stared over at him from the copilot's seat, shaking his head in disbelief. Just then the lead plane began a turn to the right.

"We're going around again," Roy muttered dismally into the inter-phone.

"Oh, shit," someone said.

They still had seen no fighters and no flak.

The entire Ninety-fourth E Combat Wing was abandoning the bomb run, commencing a 360-degree turn to the right.

Suddenly they were there, ten, fifteen fighters. No one had picked them up. The 109s roared directly at the lead box, making a head-on pass. Roy watched them, mesmerized, as they came screaming straight at him. As they shot through the formation, the deputy wing lead, just above him and to the right, began to smoke. An engine was on fire. The plane winged over, sliding into a dive. Puffs of flak smudged the sky. Wherever they were shooting from, the bastards had the range, they had the altitude. Seconds later the lead plane, Colonel Cobb's ship, shuddered violently. Black smoke poured from somewhere in the fuselage. Chunks of aluminum, Plexiglas, and rubber flew off in every direction. A black object shot past. A wheel. "They took a direct hit," Larry yelled. In an instant Cobb's aircraft, out of control, zoomed up through the high squadron. Planes scattered. Then Cobb's plane nosed over and began a long agonizing spin. It had not reached the ground when it disintegrated in a rippling explosion. "Any chutes?" Roy called out. "Anybody see any chutes?" There was no answer.

They were now the lead plane, he realized, when he felt a bone-jarring jolt, then another. The plane staggered. It seemed to skip sideways. The gunners were calling out bandits again, but he could not see them. Bursts of flak surrounded them. Smittie was on the interphone.

"We got a major-league hole in the fuselage just above the wing near the radio compartment," he said. "Fire's spreading along the right wing."

The plane began to porpoise. Roy couldn't hold it level; the elevators were out.

Joe called: "What's the matter?"

"We've got to get out," Roy heard himself say.

"Is it that bad?"

"I can't control the pitch. . . . Fire over the right wing. Get going!"

Roy reached forward and hit the bailout button. "Abandon ship," he said over the interphone. He got no answer.

From the nose Joe and Larry were crawling toward the forward entrance hatch. Plum dropped down from the top turret and joined them. Verne climbed out of his seat. He patted Roy on the shoulder with his gloved hand and sidled through the narrow passage toward the hatch. Turning, Roy could see him adjusting his parachute straps, pulling them tight against his crotch. The aircraft was bucking now, and he struggled to keep it level, jockeying the throttles. They were heading east, into the sun. He radioed again through the plane. Static crackled through the headset. The boys in the back must have already jumped, going out the bomb bay or main entrance door on the right side. He was alone in the crippled B-17.

The ship began to waffle, losing altitude. At any second the fuel tanks in the right wing could blow. He flipped the switch, engaging the automatic pilot. He pulled off his headset, his oxygen mask. He squirmed out of his seat, edging off the flight deck. Wind howled through the open bomb bay, an eerie keening sound he had never heard. The engines were hammering. He dropped down on his knees and peered out through the bomb bay. Landscape slid beneath him in a haze of muted colors. He tightened the straps and looked down again. He had never used a parachute before. "What the hell am I doing?" he thought. Then he took a deep breath, inched forward and jumped.

As soon as he cleared the plane, he fumbled for the release handle on his chute, found it, and tugged as hard as he could. For what seemed an eternity, nothing happened. Tumbling head over heels, gasping for breath, he fell through space. Then the risers of the chute slapped against his face like the tails of a whip and the harness straps bit into his crotch and he was jolted upward as if an unseen hand had yanked him to a halt in midair. Dazed, he looked up to see the white canopy blossom above his head.

As he drifted down, he watched the plane, trailing a long streamer of black smoke, disappear beyond a swath of woods several miles away. It did not go into a steep spiral but seemed to sidle along, easing itself downward as if trying to find a place to land. He did not hear the explosion, but within seconds a column of oily smoke rose in the distance beyond the trees. Craning his neck, he searched the sky all around him. FWs and 109s sometimes trailed chutes down, firing as airmen dangled helplessly in midair. But he saw no German fighters and no other chutes.

After the roaring of the engines and the howling of the wind as he crouched over the bomb bay, he was stunned by the sudden quiet. A deep, all-embracing stillness enveloped him, and the tranquil landscape below seemed as silent and serene as a snapshot. A tidy grid of yellow fields and green woods, threadlike roads and neatly delineated farms spread out beneath him, stretching as far as the eye could see. Nothing moved. But as he descended, he seemed to pick up speed, and the gentle landscape that only seconds before appeared peaceful and smooth resolved itself into an ominous maze of mammoth trees and gullies and rough rolling hillocks. A grove of giant trees seemed to materialize out of nowhere, rushing up at him like rockets. He tried to control his drift, to steer his chute toward an expanse of open terrain, a wheat field, he thought. Hoping to clear the trees, he tugged hard on the riser in his left hand, but instead of carrying him to safety, the chute began to oscillate wildly and for an instant he swung like a pendulum beneath the canopy, waiting for it to collapse. Finally, he managed to stabilize his fall.

Then he hit the trees.

Crashing through the upper branches, limbs snapped and scraped against his head and chest, tearing at his arms, jamming one leg back into his gut. He tumbled through the dense foliage, flipped over, and dangled for a moment upside down, before finally slamming, back first, against the tree's massive trunk. For several moments, he hung suspended in a snarl of broken branches and tangled shroud lines. His tattered chute was snagged in the boughs high above him, but when he looked down, he was amazed to find himself only about ten feet from the ground. Twisting to right himself, he braced one foot against a branch, found the metal clasp of his parachute harness, and tried to sidle out of the straps. Gingerly he climbed down, jumping the last few feet to the spongy forest floor.

It was surprisingly cool and dark in the woods. Patches of pale sunlight filtered through the trees, and the only sound was the insistent humming of insects. Roy dropped to one knee on the soft carpet of pine needles and tried to collect his thoughts. He looked around. Nothing moved. Of all the terrifying possibilities of combat, he had never given any real thought to this eventuality. He had lost his aircraft, his crew, and now he, Roy Allen of Philadelphia, Pennsylvania, was as alone as anyone could be, crouching beneath a tree somewhere in German-occupied France.

Before each mission the crews were given instructions about "escape and evasion"—what to do if shot down, how to navigate cross-country, how to make contact with civilians. "Move about only at night. Find a church, a priest," the evasion officer said. "Avoid groups. If possible, make contact with an individual." Roy reached into the zippered leg pocket of his flight suit for his evasion kit, a waterproof pouch issued for every mission containing items he would need if shot down. Opening it, he found a cloth map of France and the Low Countries, a French-English phrase card, a few French francs, a first-aid kit, a Benzedrine tablet as big as a quarter that would keep him awake for seventy-two hours—and a compass as small as the prize in a Cracker Jack box.

"Conceal your chute," he could hear the briefing officer say. "Bury it if possible, but get away from the scene as fast as you can." Roy glanced up at his chute, hopelessly tangled in the branches. There was no way he could retrieve it, much less hide it. And he couldn't waste any more time here. The Germans had obviously seen the plane and the chute and their patrols would be out searching. Without any clear idea of where to go, he crept forward, found what appeared to be a path through the underbrush and began walking. He did not carry a pistol when he flew, although many of the pilots did. With all the other gear he had to wear, it was just too clumsy and, besides, he didn't think he could hit a barn with his army-issue .45. He was better off without it.

Moving as quickly and quietly as possible, he picked his way through the woods, but as he walked a dull throbbing began in his lower back. With each step his back seemed to stiffen. His progress along the trail was slow and labored. He decided to discard his fleece-lined flying boots, hiding them in the underbrush. Beneath them he wore a pair of comfortable regulation shoes, and although the walking came easier, the ache in his back would not subside.

Pausing at a bend in the trail to catch his breath, he thought he heard something behind him, a snapping sound. He stopped and listened. Someone was thrashing through the underbrush not far away. Shadowy figures flickered through the trees and the voices of men calling out to one another rustled through the woods. They seemed to be searching. Diving into a shallow gully, he peeked over the lip. He could see nothing. The voices were loud but indistinct and he could not decide whether they were French or German. They came from the direction of his chute.

Sliding down deeper into the ditch, he tried to decide what to do. He couldn't make a run for it. His back, he realized, was too stiff for that and, anyway, which way would he run? The patrol behind him— if it was a German patrol—might be trying to flush him out, chasing him into a trap. Leaning back against the soft moist wall of the culvert, he curled up and waited. For what seemed like hours he crouched there, not daring to move, listening to the sounds of men crashing through the underbrush. From time to time he caught glimpses of figures, specters drifting through the trees. At times the sounds faded and he thought they were gone, but then the muffled voices would echo from another corner of the woods. Finally, the voices stopped and the woods fell silent. Roy sank back against the wall of the ditch and closed his eyes.

He did not know how long he had been out, but the light in the treetops had grown brighter. The sun was directly overhead. He could no longer hear voices. Climbing stiffly to his feet, he dusted himself off. His back was aching badly now, but he could not stay here. They would be back. He pressed forward. Reaching the edge of a small unpaved road, hardly more than a trail, that cut through the woods, he paused, wondering what to do. Should he follow it, keeping just inside the tree line or cross over, keep going through the woods? While he hesitated, a figure—a man—appeared suddenly off to his right, walking along the road. The man wore a cloth cap and civilian clothes. He was pushing a bicycle. His face was young—early twenties, Roy guessed—and he was peering into the woods on either side as if searching for something, someone. He didn't look German.

Roy stood out of sight, waiting until the man passed beyond him. Then he decided to take a chance.

PART II

A VILLAGE
IN FRANCE

CHAPTER 4

Un Aviateur Américain

June 1944

Colette's brother André was breathless from running, his shoes gray with dust from the road. For over a year he had rarely ventured into the village, except at night, not since he had evaded the STO, the compulsory labor service in Germany, and had taken to hiding in the forest. So when he appeared in the doorway to the classroom, Colette knew something was wrong.

She could hear the girls outside in the small stone courtyard behind the École des Filles, playing at the end of their school day. The headmistress was upstairs in her apartment, keeping, as usual, her own counsel, and Colette was straightening up her desk in one of the two deserted classrooms. It was almost five o'clock.

There was an American, André whispered, an American aviator. Had she not seen the planes or heard them all through the morning, formation after formation, droning high overhead, bombing, as they had done for days now, in the vicinity of Paris? It was a little after eight o'clock when he first saw the planes. Then they were no more than a cluster of bright sequins high above the horizon in the west, but as he watched, one plane, trailing a teardrop of black vapor through the sky, dropped away from the others, wobbling as it descended. André watched as it veered eastward, growing larger and larger, heading directly toward him. The huge plane seemed to skid as if on a sheet of ice until it vanished behind the trees of the Fôret de

Jouy. People all over the area must have watched it come down and some may have seen parachutes and would be searching for the aviators, trying to reach them before the Germans could find them.

André had hurried off in the direction of Chenoise, where the plane must have crashed. He saw nothing along the way and he spent some time in the village but no one there mentioned the plane. Then, in the early afternoon, as he was making his way home, walking along the dirt road that sliced through the forest toward Petit Paris, a figure suddenly materialized out of the dense woods, a tall man in olive-brown flying clothes.

"*Françieuse?*" the man called out in an almost comical accent, "*Françieuse?*" His voice boomed in the stillness. André held out his hand and smiled. He tried to speak slowly, but in his excitement the words just tumbled out. "*Camarade,*" he said, patting his chest. "*Camarade,*" but it was clear that the man did not understand. They stood facing each other on the dusty fringes of the narrow dirt road.

From a pocket in his flight overalls the man produced a small yellow card and after studying it for a moment, pointed for André to look. The card contained sentences in English and French, and the man's finger traced the line "*Je suis américain.*" André squeezed the man's arms in a gesture he hoped would convey friendship. He pointed to the sliver of blue sky above them. "Parachute?" he asked, and the man, grinning back now, nodded yes. "Parachute," he said. André glanced into the woods, but he could see no trace of a parachute. The American parachutes were as white as mushrooms. The German *Fallschirme* were mustard yellow. André saw neither. Maybe the man had buried it or hidden it in the bushes. They would have to find it before the Germans did. He would return later to search.

Scanning the card, André found the sentence "Will you give me food?" and pointed. "*Voulez-vous manger?*" he asked. The American shook his head vigorously. André motioned for him to follow. "*Bon, bon, allons-y,*" he said, and keeping to the edge of the road, the aviator trailing several meters behind him, he led the way to the house of his parents, just a short distance away. There they had hidden the aviator, and he had come to get Colette.

It was not until she had finished her paperwork—even in a tiny two-room school for girls there were always the forms—and the headmistress, leaving for the *boulangerie* on the square across from the church, had dismissed her, that Colette was able to slip away. She climbed onto her bicycle and hurried down the winding lane that led from the school past the water tower. She passed the cluster of dreary houses and tool sheds that lined the rue des Fosses, and within minutes she glided past the deserted chateau at the edge of town, its mournful shuttered windows closed behind its stone walls and iron gate.

Beyond the chateau, fields yellow with summer wheat rolled like ocean swells as far as the eye could see. On the horizon columns of towering poplars rose to mark the fringes of farmers' fields and the roads to the neighboring hamlets, Bannost and Petit Paris. The house of her parents was seven kilometers away in the Fôret de Jouy, a good half-hour's ride if she were not stopped. The German *Feldgendarmerie* were out in force, André had warned her, scouring the area for the aviators. As she pedaled along the dusty road toward the woods, she watched for any sign of their patrols.

Her parents' farmhouse was long and low with high shuttered windows and rough plastered walls and a roof of orange tile, burnished a tawny brown from weather and four years of wartime neglect. The house was the official residence of the forester of the southern Chenoise district and stood in a clearing far from any other dwelling.

At the edge of the wood line, her younger brother René, hardly more than a boy, was standing guard. He was watching the northern approaches to the house. André, he told her, had taken up a position on the road to the south. Colette rode past the familiar rabbit hutches and outbuildings and skirted the ragged vegetable garden behind the house. She leaned her bicycle against a wooden pillar of the covered back porch and looked up to find her father framed in the open door to the kitchen. Wearing his coarse riding breeches and mahogany-colored boots and drawing heavily on his pipe, he held the door open for her and followed her inside. In the cluttered *salon* that passed for a living room, she found her mother at the front window, peering nervously through the sheer curtains toward the road to Chenoise. Sitting in the cushioned armchair across from the fireplace was Monsieur Jonckheere, the captain of the local gendarmerie. Rémy Jonckheere was a broad-shouldered, heavyset man of forty, with a wide, pleasant face. Though he was growing heavy and dark circles under his eyes bore testament to many sleepless nights, he gave off an air of robust energy. With him was one of his men. They had been waiting for her since André returned from the village.

Taking in the familiar faces with one quick glance, she focused on the stranger who stood in the corner of the low-ceilinged room rubbing his large hand across his lower back. The man shifted his weight uncomfortably from one leg to another, as if he were in great pain. He was tall, towering above her father and brother, taller even than Monsieur Jonckheere. His dark hair was not close-cropped in the usual military style but long and wavy, and his broad, handsome face, though haggard with exhaustion and strain, was unmistakably American. His expression was utterly lacking the sullen, guarded look of a French peasant. In this the man reminded her of Bob Leasman—the aviator from Atlanta, Georgia, whom she had sheltered briefly in December of 1942.

None of the men assembled there could speak more than a word or two of English, and Monsieur Jonckheere expected her to converse with the American. *"L'américain ne parle pas un mot de français,"* he whispered in exasperation. For hours they had struggled to explain the situation to him and to ask him questions, but he understood little and they could not follow his attempts to respond.

And so, with lookouts posted at the windows, the men gathered expectantly around the stranger in a tight semicircle. They put their questions to Colette and, drawing on her schoolbook English, she did her best to translate. What was his name? Where was his crew? How had he been shot down? What sort of plane—they thought it was a Fortress—had he flown? Had anyone else seen him on the ground? Where was his parachute? Monsieur Jonckheere was concerned because his men had gone back into the woods and had been unable to find it. Someone must have found it. The Germans perhaps—they were certainly combing the area—or perhaps a local. The nylon was valuable in occupied France.

In their excitement, the men spoke quickly, and Colette, regretting that she had no dictionary to help her, felt that her efforts to translate were stumbling and clumsy. She was not at all convinced that the stranger understood, even when he tried to answer. Worse still, as she listened to him speak, she began to lose confidence in her English. She had learned formal English in Melun during her teacher's training, basic grammar and a smattering of Victorian poetry and Shakespearean plays, and since she had taken up her position at the École des Filles in Jouy, she gave language instruction to the young girls of the village. But she had virtually no experience with conversational English.

She listened as often as she dared to the BBC on the small radio in her sitting room above the school, though it was dangerous to do so, especially with the headmistress's rooms just across the hall. But mostly she tuned in to the BBC's French language broadcasts every night, with their news of the war and their coded messages for the French underground. The English was just too demanding. But if the BBC announcers, with their cultivated diction, were difficult to follow, this tall man, speaking quickly in an accent as American as his face, was simply impossible. After several false starts, he motioned for a pencil and paper and jotted down a few words.

He wrote in a surprisingly neat hand, she thought. His name, she read aloud, was Roy W. Allen, and his address was a strange-sounding jumble of numbers—2223 Seventy-seventh Avenue, in Philadelphia, Pennsylvania. The men stared blankly at her. No one in the room had any idea where this exotic place was. The Germans, Monsieur Jonckheere reminded her, sometimes planted one of their specially trained counterintelligence men to pose as downed Allied airmen, usually British but sometimes American. They must be treated with caution, especially when, as in this case, no parachute could be found. Yet this Roy W. Allen—how, she wondered, did one pronounce a "w" in English?—had apparently already reassured Monsieur Jonckheere and the others, and so she did not worry.

She looked over Roy Allen's shoulder as he wrote out a question for them, which she studied and then translated. "Do you know where the other men are?"

There were ten men on the crew, he explained, holding up both hands with fingers spread to indicate the number, and he believed that they had all managed to jump free of the plane. With Colette interpreting, Monsieur Jonckheere assured him that others in the area, *résistants*—patriots in the underground—would be out searching, but he did not know if other aviators had been found. How was it that Lieutenant Allen had come down alone, they wanted to know. Had he actually seen the others leave the plane? Roy Allen spoke with great calm, yet very fast, and she did not understand and so again he wrote out a few words on the sheet of paper, and these she could read. "The pilot always jumps last," she explained to Monsieur Jonckheere, who nodded.

More questions would come later, but for now they had to decide what to do with their guest. He could not stay here at the forest house. A bomber had crashed in a field just to the southwest of the forest, near the village of Combles, Monsieur Jonckheere had learned during the afternoon, and that, he reasoned, was Roy Allen's plane. Although the house was secluded, far from neighboring farms and enclosed by the forest, it stood at a crossroads between Chenoise and the busy route nationale 4. Through the years of occupation, German soldiers, driving on motorbikes or sweeping through the woods in search of "terrorists," would stop to demand a drink or something to eat. The house and its outbuildings had been searched many times. Sometimes the Germans would take raspberries from the garden or a rabbit from the hutch. Sometimes they would simply poke around the sheds or peek quickly into the house. They could arrive at any moment, their trucks crashing to a halt at the crossroads. It was something of a miracle, they all agreed, that the Germans had not already come to the house in the afternoon.

It was decided that Colette should take the stranger into the village, to her rooms above the school. There were no Germans billeted in Jouy now, and she had hidden others there before. It would be risky, with the headmistress's rooms just across the corridor, but she could do it. Colette explained to Roy Allen that later, after dark, they would leave for the village. At sundown—roughly eleven o'clock by the official German war time under which France operated—the *couvre-feu*, the curfew, would be in effect, but trying to walk the seven kilometers back to Jouy in the daylight without civilian clothes for him was simply impossible. Roy Allen seemed to understand, for he nodded and, grabbing the pen, wrote: "We will go to your home tonight?" She nodded, and he seemed to relax. They settled down to wait.

Her father produced a bottle of wine, which he kept under the shelter of the back porch, and Madame Florin busied herself in the kitchen, stoking the mammoth black oven with splinters of wood. Colette recognized the aroma of rabbit stew, which they had eaten so often since the war and the rationing of food. They were fortunate in the country to have the rabbits and the few chickens that her mother kept, as well as the garden, which gave them vegetables and raspberries. In Paris the greengrocers and butcher shops, Monsieur Jonckheere had told her, were all but empty, and even in Provins and Nangis, the larger towns of the district, which she occasionally visited, the people scrambled to make do with the meager ration cards and deals on the black market.

Sitting at the rough-hewn table, the American ate the stew, sipped the bitter ersatz coffee, and made numerous grateful gestures toward the kitchen. Although he tried not to complain, it was obvious that his back bothered him a great deal. He had hurt it, he told her, when his chute crashed into the trees. All through the later afternoon and into the evening Madame Florin, apologizing that they had no medicine, not even aspirin, fed him wine that she warmed over the stove.

Before dropping into the worn armchair beside the fireplace, Roy Allen awkwardly stripped off his flight overalls, revealing underneath what appeared, to their astonishment, to be a dress uniform—dark brown trousers, a khaki-colored shirt, with smartly pressed pleats, and even a tie, pulled, even now, only slightly askew. Looking him over as he stretched out in the chair, his long legs extending into the room, they were all concerned. The man would not be easy to disguise. Big and broad shouldered, he was far too robust and well nourished to pass for an inhabitant of occupied France. Her father was already wondering where they would find clothes and civilian shoes for this giant of a man. Monsieur Florin had contacts in Provins, a clothes merchant with whom he bartered food from the garden for items of clothing, and he would try, but the shoes, he kept muttering, the shoes would not be easy.

Toward dusk Monsieur Jonckheere and his deputy left for Jouy, the heavy wooden shutters were drawn, and in the closeness of the low-ceilinged room the aroma of the wine and the strong tobacco of the cigarettes settled around them. There was no electricity in the forest house, and the kerosene lamps flickered and waned, bathing the room in a sleepy yellow light. Gradually the conversation lapsed, and as the Florins watched, Roy W. Allen, exhausted and lulled by the wine, dozed.

Just a few kilometers away, in the tiny crossroads hamlet of Bannost, André Knisy had spent the afternoon listening to the planes rumble overhead. The Americans were attacking somewhere in the area, the airfields or the railway junctions around Paris, he guessed. It had been this way for days, since before the invasion, and now the raids had intensified as the Germans rushed troops along the highway just to the north. They tried to stay off the roads during the long daylight hours, when American fighters roared down out of the clouds to strafe anything that moved, but after dark, Knisy could hear the German convoys groaning along the tree-lined roads, heading westward toward Normandy and the front.

Knisy was fifty, a veteran of the Great War and the proprietor of a general store just across from the church on the broad sloping square of Bannost. He also doubled as a milkman, delivering milk from the local farms to shops in the villages that dotted the area. He was known to everyone in the region. They saw him almost daily in his horse-drawn wagon, plodding along the empty country lanes, the cumbersome metal canisters of milk rattling under the heavy canvas tarp. A corner of his store at Bannost also served as a café, where Knisy dispensed wine and sometimes, on special occasions, a bottle of champagne from the vineyards just to the east. On weekends and holidays the locals from the surrounding farms and villages brought their wives and girlfriends to Knisy's café to drink and jostle across the small parquet dance floor. Sometimes there was a small local band, but usually the music came from the radio or Knisy's ancient gramophone.

Standing at the bar in his black beret, Knisy would watch them dance, polishing glasses, pouring the occasional drink, chatting with the traveling timber salesmen, the merchants, the farmers. He knew everyone, and each believed they knew him. But they did not know that beneath the rectangular patch of parquet where they danced, a container of arms or a radio transmitter might be hidden. They did not know that upstairs in the corner room that faced the square, a British agent known to Knisy only as Camille and his radio operator called Jackie would stay when they passed through. They did not suspect that for over a year Knisy's establishment had served as a *planque*, a safe house, for the underground and a haven for downed Allied airmen, a stopping point on one of the many escape routes used to aid fliers and others seeking to flee occupied France. There, in the rooms he rented above the café and dance hall, he would hide them until a contact from Paris would arrive to move the men a little farther along the circuit. Knisy did not know where they went once they left his café.

So in the late afternoon of June 14 when the telephone rang at the café and he heard the husky voice of his friend Bertheau, the postman at nearby Champcenest, he understood.

"There are five cumbersome packages here in the office," Bertheau said. "You need to pick them up."

Within minutes Knisy had hitched his horse to the wagon and set off. All along the way he saw German trucks brimming with soldiers, but they paid him and his familiar wagon little mind. Still, with so many German patrols moving through the fields he hoped he was not too late.

At the little post office at Champcenest he learned the details that he had expected to hear. An American plane had been shot down, and its crew had bailed out. The bomber—it was a Flying Fortress, Bertheau told him—had crashed near Chenoise, and five of its crew were being hidden in the oat fields nearby. When it was safe, after dark, the farmers would slip the Americans into the village.

So Knisy waited patiently at the café beside the post office. When the Americans arrived, he would load them into his wagon, beneath the canvas tarp, put cloth sacks over the hooves of his horse to muffle the sound, and begin the short trip back to Bannost and his café. After the curfew the only traffic allowed on the roads were German military vehicles or the automobiles of prominent collaborators, but he would take his chances, as he had on other nights. Luckily there were no Milice in the area. These Vichy paramilitary units, black-shirted French fascists, were as bad as the SS.

He rolled a cigarette, smoked it, and then another. He read the regional newspapers, *La Seine-et-Marnais*, from Melun, and another from Provins, both filled with Vichy lies and foolishness, he thought. He drank from the bottle of local cider put before him on the table and waited.

It was almost eleven o'clock before the sun dropped below the line of poplars on the horizon. Hay wagons from the fields rattled along the narrow streets of the village in the gathering dusk, and hidden in one of them were five American aviators. From the farmers who delivered the sweat-stained and dirty men to him Knisy discovered that two of the Americans had come down in one field, while the other three had landed not far away. All through the long hot afternoon, while the Germans swarmed through the area like locusts, the farmers had hidden them, bringing them water and telling them, as best they could, to stay down, to be patient. A German patrol had come within a hundred meters of the Americans, who were pressed into a shallow gully in the field, but it had passed on by.

Knisy did not speak English, only a few military phrases and ribald expressions he had picked up during the Great War, but he understood that they were from a B-17, that they had been on a mission to the vicinity of Paris, that they had been shot down by German fighters. Standing in the darkened barn just behind the dilapidated post office where his wagon waited, he asked the exhausted men where they were from, and he listened with pleasure to the exotic American names: Kentucky, Oklahoma, Maryland, Ohio, and Illinois.

The moon had risen when the men crawled into the wagon amid the empty milk canisters, and Knisy, hoping the Germans had long departed, began the slow journey back to Bannost.

It was almost midnight when Colette and Roy Allen left the forest house for Jouy. They moved silently through the dark woods, alert for any sound, any signal that might indicate trouble. Monsieur Jonckheere did not believe German patrols would be out after dark, certainly not in the forest. The woods had become havens for the *réfractaires*, young men who had gone into hiding to avoid compulsory labor service in Germany. Many were armed, and although the Germans would occasionally swoop down from their garrison at Provins and mount searches for these "terrorists" during the day, they rarely ventured into the woods at night. Colette knew that the German military police, the *Feldgendarmerie*, set up roadblocks along the chalky country lanes that crisscrossed the region, checking papers, enforcing the curfew. Anyway, it was too late to follow the main road back to the village.

When they reached the edge of the woods, they walked along the fringes of a narrow lane that led through the fields toward Jouy. Colette wished that they could follow the deep rutted wagon tracks that meandered through the crops, but the fields were high with wheat and she could not find the paths in the dark. They would have to take their chances and stick to the road. She had traveled this road many times, though rarely at night—and never after curfew—and at first they moved cautiously. Colette led the way and the American followed along several paces behind her. There was no sign of life on the main road off to the east, but ahead of them lay Petit Paris, where half a dozen farmhouses lay clustered around a sharp bend in the road. They would have to walk directly through the hamlet. What would they do, she worried, if the dogs barked and the farmers threw open their shutters? But Petit Paris was silent and dark as they approached, and they passed quickly among the houses without incident. The road now stretched out straight toward Jouy, the last leg of their journey, and they quickened their pace.

As they trudged along in silence a light drizzle began to fall, and a breeze kicked up, making a rustling sound in the flowing wheat that bordered the road on both sides. They were only four kilometers from the school. Another twenty minutes, maybe thirty. She longed to speed up, but the American was limping badly. Out of the corner of her eye she could see him breathing heavily as he tried to keep up. Still, he did not complain.

It was then that she heard the first coughing of a motor. She stopped dead still and listened. From the direction of Jouy the distinct clamor of an engine rolled across the fields, and as she squinted to look, two shafts of light appeared in the darkness, moving slowly along the road. There were no trees or bushes on this exposed stretch, no place to hide, nowhere to run. The vehicle advanced steadily toward them, its lights on low beam and hooded according to the blackout regulations. "Be quick," she heard herself say, and she grabbed Roy Allen by the arm. They jumped the shallow ditch beside them and waded into the waist-high wheat. Dropping to the ground, they lay shoulder to shoulder among the broken stalks and stubble no more than five meters from the road. The yellow lights grew larger, and Colette pressed her face hard into the damp earth and listened. On the wet pavement just beside them tires whined, and the vehicle seemed to stutter, changing gears with a groan, almost choking to a halt. Then the engine caught, and the vehicle picked up speed once again and continued on. Cautiously raising her head, Colette caught a glimpse of a motorcar fading in the rain. It was her neighbor, she thought, the veterinarian on his way to an emergency.

They lay for some time in the field catching their breath, waiting. Neither spoke. The rain subsided and the moon reappeared through the clouds. "We should go now," she said at last. Collecting themselves, they brushed the wet chaff from their clothes and climbed back onto the road. They walked on in silence. Ahead of them no hint of light rose from the dark forms of the village. Only the ghostly, whitewashed silos of Jouy's giant grain elevator loomed like an apparition in the moonlight, and the only sound they heard as they crept along the road was the calling of night birds, already anticipating an early dawn.

Moving as swiftly and silently as she could, Colette led the American down the deserted village streets. He was limping terribly now, almost staggering, and although he tried to walk softly, his movements were stiff and his breathing labored. In the early morning quiet the sound of his leg dragging over the grit of the rue des Fosses pierced her ears like the screeching of chalk across the classroom blackboard. Occasionally a splash of ochre light spilled from beneath closed shutters, a violation of the strict blackout regulations, but no doors opened and they met no one. She hoped that no unseen eyes were watching.

Approaching the darkened schoolhouse from behind, they slipped past the water tower and the outhouse, into the courtyard, where the school's small trees, now in full leaf, cast shadows on the moonlit gravel. The headmistress's rooms looked out onto the courtyard, but there was no trace of light from her windows, no sound from behind the drawn shutters.

Standing in the shadows, Colette wondered if Roy Allen understood what she had told him about the headmistress and the school. She had never known what to make of Mademoiselle Berthe. They had lived and worked alongside each other for almost three years now, and twice Colette had hidden *résistants* in her rooms for several days. In November she had sheltered two Gaullist agents who arrived by Lysander from England and in February three more. Did Mademoiselle Berthe suspect anything? Did she hear them moving about in the little suite of rooms just across from hers? Sometimes Colette thought it was impossible that she did not know. Maybe she believed Mademoiselle Florin was concealing her brother André or another friend who had avoided the STO. Since February 1943, when the Germans had initiated the hated Service du Travail Obligatoire, many people in the countryside had someone to hide, a brother, a son, a lover, who did not relish spending the war as a forced laborer in the Third Reich. Colette was always careful, and her visitors from the resistance had been extremely cautious during their stay. Even the girls in the classrooms below had not heard them moving about. Colette knew nothing about Mademoiselle Berthe's views on politics, on Vichy, on the war, on anything except school matters. Like almost everyone in occupied France, the headmistress thought it prudent to keep such things to herself.

Colette had tried to explain to Roy Allen before they left the forest house, to impress upon him the danger, even once inside the school. Pointing now to the bank of shuttered windows above them, Colette whispered to him, "The headmistress sleeps there," and pressing her finger against her lips, added, *"Nous devons nous taire.* Very silent!" In the dark she could not see his face clearly, but Roy Allen nodded as if he understood, and they darted the last few steps to the doorway. Easing her key into the lock, she pushed open the heavy oak door, and they stepped inside. The vestibule was dark, and the smell of chalk dust and dried paper hung in the motionless air. She paused, waiting for her eyes to adjust, but even after what seemed like minutes, she could see absolutely nothing. Grasping his hand and keeping her right shoulder against the wall, Colette started up the first short flight of steps. The shallow wooden stairs creaked and groaned as they climbed. Only six small steps, but their progress was agonizingly slow. At the landing, they paused, listening, but there was no sound from the headmistress's bedroom. Colette squeezed his hand and they started ahead, inching their way upward. At the top of the stairs they stopped again. Then, hardly daring to breathe, they crept along a corridor so black they might have been at the bottom of a well.

At last the wall against her shoulder gave way to a doorframe. She pushed open the unlocked door and they stepped inside. In her rush to leave earlier in the afternoon, she had forgotten to draw the shutters and silvery moonlight poured into the room. After the dense murk of the corridor, the little kitchen seemed to glow, and the gray forms of the sink and stove and table were outlined distinctly in the pearly light. She pulled aside the sheer curtains and peered out into the street just below. The rue de la Gare was empty and the large stone house of the veterinarian just opposite stood in stillness. Pulling the shutters closed, she retraced her steps and fumbled with the light switch. When it clicked, the room was flooded in a glare so harsh she was forced to squint.

Then Colette turned to face Roy Allen.

In the tiny kitchen, the American seemed enormous, a gigantic presence looming above her, and she found herself staring up at him as if seeing him for the first time. For a moment she wondered what she had let herself in for. The other American, Bob Leasman from Atlanta, Georgia, had been concealed near the forest house and for only one night. The others, the *résistants* she had hidden in the school, were, after all, French. They knew the ropes and she had kept them for only three days. Somehow, as Monsieur Jonckheere explained it at the forest house, it had seemed perfectly logical, the only real alternative. But now, standing alone with this strange man in the closeness of her rooms, Mademoiselle Berthe only a narrow corridor away, the stark reality of it hit her and a thousand problems presented themselves.

While she stared, Roy Allen suddenly winced and grabbed at his lower back. The trek from the forest house had taken its toll on him.

She motioned him to sit at the table, and while she poured a cup of wine for him, he eased himself stiffly into a chair. "You must sleep," she whispered. "You will feel better with rest." He shook his head grimly and, cradling the cup in both hands, took a sip of the wine. He would be asleep in a matter of minutes, she thought.

Leaving him at the table, Colette opened the door to the adjoining room. Her suite consisted of three small rooms on the west side of the corridor. Beyond the kitchen was a sitting room—she called it the studio—with a chair, a divan, a small bookcase, and a credenza. Her own bedroom was across the corridor, just beside Mademoiselle Berthe's kitchen. She closed the shutters of the studio window, switched on the light, and began to arrange the divan for him. He would sleep here tonight, but she would have to speak to Monsieur Jonckheere tomorrow, after the school day. She would explain the situation to Roy Allen in the morning, to impress upon him that he must be absolutely quiet while school was in session, must not move around, play the radio, that he must use the pail in the corner, the chamber pot. How would she tell him that?

Then, from the kitchen, the quiet was broken by the groan of pipes and splashing water. Colette leapt into the kitchen and stopped in utter astonishment. The American stood at the sink, his back to her, naked from the waist up. Water cascaded from the faucet, and she caught herself before she cried out. He turned toward her, holding something wet in his large hands.

"*Mon Dieu,*" she almost sobbed. "What do you do there?"

He looked at her, casually turning off the water and wringing out the wet clump over the sink.

"I wash out my shirt every night," he said calmly. "Always have."

"*Mais pas ici,*" she cried, "not now!"

He smiled at her and draped the shirt over the edge of the enamel sink. Still stunned, she listened for a sound from across the corridor but could hear nothing. He looked around her into the studio at the divan.

"You sleep here," she muttered.

"And you?" he asked.

She blushed. "I am sleeping across the hall, in my bedroom."

"Then you'd better get going," Roy Allen said, and brushed past her into the studio.

Colette stood as if frozen to the spot. He was a powerfully built man and utterly unself-conscious. For a moment she stared as he stretched out on the divan. Then she turned and fled across the pitch-black corridor to her room.

When Roy awoke, he had no idea where he was. He lay in a narrow bed in a small room with watery sunlight pouring in through an open window. A sheer curtain trembled in a breeze he could not feel and all around him intricate patterns seemed to swim dreamily from the silver-flocked wallpaper. From somewhere below, children's voices rose in a murmurous chorus. He lay back and listened. After three years of being jolted awake in barracks and Nissen huts to the rough animal clamor of men rising, grousing, fumbling with their clothes and gear, the soft rhythmic chanting—they were reciting—was a shock. And yet it was not the sweet singsong of the children's voices that struck him but the profound stillness beyond, as if he had awakened, a child himself, on a winter morning when there had been snow in the night.

Closing his eyes, images flashed like tracers before him—the burning plane, the parachute, the farmhouse, the fields, the young French woman, hardly five feet tall, leading him down the deserted village streets and into a darkened building. Funny, when the shells hit—he could not tell whether from flak or fighters—it didn't seem particularly bad, nothing like the bone-jarring shocks they had taken over Dessau or Berlin. It all happened so fast, the plane lurching upward, the controls going suddenly, sickeningly soft in his hands. The moment seemed unreal. He could hear Joe's voice over the interphone, asking in his casual Texas drawl if it was really bad, and he remembered hitting the bailout button, the three long bursts called for in the manual. In a blur he seemed to see Verne pry himself out of the copilot's seat, tossing his flak helmet aside, staggering as the plane lurched. From somewhere below and behind him he sensed the others—Joe, Larry, Plum—fumbling with the escape hatch. When he at last released the controls and edged along the flight deck toward the bomb bay, they were all gone.

Drifting down, he had seen no other chutes. The men in the farmhouse tried to tell him something about this last night, but he couldn't fully understand. Maybe the others had been picked up by the resistance too. Maybe they were close by, hidden in an attic or cellar or hayloft. The plane must have been very low—no more than two thousand feet—when he jumped. That might explain why he didn't see the others. He hoped they had been lucky too.

Sitting up, he swung his legs over the edge of the bed. It was, he realized, a sort of sofa, a daybed his mother would have called it, and the springs groaned as he stood up. The room was small and neat and simply furnished. Across from the bed stood a low bookcase and a narrow upholstered chair and beside the window was a credenza with large brass knobs, as round and shiny as Christmas tree ornaments. A small radio with an oval dial rested on top. He stepped to the bookcase. His back was stiff and sore. Leaning down, he ran his finger absentmindedly along the neatly shelved books. The titles were mostly French, but he found a number of books in English—collections of poetry, a thick volume of Shakespeare's plays, a novel by John Galsworthy.

He looked up and his eyes were drawn to a framed photograph that stood on top of the bookcase. It was the mother and father and the girl, Colette, posed in front of what appeared to be the farmhouse from yesterday. There was another picture of the two brothers— André, who had found him on the trail, and the younger one, he could not remember the name, who had sat at his side throughout the evening, understanding nothing but obviously entranced by the uniform, the flight gear, the exotic American suddenly dropped into the family's midst.

Stepping over to the credenza, he looked at the little radio with its large oval dial. Instinctively he reached out and turned it on. Static sizzled through the room, followed by an earsplitting peal of incomprehensible French. He grabbed at the knob, adjusted the volume, then slowly turned the dial. At first there was more French, then a staccato burst of German, and finally a wave of dance music. He did not recognize the melody and the singer was French, but it was pleasant and it *was* dance music and so he left it on and wandered into the kitchen.

The shutters were open and a fresh breeze ruffled the pages of a magazine on the kitchen table. His shirt was draped carefully over a chair near the window, drying in the morning sun. Resting his elbows on the windowsill, he looked out at the empty road and the row of stone-and-plaster houses across the way. It must have rained again during the night while he slept. The narrow road was black with moisture and wisps of steam rose from the pavement where the sunlight hit it. Off to the right a church tower rose above the slanting rooftops of the village. He wondered where he was. In the struggle to keep control of the ship after they were hit, he had lost all sense of direction.

But the turn, the three-sixty the formation made as they approached the target, would have taken them well east of Paris, away from the sprawling urban smudge he had seen through the morning haze. The girl, Colette, had mentioned the name of the village but it meant nothing to him.

While he watched, a bicycle crept along the road, heading into the center of the village. The rider was an elderly man in a black beret and he labored as he pedaled up the slight incline of the road. The old man did not look up but concentrated on the road and Roy watched him until he turned out of sight. Roy was still standing at the window when the young woman burst into the room.

"*Attention!*" she gasped. Darting toward him, she tugged him away from the window. "*Vite, vite!* Be quick! You must not be seen here."

Roy stepped back and frowned. "You said there were no Germans here," he protested, gesturing toward the open window. "I haven't seen any Germans."

"No, monsieur, there are no Germans in the village. It is not the Germans who worry me," she said. "Jouy is a small village. One thousand citizens are living here, perhaps more, but we can rely on only a dozen or so. One must be careful. Always. There are *collaborateurs*, people who are loyal still to the government in Vichy. Fewer than before, it is true, but others will denounce you. Word travels fast in such a village.

"Even here in the school you must be cautious. You must not walk around while the children are below in the classroom—they will hear you and will ask questions and tell their parents when they go home that Mademoiselle Florin has someone in her room. People talk. There will be questions."

As they stood facing each other at the edge of the kitchen table, the lilting dance music stopped and an announcer's voice boomed from the open door to the studio. Colette stared through the doorway as if hearing it for the first time. "And you must not play the radio during the day," she scolded. "The children have heard it already this morning. They are looking up at the ceiling and then at me as if waiting for an explanation. Even the headmistress must not know that you are here."

"Is she a collaborator?"

"No, I do not say that, but in France today one does not know for certain, not only about strangers but about anyone. Here people betray others for many reasons. Sometimes it is politics, sometimes petty jealousies or old grievances. An envious colleague, a jilted lover, an angry neighbor tired of hearing your dog bark in the night makes a *délation anonyme,* and the damage is done. It is a way to cause trouble, to settle old scores."

"Any word about my crew?" Roy asked.

"*Non,* monsieur," she said. "I am afraid that we have heard nothing. They have found your plane. A Fortress. It is in a field just south of Chenoise, not far from the house of my parents."

Roy frowned. "And no one was in it?"

"No, they found no bodies in the wreckage. Perhaps the others will yet appear."

She turned to the cupboard beside the small stove, removed two plates, and set them on the table. Then she placed a knife and a cutting board and a long loaf of bread in the center.

"How are you feeling this morning? Does your back give you pain?"

"It's okay. A little sore, that's all." He watched her run water over a handful of raspberries in the sink and place in them in a colander to drain.

"They are from the garden of my parents," she said proudly.

"Where exactly are we?" he asked, gesturing toward the window.

"Jouy-le-Châtel," she answered. "The village is seventy-five kilometers southeast of Paris, in the Département Seine-et-Marne." She was warming soup on the stove, stirring the pot with a large wooden spoon. The scent of cabbage filled the little room.

He did a quick mental calculation. The briefed course called for the formation to approach the target from the southeast. "Yes," he muttered, "that would be about right."

"We must eat now," she said. She poured the soup into bowls and placed them on the table, and Roy, pulling on the damp woolen shirt, sat down across from her. He was surprised at his own sudden hunger, and he ate quickly.

Seventy-five kilometers southeast of Paris. How far, he wondered, was that from Normandy? He had left his evasion kit and the waterproof map at the farmhouse last night but he would retrieve them. It was his duty to try to return to Allied control. He had heard plenty of stories about guys going down and being presumed dead, then showing up at the base two, three months later. The French underground had organizations that helped downed fliers make it back. Maybe the little group in Jouy had plans for him.

"How long will I be here?" he asked. Colette was still sipping her soup and the question seemed to surprise her.

"Monsieur Jonckheere—he is the chief of the local gendarmerie. You met him at the home of my parents yesterday—paid me a visit this morning. It was he who told me about the Fortress. It appears that you will be staying here for some time. I thought that perhaps you would be moved to the farm of Monsieur Pivert, the mayor, who lives to the south of the village, but that is not to be." She looked at him seriously. "You will stay here until . . . until other arrangements can be made. That may take some time."

While Roy stacked the dishes in the sink, Colette took a small booklet filled with colored coupons from her bag. Sitting at the kitchen table, she studied them carefully, her lips working noiselessly as she made her calculations on a pad of paper. Roy stood above her, his hand resting on the back of her chair. She glanced up.

"*Tickets d'alimentation,*" she explained, "Rationing. We must have the tickets for everything." She studied the book of coupons. "If you are to remain here we will need extra tickets," she said at last. She held the coupons up for him to see, sheets of numbered pink and yellow and orange coupons with stark black lettering that read *pommes de terre, fruits et légumes, pain, fromage.* "They are issued each month at the *mairie.* As mayor, Monsieur Pivert—he is the leader of the *résistance* in Jouy—is in charge of the system. He will see that I get them.

"Everyone must carry this *carte d'alimentation,*" she explained, holding up a small red card with an "A" stamped prominently on it. She pointed to her name, the village, and her occupation, instructor. "All the population is divided into groups, categories that determine how much and what sort of food one is entitled to. There are limits on everything. Since I am between twenty-one and seventy, I fall into category A. *Travailleurs,* manual laborers, have a separate category and farm laborers, *cultivateurs,* too. They receive more. There are categories for infants, for older children, *jeunes,* but these I do not know so well.

"Even in Jouy there are shortages, and the people must make do. In the larger towns, in Provins or Nangis, people stand in long queues at the Food Office. They wait for hours, the queue crawling like a snail, centimeter by centimeter. I have seen this in Provins, where the women—they are mostly women—stand for hours. The newspaper announces what will be available and the women come and wait.

Sometimes they compare their tickets, wondering whether it is safe to trade—this is forbidden, you must understand—and they complain as they edge their way toward the entrance. Once inside the door, they dart to the counters to claim the different cards. Then they must go to the shops and wait again. Often there is nothing left when they reach the front, or it is not what they need." She paused, looking up at him, and smiled for the first time. "But you must not worry. There will be some food from the farm and the extra tickets from Monsieur Pivert. *Nous nous débrouillons.* We will get by."

Later they could hear the girls returning from their lunch, and Colette went below again. He tried to sleep but could not. He thumbed through the magazines he found in the studio, full of photographs of French movie stars and stylish women, but he could not read the captions. He could find no stories about the war at all, no pictures of the battlefronts, no maps depicting the positions of the armies. Each issue carried several cartoons, some of which he could figure out, and he looked longingly at the crossword puzzles in the back pages of the magazines. Through endless evenings in the barracks and the countless hours of riding from base to base in the packed troop trains, he had worked the crosswords. He had done them since he was a kid in Philly, in the discarded newspapers he found on the buses and trolleys. In training he found that they cleared his mind, gave him a diversion from airplanes and the war and somehow—he did not know why—made him less homesick.

Sitting at the kitchen table, he decided to try to compose one for himself. He understood the basic structure of the puzzles and, rummaging through the small bookcase in the studio, he found pencil and paper, a French-English dictionary and what appeared to be an almanac for the year 1939. After several false starts with the names of rivers and capital cities and prominent political figures, he hit upon the idea of using the lyrics and titles and singers of popular songs. He always listened to the music programs on AFN, and he always sang along. He knew all the words. Humming now to himself, he began by writing out a list of songs from the Hit Parade—"Till Then," "How Blue the Night," "Don't Fence Me In," "GI Jive," and his favorite, "Long Ago and Far Away." He jotted down the bands and the singers for each, even the songwriters. Then, using the edge of a magazine as a ruler, he drew a large square and blocked out the boxes for the letters. He worked for much of the afternoon.

When he tired of the crossword, he turned again to the almanac, to its colorful map of France. He identified Normandy and the Cotentin Peninsula, where the Allied armies were fighting, and, using the scale, measured the distance to a point he estimated to be eighty kilometers southeast of Paris. Jouy-le-Chatel did not appear on the map, but Nangis did. According to his rough calculations, he was roughly four hundred kilometers due east of the invasion beaches. A long way. The Pyrenees and the Spanish frontier were even more remote, in the distant southwest corner of France. Some fliers had escaped over the Pyrenees and been returned to England, others had somehow made it across the Channel by boat, leaving from Belgium or points on the French coast. All this he knew vaguely from evasion briefings and from talk around the base. He would ask Colette about it when she returned at the end of the day.

Later in the afternoon he watched the girls leaving the school, their books slung in packs across their shoulders like soldiers. As they bounded up the street, laughing and shouting to one another, a truck rumbled into view and the children scattered. The truck wheezed slowly along the road, groaning as it climbed the gentle rise toward the village. As it passed directly below his window, Roy could see a bizarre cylinder-shaped contraption attached above the back fender as if an American water heater had been bolted upright to the bumper.

"*C'est un gazogène,*" a voice behind him said. He jumped. "Please, you really must come away from the window," Colette said.

"I didn't hear you come in," he said, stepping back into the room. "What is that thing?"

"A *gazogène*, I do not know the English." She thought for a moment. "There is no petrol in France today. Only the Germans and the collaborators have petrol. Maybe a doctor or, in the country, a veterinarian. But the bakers and merchants and others must rely on the *gazogènes*. For the *voitures*, the motorcars, and autobuses, too. Some are powered by burning charcoal, some by wood." She tried to explain the engine's internal functioning, the conversion of the combustion into fuel, but the language was too difficult.

"You have been very quiet this afternoon," she said, changing the subject. "That is good. Have you slept?"

"No," he replied. "I've been working on a crossword." She stared blankly, and he showed her the puzzle. "It's not finished yet," he said, "but it's something to do."

"*Ah, bon,*" she said, "*mots croisés.* I see." She looked up at him, shaking her head in appreciation.

"Mostly I've been looking at magazines. At the pictures, but I don't know who anybody is."

One of the magazines was still on the kitchen table and he pointed to the cover. An aged military man stared out of pale blue eyes at the camera. Resting in an ornate chair, he wore a simple greatcoat, gloves, and the red gold-braided hat of a French field marshal. She glanced down at the magazine and looked back at him, clearly surprised.

"That is the Maréchal Pétain," she said. "You must know him. He is the head of the French state, of the government in Vichy." She paused. Roy showed no sign of recognition, and she continued. "My father believes he is a tragic figure, a misguided patriot who is used by the truly wicked ones, the real *collaborateurs.* He is an old man now—he has eighty-nine years—but earlier, in the Great War, the *maréchal* was the hero of Verdun, 'the savior of France,' as the song goes. You will hear this song many times—'*Maréchal, nous voilà!*' It is played every day on Radio Paris. The station is controlled by the Germans and is full of collaborationist propaganda." She began to hum a rousing marching song.

"What does it say?" he asked.

She hummed the melody softly to herself for a moment, then said: " '*Maréchal,* we are here. We swear to serve and follow your steps, for you have renewed hope: the fatherland will be reborn!' And the chorus, ah monsieur, in the chorus," she said, shaking her head in disgust, "they sing, 'Pétain is France and France is Pétain!' "

As she spoke, she thumbed through the magazine, scanning the pages, pointing out different Vichy political figures. Roy did not recognize the names. Finally she found the photograph she was looking for and tapped the page. A cluster of officials posed on the steps of an ornate columned building. At the center of the group stood a swarthy, slump-shouldered man with thick black hair and a dark mustache. He wore a rumpled black suit with a bone-white shirt and, oddly it seemed to Roy, a white silk tie. He looked like a Chicago gangster. "That is Pierre Laval," she said, "the prime minister of Vichy. He is the most reviled of all the collaborators, the most evil. He manipulates the *maréchal* and works hand-in-glove with the Germans."

Roy tried to follow Colette's explanations, but as she talked on, it was clear just how little he understood the situation in France. At the base the Group information officer had organized lectures about the politics of the war—the Western Alliance, the courageous Soviets—and the crews were urged to attend. Few did. Sometimes *Stars and Stripes* would carry a human-interest story about oppression in German-occupied Europe, about a Danish family devastated by Nazi brutality or the plight of Warsaw or the heroic French underground, but nobody in the crew paid much attention. At briefings, the intelligence officer would always have a word to say about resistance forces on the Continent—in Belgium, Holland, and France, wherever the Group's target for the day was located—but these remarks were of a distinctly practical nature, how to survive on the ground if shot down, how to evade capture, how to make contact with friendly forces. He recalled nothing about the politics.

He asked questions, embarrassed at his own naïveté, and Colette listened carefully. She was patient and tried to explain. At first the answers were awkward, as she struggled to find the words, but as they talked through the late afternoon hours she became more confident of her English and his accent no longer baffled her.

"What about the Germans?" he asked. He was sitting at the table with the crosswords still spread in front of him. The light pouring through the window had turned lilac, and Colette adjusted the sheer curtains. "Aren't there any Germans around?"

"Oh yes, monsieur," she said, taking a seat across from him. "You will see them. Their *Kommandantur*, their headquarters for the district, is in Provins, just a few kilometers away, and their patrols and police can appear anywhere. But there are no soldiers billeted in Jouy. In the early days, just after the armistice, their troops were everywhere—in the streets, the *tabacs*, the cafés. The fashionable shops in the big towns were filled with them. Their money had great value, and every day they were buying perfume and silk scarves for their wives and lovers and shoes for their children. Some even attended mass in the church. It was a great shock to see them taking the sacraments in their gray uniforms.

"Those were happy times for them, when France had fallen and England stood alone against them. In those days they were still on their best behavior. Their newspapers were full of propaganda proclaiming friendship between the French and German peoples and stirring up bad feelings about the English. On walls all over the district they plastered giant placards saying '*Voyons, mon petit, tu ne vas tout de même pas aller te faire tuer pour les Anglais*'—'Look, little one, don't go and kill yourself for the English.' Another one was showing a

German soldier with children all around him, saying 'Forsaken people, put your trust in the German soldier!'

"In Chenoise—it is close to where your plane crashed—soldiers were billeted in the town. The people were forced to give them their bedrooms. Sometimes the soldiers simply came and took the mattresses. If the owners had fled during the evacuation of 1940, the Germans took over the house. The *Kommandantur* was in the doctor's house and the canteen in the school. The grounds of the chateau were full of soldiers and their horses. In Provins there are still Germans. They do not stand in the queues or worry about rationing tickets, but times are hard for them, too, I think.

"For years German soldiers stopped at the farmhouse, demanding eggs. I have never seen a people eat so many eggs. Once several stopped when I was outside picking raspberries and they came into the house. Over the mantel there is the picture of my father in his uniform from the Great War—you have seen it hanging there—and they asked questions about it, where he had fought, if he was wounded, what the medals were for. They were very impressed. After that, almost every day at twilight, German officers came to the house on their way to hunt in the forest. As forester, my father was obliged to go with them and show them where there are rabbits and pheasants. But they no longer come. They are afraid of the woods now. There are terrorists there, they say.

"Two years ago—it was November of 1942—things began to change. The Allies landed in North Africa, and the French colonies there were liberated and everywhere there was a sense that the Germans could lose the war. Until then they had occupied only a portion of France, the Atlantic coast and the northern areas around Paris. The government in Vichy controlled the rest, the so-called unoccupied zone. But when the Allies came into North Africa, the Germans rushed to occupy all of the country. Then in January, they introduced a forced levy of French men to work in Germany—the STO—and many young men fled into the forests or hid. The maquis, the armed resistance groups in the south, sprang up then."

The resistance group in Jouy had begun even earlier in 1942, she said, when Messieurs Jonckheere and Pivert hid a Canadian aviator at the mayor's farm until they made contact with a group that took him to Paris. Now it was involved in many plans, she said, plans made by Captain Paul, but she would not elaborate.

"Who is Captain Paul?" Roy asked.

"He is the leader of the *résistance* in the area. Perhaps you will meet him someday."

"Does he live here in the village?"

"Oh, no," she responded, "I do not know where he is living. I myself have never seen him. But Monsieur Pivert is in contact with him."

Curfew had passed and they were sitting over wine when the gendarme from yesterday appeared at the apartment. Colette poured Monsieur Jonckheere a glass of wine from the nearly empty bottle, and he joined them at the table. He had come to check on their guest and to report, with regret, that nothing had been heard about the crew. This did not mean that they had been captured, he insisted. The *résistance* worked in compartmentalized units. It was possible for one *réseau* to operate side by side with another without necessarily knowing its counterpart's activities. This was done for security. He had feelers out. He would see what he could discover. In the meantime, he urged Lieutenant Allen to rest, to relax.

"How long *will* I be staying here?" Roy asked. He waited for Colette to translate.

"One cannot say just now," the gendarme replied. "Let us wait and see."

"But you have handled fliers before, haven't you, helped them escape back to the Allies?"

"It has been done," Jonckheere answered. "But we will speak of it another time. For now you must rest. Mademoiselle Florin will take good care of you," he said, raising his glass of wine to Colette. He spoke to her for a moment in French and she nodded in agreement. Then he rose from the table and was gone.

While clearing away the evening's dishes, Roy felt suddenly very tired. Woozy with wine and exhaustion, he excused himself and stumbled toward the studio and bed. He peeled off his shirt and tossed it onto the upholstered chair.

"Good night," he said, turning back to Colette from the doorway. "Maybe they'll find something out about the crew tomorrow."

"I am hopeful, monsieur," she said. "Sleep well."

"Yes," he muttered, sitting down at the edge of the bed and removing his shoes. "Thank you." He smiled up at her. "Thank you for everything."

"*De rien*," she said, "it is nothing." But he did not hear the words. Sprawled diagonally across the divan, the American was sound asleep.

Before returning to her room that night, Colette washed his shirt in the sink.

In the days that followed, they settled into a routine. He would rise early, listening to the mourning doves that settled on the roof of the school in the first fresh light of dawn. In spite of Colette's repeated warnings, he would stand in the window and peer out to the west, to the lush green-and-yellow fields that began only a few yards from the edge of the village. Roosters crowed from the nearby farms, and just after daybreak the distant clatter of an early morning train whined somewhere off to the south. There was rarely any traffic on the sleepy streets of the village. Occasionally a bicyclist would pedal by, heading for the square, or a horse-drawn cart would lumber along, but there were no cars, no trucks—except for the solitary *gazogène*—nothing to break the all-pervading quiet.

Sometime later, Colette would cross the corridor from her room and they would share a meager breakfast of bread and margarine and drink cups of the bitter coffee. Later they would hear the girls arriving for school, and Colette would gather her books and go below to her classroom. Sometimes he heard Mademoiselle Berthe stirring in the hallway and bits of conversation between the two women as they descended the stairs. At noon Colette would return to warm a pot of watery soup and they would talk until she had to go below again.

During the long afternoon hours, when the electricity was on—it seemed to him to come and go without any particular pattern—he listened to the radio. At first Colette objected, but it did little good. Finally she relented, extracting a promise from him that he would keep the volume very low. So every day he would turn on the little set and listen. He tried to pick up the BBC's English-language programming for the war news but the static was bad during the daylight hours and anyway listening to the English was particularly dangerous. Instead he scanned the channels for music.

When he could find no music on the dial, he sang to himself. Walking from room to room or settling in at the kitchen table, he sang all sorts of songs, tunes from the Hit Parade, Christmas carols, snatches of church hymns he could remember. Later Colette would complain bitterly, cautioning him to be quiet. She could hear him in the classroom down below. She was sure the students could hear him. But it was a losing battle.

Sometimes she brought newspapers and well-thumbed magazines for him. Usually several weeks, even months old, the magazines were thin and their flimsy pages greasy and filled with photographs of French film stars, singers, and socialites. Occasionally there would be a photograph of devastation attributed to Allied bombing—shattered buildings and crumpled bodies. French civilians killed by the Anglo-American forces in Nantes or Marseille or St. Nazaire, the caption read. It was an odd sensation, looking at these photographs. Whenever he saw them Roy could not help but think how the crew had always hoped for a nice safe target in France.

But aside from these occasional shots and the stories that accompanied them, he could find no real coverage of the war itself. Sometimes the papers printed official German military communiqués, offering vague summaries of actions on the eastern front or commentaries on the air war. But while the most decisive battle of the war raged in Normandy and Allied armies were fighting now on French soil, the newspapers, the magazines, even the radio, were filled with sports and fashion and scenes of French country life.

It was harvest time and every afternoon the farmers brought their wheat in horse-drawn wagons to the grain silos behind the school. They came, wagon after wagon, in a constant procession, plodding along the rue des Fosses until the late afternoon light was suffused with flecks of airborne chaff, giving the air itself a grainy golden cast. Even as the last light was fading and the evening shutters were drawn, he would hear the steady clatter of the horses over the cobblestones of the village streets.

In the evenings, with the children gone and Mademoiselle Berthe settled in her room across the hall, they talked. Unless the schoolmistress stood in the corridor just outside their door, it was unlikely that she could have heard, but still they spoke in hushed tones. At 1930 and 2115 they listened to the BBC's French program and Colette translated the war news as best she could, explaining, too, the system of coded personal messages—the *avis*—for the *résistance*. But mostly they talked. She told him about her childhood, her family, her teacher's training in Melun, her life in the village, and Roy told her about May and the baby, about the old neighborhood in Philadelphia, about the boys in the crew. She would interrupt with questions about

America, about the army or about some expression she did not understand. She tried to teach him a few French phrases, without much success, and begged him to teach her colloquial English. She was a very good pupil, Roy joked, but he was a very bad teacher.

After several days of confinement in his two tiny rooms, Roy grew restless. His back had begun to bother him again. A dull throbbing ache had settled at the base of his spine. He was desperate to move around, to get a change of scene. Colette spoke to Monsieur Jonckheere. It was obvious that Roy could not be allowed out during daylight hours, but whenever he could get away, Monsieur Jonckheere stopped by the school after curfew and the two men would make "an excursion." Through a contact in Provins, Colette's father had managed to find civilian clothes for him—shirt, pants, jacket, even a beret, everything except shoes—and they polished Roy's regulation oxfords with dark oils until the military brown had faded.

It would be almost midnight and the streets deserted, and the two men would slip down the stairs, past the closed shutters of the houses, and into the surrounding countryside. Sometimes they strolled along the cart paths through the fields to Vimbré, Monsieur Pivert's farm just south of the village, or took the desolate back road to Petit Paris or wandered through the apple orchards not far from the school. During these outings Monsieur Jonckheere always wore his blue gendarme's uniform. That way, if someone became inquisitive, he could explain that the stranger was his prisoner.

Whenever the men visited Vimbré Colette would come along to translate. The mayor's farm was a rectangular compound of low-lying buildings arranged around an expansive courtyard, and as they approached through the fields in the starlit June nights the farm seemed to rise before them like an island in a sea of wheat. It was there, Colette told him, pointing to a long sloping meadow, that the little planes, the Lysanders, had landed, bringing agents of the *résistance* to France and carrying others away.

Roy enjoyed these excursions with Jonckheere, especially the visits to Vimbré. Madame Pivert and her daughter would prepare a meal in the large country kitchen and the men would drink wine and talk to Roy about the war. Roy did not say much about his missions, though the men were always eager to hear and were especially impressed to learn that he had been to Berlin, that he had dropped bombs on the capital of the Reich. On these evenings Roy always asked about the crew, but with each passing day his hopes of seeing them again faded.

Although the men would never say so directly, it seemed likely that they were either dead or in German hands. Perhaps Captain Paul would have some information about them, Pivert suggested. He would be in contact soon.

The men, in turn, told him about their organization and its activities, about their security measures, about the Gestapo and the informers around them. They spoke in general terms, avoiding names and dates and addresses, but regardless of what meandering course their stories took, they returned time and again to Captain Paul. They spoke of him often and always with great reverence. He was a Frenchman, Monsieur Pivert believed, but he worked for the British, for the War Office, and he was the leader of the regional underground. A tall, slender man of great energy and courage, he had come in the spring, breathing life into the *résistance* in the area. He communicated directly with London via radio and had arranged for parachute drops, bringing weapons and ammunition to the *réseaux*. He had armed and trained teams of *résistants*, and after the *débarquement* in Normandy he had led them in many actions against the Germans, ambushing convoys, derailing trains, and cutting telephone lines. Perhaps, Pivert said, Monsieur Roy would meet him at the farm on one of his swings through Jouy.

Was it possible, Roy wondered aloud, for Captain Paul to arrange for him to be moved into Paris and then on to neutral Spain? Maybe he could even manage a Lysander pickup here at the farm. No evening at Vimbré ever passed without Roy pressing to be returned to his base in England or to Allied lines. Pivert always listened attentively and his words were sympathetic. He understood that Monsieur Roy wanted to rejoin the war, but there had been no Lysander landing at Vimbré since February, and everywhere the resistance was busy preparing for the uprising that would lead to liberation. He would make inquiries about the possibilities for his movement—there were groups whose special task it was to help downed aviators and others on the run—and he would speak to Captain Paul at the first opportunity. But the evening always concluded with a plea for Roy to be patient.

Days passed in this way. Then a week. Then another. The weather was cool and rainy and in the early mornings mist clung to the red tiles of the houses. Some mornings long vaporous contrails spread across the sky from horizon to horizon. The Eighth was up in force, heading for targets in eastern France or western Germany. The BBC reports on the air campaign were sketchy, but the Allies were still hammering transportation targets in support of the troops bogged down in Normandy. Helpless, Roy could only sit and watch. He was relatively safe and comfortable in the École des Filles, and he was grateful to Colette and the others—they ran terrible risks for him every day—but it had begun to sink in that he might never leave Jouy. Jonckheere, Pivert, and the others were content for him to sit out the war in the village, waiting for the Allies to arrive. It would not be long, they insisted.

But the campaign in Normandy was not going well—there had been no movement for weeks—and he hated doing nothing, sitting day after day with his crosswords and lists of songs, listening to French dance music. He was increasingly tortured by thoughts of home and May. By now she would have received the telegram from the War Department, reporting him missing in action. Maybe others in the formation had seen the parachutes and that would give her some hope, but he was not sure whether the War Department provided this kind of information. Seven months pregnant, she would be waiting in the sweltering Philadelphia summer for news of him and here he sat, helpless.

He tried to remain quiet, but the hours in the school crawled by and he couldn't keep still. He rumbled around the rooms, humming and singing to himself. He grew reckless. One evening Colette found him standing in the window smiling broadly and waving to the soldiers in a passing German convoy.

"How long would it take me to get to Normandy?" he asked one rainy afternoon. He had been studying the map in the almanac again.

"It is far away, Roy," Colette said, "and the German army stands between Jouy and the front. Besides, you have no papers."

"You could take me," he replied. A smile flickered across his face but there was an edge in his voice. "We could go together."

"Surely you are not in earnest," she said

"I'm serious," he continued. "We would go as husband and wife or brother and sister. If we got into a jam, you would do the talking."

She could only stare.

Several days later the wife of the surveyor Gittard fell in beside her as she walked toward the bakery across from the church. The Gittards lived on the rue de la Gare, just down from the school. Madame Gittard made small talk, as was her custom—the weather, the harvest, the mass on Sunday. Then, looking straight ahead as they strolled into the square, her voice dropped and she said, "You must tell the American to be more careful."

Colette was stunned. A neighbor, an elderly lady who lived just down from the school and who liked to talk, had seen someone at the window, Madame Gittard reported. "Mademoiselle Florin has a man there," the old woman had told her. "Oh, it is probably her brother André," Madame Gittard had responded, "hiding from the STO. He is sometimes there." But the liverish old busybody would have none of it. "*Ça ne parle pas français*," she hissed. "It doesn't speak French."

That afternoon Colette went alone to Vimbré. The Piverts were alarmed at what she told them.

"He must be careful, and he must stay at the school," Monsieur Pivert said. "He cannot leave. This is out of the question." He hesitated. "Are things not good between you?" He looked at Colette. "Perhaps if he were happier, more satisfied, in the school, he would not be so anxious to leave."

Colette blushed. "There is no trouble between us," she said. "He wants me to take him to Normandy."

"What did you say to this madness?"

"*C'est impossible.*"

"*C'est lui qui est impossible,*" Madame Pivert blurted out. "Does he not know that if he is caught—and of course he will be caught—he endangers us all?"

"I have explained this to him many times," Colette said.

Monsieur Pivert sighed. "I will talk to Captain Paul. Perhaps he can set Monsieur Roy straight."

It was growing dark when Colette reached the school. She did not speak to Roy about her visit to the farm. They talked as they did every night but her heart was not in it, and later, lying in her bed, she could not sleep. The Gestapo was coming, she was convinced, bearing down on the school at that very moment. In the darkness behind her eyes she could see their black Citroëns arriving from Provins and the men in their long leather coats bounding up the stairs. She could hear their fists pounding on the door and the shrieks of Mademoiselle Berthe from the corridor. Her eyes snapped open and she sat bolt upright in the bed. Gray light seeped through the shutters, and specters danced in the corners of the silent room. Beneath the summer duvet she shivered. She pulled her knees up against her chest and hugged them tight. There would be no sleep tonight. Something would have to be done. Maybe Captain Paul would have the answer.

CHAPTER 5

MINISTER

July 1944

M y friends tell me that you want to leave us," Paul Guérin said to the American sitting before him. It was late in the afternoon when he arrived at the school. The gendarme, Jonckheere, had led him from their rendezvous at Vimbré. It had already been a long day. He had left Melun just after dawn, touching base with his team leaders in villages throughout the region, reviewing their readiness, inspecting their arms caches. At Nangis he had met with Mimi, his courier, who rode with him to visit the little group in Jouy.

He did not need another aviator, not now, and an American to boot. The man was anxious to return to England, to his unit, or to Allied lines, relentlessly pressing the *réseau* in Jouy to help him. The American's fantastic plan of going together with the girl to Normandy was foolish. And yet he knew that this was not uncommon among concealed aviators—or wireless operators for that matter. Hidden for weeks, sometimes months, confined to a safe house or maybe even a single room, they would go stir crazy with boredom and were, to the horror of those who harbored them, prepared to take any sort of risk just to be out, to *do* something. He had known of Allied fliers who, after a week or so of hiding, would slip away from their handlers and be found by their frantic hosts sitting calmly in a café or emerging from the cinema.

When he was operating in Troyes well-intentioned people who were hiding Allied aviators frequently showed up at his doorstep, imagining that he could dispose of them quite easily. He had helped over two dozen of them, finding false papers, civilian clothes, and safe houses. Still, he could not be responsible for them. SOE operated small escape lines for its agents and would sometimes handle others, but this was rare. So, after hiding the aviators for a short time, he passed them on to a local Gaullist organization that convoyed the men into Paris and then on to Spain. He hoped they made it home.

The American shifted in his chair. "Well," he said, "I do want to get back to my unit. I'm no good to anybody here, sitting, doing nothing."

"You are a man of action, Lieutenant. I understand this, but at this moment patience must be our watchword. The time for action will come, and then there may be a role for you to play. Meanwhile, your friends in Jouy are making preparations. All over the region the *réseaux* are mobilized, waiting for the signal to strike."

"You think the Allies will be here soon then?" the American asked, hardly bothering to disguise his skepticism.

"But of course," Paul Guérin answered, wondering as he spoke whether he actually meant it. "Within the month. Any day now the breakout will come and the Germans will fall back and we will be ready." He paused to light a cigarette, leaning forward to touch its tip to the candle at the center of the table. His movements were deliberate, and when he exhaled his eyes followed the blue smoke as it coiled to the ceiling. He looked back at the American. The man was powerfully built and the civilian jacket the *réseau* had found for him pinched at the shoulders. He would not get far out in public.

"Besides," Paul continued, "moving about is very dangerous now. Since the invasion the Germans are everywhere. Their convoys fill the roads, especially at night, and everywhere they tighten their security. There are many controls."

"I understand that," Roy Allen answered, an unmistakable edge of stubbornness jutting into his voice, "but I'm willing to take my chances. I was told that you might be able to help, to arrange passage into Paris and on to the south, to the Pyrenees."

"Your courage is most impressive," Paul Guérin said, speaking with all the patience he could muster, "but I am afraid we can do nothing at this time." True, the *débarquement* had gone well, but the breakout, which everyone assumed would come quickly, had not yet occurred.

The Allies were mired in the tricky *bocage* country of Normandy, and the Germans, frantic in their mounting fury, were lashing out at the resistance all over the country. Many in France who had not been involved before were seeking out resistance groups, ready now to help in the liberation they assumed was imminent. The *réseaux* were swamped with new recruits. Many were incautious, security had deteriorated, and the Germans were reaping a harvest of the indiscreet. It was a dangerous time.

"I urge you to sit tight, *mon ami*. You are well taken care of here in Jouy," he said, "and you have companionship." He smiled, glancing across the room at Colette. She busied herself in the little room beyond the kitchen. Mimi sat on the divan and smiled seductively at the American. "You live in a golden prison," Paul Guérin continued. "Be patient. The war will come to you soon enough."

He wished there was something more to say. It was a simple matter of priorities. Only a few short weeks ago he might have taken time to deliver the aviator to an escape line, but not now. In the spring, when the Allied bombing of French targets intensified—a prelude to the D-Day landings—the *réseaux* were inundated by a torrent of downed airmen. Night and day parachutes filled the sky. Allied aviators seemed to be everywhere, hidden in barn lofts, concealed in cellars and attic rooms, waiting for a passage over the Pyrenees to neutral Spain.

The lines—*chaînes d'évasion*—were very active then. Some were operated by the Free French, some by the British—an entire section of British Military Intelligence, MI-9, was devoted to "escape and evasion"—and a few were even run by freelancers who had hidden Allied fliers. The successful lines—the incautious or unlucky ones were invariably discovered and their agents shot—operated on the same general principles. Each line created a network of safe houses where the aviators or other escapees—Jews, *réfractaires*, and French nationals on the run from the Vichy authorities—could be hidden. They were to be kept in seclusion, outfitted in civilian clothes, and provided, if possible, with false papers. Contact with the next link in the chain would be made by coded message and, after a short time, usually no more than ten days, a guide would arrive to escort the aviators either to another safe house along the line or directly into Paris. There the aviators would be distributed among a number of safe houses scattered around the city until they could be convoyed, usually in small groups, south to the Spanish frontier. It was an extremely hazardous operation, and many lines had been infiltrated.

Some *chaînes d'évasion* were still in operation, he knew, but after the invasion, the situation had changed. With the Allies in Normandy and German troops rushing westward into the area, it hardly made sense to move airmen along the usual escape lines. It was time for the fugitives to stay put, to let the Allies come to them. Besides, the resistance had other, more pressing duties now.

There was still much work to do in preparation for the uprising, weapons to be distributed, teams to be trained, targets to be hit. Jouy-le-Châtel stood in the very heart of the area that he would seize and hold as the Allies approached, an area that stretched from Meaux in the north to Provins in the southeast and Fontainebleau in the southwest. The *réseau* in Jouy was affiliated with the Gaullist BCRA but now, on the ground in France, such distinctions made little difference. They cooperated in all things. The group had done good work, finding drop zones, stashing weapons, and recruiting *résistants*. Pivert reported that the groups in and around the village could count on as many as one hundred men.

It was all coming together, the organization, the planning, the training, everything he had worked for since that March night when his chute snapped open and he drifted into a moonlit field near Troyes. Clutching the straps as he swung in the blustery slipstream, he had seen the other chute, below and off to the right, swaying like an apparition in the starlight. In a heartbeat he crashed into the frost-covered field, rolling as he had been taught to break the impact. Within seconds the reception committee was racing toward him. *"Bienvenu,"* the dark figures shouted, crowding around. *"Bienvenu, camarade.* Welcome to France." Perhaps fifty meters away, at the edge of the wood line, Charles, his wireless man, was gathering in the billowing folds of his chute, checking his equipment. The reception committee did its job well, and within minutes they were on their way to a safe house in the vicinity of Troyes.

The next day, while Charles waited on the outskirts of the city, Paul Guérin made his way to the home of a trusted contact. Robert Vassart, the public prosecutor in Troyes, had been active in resistance circles for some time, and Paul had worked with him on various occasions, turning to him for information about police investigations, judicial proceedings, and other matters. Vassart was surprised to see him.

"Pierre Mulsant!" he exclaimed in amazement when Captain Paul entered the room.

"No longer," Pierre responded, smiling. "Today you see before you Paul Guérin, captain of the British War Office."

"*Bon, bon,*" Vassart replied. "Whether British or French, I am happy to see you again. I am glad that you are back."

When the men were settled in Vassart's study, Pierre gave a brief report of his activities in England and explained the general outlines of his mission. He asked Vassart for the name of a reliable man in the Département Seine-et-Marne, just to the north, someone who knew the region, who had contacts there, and could be trusted. Vassart considered this for some time.

"Yes, I believe there is such a man," he responded at last, "an attorney I know in Melun. As far as I know he has not been involved in resistance activities, but he is a patriot, a man with an excellent knowledge of the district and many connections. His name is Roger Veillard. Before the war he traveled in prominent socialist circles. He was familiar with Léon Blum, the premier, and many other notables in the party. He remains very active in his legal practice and has defended many patriots in the courts. He has offices in both Melun and Paris. I will contact him."

The next day Vassart sent a letter requesting an urgent meeting, and Veillard responded immediately, inviting them to meet him in Paris, at a small brasserie near the Gare de Lyon. On March 14, Pierre, Charles, and Vassart boarded an afternoon train from Troyes. It was a rainy Sunday, and the train was packed with the usual weekend travelers returning to Paris. Billowing smoke into the leaden sky, the train steamed slowly along, stopping at one busy station after another. Throughout the train weary passengers jammed the crowded compartments and narrow corridors, pressing against the gritty windows. Most carried bags bulging with food bought or bartered in the countryside— a rabbit, a chicken, eggs, a handful of potatoes, anything to supplement the meager rations allowed by the regime. It was safer to take the train on Sundays, when the crush of travelers made controls at the stations more difficult, and as they lumbered through the grim industrial suburbs, Pierre was filled with mounting anticipation. If the attorney was as well connected as Vassart said and if he was willing to help, he would be invaluable in getting the circuit up and running.

They arrived at the Gare de Lyon in the failing light of late afternoon, and, pushing through the crowd, found the little brasserie in a street just opposite the station's domed clock tower. Standing in the entrance, Vassart scanned the nearly deserted restaurant, then led the men to a corner table where a distinguished-looking man in his mid-thirties sat alone over a pastis and a small carafe of water. He had chosen his spot well. Except for a knot of travelers standing along the zinc-topped bar and an elderly couple seated near the entrance, the room was empty, and the four men at their corner table could talk unnoticed. Only the tepid afternoon light from the windows illuminated the shadowy room, and after Vassart made cursory introductions, the men sat facing one another around the oval table.

"I believe we have 'urgent business' to discuss," Veillard said at last, and, speaking low, his face only a few inches away from the attorney's, Pierre began to outline his mission to France. As he talked, he studied the man they had come to meet. Reserved and self-possessed, Veillard listened with a palpable air of skepticism. Even when Pierre concluded, Veillard did not speak for some time but sat staring straight ahead. Then, without commenting on what he had heard, he explained his position. Until now he had refrained from active participation in the resistance, he said, feeling that someone so well known in political circles, especially on the left, simply could not undertake clandestine activities. Early on in the war he had been closely watched by the Vichy security forces, his movements monitored. He had chosen to help in other ways, defending his countrymen in the courts, passing on information gleaned from his extensive police and judicial sources.

As he listened to Veillard, Pierre's heart sank. Everything about the man's manner, his expression, his speech suggested a personality of colossal conceit, both about his political past and his present contacts. He seemed cold and aloof, supremely sure of himself and his own best interests, and hardly eager to help. But, after a pause to light another cigarette, Veillard surprised him. The situation was changing, he said. That was clear. The decisive moment of the war was fast approaching, and Pierre's mission intrigued him.

"Perhaps it will not be considered too much, Captain Guérin, if I seek some sort of sign, some verification that you are who and what you claim to be," he said at last.

"*Naturellement*," Pierre responded. "One must be careful."

"You could arrange, I assume, to have the BBC transmit a message, an *avis*, during the French program in the coming days?"

Pierre nodded. "Yes, that is possible." Charles could contact London.

"*Très bien*," Veillard responded. "I will choose the text." He thought for a moment. " '*Je n'ai confiance qu'en moi.*' " He smiled dryly. " 'I trust no one but myself.' How is that for a message? Appropriate both for the situation and my distrustful nature, *n'est-ce pas?* But, as you say, one cannot be too cautious."

That night Charles relayed the message to London. They did not have to wait long. Within days, the BBC broadcast Veillard's text among the "personal messages" of the *Les Français parlent aux Français* segment of its French program. Veillard was impressed. Without hesitation, he invited Pierre and Charles to stay in Melun, to use his home in the rue Henri Chapu as their base of operations until they could find other safe houses and establish themselves in the area.

For over a month they stayed with Veillard in Melun. He introduced Pierre to people in the town who, he believed, would be useful for the circuit. He helped find safe houses where Charles could make his transmissions and others that would serve as "letter boxes" where messages could be dropped. It quickly became apparent that Veillard was not only well informed and intelligent but energetic as well—and he wanted to play an active role in the circuit. Night after night when Pierre returned to the house, Veillard briefed him on the situation in Seine-et-Marne.

"There are no maquis units in the region," he explained as a cold March rain rattled against the windows. "The country is flat and the roads are good. The Germans run numerous patrols and constant surveillance in the countryside, making it impossible to establish permanent armed camps such as the maquis have created in the south. On the other hand, it is possible to travel the region without too much trouble. You will not find so many controls in the trains or stations in Paris," he said. "Sometimes the Germans are on the lookout for deserters in the stations—Czechs and Austrians mostly—and occasionally the *Feldgendarmerie* carry out controls on the roads, but the situation is manageable. You should be able to move about.

"But," he warned, "the Germans are hardly the only problem in Seine-et-Marne. Morale in France is approaching a crisis stage. This you will see. The people are exhausted, worn down by the privations of the war. They are furious with the collaborationist government in Vichy but frustrated by the inaction of the Allies. They wait for the invasion, but I tell you it must come soon or there will be a revolution inside France.

"You will find many recruits for your mission, of this I am certain, but many still listen to the government's propaganda, especially the radio addresses of that swine Henriot." Pierre nodded knowingly. Philippe Henriot was Vichy's Minister of Information and Propaganda, a skillful orator and a collaborator of the first order. He was a clever, dangerous man, remorseless in his attacks on the Allies. Pierre had heard his high nasal voice on Radio Paris many times. "Even now," Veillard continued, "his broadcasts have an enormous effect on the peasant class. The workers and the bourgeoisie are unmoved by them, but the peasants, ah, the peasants live for their crops and believe that if the Allies arrive, they will seize or destroy the crops in the fields. For them this would be a catastrophe beyond measure." Pierre nodded. The socialist politician of prewar days was slipping through, he thought. "Still, patriots are numerous," Veillard continued, "keen and willing to fight to the last drop of their blood, but arms—and leaders— are needed to make their efforts successful."

"But of course," Pierre responded. "This will be our task."

From his work in the courts, Veillard was convinced that practically all the gendarmerie in Seine-et-Marne were sympathetic to the resistance and could be relied upon. In Nangis, where Veillard had many contacts, the chief of police was probably involved in resistance activities. He could be approached. As for the Milice, Vichy's hated paramilitary police, there were no more than thirty or so in the entire *département*. "They are all extremely poor types," he added. "They work hand-in-glove with the Gestapo and act as informers, but the scum have few supporters."

Armed with leads from Veillard, Pierre set to work. Within the following weeks he systematically expanded his contacts from Melun to the outlying towns. It was axiomatic in SOE organizational procedure that a circuit was to be kept small. Recruits had to be chosen with care and made to understand that under no circumstances were they to recruit on their own. But his mission was to build up a circuit in Seine-et-Marne as quickly as possible, to be ready to attack D-Day targets throughout the area, and this required an extensive set of contacts.

The men and women he hoped to recruit would not have to leave their homes and identities behind. They would not become maquisards living in the woods in armed bands. Instead they would continue their everyday lives in their towns and villages, going about their business in the fields and shops and offices as before. But they would be living a double life now, a clandestine life that carried enormous risks and demanded special qualities.

As in Troyes, gendarmes and priests proved the most eager—and useful—contacts. In Cessoy and Maison Rouge the local abbés were won over, and in Donnemarie he recruited the entire gendarmerie for the circuit. In Courpalay the mayor agreed to organize reception committees; in Gastins a safe house was found where supplies could be stored; and in Nemours, Bray-sur-Seine, and Jouy-le-Châtel Pierre mobilized the cadres who would find landing grounds, form reception committees, and organize sabotage teams.

He found his most important contacts in Nangis, a town of two thousand inhabitants just east of Melun, which gradually became the base of his operations for the entire region. There the local priest helped Pierre identify possible recruits, and none proved more courageous or energetic than the baker Marcel Ballaguet. Ballaguet, who had done work for the Gaullist organization in the area, quickly became Pierre's chief lieutenant, and his *boulangerie* in the rue de la Poterie came to serve as the circuit's headquarters. Ballaguet and his wife, Madeleine, lived in rooms in the shop but also maintained a small apartment above the L-shaped courtyard just behind the bakery. With one entrance through the shop and another that opened onto a side street, the little apartment was a perfect *planque,* a safe house, for the group. Whenever Pierre or Charles was in town they stayed in the small apartment on the second floor, where Charles installed a wireless set.

Just as useful, Ballaguet owned both a truck and a motorcar that he put at Pierre's disposal. In April they toured the area around Nangis for suitable dropping grounds. Several farmers—friends and relatives of Ballaguet—proved willing to offer their fields for airdrops and their barns and grounds for arms depots. The brothers van den Avenne provided horses and wagons for reception committee work and also hid containers dropped in their fields until they could be distributed to the group's various supply dumps. Pierre chose Alix van den Avenne's farm at Montepot, code-named **XAVIER** by the RAF, as the primary dropping ground for the circuit, and Georges Godé's farm, just east of Nangis, served as a supply depot and safe house. Georges Duchatelet built an excellent arms dump on his property, and André Dubois offered his farm as a second hiding place for weapons and a site for Charles's wireless transmissions.

Ballaguet also introduced Pierre to a number of like-minded friends in town, capable men he trusted. Alfred Bertin, a *transporteur* who owned several trucks, not only delivered weapons from the dropping grounds to the group's arms depots but formed a team of commandos responsible for railway sabotage. When the time came, he would also sever the underground telephone cables. A local electrician, Roger Lamaur, handled the recharging of batteries for the radios and S-Phones and together with a shop assistant and his wife, Jeanne, assumed the task of cutting overhead telephone wires.

In May radio traffic with London intensified and the increased contact brought new risks for Charles and the circuit. The Germans had organized a special radio detection unit, the *Funkpeildienst,* which employed an efficient system for tracing wireless transmissions. Dividing France into a series of small grids, they established direction-finding (D/F) stations that could track a signal to within an area of twenty square miles. If an operator made several transmissions from the same site and used the same wavelength, and if those transmissions lasted twenty minutes or more, the technicians of the *Funkpeildienst* would determine the general location of the radio during the first session. During the second transmission, they would zero in on the position, and during the third they would dispatch a vehicle equipped with electronic detection sets to the area. When the vehicle, often disguised as a delivery van, a wine or timber merchant's lorry, or an ambulance, came within several blocks of the signal, agents armed with direction-finding sets would climb out and follow the signal on foot.

Despite the camouflage, the detection vans, *camions goniométriques,* or *gonios* as *résistants* called them, were easy to spot. As the slow-moving vehicles cruised the streets, the equipment inside emitted a distinctive high-pitched whine, punctuated by a series of shrill electronic chirps, and a distinctive ring-shaped antenna peeked from their roofs. Charles had seen them many times in Troyes and Melun and the men in trench coats and felt hats who jumped from them, pacing trancelike along the sidewalks and roadsides, their eyes glued to the dials on their chest sets.

SOE guidelines called for W/T operators to post lookouts whenever transmitting, but Charles found this impossible. Most important of all, he felt, was to keep the length of transmissions to a minimum and to establish several sites from which to transmit, sites as far from one another as possible. By 1944, the German D/F apparatus had become so terrifyingly accurate and swift that SOE instructed its agents to keep all transmissions to no more than five minutes.

There was no voice communication with London. Charles transmitted his messages on SOE's basic shortwave Morse transceiver—a set that contained both a transmitter and a receiver. It weighed a hefty thirty pounds and, with a length of two feet, could be carried in an ordinary suitcase. He had to be creative about the aerial. It required some seventy feet, generously spaced during transmission, and the German D/F teams were always scanning the rooftops and back alleys for them. So, except in rare cases, he deployed the aerial inside, coiling it over the dresser, the bed, the armoire, and sometimes into the hall.

During his first weeks back in France, he made his transmissions from Veillard's house, then from the home of a baker in the rue du Palais de Justice just across the street from a school used by the Germans as a headquarters. Standing at the second-floor window peering through the sheer curtains, he watched them come and go in their shiny boots and field gray uniforms and listened to the idling of their motorcycles in the narrow street not twenty meters from his wireless set. In time other sets were dropped. Most were the more compact 3 Mark II's, which were housed in small black briefcases and could be carried from place to place without attracting attention. Scattered in safe houses throughout the area—in Malesherbes, Nangis, Rozay-en-Brie, Mitry, and Meaux—they allowed him to alter the locale and frequency of his signals.

Sitting in the cluttered apartment behind the Boulangerie Ballaguet or amid the bales of hay in a barn outside Rozay, Charles would spread his silk code sheets before him, arrange the antenna, and tap out his signals. At a rambling country estate near Grendon on the Bucks-Oxon border, F-Section's Home Station would be listening. There teams of wireless operators dispatched messages to British agents all over France. The Royal Corps of Signals provided some personnel at Grendon but most of the wireless operators were young women, recruited from the First Aid Nursing Yeomanry (FANY) and Women's Services. Charles's sister Joan worked as a coder at Grendon and whenever he sent his signals, he liked to think of her at the other end, listening for him.

In fact, whenever Charles transmitted his elaborately coded messages at the prearranged times—his sked—the same operator at Grendon would be listening for him. This was his "godmother." As a security check, she would ask for the password in the form of a question, the response to which was a non sequitur. "How is the weather in the highlands" was to be answered by "Uncle Jacques's nose is red." Charles also embedded a second security check in the message—a misspelled third word or a missing vowel in the second. If he fell into enemy hands, he might in good conscience reveal the first check, the password, to satisfy his German interrogators, knowing that if the second were omitted from any transmission, Home Station would realize that something was wrong and be on the alert for an impostor. Over time, Charles's godmother would also come to recognize his distinctive touch on the Morse key. That touch—his "fist" they called it— was as individual as a fingerprint, and if it seemed different, she would suspect an impostor.

Having passed through these elaborate security checks, Charles's godmother would take down the coded message. She would have no idea what the groups of letters meant and so would pass the message on to the decoding officers who worked in a different wing of the same house. They deciphered the groups of letters exactly as they read them. Apparent misspellings, fragments, or mutilated words were to be left untouched. The messages were then teleprinted to Baker Street, where Buckmaster and his small staff would analyze them.

This, at any rate, was the theory. Working under severe time restraints, Charles and Home Station had to work fast, and messages to and from the field were frequently so garbled, with letters or whole words missing, that rigorous adherence to the security procedures proved impossible. Sometimes Charles could hear the signal beamed at him, but it was clear that Grendon could not hear him or had received only part of his message. Sometimes the whole password sequence was so jumbled or truncated that it was virtually useless. As he often complained to Pierre, if he and his handlers in Britain had suspected a spy whenever they failed to receive the full security check and countercheck, they would never have been able to communicate.

Charles never used the same set or the same frequency for two days running. Riding his bicycle or in the lorry with Marcel Ballaguet, he traveled from safe house to safe house, carrying with him only a microfilmed copy of his transmitting schedules. He was glad to be out, on the move. During his time in Troyes he rarely went out. His contacts with the outside world were largely limited to the *réseau*, and the monotony of the routine gradually wore him down. He complained about the loneliness and the tedium of the job, always pressing Germain for more responsibility, more contact. Back in Britain between missions, he had argued that the wireless operator was underutilized in SOE circuits, that he could be of more use to his team leader in the field. After all, the sked only required him to transmit three or four times a week, and in between those transmissions much of his time was spent in seclusion. The circuit's "pianist" should be out in the field, helping the leader to recruit, to train, to organize. Pierre needed little persuasion, and so whenever possible, Charles accompanied him on his rounds, sending signals to London on the sets he distributed throughout the region.

Shortly after establishing contact with Home Station, Charles received a message indicating that the team's third member was en route. **FLORIST**, the courier for the circuit, had left Britain and would be arriving in Paris shortly. Pierre was to rendezvous with the courier there at the prearranged location. On a raw afternoon in late March, he entered a crowded café just off the Place St. Michel and surveyed the loud smoke-filled room. For several days he had visited the café at the agreed upon time, waiting to be approached with the password. On this day no password was necessary. From a table beside the steamy mullioned windows a familiar face appeared in the blue tobacco haze. **FLORIST**, as Pierre had hoped all along, was none other than Nenette from Troyes.

In late February she had completed six exhausting weeks of SOE training, and after a final briefing at Orchard Court, she had joined several other agents who were escorted to Torque, on the south coast of England. There they were housed in an ancient resort hotel, empty and cold in the blustery off-season weather, until the little group was delivered to the naval base at Falmouth. In the early afternoon of March 21, the party boarded a depot ship of the Fifteenth Military Gun Boat (MGB) Flotilla, where their clothes and equipment were given one last check. Then, the group was transferred to a smaller vessel that had pulled alongside. Bristling with wires and antennae, the craft was a specially outfitted gunboat just over one hundred feet long that would carry them to their rendezvous across the Channel.

Since mid-1943 SOE's escape section had run this operation out of Falmouth under the code name **VAR**, ferrying agents to a spot on the rugged Breton coast and picking up others for the return trip to England. These trips, Nenette understood from her briefing, were made only on moonless nights. No lights were allowed once at sea. About fifteen miles from the French coast, the main engines would be cut and the boat would proceed on auxiliaries, muffling the sound and minimizing the wake. Close to shore, the ship would attempt to contact the reception committee via S-Phone. If that failed, those on the beach would beam the agreed-upon Morse letter by flashlight and the landing party would disembark.

Low clouds and light mist hung over the Channel as they plowed into enemy waters, shielding them from aerial observation. They encountered none of the speedy German E-boats that regularly patrolled the coast. They had been running on auxiliaries for some time when at last the churning of the engines ceased, the MGB stopped dead in the water, and Nenette heard the anchor slide into the sea. In the cramped compartment where the agents sat waiting amid their gear, a seaman issued them close-fitting slickers, and then Nenette and the others climbed onto the deck. Topside no one was allowed to speak or smoke, the seaman warned them, and the small group huddled in silence as the boat pitched and yawed in the choppy current. Shivering in the sea air, Nenette could see a beam of light flash from the murk beyond the breakers. While she stared into the darkness, two small rubber boats were lowered. A team of armed sailors, clad in black, their faces smeared with charcoal, climbed into the first boat, and on a signal from the crew, the agents slipped over the side into the second.

Following the lead boat and rowing with muffled oars, the seamen guided them toward the beam, riding the waves until the bow slid onto the beach. They worked quickly to secure the boat and then, just as the briefing officer on board had explained, carried the waiting agents the last few yards through the surf. There were to be no sea stains on their shoes or clothing. Standing in a patch of rough shore grass, Nenette and the other agents remained quiet and tried to stay out of the way. In the gathering fog, a group of outgoing passengers, dark shapes that slipped like shadows over the sandy pallor of the beach, rushed out to the rubber boat and climbed aboard. They did not look at the new arrivals or make any effort to speak. The seamen were on the beach for no more than three to four minutes and, as they pushed the boats back through the breakers, other figures emerged from the darkness, motioning Nenette and her companions to follow. They walked quickly away from the beach, leading the landing party through a landscape of sandy hummocks and windswept brush to a nearby cottage where the outgoing agents had been waiting. As always, the landing had been made on a rising tide to minimize foot-prints and, at first light, when Nenette and the others awoke from a brief rest, a member of the reception committee returned to the beach to check for any traces of the landing.

The beach was on the rugged northwestern coast of Brittany, near the town of Morlaix. The Germans had established a *zone interdite*, a forbidden area twenty-five kilometers deep, all along the coast, and special papers were required for everyone within it. The next day a guide arrived to lead Nenette out. He provided her with the obligatory safe-conduct pass and briefed her on their journey. The escape line maintained several safe houses in Brittany and a network of operatives to convoy, hide, and assist agents in transit across the *zone interdite*. It had been in operation for over a year and had suffered periodic setbacks, but on this trip, all went smoothly.

From Brittany, she made her way by bus to Rennes and then by train to Paris, passing through the numerous enemy controls without incident.

During training in Britain she had been Yvonne Fauge, but the forged papers she now carried were for Yvonne Ferande Cholet. Like Pierre and Charles, she had been given a new identity, a new past, and an intricate cover story complete with family photographs, old letters, and ration cards in her new name. Her operational name was simply Mimi. Looking at her familiar face in the crowded Parisian café, Pierre was happy to see his old comrade.

Her SOE handlers in Britain were mixed in their evaluation. One instructor concluded that she was "absolutely reliable, intelligent, and agile minded," but another found her "a very temperamental person . . . who could be useful if the right job were found for her." The most compelling aspect of her personality was, Pierre understood, the most potentially troublesome for SOE. "The most interesting person here and probably the most intelligent," her instructor at the Special Training School in Scotland had written. "A lively and indefatigable talker . . . , her conversation is not, however, of an indiscreet character, but bears on her emotions, bruises, aspirations, and amusements. . . . She likes a great deal of attention from those whom she is pleased to call 'les boys' . . . and uses her personal charm unabashedly to get her places." The final entry in her file was typical: "Her character is strong and she seems determined but she is egocentric, spoilt, stubborn, impatient, conceited, and anxious to draw attention to herself. . . . She might work well as a subordinate to someone whom she liked and trusted. She would, however, always require strong leadership." Pierre was pleased to see that she had requested "to serve again with her former chief," and now, back in France, he was delighted to have her with him again.

In the following weeks Mimi proved invaluable as a courier. Since women were not required to carry demobilization cards or work papers, they were rarely stopped by the *Feldgendarmerie,* and Mimi assumed responsibility for maintaining contact with the *réseaux* in the circuit. In late April Pierre summoned her to Nangis, where she took up residence in the little apartment behind the Boulangerie Ballaguet, using it as the base for her activities. Arriving by bus or bicycle or riding in Bertin's truck from Nangis, she visited **MINISTER**'s groups all over the region, checked the "letter boxes," and did reception committee work whenever necessary.

In April the airdrops of material began. Pierre never ceased to marvel at the simplicity of the system devised by SOE. Once an appropriate drop site had been found, Charles radioed to Home Station, giving the location by a set of coordinates taken from an ordinary Michelin map. He began by indicating the number of the map, then pinpointed the position using the horizontal letters and vertical numerals on the edges of the map. Finally he gave the nearest village and its relation to the drop zone. The position of the field on Robert Pivert's farm just outside Jouy was map 77, Y28, NW of Provins, 1.5km SE of Jouy-le-Châtel. The RAF would check the coordinates and, if possible, take aerial photographs of the site. A radio message from Home Station would then confirm.

During that first month, Special Operations Squadron at Tempsford dropped twenty containers in the area around Nangis, bringing supplies of all sorts—everything from small arms, explosives, and ammunition to boots, batteries, socks, soap, cigarettes, chocolate, and bicycle tires. The most prized items were the weapons, especially the Sten submachine guns. Not much to look at, the Sten's black barrel was only seven inches long, much shorter than the magazine that jutted out from its left side. Its crude metal stock was, in many models, merely a thin iron pipe twisted to conform to the shoulder. When properly used, the Sten produced a high rate of fire—550 rounds a minute—perfect for short-range guerrilla combat. Equally important, its ammunition was interchangeable with the German Schmeisser. The Stens arrived in their containers, well oiled and in three pieces, along with four fully loaded magazines and a multilingual instruction sheet about how to assemble and use them.

The large cylindrical containers in which the weapons and other supplies were dropped were heavy and unwieldy, some weighing as much as a ton. The reception committees—in keeping with SOE guidelines, Pierre employed only seven to eight men—had to work quickly to remove the outer shell in the field and disburse the smaller, more manageable canisters found inside. The canisters were then taken by horse-drawn cart or, more often, by truck to the arms depots where they would be stored until they could be distributed to the group's teams. The containers themselves would then be buried or dumped in the nearby Seine. Between April and the first days of June **MINISTER** received over one hundred containers in twelve drops.

Pierre had seen everything during these nighttime operations. In Troyes he had attended drops organized by the local Gaullists where as many as thirty people were involved. Whole families might show up to watch the containers drifting down, spreading picnic blankets in the fields at the edge of the woods. On other occasions the reception committee would find itself surrounded by a ring of cows. Surprised to find anyone abroad in the moonlit field, the huge white beasts would lumber up to them and stand, silent as specters, until someone shooed them away. In no time they would be back, materializing out of the wood line as if conjured by a sorcerer. Once an enormous wild pig had come snorting and stamping out of the underbrush, scattering the startled reception committee all over the field.

On one night drop near Nangis, several parachutes landed in the courtyard of a nearby farm, and the reception committee, armed with pistols and Stens, had to threaten the astonished farmer into silence. On another occasion Pierre watched helplessly as containers drifted into the trees beyond the landing zone. Draped among the branches, the containers and their parachutes dangled high above the ground, and all through the night the reception committee scoured a six-kilometer area in a frantic search for them. If all were not retrieved before sunrise, the Germans would surely find them, the landing ground would be lost, and the group compromised. The hunt dragged on until the early morning hours before all the containers—*les pippens,* as the farmers called them—were retrieved and unpacked and the weapons loaded into Bertin's truck for dispersal. The abbé Henri had surprised everyone with his agility that night, shinning up tree trunks like a squirrel.

Burying the containers was hard work and could take hours, so whenever possible the reception committee bundled the empty shells into the back of Bertin's or Ballaguet's truck and drove twenty-five kilometers to the bridge at Balloy, where they slid them into the murky Seine. They never encountered any trouble on the road or at the bridge. But one Sunday afternoon, as Ballaguet and his wife, Madeleine, were

"Mademoiselle Florin," he said, nodding his head in recognition. "I hope that you are not ill."

"*Bonjour,*" she said. "No, thank you, *docteur,* I am well. But I am in need of your help. I wish you to see someone. He is sick with fever, and I don't know what to do."

"Who is this person I am to see?" the doctor asked.

"You do not know him," she said.

He waited but she did not elaborate. Alert now, he scrutinized her warily, though his tired face remained without expression. "Where is this person without a name?"

"He is at the school," she said, "in my rooms."

Her answer seemed to surprise him, and he did not respond for some time. He clearly wanted to know what this was about, what he would be getting into, and yet it was often best in these times to know as little as possible. Colette watched him as he struggled with his thoughts, but she did not offer anything more.

"You go on ahead," he said at last. He was unhappy but he would come. "I will get my bag and follow."

She hurried along the streets toward the school, hoping that Mademoiselle Berthe would be out, and she was relieved to find the École des Filles quiet, its corridors deserted. Within minutes footsteps resounded in the stairwell, and Dr. Lecocq, medical bag in hand, stepped into her apartment.

"This way," she said, leading the physician into the studio. Roy lay on the divan, his face glistening with sweat. His cheeks were flushed, and his watery eyes were rimmed with red. "Hi, Doc," Roy said weakly, raising himself on his elbows. Dr. Lecocq shrank back as if scalded by a stove and shot a furious glance at Colette. He wanted no part of this. Maybe he thought it would be her brother André or another *réfractaire* from the village, maybe even a lover she wished to hide, but he had not bargained for a soldier. If Colette had not been standing in the doorway, he might have bolted out. After a moment, he seemed to compose himself. Without uttering another word he unpacked his double-handled bag and produced a thermometer. He took Roy's temperature; he felt his pulse and peered into his throat.

"*C'est son dos,*" Colette said, pointing to her back. "His back is inflamed."

The physician turned Roy onto his side and probed along his spine. Roy winced.

"This man needs to be seen at a hospital," the doctor said, closing his bag. "I can do nothing for him. I have nothing to give him, no medicines, not even aspirin. There is no one, no physican anywhere in the region with medical supplies." He shook his head. "All I can recommend for the back, to relieve the pain, is hot bricks."

Colette looked bewildered.

"Press hot bricks against the area here," he said, touching his own lower back. "It will ease the pain a bit, but he needs to be seen at a hospital."

"But that is impossible," Colette said. They both knew that the only hospital was in Provins and the Germans controlled it. The doctor shrugged. His visit was over. He had done his duty, and now he wanted to be out of the school and away from the American as quickly as possible. He would not be coming back.

When she explained the doctor's prescribed treatment, Roy managed a rueful smile. "Hell of a heating pad." He grimaced and shook his head, but after applying a cool compress to his forehead, Colette left him to begin her search. When she returned in the early evening her basket contained two dusty, discolored bricks. She found them in an alley off the rue des Fosses among the rotted timber and crumbling masonry of an abandoned house she had passed many times. She cleaned them at the sink, scraping away the grit and mortar, and heated them slowly on the stove. Then she wrapped them gingerly in a thin towel and pressed them to Roy's lower back.

Together they passed another grueling night in the airless studio, but in the early morning, as the first faint light began to seep through the shutters, Roy's fever broke, and he tumbled into a deep sleep. He was still asleep when Colette returned at lunch and again at the end of the school day, but it was the beginning of his recovery. The fever seemed to drain out of him in the sultry July heat, and with each passing day he grew stronger. The pain lingered on, but each day Colette warmed the bricks and pressed them against him and the pain gradually dwindled, shrinking finally into a dull soreness at the base of his back.

As soon as Roy felt able, Monsieur Jonckheere came again to the school, and they resumed their excursions to Vimbré. The little group of *résistants* were relieved that he was on his feet again and could join them at the farm. Captain Paul had recently returned to Vimbré and expressed his hope that Roy was recovered and content at the school.

"Your Captain Paul is an impressive man," Roy told them. He had about him that unteachable air of leadership Roy recognized in the best officers he had known, an aura that inspired confidence and made men want to follow. Colette seemed to think that there was something aristocratic about him—his tall, angular build, his bearing, his language—but Roy could not judge this. He knew only that Paul Guérin was one of those rare men able to lead by sheer force of personality, and he had uttered his final judgment on Roy's position.

"You live in a golden prison," he had said as he departed, and for the little circle of *résistants* Captain Paul's word was final. Roy knew that this was prudent advice. As long as he remained in Jouy he was safe and he was out of the way. For Paul Guérin it was a simple matter of military priorities, and Roy could not quarrel with the logic. Still, he found it hard to swallow. It had been over a month since D-Day, and the Allies were still bottled up in Normandy. The BBC put the best possible face on the situation, but Roy could not hide his disappointment from his friends at Vimbré.

During this time there was much speculation at the farm about Roy and Colette, only some of which he could glean from their animated conversations. Out of Colette's earshot, they dropped broad hints about his life with her at the school, suggesting that if he were satisfied as a man, he would be willing to stay put and out of trouble. Paul Guérin, they indicated, agreed. Roy would not be drawn into these conversations, but there had been a moment during Captain Paul's visit when it occurred to him that Mimi, the captain's courier, was being dangled in front of him. It did not seem out of the question to Colette, who conceded reluctantly that Captain Paul's courier struck her as *"une femme avancée."* Pivert even hinted that a young blond woman who worked at the farm was willing to spend time with Monsieur Roy. Her fiancé, a young man from a nearby village, was a prisoner of war in Germany and had been gone since 1940. The girl was lonely. But Roy demurred, pointing to the small of his back. *"C'est dommage,"* the men at the farm commiserated, "that is too bad. Perhaps sometime soon the back will improve."

Even the Florins could not hide their curiosity about his life with Colette. One Sunday they visited at the school, bringing a basket of food from the farm. It was a lovely afternoon, clear and bright, and Mademoiselle Berthe was away for the day. The mood was festive. They sat in Colette's rooms and listened to the music on the radio and ate roasted chicken and drank champagne. At one point, as they finished off a bottle, Monsieur Florin, smiling mischievously, asked Colette a question and she blushed. Then he said something more, waggling his finger lasciviously toward the doorway to the corridor, and the others laughed and laughed. Even Roy joined in, though he did not know why. He wanted to know what was so funny, but Colette refused to translate.

"*Ce n'est rien,*" she said huffily; "It is nothing, just silly foolishness," and shook her head at her father, admonishing him in his shamelessness. But Monsieur Florin persisted, prodding her on.

"Come on," Roy said, shooting her an encouraging smile.

"My father asks if we are . . . are being together," she said, deeply embarrassed. Monsieur Florin was looking on expectantly, a broad grin arcing across his face.

"And what did you tell him?" Roy asked, smiling.

"Of course not, I told him."

"And what did he say? Why was he pointing at the door?"

" 'Maybe he likes his girls big,' " she translated, pointing as her father had done to Mademoiselle Berthe's apartment.

"Ah," Roy said, and when the others saw that he understood, they laughed all over again.

Roy laughed too but it was a thin, awkward laugh. For almost a month they had lived together in the forced intimacy of the school. Rarely apart for more than a few hours night or day, they had learned each other's moods and habits and smells. They had grown to depend on each other, to trust each other, and each day brimmed with an intensity peculiar to this shared secret existence. There was an undeniable tension between them born of their relentless physical proximity, but they never talked of it, never acknowledged it. In all the closeness of their life together at the school, an unspoken boundary remained, and they did not cross it.

Colette was relieved that the school year was drawing to a close. It was time to get away from the village. The circle of people in Jouy who knew about Roy was expanding dangerously—Mademoiselle Berthe, Madame Gittard, Dr. Lecocq, the old biddy down the street, maybe more. So far there had been no repercussions, but one could never tell. Recovered from his fever, Roy was anxious to be out of the school and began to press again about leaving Jouy. The very walls of their two small rooms seemed to be closing in around them.

Jonckheere came some nights and they walked into the country, but each of their excursions carried with it the risk that he would be seen. Once as Roy made his way up the darkened stairs after a visit to Vimbré, he stumbled directly into Mademoiselle Berthe. For a moment they performed an awkward minuet around one another on the tiny landing, and the headmistress, as startled as he, blurted out in English, "Oh, I'm as big as a horse," and laughed giddily.

So the last days in the school were tense. Mademoiselle Berthe avoided Colette, averting her eyes when they passed in the corridor, speaking only when absolutely necessary. During the long hours of silence, while the girls wrote in their exam books, Colette thought that she could hear Roy rumbling about up above, singing, playing the radio. The girls did not seem to notice, and Mademoiselle Berthe said nothing. It was clear that when the school closed, Roy would have to be moved, but he could not go to Vimbré. Monsieur Pivert was adamant about that. He would have to go with Colette to her parents' house in the Fôret de Jouy. In the division of labor within the group, the American was her responsibility, and she was glad.

The school year ended on July 13, a rainy Thursday, and early the next morning, a truck arrived in the courtyard behind the school. Roy and Colette hurried out and climbed in beside the driver. The man behind the wheel was a baker from Chenoise, and the cab of the truck smelled of warm bread and smoldering charcoal from the *gazogène*. Monsieur Florin had arranged for the baker, a man he trusted, to make the pickup on a delivery run to the *boulangerie* in Jouy. Taking the small back road that ran south of the village toward Petit Paris, they would follow in reverse the route that Roy and Colette had walked on that first night one month before.

It was not a long trip, but the *gazo* churned along at a leisurely pace through the freshly mown fields toward the distant woods. Far to the left, Roy could see a cluster of low buildings nestled in a grove of trees, which he recognized as Vimbré. In the light of day, the farm seemed much closer to the village than it had during his moonlight excursions with Jonckheere. "There," Colette said suddenly as they rumbled down a long straightaway. "Look there!" Roy leaned forward to see past the driver and she pointed to the spot, now a barren expanse of stubble, where they had hidden in the wheat on June 14. It seemed like a year ago. They passed through Petit Paris, deserted except for a solitary farmwoman who wiped her hands on her apron and watched them from behind a crumbling stone wall. She did not wave or move her head but her eyes followed them until the *gazo* disappeared around the curve that marked the end of the hamlet.

Just beyond the houses of Petit Paris, they entered the woods and turned off the paved road. Shaded by a dense canopy of overhanging branches, the *gazo* bounced down a dirt and gravel lane no wider than a cart path. Bushes slapped at the sides of the truck, and grass grew in the center between the tracks. Roy had no clear memory of the place where he had been sheltered on June 14, but as the lane widened at a clearing, a house came into view and he saw Monsieur Florin and his wife and René standing beneath the overhang of an open back porch.

After weeks of being confined in the two claustrophobic rooms above the school, Roy was ecstatic to be out. He luxuriated in the sense of openness. In the secluded forest house he did not have to worry about being seen or keeping quiet. He could walk from room to room, sing, or chat with the Florins. At certain times of the day, he could even venture outside. Although someone had to be with him at all times, he could stroll into the garden or take walks in the woods with Colette or her father or André when he came to visit. He slept in the front bedroom with René, who had kept Roy's leather flight jacket and gloves and evasion kit hidden and asked him question after question about B-17s and flying. He hung on Roy's every word. Despite the risks, the Florins seemed genuinely delighted to have him in the house, and slowly Roy began to decompress.

On one of their walks in the woods Monsieur Florin led him along a maze of trails that wound away from the house and deep into the woods. It was important that Roy know his way around them. There were dangers here in the country, too, Monsieur Florin warned, as they stopped at the spot where Colette had hidden the other American, Bob Leasman, almost two years before. The narrow unpaved road that ran beside the house and through the woods made a shortcut between Jouy and Chenoise, and the Germans sometimes stopped there. They would search the house and outbuildings, sometimes sending patrols into the woods, sweeping the area for "terrorists." Usually though, Monsieur Florin added with a wry smile, they were looking for rabbits or chickens from the hutches or vegetables from the garden, and they took whatever they wanted.

There was no electricity in the forest house, and Roy could not listen to the radio. Without the music and with no news of the war, he worked on his crosswords, which were growing more and more elaborate, and he sang, much to the delight of Madame Florin. She did not understand the lyrics, but it made no difference. He sang song after song, loudly now, and his voice, Colette marveled, was surprisingly deep and rich. Occasionally Monsieur Florin reported on things he had heard in the neighborhood, but these stories were hardly more than rumors. Roy wondered what was happening at the front. Had the Allies launched their offensive to break the stalemate in Normandy? Had the Germans counterattacked? No one seemed to know. There were no more excursions to Vimbré—it was too far—and he no longer saw Jonckheere. Tucked away in the Fôret de Jouy, he was safe and relaxed, but as the days passed, he felt increasingly isolated.

Perhaps recognizing Roy's restlessness, Monsieur Florin mentioned in passing one afternoon that he had recently seen the wreckage of what he believed was Monsieur Roy's plane. It was not far away, in a field just beyond the woods to the southeast, near Combles. The Germans had combed through the wreckage and scavengers from the area had stripped away everything they could use, but the remains of the aircraft were still there. It might be possible for Monsieur Roy to see it. After a long, animated discussion between the Florins that Roy could not follow, Colette told him that her father would try to arrange a visit to the site of the crash.

Several days later, in the early morning, the baker from Chenoise stopped by the forest house in his *gazo*. He would take Roy and Colette to the crash. No one, the baker insisted, would be allowed out of the truck. The Germans might have the site under observation, and it was dangerous enough for Roy to be there at all. They would not stop for long.

Roy was excited as they left the house but did not speak as the *gazo* ground through the woods, turning from one narrow dirt lane into another. Monsieur Florin had showed him the position of the crash on his forester's map, and they seemed to be heading due east, skirting the major road that led to Chenoise. They had not gone far when the baker turned south and the woods gave way to a vast yellow wheat field that rolled out to a distant tree line and there, at the center of a ragged pool of debris, lay the charred skeleton of a crashed aircraft.

Shards of shattered Plexiglas and bits of aluminum, melted into pulpy unidentifiable clumps, lay strewn across the field, leaving a trail of rubble that stretched out of sight. Perhaps fifty meters from the road a gnarled propeller had plowed into the soft earth, and nearby, warped into a clot of burned rubber, a landing gear jutted from a hunk of metal as big as a jeep. One wing, its engines lost, its aileron burned away, lay at an angle beside what remained of the fuselage. The other wing was simply gone. The nose of the plane had been torn away, disintegrating into a ganglia of twisted wiring and jagged metal, and the center section of fuselage was ripped open and gutted, revealing the ribbed interior of what had been Smittie's radio compartment. Only the giant vertical stabilizer at the tail of the aircraft distinguished the wreckage as a B-17. It rose out of the rubble like a tombstone, the 457th's diagonal blue stripe and call letter, "U," clearly visible on its aluminum skin. Above the U, six neatly painted black numerals, 297579, identified the aircraft as Roy Allen's.

While the *gazo* idled noisily at the side of the road, Roy stared out at the field of debris, unable to speak. No bodies had been found in the wreckage, Jonckheere had assured him, but as he looked out at the tail gunner's compartment where Grimes had ridden, crushed flat beneath the vertical stabilizer, he found it incredible that they had all managed to get out. Even Paul Guérin had been unable to tell him anything about the crew. There was no news, no communication through resistance circles that they were safe or had even been seen. Sitting in the steamy cab of the truck, his shoulder pressed against the door, he fought the impulse to get out and have a closer look, as if sifting through the shattered remains of the aircraft would give him some clue, some new understanding of what had happened on that day a month ago. But the baker was anxious to go, and Colette, sitting closely beside him, touched him lightly on the shoulder. "It is time," she said. Sunlight sparkled on the remains of the silver fuselage as the baker swung the *gazo* around at a wide spot in the road, and Roy turned back, watching until the field and all it held disappeared behind them.

Roy was dozing in the front bedroom when he heard the vehicle approaching. It was not the familiar coughing of the *gazo* but a deeper, fuller rumble. Then he heard the whining of brakes and tires skidding to a gravelly halt. He stood up and slipped the curtains to one side and peered out. A wispy cloud of dust from the road had begun to drift across the front garden toward the woods. He could make out the back of a vehicle, gray-green and mottled with camouflage paint. At that moment Colette burst into the room. *"Les Allemands sont là,"* she whispered breathlessly. "German soldiers. They are coming to the back door." Monsieur Florin had gone out to meet them, to head them off. Roy could hear already a smattering of both French and German. "Be quick," Colette said, pointing to the window.

Roy pulled on his shoes, pushed aside the blue-and-white-checkered curtains and swung open the double windows. Leaning out, he looked toward the road. No Germans were in sight. He jumped clear of the window and then, crouching as low as he could, darted across the front garden. Dodging the rows of peas and pole beans, he headed toward the trees. At the edge of the garden he leaped a ditch, crossed the broad path that bordered the woods, and slipped into the underbrush just inside the wood line. For several moments he did not move. He lay on the ground, breathing heavily, and listened. He could hear voices coming from the rear of the house, and after he collected himself, he crawled along until he could see both sides of the house and the truck idling in the dusty road.

Like an Alpine chalet, the back roof of the forest house sloped sharply downward, forming an overhang that sheltered a small open porch. A German officer with immaculate boots stood in a swath of shadow at the edge of the porch, locked in conversation with Monsieur Florin. A dozen soldiers had jumped from the back of the truck and fanned out across the back garden. Working in pairs, they nosed around the sheds and outbuildings, slowly opening the heavy plank doors with the muzzles of their rifles. Roy looked around behind him. A narrow trail he had walked with Monsieur Florin wound just to his left. If the soldiers moved toward the wood line, he would slip down the trail, deeper into the woods. What he would do then, he did not know. "I hope they don't have dogs," he whispered to himself.

When he turned back toward the house, the officer, accompanied by one of his men, was just disappearing beneath the eaves of the porch. They're going to search the house, Roy thought. Had he left anything behind in the bedroom? Earlier he had been working on his crosswords, and, he realized with a start, all his papers—the lists of songs and lyrics—were lying beside the hurricane lamp on the small bedside table. Maybe Colette had noticed them. Had he left other things around? He patted his chest. His dogtags were still there, but where did René hide the flight jacket and gloves and evasion kit?

He watched the house, waiting. The soldiers had dispersed, taking up stations at intervals around the grounds, and he tried to keep them all in view. Within minutes two soldiers appeared at the front corner of the house, closest to the road, and one of them began to pick his way cautiously through the trellises and vine-covered tripods of the garden. At first his eyes appeared to be riveted on the ground, as if he was following a scent, and whenever he raised his head, as if sniffing the air, his glasses glinted in the sunlight like mirrors. He stepped tentatively toward the front door. In a flash Roy noticed that the double windows to his bedroom, just beside the door, were no longer ajar. Colette must have had the presence of mind to close them when he jumped out.

The soldier bounded up the three stone steps to the door, turned, and looked out again at the garden. For an instant he stood framed in the recessed doorway, and then, moving along the plaster façade, he halted at the front bedroom window. Shading his eyes against its reflection, he peered inside. For a moment the soldier did not move. Then he turned slowly and squinted toward the trees where Roy lay hidden. Edging his way to the ivy-covered corner of the house nearest the woods, he surveyed the tree line. He studied it for some time, his rifle poised. Roy hunkered down, hardly breathing. Then the soldier heaved a deep sigh, pushed back his steel helmet, and leaned into the cool ivy. Tilting his blond head from side to side, he slipped his rimless glasses off one ear at a time, and with the back of his hand he wiped his eyes. He seemed to relax.

Roy thought of making his move now, while he still had the chance, but he decided against it. He would wait and see. He lay prone on the forest floor, peering through the underbrush at the Germans, trying to account for each of the soldiers. While he was counting, the officer, followed by the Florins, reappeared at the entrance to the back porch. He was speaking to Monsieur Florin, who listened with an air of great calmness, a cigarette dangling casually from his lips. They had obviously found nothing in the house. The officer spoke for some time, then, turning smartly in the dust, barked an order to his men. Instantly the truck's engine kicked into gear, and the soldiers scrambled into the back. With one last look at the forest house, the officer made a hurried half-salute toward Monsieur Florin and climbed in beside the driver. Within seconds the truck was gone, disappearing down the narrow lane in the direction of Petit Paris.

Roy pushed himself up on his elbows and looked toward the house. He watched the approaches to the clearing and listened to the sounds in the woods around him. For a time the Florins stood in the back garden, ostentatiously engaged in small chores. Then Colette appeared from the kitchen, and together they busied themselves in the sheds, feeding the chickens and rabbits, checking the meager rows of vegetables that stretched out in between. They gave no signal to him, and he watched them without moving. Toward dusk they returned to the house. Still he waited. It was well after dark when Roy finally crept forward, slipping through the shadows of the back garden toward the blacked-out house.

Gathered in the yellow kerosene light of the kitchen, the Florins were waiting for him. They knew that he would hide until nightfall then sneak back to the house. They were confident, Colette said as her parents embraced him, that Roy would know what to do. The soldiers, of course, were looking for "terrorists." The officer had asked her father if he had seen anything suspicious. When Monsieur Florin had nothing to report, the officer delivered a warning. The *Kommandantur* in Provins had received reports, many of them anonymous, of armed terrorists in the area. Unfortunately there had recently been an outburst of terrorist activity all over France, the officer lamented, and now very stern measures were being taken not only against individuals but against whole villages where the terrorists were harbored. These reprisals had been carried out by SS units, freshly arrived from the eastern front, where such methods were common. It would be a tragedy for such things to happen here.

The Florins were relieved that the Germans had found nothing— the soldiers had hardly even looked in the house—and they were proud that Roy had managed to slip out of the trap. Producing a bottle of wine from the sheltered porch, Monsieur Florin insisted on drinking a toast to Roy's "adventure," to his athleticism—jumping out the window, in spite of the lingering pain in his back. They laughed and drank the wine, but beneath the joviality the Florins were clearly shaken, and to Roy, the forest house no longer seemed a haven.

"You and your guest have missed all the excitement at the school, Mademoiselle Florin," the surveyor said conspiratorially. Colette looked up, puzzled. She had ventured into the village to pick up some odds and ends she had left behind at the school and had run into Monsieur Gittard, the surveyor, on the street before the Hôtel de Ville. The reference to Roy caught her off guard, even though she had long suspected that Monsieur Gittard knew. It was his wife, after all, who had first warned Colette that her neighbor in the rue de la Gare had seen the American. "Yesterday the Germans came into the village," he continued as they walked along toward the church. "A troop of soldiers bivouacked at the school. Many bedded down in the court-yard, but the officers slept in the rooms at the school. The whole street smelled of sausage."

"Are they still there at the school?" Colette asked, trying to conceal the alarm she felt. Before they left for the forest house she had scoured the apartment for any trace of Roy's presence, but the idea of German soldiers in the rooms was disturbing.

"They left before dawn this morning," the surveyor said, "heading north. By the way, I am told that your guest is looking for a way home."

Colette had let the first mention of Roy pass without comment. Now Gittard clearly expected a response and she did not know what to say. The surveyor was involved with the *réseau* but just how she did not know.

"Perhaps I can help, if you are interested," he went on.

"What do you mean?"

They passed the *tabac* on the corner and turned into the rue de la Gare. Heavy clouds, as black as the inside of a stove, were advancing toward them over the fields to the west, and the first hesitant drops of rain began to fall, darkening the moss-covered stones of the church.

"A friend from Nangis is bringing another guest, an *aviateur,* to my house on Sunday. This guest is staying now in Fontains, but on Sunday he will be brought to my house here in the village. I will escort him then to another friend in Bannost, who will make sure that he has transportation to Paris."

Colette glanced up at him as they walked. For days Roy had been pressing her, gently at first and then with greater vigor, about Paris and an evasion line that could get him into the city. Aggravated by his jump from the window, his back had flared up again, and he was in considerable pain. Maybe, he argued, he could get medical attention in Paris. Maybe the resistance had contacts at hospitals there. And after the incident with the Germans, it was hard to argue that he was safe at the forest house.

"Are you sure of these friends?" she asked.

"Yes, I have known them for many years, and they are to be relied on." Colette knew better than to ask the name of the contact from Nangis or of the person they would meet in Bannost. They had stopped in front of the deserted school. Gittard's house was just down the street. "If you wish, I can arrange for your guest to join us, but I must know quickly." Beyond a distant line of poplars, delicate veins of lightning spread along the horizon and a peal of thunder rolled across the fields toward them. "Sunday is the day after tomorrow," he said, turning up his collar against the rain,

Blinding, windswept rain fell all afternoon, drenching her as she bicycled home from the village. All the way she agonized about what to do. She did not have to tell Roy about Gittard. That would be the simplest solution. He might never learn of the surveyor's offer, and with luck, the Americans would be arriving any day now. Besides, leaving Jouy was fraught with danger. Roy knew that. It was true that the pain in his back had worsened, and he *did* need medical attention, but the idea that he could get treatment in Paris seemed as fantastic as his earlier suggestion that she take him to Normandy. Although staying at the forest house was not without risks, he would be in infinitely greater peril out on the road. Keeping Gittard's offer to herself was, therefore, the most prudent course of action. Yet, that would be a form of betrayal, wouldn't it? It was what he wanted, what he had been yearning for since he dropped into her life almost six weeks ago. When she arrived at the forest house, soaked to the bone and spattered with mud from the road, she did not know what she would do. She knew only that she did not want him to leave.

That night, when the evening dishes had been cleared away, and the family sat at the table and Monsieur Florin had opened a bottle of cognac, Colette relayed the surveyor's message to Roy. Perhaps she should have consulted her father or Monsieur Pivert. But sitting in the amber lamplight, surrounded by her parents and her brothers, she could not hold back. She spoke with great reluctance and did not try to hide the deep anxiety she felt. She laid out, as forcefully as she could, the reasons why Roy should stay, and the others joined in.

"Here in Jouy, you are surrounded by friends," Monsieur Florin began, "people you know and trust. If you set out with Gittard on this *chaîne d'évasion*, you put yourself in the hands of strangers. You will be passed from contact to contact, and at each step along the line the danger of denunciation is great."

Colette translated as her father spoke, but she was sorry that they had no news of the war to support their arguments. In the week since they had left the school, she had heard no radio news and seen no newspaper. Still, the Allies would be coming soon, they all agreed. It would not be long.

"Besides, you have no papers—identity card, ration card, demobilization card, and more," Monsieur Florin continued. "Without papers you are a dead man in France. Gittard's contacts will certainly try to provide them when you reach Paris—if you reach Paris—but the *Feld-gendarmerie* has many controls on the roads and the trains are closely watched. I am not a betting man, my friend," he said, drawing heavily on his cigarette, "but I would not give good odds on your reaching Paris."

"Yes," echoed André, "Paris is a dangerous place. The Gestapo is very active there and the Sûreté, the Vichy security police, works closely with them. In Paris you can trust no one."

"And even if you should survive the trip to Paris," Colette said, "even if you have possession of the necessary papers and make the contacts to take you on to the border, the journey to the Pyrenees is long and even more dangerous. The Germans patrol the trains and the border and many are caught before they reach the frontier. I have heard Monsieur Pivert and the others speak of this many times."

Roy listened without speaking, hardly touching the cognac that sat before him on the table. After weeks of pressing to leave at every turn, he seemed surprisingly subdued now at the prospect of actually going. He would sleep on it, he promised, as he rose stiffly from the table. His back was bothering him tonight. "We'll talk in the morning," he said, touching Colette gently on the shoulder. Followed by René, he drifted into the bedroom and closed the door. The Florins sat in silence. The drumming of the rain on the roof had stopped, and with the lamps extinguished and the room lit only by candlelight, Colette pushed open the door to the back porch. She took a deep breath, inhaling the sweet storm-driven air. Her mother came and stood beside her for a moment in the doorway.

"Will he stay?" she whispered, as the others wandered off to bed in the semidarkness.

"No," Colette heard herself say. "In the morning he will tell me that he must go."

The next day she rode her bicycle again over the muddy, rutted roads back to Jouy. She had to tell Monsieur Gittard that he should prepare for another guest. On the way she stopped at Vimbré. Monsieur Pivert was shocked by what she told him. He thought that Paul Guérin's visit had settled matters, that Roy was reconciled to his situation in Jouy. She stood with the Piverts in the courtyard of the farm, steam rising from the puddles and the soggy hay wagons in the surprising morning heat.

"He is determined to go," Colette told them, "more determined than ever. And now a possibility has arisen."

"What possibility?"

"Monsieur Gittard, the surveyor, has a contact in Nangis who is hiding an aviator. On Sunday the contact will bring the aviator to Jouy and then on to Bannost. There he will be picked up by a Paris connection. Monsieur Gittard has great faith in the man and has offered to take Roy along."

"I do not like this," said Monsieur Pivert. "I do not like this at all." He wore his knee-high farm boots, caked with mud and manure, and his tattered corduroy britches that had grown too tight. The scent of a wood fire filled the damp morning air, and a wisp of smoke curled from the kitchen chimney. "Here he is safe, but on the move, with a *chaîne d'évasion,* he runs great risks. These evasion lines are riddled now with traitors, German spies and worse. Besides, German troops are everywhere these days, on the roads, in the villages, in the fields. It is worse than '40. He must understand this."

"I have tried to make him see," Colette said, "and my father has talked to him, but he is stubborn."

"He is a difficult man, this Monsieur Roy of yours," the mayor agreed, shaking his head.

"A poison gift," his wife snapped, wringing her hands in her apron, "and he will get us all caught yet!"

"There is something more," Monsieur Pivert said. "Gittard's heart is in the right place, and he is brave. He has done his part for us." His face clouded. "But he sits too much in the cafés. He likes his wine, and when the wine has him, he talks." Colette knew this to be true. She had seen him many times at his table in the café on the road to Chenoise, holding court.

"Must you tell him?" Monsieur Pivert asked. "Does he know already of Gittard's offer?"

"I have told him," Colette said. "I had to." Her voice was firm, but she wondered, as she had all through the sleepless night, if she had done the right thing. She was glad she did not have to explain. "I am meeting with Monsieur Gittard this morning, to confirm the arrangements for tomorrow. We will keep trying, my parents and I, to dissuade Roy but there is so little time."

"He is a fool if he leaves Jouy," Madame Pivert grumbled, turning away toward the house.

"I wish him *bonne chance*," her husband said. "He will need it."

They rose early at the forest house on Sunday. No one had slept much. Before dawn Roy could hear Madame Florin stirring in the kitchen and smell the bitter aroma of the chicory. He lay on his back, staring up at the streaks of shadow that wavered across the ceiling. His heart was racing as it did in the anxious hours before a mission, when he would lie wide awake in the darkness, waiting for the CQ to enter the hut to rouse them for briefing.

After six weeks in hiding he would be leaving Jouy, leaving Colette and the Florins and the security they had provided. They had talked long into the night again, and, for hours after the lamps were extinguished and he crawled into bed, he mulled over his options. He weighed them, analyzing them from every angle as he had done from that moment on Friday when Colette told him of Gittard's offer. For the past thirty-six hours, the Florins had pressed their arguments with great fervor. They invoked the warnings of Pivert and Captain Paul, who had experience with the evasion lines and who had insisted that leaving Jouy now, with the Allies poised to break out of Normandy, was madness. He would have to make a long dangerous journey to the south. The Germans and the Vichy authorities conducted many spot searches on the trains and in the stations, especially in the border regions, and they knew how to spot false papers. Then there were the mountains. The Pyrenees were over five thousand meters high, Monsieur Florin had told him with an ominous edge to his voice, fifteen thousand feet. Could Roy imagine himself, with his ailing back, scaling these cold rugged peaks with a paid Spanish guide who would betray him if he got a better price from the Germans?

They had made a compelling case. The Florins were his friends, and he trusted their judgment. They were probably right. But as he lay in bed listening to the muted voices of Colette and Monsieur Florin beyond the door, he realized that there had never really been a decision to make. Within thirty seconds of hearing Gittard's offer, he had known that he would go. He wasn't kidding himself. He understood the risks. It *would* mean trusting people he didn't know. He *didn't* have papers and *could* be caught before he even reached Paris. Or he *might* fall into the hands of the Germans in the city or on the way to Spain. He might freeze in the mountains or be sold out by a guide, as Monsieur Florin warned. In the end he knew only that he had to go.

He had his reasons, thinking them through one by one in the darkness as he waited for the day to begin. May would have received the MIA telegram from the War Department by late June, a month ago, and would be pacing the floor in her parents' row house, waiting on tenterhooks for another telegram. She would be watching for the boy from Western Union, praying that the next communication from Washington was not one which began: "The Secretary of War regrets to inform you . . ." The baby was due in September, and he had to somehow get word to her that he was alive.

Then there was his back. In the week since they had left the school, the pain had not only returned, it had changed. No longer the bone-deep soreness at the base of his spine, it was now a sharper, searing pain that came in sudden spasms, spreading from his back all along his side. The hot compresses that Colette applied daily offered just moments of relief. He couldn't shake the feeling that something was wrong, that this wasn't just a wrenched back from the jump. They couldn't do anything for him here, but maybe it would somehow be possible in Paris.

And, finally, there was still a war on. For over a month he had sat in Jouy and watched the vapor trails spread across the sky, wondering where they were going today. While at the school he had listened to the BBC report that Allied raids on transportation and communications targets in France were continuing. There were also attacks on the synthetic oil refineries in Germany, at Merseburg and Leipzig, places he recognized from the briefing maps. Now he could not follow the reports. He could only stand at the window and watch for the silver flashes of the formations as they arced across the sky. Never had he experienced such helplessness, such idleness. It was his duty to get back to his unit. Evading capture from Jouy to Air Station 130, thought of as a whole, seemed like a long shot, but broken down into its different stages—Jouy to Paris, Paris to one of the border villages, the trek over the mountains, then a flight back to England— it seemed doable. He had heard of guys who had done it, guys from the 457th.

All of these were good, plausible reasons, but it was an empty exercise. He had simply known, even before the reasons materialized, that if the opportunity to go came, he would not let it pass, and today, in just a few hours, he would be on his way.

Roy wore a dark suit, a little tight at the shoulder, a white shirt that pinched his neck when he tried to button the collar, and a tie that he loosened and tugged to one side. His shoes were polished black, and on his head, pulled forward toward his eyebrows, was the black beret that he wore on his trips to Vimbré and that always made him feel slightly foolish. He and Colette walked side by side at the edge of the paved road leading to Jouy, and he was glad the rain that threatened in the early morning had held off. They were expected at Gittard's before noon. As they passed through Petit Paris, it struck him that he was not at all concerned about being caught on this leg of his journey, though it would be ironic, indeed, after all his worries about Paris and the Pyrenees, to be captured on the walk from the forest house into Jouy.

At first Gittard had suggested that he would come to the Fôret de Jouy for Roy, but Colette refused. Although it meant that they would have to walk into the village, she did not want to say good-bye at the forest house, and Roy was glad. It was hard enough taking leave of the Florins. Standing on the back porch in the early morning light, they had been a portrait of dejection, and he couldn't shake the feeling that by leaving he was somehow betraying their trust. There had been tears and kisses and hugs and he was shaken by the time they strode through the back garden and headed down the lane through the woods. He and Colette did not talk much on the road.

As they walked, he hummed softly. Shortly after waking, he had sat at the edge of the bed, anxious for the day to begin, and shuffled through the crosswords and song titles he had jotted down during his weeks in Jouy. He wanted to leave nothing behind. He folded the papers neatly and tucked them into his coat, which hung on the chair at the foot of the bed. He intended to stuff them into the flames of Madame Florin's stove, but in the excitement of the morning, they had slipped his mind. Now, walking with Colette along the road toward Jouy, he patted his coat pocket, and the papers were there.

They passed the deserted château at the edge of the village, its grounds now overgrown with weeds, and moved swiftly along the winding back street that led to the school. There was no sign of life at the École des Filles. A trio of carefully pruned plane trees cast their shadows across the vacant courtyard, slanting toward the school, where the windows were shuttered against the summer heat. Only a few morning bicyclists, perhaps on their way to early mass, passed them as they turned into the rue de la Gare. No one paid them any attention.

Gittard lived just beyond the school, where the village tapered into a single row of houses that trailed off into a swath of orchards and oat fields. The surveyor was waiting for them, and when they tapped at the door, he eagerly ushered them inside. He made a hasty, agitated gesture of welcome to Colette and gave Roy a nervous, appraising glance. His whole body seemed to vibrate with excitement. Two men sat at a table in the cramped dining room, but Gittard made no effort to introduce them and they did not speak. Roy thought he recognized Madame Gittard when she appeared from the kitchen carrying a tureen of soup. Maybe he had seen her from the window at the school. While the men sat in silence, she bustled back and forth, placing bowls and spoons and a cutting board with bread on the table.

Finally one of the men spoke in French to Monsieur Gittard, but the other, like Roy, sat quietly, taking everything in. A particularly foul smelling cigarette burned in an ashtray directly in front of him, but he did not seem to notice it. His clothes were ill-fitting and there was something about his face that struck Roy as distinctly English. While Madame Gittard poured the wine and the men settled in to eat, the surveyor spoke briefly to Colette and she translated.

"He has instructions for your trip," she said. "They are extremely important and you must follow them exactly. If you have a question, you must ask it now, not when you are out on the road." Roy nodded, and the other aviator leaned forward, listening as well. "You are not to speak, not to anyone, not even to one another. Stay close to Monsieur Gittard and take your lead from him. You will bicycle to Bannost. It is a small village only a few kilometers from here. There you will meet the next contact. That is all I can tell you."

Roy barely touched the soup or the bread laid out for them. He wanted no wine. While the others ate, he looked across the room at Colette, who had risen from the table and stood against the window, conversing with Madame Gittard. She had no appetite either. He owed so much to her. She had taken him in, fed him, nursed him back to health. She had taken chances for him, put herself and her family in grave danger, and even now, against her own better judgment, had done what he had asked: she had arranged for him to leave. Watching her day after day as she negotiated her life in the school, in the village, in the resistance, he was awed by her tenacity and resourcefulness, by her simple, unflagging courage. It was not the courage he had seen in combat but a more subtle form, all the more powerful for being submerged beneath the unruffled surface of her daily life. He tried to think of something to say, but the room was crowded and anyway the time had passed. He wished he had said something to her on the walk, thanked her, told her how he felt. Watching her now as she spoke to Madame Gittard, he knew only that he hated to leave her like this.

The meal was over and Monsieur Gittard rose from the table and said something to the contact from Nangis. Everyone stood at once, filling the already crowded room. It was time to go. Colette waited for him beside the door and together they stepped into the street. Several bicycles stood propped against the side of the house. Gittard pointed toward one. At the base Roy had ridden such a bicycle, with its tricky English hand brakes, but the seat, obviously adjusted for a much shorter man, was too low, and he could not fully extend his legs to pedal. He tried to raise the seat but could not, and while the others waited, he climbed on and pushed off in the little alley beside the house to test it. His knees bowed out and the bike wobbled as he pedaled, but he would manage.

The men were already mounted on their bicycles, ready to leave, when Monsieur Gittard suddenly muttered something to his wife, who hurried back into the house. When she returned she carried an ancient box camera. Monsieur Gittard, to Roy's astonishment, wanted a picture. After a moment of fumbling and hurried instructions that he did not understand, Roy and the other aviator were posed side by side against the wall of the house. Roy pulled off the black beret and looked out at the camera. He could not quite manage a smile. After all the stress on security, the photograph struck him as more than a little inconsistent, even unsettling.

Colette shook her head in disbelief. She was standing with Madame Gittard in the street at the corner of the house, watching. As the men once again climbed onto their bicycles, Roy shot a quick glance at her. After weeks of waiting, everything was moving much too fast. He had not had a chance to thank her, to say good-bye, to give her a parting hug. As the others pushed off into the street, Roy paused beside the two women.

"I wish you good luck," Colette said to him. Her voice was strained and brittle.

Straddling the bicycle, Roy leaned over and kissed her on both cheeks, as he had learned to do, in the French fashion. "I, I . . ." he faltered, "I'll see you again." He looked down at her and tried to give his best jaunty smile. It didn't work. "You take care of yourself."

Madame Gittard stood just beside them, almost touching Colette's shoulder, watching. "*Bonne chance,*" she chirped. "*Bonne chance,* monsieur."

Colette stepped away from the bicycle, and Roy turned back toward the street. Gittard and the others were already pedaling away up the incline toward the village, and he would have to rush to catch up. He glanced again at Colette and smiled grimly. Then he turned and headed up the street. He did not look back.

He caught Gittard and the others where the rue de la Gare swung toward the square, and they wove their way through the near-empty streets of Jouy. Pedaling two abreast, they rode out of the village in brilliant sunshine and turned onto the main road that ran to Chenoise. A string of cyclists, like scattered beads on a necklace, stretched along the road before them, but they saw no cars and no Germans. Heading south, they passed the main entrance to Pivert's farm and the fields where the Lysanders had landed. Roy had never seen Vimbré from this vantage point, and he wondered what Pivert and his friends at the farm would say when they learned that he had left.

They had not ridden far beyond Vimbré when Gittard led them into a narrow lane that meandered lazily to the east. As the road wound through the now rolling fields, Roy struggled to find a pedaling rhythm and he had to work to keep pace with the others. Winded, he paused for a moment at a rise in the road and looked back out across the yellow fields toward Jouy. In the distance, the brown, blunt-nosed church rose above the surrounding rooftops and the giant grain elevators shone white as a sand dune in the morning sun. Beyond them he could just make out the water tower behind the school. He pedaled on, trying to catch up. When he turned to look again, Jouy had disappeared from view.

The low two-story buildings of Bannost lined a broad, open square, and Gittard stopped in front of a row of shops just across from the church. The men pulled their bicycles into a courtyard behind the corner building and followed the surveyor inside. They entered what appeared to be a sort of general store, one wing of which had been converted into a café with a small parquet dance floor at the center. Two men stood at the bar, one wearing a black beret, and three others sat at a small table wedged into the corner. While Roy and the other aviator took seats at a table close by, Gittard conferred with the man in the black beret. He was clearly the proprietor and as they talked he poured out a drink for his guest. They did not speak for long. Then the surveyor turned, barely glancing toward Roy's table, and strode out of the room.

After several moments, the proprietor looked out the front window, and then turned and nodded to his companion at the bar. The man took a last sip of coffee, and made his way through the store toward the courtyard. The men from the other table followed. Roy and the other aviator looked at each other, then rose and joined them.

In the courtyard, the men stood in a tight semicircle. "I am Robert," the man from the bar said. "Listen carefully and do as I say." He seemed to be looking directly at Roy. "Watch me. Stay close and follow my lead. We will travel to another village. There we will take a bus. Then we will board a train for Paris. Don't speak under any circumstances." Roy glanced at the other men. They were *résistants*, operatives of the evasion line, come to fetch him and the other aviator, he assumed. "You will leave the bicycles here," Robert continued. "Come," he said, motioning toward the rear of a truck that was backed into a shed at a corner of the courtyard. "There is not much time."

The men pulled open the back gate of the truck and clambered inside. As Roy climbed in, Robert handed him a burlap sack. It was tied at the top and surprisingly heavy. "Here," Robert said, "you take this with you. Hold on to it." Then someone, Robert perhaps or the proprietor who had joined them in the courtyard, closed the gate behind them. The men arranged themselves among the barrels and crates and enormous wheels of cheese that were stacked virtually to the canvas roof. A powerful odor of damp cloth and mold pervaded the dark space inside the truck. They rode for some time, jouncing and lurching from side to side as the *gazo* heaved along the winding country roads. Occasionally someone grunted or swore to himself in no discernible language but no one spoke.

At last the truck slowed, grinding through a series of tight turns, and they felt it back to a halt. The rear gate swung open and Robert motioned for them to climb out. They found themselves in a brick courtyard at the edge of a road. They waited there until they heard a vehicle approaching. Then Robert stepped out into the road and the bus stopped and they climbed aboard. The bus was filled with country people, farmers in ill-fitting Sunday clothes, women in peasant black with weathered faces and swollen legs. Pulling his hat down over his eyes, Roy leaned his head against the cool windowpane and tried to sleep.

The bus made many stops, pulling to the side of the road in hamlet after hamlet, disgorging passengers and picking up others. Many carried suitcases or canvas bags bulging with produce, and the smell of potatoes saturated the crowded bus. After a time the bus pulled into a little town and halted beside a railway depot so small and disheveled Roy could not even see a sign. He had no idea where he was or what direction they had taken. Robert disappeared into the depot, and the men milled around on the crowded platform, looking absentmindedly at the depot's peeling propaganda placards and the official proclamations, printed in French and German, whose dense black lettering had faded in the summer sun.

They had not waited long when a whistle screeched and the little crowd on the platform rustled forward in anticipation. When the train arrived, hissing to a stop in an explosion of steam, the men followed Robert as he climbed on board and pushed forward along the narrow corridor. By a stroke of good fortune, they found an empty compartment, and the little group occupied all six seats. Roy placed the burlap sack on the floor beside his feet and, exhausted, fell back into his seat.

At every stop more passengers pressed into the train. Roy watched as they filled the corridor outside the compartment until at last no movement was possible at all. Many carried bags, just as he did, or baskets or valises with the stalks of unidentifiable vegetables protruding from them. Robert sat just across from him, reading a paper. Roy pressed his face against the window and watched the towns slide by. So far so good, he said to himself. A surge of excitement shot through him. It was Sunday, July 23, and he was on his way to Paris.

PART III

PARIS

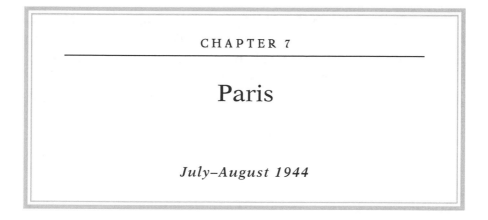

CHAPTER 7

Paris

July–August 1944

It was late afternoon when the train eased into the cavernous station, grinding to a halt under a canopy of frosted glass and ornate steel beams. Hot and irritable, passengers poured from the crowded carriages onto a platform already brimming with bicycles, baggage carts, and heaps of luggage. Struggling in the heat with their baskets, valises, pillowcases, and canvas sacks bloated with the bounty of a trip to the country, they jostled along toward the control gates at the entrance to the platform.

Stepping down out of the stifling carriage, Roy found himself swept forward, surrounded by Robert and the others. A great crush of passengers had already collected at the exit, passing slowly through the control gate like sand through an hourglass. Pushed along in the thickening crowd, unable even to lift his arms, Roy could see far ahead a small knot of harried ticket collectors, examining papers, making the occasional perfunctory check of a sack or suitcase.

Just beyond the control barrier, several men in civilian clothes stood gazing down the crowded platform. At first glance they might have been meeting friends or relatives returning from a Sunday excursion. And yet there was something in their demeanor, their bearing, that made Roy take a second look. As he watched them, the men peered steadily out into the crowd, their eyes sweeping like searchlights across the mounting wave of passengers. Sometimes one would

173

step forward, glance down at the papers offered up to the ticket collectors, examine the face of the passenger, confer, then retreat back to his post.

"Gestapo," Robert whispered, and Roy felt a tightening in his stomach. He had no papers, no identity card, nothing. Only a heavy burlap sack. He would remain quiet, play his role, let Robert do the talking. As they were propelled closer and closer to the control point and the steely-eyed Gestapo officials, his heart pounded. He hoped Robert knew what he was doing.

Then, with the gate only a few meters ahead of him, Roy watched as the overwhelmed ticket collectors suddenly relented and began motioning the passengers to move on through. They barked impatiently at those at the head of the line, and two, then three, then half a dozen passengers stepped through the control point without stopping. At random intervals one of the officials would raise his hand, halting a passenger and demanding to see papers, and the line would stutter, then surge forward again. The Gestapo agents stood to the side, watching.

Robert was ready to step past the gate, when one of the ticket collectors, his thin face glistening with sweat, blocked his path. He uttered a few words and held out his hand, tapping his fingertips to his thumb. With a weary calm, Robert reached into his coat, producing a small booklet of papers. At that moment, the Gestapo agents darted forward. Roy's heart froze. Wedged into the crowd, there was no place to run, no escape. Colette had warned him, Paul Guérin had warned him, and now, on a sweltering train platform in Paris, his luck had at last run out.

The Gestapo men strode directly toward him. Roy let the heavy burlap sack slip to his feet and braced himself. Brushing past the ticket collectors, the leader of the two gripped Roy's shoulder and shoved him roughly aside. Stunned, Roy did not dare move. Out of the corner of his eye, he saw them approach a well-dressed elderly man. A momentary grimace rippled across the man's lips as the Germans pulled him aside, but he was composed, almost serene as they led him through the silent crowd toward the control gate. All along the platform, the Sunday passengers averted their eyes.

When the Germans had passed, the weary ticket collector glanced up at Robert and, with a distracted sigh, handed him back his papers. Then, turning directly to Roy, he waved him through the gate. Roy picked up the sack and, following Robert, walked briskly past the

Gestapo agents and the elderly gentleman, past clusters of German soldiers, and into the busy terminal.

Outside the station, the little group wove its way through a maze of two-wheeled carts and horse-drawn wagons and endless racks of bicycles. A black Citroën, its long polished hood gleaming in the late-afternoon sun, idled near the side exit, tended by two men with the unmistakable look of Gestapo. No other automobile, no bus or truck, was visible on the street that led away from the station. At the corner, beneath a sign reading Taxi, an elegantly dressed woman clutching a hatbox stepped into a cart harnessed to a bicycle, and a young man in shorts and high stockings climbed onto the bike and pushed out into the street. A rickshaw, Roy thought in amazement, they're driving rickshaws in Paris!

Without looking back, Robert plunged into a series of narrow serpentine streets where the shops were closed and shuttered and rivulets of water ran in the gutters. Sunlight slanted across the balconies of the upper floors, high above the deserted bakeries and greengrocers, but the streets below were draped in shadow. Even in these shaded byways the shallow sidewalks bustled with people, and the wooden soles of their shoes striking the cobblestones rang out like the clip-clopping gait of horses' hooves.

Robert kept up a brisk pace and Roy's back ached under the weight of the burlap sack. He was sweating heavily, and the surge of adrenaline that had sustained him at the station had long subsided, but he could not ask the others to slow down or stop. When at last they emerged from the winding streets into a broad tree-lined boulevard, Roy paused to catch his breath and looked up at the scene before him. As far as the eye could see, bicycles swept along the sun-dappled street. Ridden by well-dressed men, attractive young women, gray-clad nurses, adolescent schoolboys, even a trio of nuns whose black habits billowed in the breeze behind them, bicycles swarmed past, and the metallic whirring of their tires filled the air like the hum of summer insects. Occasionally a solitary *gazo* would stagger by, scattering the cyclists, but these were rare.

They walked for blocks along the Avenue Daumesnil without seeing a car, passing small sidewalk newsstands and crowded outdoor cafés where people sat over coffee at round, red-topped tables. Hardly noticing, Roy stumbled on, and with each step, his suffering intensified. No longer confined to his back, the pain slashed through his side into his groin. A shot of bile surged into his parched throat, and his bowels contracted. He was afraid he was going to vomit, but he trudged on, his eyes locked on Robert leading the way along the broad boulevard.

At length, Robert turned into a small cross street and stopped in the middle of a short block just a few meters off the Avenue Daumesnil. Standing beneath an arched stone portal at number 47, he looked quickly along the sidewalk behind them and turned the key. One by one the others stepped inside. Without speaking, Robert strode quickly through the darkened vestibule, pushed open the glass-paneled inner doors, and began to climb a broad, winding staircase to the right. Trudging after him, the men tramped up flight after flight of groaning wooden stairs. By the time Roy reached the dingy landing at the fourth floor, breathing heavily and staggering with fatigue, he could see an open door on the landing just above him. It was the top floor and the men were filing in. Sweat stung his eyes and the burning pain in his back and side was excruciating. At the doorway a young woman beckoned to him, and Roy stumbled across the threshold.

Inside, the apartment was crowded. Robert waited with Roy's four companions from the train in the narrow foyer, while another three men stood in a cramped living room. Two women hovered in the doorway to what appeared to be a kitchen. At first no one spoke, but when a slender, intense man of roughly Roy's age emerged from a back room, the apartment erupted in excited talk. Robert and the other man laughed and spoke with great animation, their sentences exploding in staccato bursts. As he spoke, Robert gestured toward Roy and his companions from the train, and the man's dark eyes took each of them in, sizing them up with a rapid, appraising glance. Looking down at the burlap sack resting at Roy's feet, he asked, *"Et qu'est-ce que tu nous apportes dans le sac?"*

"Produits du terroir," Robert responded, smiling broadly.

"Ah, bon, bon," the man muttered, stooping down to inspect the sack. He staggered slightly as he tried to lift it, and Robert helped carry it to the kitchen table. *"Mon Dieu,"* the man swore, *"c'est du béton?"* The others crowded around as the contents of the sack spilled out onto the table. From Roy's vantage point at the rear he could see over the shoulders of the men, and as he watched, Robert pulled what looked like slab after slab of dried beef from the coarse burlap. Colorless and stiff, the meat was hardly appetizing to look at, but a real delicacy in wartime France. Then, from between the tightly packed meat Robert produced a small cloth sack, then another and another. As the

men leaned forward in anticipation, Robert untied the first sack to reveal three well-oiled pistols. The others contained several carefully wrapped boxes of ammunition and three more pistols.

Roy could only shake his head. Not only had he passed through the controls at the railway station without papers, he had been carrying weapons in the bargain. What would Robert have done if the Gestapo agents had seized him? Would he have simply slipped away in the crowd? But that hadn't happened, and the occupants of the apartment were in a mood to celebrate. It had been a successful day. They had convoyed Allied aviators from the Département Seine-et-Marne to Paris and Robert had delivered weapons and ammunition to the *réseau.*

Exhausted and struggling with the pain in his back, Roy slumped in a large overstuffed chair in a corner of the living room while several bottles of wine appeared from the kitchen and glasses were passed around. Although Robert made sporadic efforts at introductions, Roy was too dazed to absorb the names. The apartment belonged to Georges, the young man who had opened the sack, and his sister—or was she his wife?—Yvette. He could not be sure just how many people were in the small apartment. They milled in the cramped living room, sat in stiff-backed wooden chairs around the kitchen table, or disappeared down a narrow corridor to the back rooms of the apartment.

At dusk the sky beyond the windows darkened, bathing the room in purple light, and Georges and Yvette lit candles and closed the shutters. The electricity supply in Paris was unpredictable, Georges explained, with current available in the apartment for only a few hours each day, and, of course, the blackout was still in effect. With luck there would be electricity later, and they would listen to the war news from the BBC.

While the others laughed and talked in clouds of tobacco smoke, Yvette lingered by Roy's chair, inquiring about his condition, nodding her head in commiseration, and pouring him glass after glass of wine. She spoke no English, and in response to her earnest questions he could only smile weakly and rub his back. But she was sympathetic and the wine kept the pain at bay, and as the evening wore on the sharp stabbing in his back diminished.

Sipping the wine that Yvette poured for him, Roy gradually relaxed. He noticed that the four men from the train, the men who had accompanied them from Bannost, did not join in the lively conversation. They seemed to hang back in their ill-fitting clothes, nodding when spoken to, smiling vaguely, watching. Then it struck him with a start that they were not French at all, not *résistants*, as he had assumed, but Allied fliers just like himself. Following Robert's orders, they had not spoken all through the dangerous journey from the country. Even now, apparently safe in the apartment, they were too exhausted, too confused, and too cautious to start up a conversation. He would talk to them later, when the scene was less hectic and they were left among themselves.

He had been dozing in the comfortable chair for some time when at last the current crackled on and everyone gathered around the small radio to listen to the war news from London. It was the BBC's French program but he listened as intently as the others, watching their expressions for a sign that the news was good. On this night the bulletins from Normandy were discouraging, as they had been for weeks, and the men muttered and swore as the program came to an end.

Soon after the broadcast, Robert departed. He had to get home to the Rue Gambetta before the midnight curfew and could not afford to miss the last metro. He would return tomorrow, he assured them, with news from his contact. The contact would make the arrangements for the men to move along the *chaîne d'évasion,* probably to the south, over the Pyrenees and into Spain. He had much experience, this contact, and although Robert was not certain about the timing, Roy and the others should be prepared to move at a moment's notice.

Roy was giddy with fatigue and his head heavy with wine when the occupants of the apartment finally bedded down for the night, sleeping in chairs, on the sofa, on the floor. His back was stiff and sore and his muscles ached. As he rose from the chair, he found that he could hardly walk. It was pitch black in the apartment when Yvette led him to a bed in a small front room and helped him ease onto the mattress. Someone—he could not tell who—was already asleep in the bed and another form was curled in a chair nearby. The pillow was cool and his head was swimming as he closed his eyes. It seemed like a year since he had left Jouy.

When Robert arrived at the apartment the next morning, Roy was in agony. The scalding pain had returned with a vengeance in the early morning hours, spreading to his intestines, his bowels, and he was burning with fever. He could walk only a few steps without doubling over, and no one seemed to know what to do.

While Yvette applied wet towels to Roy's forehead, Robert reported that his contact was not yet ready to take the aviators. They would have to wait a few days. In the meantime, Georges's apartment was clearly too small to accommodate everyone. He would take four of the airmen to a safe house on the outskirts of the city, in St. Maur. Roy was in no shape to travel and so he would remain here, in the Avenue Michel Bizot, until he could be moved. When the arrangements had been made, Robert would call for him.

Throughout the day Georges and Yvette followed Roy's condition with mounting concern. The pain had become excruciating, attacking in sudden, unexpected bursts that left Roy limp and on the verge of delirium. Georges knew a doctor who could be trusted, he thought, and after much discussion, he dispatched Yvette to fetch him.

While they waited, Roy stretched out on the large double bed Yvette had prepared for him. He tried to sip a bit of wine but the pain was coming in waves now, relentlessly, shooting from his back in white-hot spurts that left him stunned and breathless.

An hour passed, maybe more, before the bell rang, and the apartment door opened and he heard voices speaking in low tones. They spoke for some time, a long, murmurous, incomprehensible conversation, and when at last Georges strode into the bedroom, he was accompanied by a woman Roy had not seen before. "The doctor is here," Georges announced, gesturing toward the tall, athletic-looking woman. She carried a battered black leather bag, worn and deeply furrowed, which she placed at the side of the bed.

"So," she said, "my friends tell me that you are a pilot."

Roy nodded, glancing uncertainly at Georges.

"I like aviators," she said. "An affinity. I, too, was once in the flying service. In the first war." From her bag she produced a creased photograph of a young woman standing with several men in flying clothes. They wore dashing white scarves and goggles pushed up on their foreheads and behind them he could make out the wooden prop and flimsy canvas wings of a biplane. Roy shook his head in appreciation.

The doctor sat on the edge of the bed beside him, and Roy tried to describe the pain. He recounted his landing in the tree, the wrenching fall, the heated bricks Colette had applied. With his left hand, he traced an arc from his lower back to his side. The woman tilted her head, pursing her lips as he described the spasms. *Je comprends,* she said. "You will stand please." Roy rose unsteadily to his feet, and with her delicate hands, she turned him to face the doorway where Georges and

Robert stood watching. "You remove your shirt now." Using her thumbs, she probed firmly along Roy's spine, pressing until he winced. At last she paused and bent over her bag. Speaking rapidly in French, she addressed the men who had edged into the room. They listened intently, shooting an occasional anxious glance at Roy. From time to time they interrupted to ask questions, and from their subdued expression, Roy understood that her answers were not reassuring.

Turning back to Roy and opening her bag, the doctor sighed. "There is little I can do," she said with a quick, almost imperceptible shrug of her shoulders. How many times, he wondered, had he seen this gesture in France, from Colette, from Jonckheere, from Monsieur Florin? What did it signify? He was never sure. "So little in the way of medicine," she muttered, and began preparing a syringe, flicking the needle with the tip of her finger. "Like the milk and the wine, the morphine is watered down," she said, motioning for Roy's arm, "but it will help with the pain."

She had brought a heating pad, which she placed on the mattress beside him. Stepping forward, Georges knelt, and plugged it into the socket behind the bedside table. The doctor glanced at her watch. "We are having electricity for only another hour now. The *Révolution nationale* has brought us so much," she said with derision. "No more decadent living for us. Each day private domiciles receive current for only two hours, beginning at noon. Only public offices have current during the day." She closed her bag and sighed. "Place the pad to your back when you can. You will feel the morphine soon."

As she left the bedroom, the doctor glanced back at Roy. "*Bonne chance, mon capitaine.*" She waved, her arm raised in a casual salute. Brushing past Georges in the doorway, she muttered, "*Ton ami doit être à l'hôpital.*"

Roy sank back in the bed, the flannel heating pad tucked up under his lower back, and felt its electric warmth begin to radiate through him. An aroma of singed cotton rose from the rumpled sheets, reminding him, to his astonishment, of his mother standing in her slip at the ironing board in the little house at Fifth and Cayuga, pressing a dress for work. Within minutes a gentle morphine haze settled over him, and he felt woozy. Like a leaf floating lazily downstream, rotating slowly in the current, he felt the room slide away from him and he drifted off.

He was not sure how long he had slept when he woke, disoriented and dazed, in a pool of sweat. From the other room he could hear the murmur of familiar voices and smell the sweet smoke of the cigarettes. The men were talking in the kitchen, and there were women's voices too. From far away the shrill singsong of a siren wailed, grew louder as it passed somewhere nearby, then faded. Lying in the shadowy stillness of the room, he heard other noises he could not place, muted scratching sounds that emanated from directly above his head. Something seemed to be moving in the shaded room. Was it a rat in the wall? In the ceiling? He opened his eyes and the room swam dizzily, the armoire and dresser bobbing in the wash of the grainy twilight. Then he heard it again, more distinctly now. It was crazy, he thought, but there it was: the unmistakable clucking of a chicken—several chickens, in fact, clucking, scratching, pecking. Lying in a Parisian apartment five floors above the Avenue Michel Bizot, Roy Allen, city boy from Philadelphia, was hearing barnyard noises. It was the morphine talking, clucking like a chicken.

Georges peeked in the room. Roy stirred and sat up, rubbing his eyes.

"*Ça va?*" Georges asked, exhaling smoke from his nostrils. "How are you feeling?"

Roy shook his head, as if he were trying to shake water from his ears. "This morphine," he began, his tongue thick and lazy, "is the damndest thing. I, uh, I hear chickens." He laughed.

"But of course you do, *oui*," Georges replied. "*Poulets. Ils sont partout à Paris.*"

Roy stared at him.

"*Lapins aussi,*" Georges went on. "In Paris the chickens are everywhere. Rabbits, too. The people raise them in their flats. Hens, hares, even ducks. All Paris is hungry. The people are obsessed with food. They talk of it all the time; they spend their days searching for it. There is, of course, the *marché noir,* the black market, but that is for the rich and the traitors. The people, they struggle. The food shops are empty and every day they are standing for hours in the queues for a few vegetables, the chance for *un petit peu de margarine,* even turnips and rutabagas— do you know rutabagas?" he asked, his eyes widening in disgust. "These yellow roots, the color of cows' teeth, that before the war were fit only for pigs. Now all of Paris waits eagerly in the queues for them. Weekends the trains are full. The people are making foraging expeditions to the country to the farmers. They visit country cousins they have not seen for years before the war. They barter."

Roy recalled the Sunday train, the fine layer of farm dust in the crowded carriage, the loamy smell of soil, the bulging burlap bags, the finely dressed men and women, old and young, carrying sacks.

"The rooftops of Paris are covered with vegetable gardens. Here, just above us"—Robert gestured with a wide sweeping motion of his arm—"all through Vincennes, through all the arrondissements of Paris, in all the public gardens—the Invalides, the Jardin de Luxembourg, even the Tuileries—they are all now plowed and planted with beans and cabbages. And, of course, the Germans, *ils nous prennent tout*. For all the years of the occupation they steal everything away.

"But the people, *ils se débrouillent*, they make do. They are resourceful. This *Débrouillardise*," he spoke the word slowly, elaborately, rolling it precisely off his tongue, "has become a way of life under the occupation. The people call it *'le Système D.'* The *avocat* exchanges his services for a chicken. The plumber repairs a toilet, and receives tobacco. Not the *tabac national* we smoke now"—he held up the roughly rolled cigarette and pinched a brown fleck from his tongue—"composed of grass and herbs, but real tobacco." He glanced at Roy to see if he was following.

"For everything there are substitutes," Georges continued, "national substitutes. Saccharine, the authorities in Vichy tell us, is *sucre national*; this dismal acorn coffee we drink now for four years is *café national*, all provided for us by the *Révolution nationale* made by Pétain and his *collus*, his *collaborateurs*. It is merde, I tell you, merde."

Roy closed his eyes, listening. Georges kept him company, sitting in the chair beside the bed talking, slipping in his excitement from English into French and back again, and Roy, borne along on a tide of morphine, glided serenely in the gentle wake of Georges's words. He dozed.

When he awoke again, the room was pitch black, the heating pad was cold and the morphine had worn off. He had slept in a fetal position, curled tightly against the pain. Afraid to move, he lay absolutely still, hardly breathing, wondering if the pain would return. For perhaps the thousandth time he went through all the possibilities—pinched nerve, slipped disc, strained back muscles. He wondered if he had made himself clear to the doctor, wondered just how much English she actually understood. Maybe she wasn't even a doctor. After all, she had offered no diagnosis, had not even speculated. He dismissed that possibility. That kind of thinking would do him no good.

Gingerly he stretched his legs, ready for the razor-sharp slash of pain. Moments passed and it did not come. With great care, he rolled onto his back. Feeling only faint twinges at the base of his spine, he allowed himself a deep breath, then another.

It was cool in the darkened room, and the air was fresh with the scent of rain. Other than the nighttime sounds of the person asleep in the chair just beside him—whether it was Georges or one of the others, he could not tell—the room, the building, the city were absolutely silent. At intervals the blanket of all-enveloping quiet was ruffled by the rumble of a train or a distant siren. Once he thought he could hear a far-off thumping sound, like artillery fire or an RAF raid. Somewhere out there the war was still going on. He dozed. Toward dawn, he could hear the chickens stirring. He smiled. So he had not imagined them after all. There were chickens in Paris. Maybe things were going to be okay after all.

The pain returned just after daybreak. Sweating and shivering, he found it hard to focus his eyes, to speak, and by midmorning he was in an advanced state of delirium. Leaning over the bed, dabbing Roy's forehead with a damp cloth, Georges looked grim. He had sent for a doctor. His friend from yesterday could not be reached and, after much deliberation, they decided to fetch another doctor. They did not know him well. He was not, to their knowledge, a *résistant*, and so Roy would have to keep silent. Under no circumstances was he to speak. That was imperative. The situation was extremely dangerous and their safety depended on Roy.

"You are, let us say, Louis Rouet, mason from Cherbourg," Georges said. "We will pick Cherbourg since it is now in Allied hands and no one can check it. You are a *sourd-muet*, a deaf-mute. Do you understand?"

Roy nodded, already in character.

Just before noon, the doctor arrived. He was a short, mustachioed man who asked no questions of Roy and uttered only a few words to Georges and Yvette. He obviously did not want to know the circumstances of Monsieur Rouet. He would perform his duty and depart. But like the first physician, he could do little for the patient, except administer a shot of morphine. Roy played his role without flaw, gesturing weakly to his back, grunting for emphasis, but otherwise holding his tongue.

He slept through much of the afternoon, rose in the evening and joined the others at the kitchen table, where he was fed a glass of wine, a thick soup, and as a special treat a slice of onion. That terrible feverish day would repeat itself for an entire week. Each morning the sharp stabbing in his back returned, and for six delirium-ridden days Georges sent for a different doctor. None were known to the group, and in each case, their only course of action was to administer morphine. The drug left him groggy, dulling the pain for several hours, but it always returned.

In the evenings, the men sat at the kitchen table or in the overstuffed chairs in the cluttered living room, engulfed in the dense smoke of the cigarettes. Roy always joined them, slipping into a chair, examining the now-familiar faces in the flickering candlelight. He could not follow the intricacies of their discussions, even though his friends peppered their conversations with comments in English, turning to him as if he had been an active participant. They asked him about the Normandy landings, about Eisenhower, about matters of grand strategy, and sometimes about the bombing.

Roy tried to explain Allied air doctrine in the most general terms, the necessity of destroying transportation targets—railroad junctions, marshaling yards, bridges—that led to Normandy. To ensure air supremacy over the landing beaches, German airfields in the west had to be destroyed. All of this meant missions over France, sometimes Belgium and Holland, even Luxembourg. Sometimes the planes missed the targets, bombs went astray—there were a hundred reasons for this—and then innocent civilians died.

Yes, this was regrettable, the men nodded gravely. But, they insisted, the people living *sous les bombes* in occupied Europe were resigned. They understood. It was the inevitable price of war, of occupation. Although Paris itself had been largely spared—the Allies had tried not to bomb the city's center—there were many targets on its fringes, and the men had seen the devastation firsthand, the shattered buildings, the mangled bodies in the rubble. The Vichy authorities, of course, made great propaganda out of the bombing, reporting in the papers and in the newsreels, the *France-Actualités* shown in the crowded cinemas, any destruction in France caused by the Allied raids.

In April bombs had fallen in Paris, some landing in the streets of Montmartre, damaging the Sacré Coeur. On his only visit to Paris since the beginning of the war, Pétain had been photographed visiting the scene, his famous blue eyes brimming with tears at the sight of the ragged craters that pockmarked the steep hill in front of the cathedral.

Mostly, though, the men talked politics. The liberation was at hand, and night after night their conversation revolved around the role the resistance would be called upon to play. They spoke with admiration and anxiety about the Communists—what they would do when the time for action arrived, whether they would cooperate with de Gaulle and the Free French. They were well organized in Paris, the Communists, and well armed, and many in the resistance were convinced they had their own plans. All the *réseaux* had caches of weapons, small arms and explosives smuggled in from the countryside, and they were ready to use them when the word was given. It would not be long now.

But the battle against the Germans was not the only war being waged in France. The nation was engaged in a *guerre civile,* a bitter *guerre franco-française.* All over occupied France patriots were locked in a desperate struggle against the forces of collaboration, against Pétain, Laval, Vichy. These names Roy had heard many times in Jouy, from Colette, Jonckheere, and the others, but here in the Paris apartment Georges and his friends rattled off a bewildering catalogue of prominent collaborators and their organizations—Jacques Doriot and his Parti Populaire Français, Marcel Déat, leader of the Rassemblement National Populaire, and Joseph Darnand, founder of the fascist Milice Française. Among them, Darnand was most despised. An implacable enemy of the Republic and an extremist of the right for years before the war, he had publicly sworn allegiance to Hitler after the fall of France, even becoming an SS officer. Now the pig was the ranking police official in Vichy. Laval had named him secretary general for the Maintenance of Order, and his Milice, armed by the Germans, had become the official security service for the collaborationist regime. Working hand in glove with the Gestapo, the *miliciens* and their spies infiltrated the *réseaux,* arrested *résistants,* deported them to the camps in Germany, or simply executed them on the spot.

As liberation neared, Vichy had become even more frantic in its efforts to "stamp out terrorism," and an escalating spiral of assassination and reprisal had swept across the country like the mistral. The violence had reached a new crescendo in June when Philippe Henriot, Vichy's Minister of Information and Propaganda, was gunned down by resistance forces in retaliation for the murder of an imprisoned resistance leader by the Milice. Henriot, the men explained, was a particularly tempting target for reprisal. Broadcasting daily on Radio Vichy, for years he had spewed venom against the decadent parliamentarians of the Third Republic, the Communists, the Jews, and, of course, the "terrorists" of the resistance. No one, the men agreed, had done more to cultivate hatred, to turn French against French. But now, after four years of oppression, the great reckoning was at hand. "There comes now a *règlement des comptes*," Georges said, "a settling of accounts. You will see. And soon."

Roy knew that weapons and ammunition were concealed in the apartment and that sometimes the men carried guns when they left. They never revealed where they were going or what they were doing, and he never asked. Then, late one afternoon, he found them gathered in the smoke-filled living room, pacing the worn carpet, speaking in animated tones.

"What gives?" Roy asked at last, standing in the doorway.

"*Une action de combat*," Georges said.

"Tonight we eliminate a collaborator," Robert added. He exhaled heavily and waved the smoke away from his face. "A local man, a spy, from Vincennes."

Roy looked at the men. They were deadly earnest. "How will you do it?"

"We will shoot him," Georges answered. "He will be lured to a small street, an alley near the park. It has been carefully selected. It is secure. He expects nothing."

"You're sure he's a spy?" Roy asked.

"He has been responsible for the deportation of many patriots," Georges said. "The resistance is riddled with such men—and women. Spies in the pay of the Germans. Some do it for the money, others for political reasons. Because of him, many are dead. The time has come to settle with him."

Like a briefing officer at AS 130, Georges went over the plan in painstaking detail, the checkpoints, the signals, routes of escape, coordinating their actions, their stories in case they were caught. After the action, they would rendezvous at the apartment before the midnight curfew. If something went wrong, if they did not return, those left behind in the Avenue Michel Bizot would move to another safe house just three blocks away in the rue de Fécamp where they would wait for further instructions.

One by one the men left in the early evening, and Roy and the others settled in to wait. The women read the newspapers in the small sitting room and talked, and Roy sat at the kitchen table. He would compose a new list, the Hit Parade tunes of 1943. "Mairzy Doates," "Shoo-Shoo Baby," "Oklahoma" . . . He hummed quietly, mumbling snatches of the lyrics to himself. It was the first time since he had landed in Paris that he had sung. An hour passed, then another. Outside it was dark, and the streets had fallen silent. The stillness of these Parisian nights always took him by surprise. Occasionally a train would clatter over the stone viaduct that arced over the Avenue Picpus just a long block away and the sound would rumble along the deserted street below and through the shuttered windows. Then the silence would return, stranger, more haunting than before.

The candles had been lit and curfew was approaching and everyone in the apartment was growing anxious when the men began returning. Robert was the first, his face flushed with excitement. The action had gone smoothly, according to plan. At the last moment, the traitor had suspected something, had tried to flee, then had pleaded for his life, offering money, a deal, but it was no use. He had been shot once, through the temple. His had been a mercifully quick death, Robert said without emotion, not like those suffered by the patriots he had sent to the Gestapo's chamber of horrors in the Avenue Foch.

With each passing day it became increasingly clear to everyone in the crowded apartment that something would have to be done about Roy. Robert's contact was not yet ready to take him, and in any case he could not be moved.

Roy listened as the men went over various possibilities, arguing points he could not understand. Their excited voices rose and fell in the incomprehensible singsong French that he had listened to for weeks, and it was obvious that they could not agree.

"There's only one thing to do," Roy interrupted at last. The conversation in the kitchen stopped and the men looked up at him, startled to see his ghostly face emerge from the darkened bedroom. "Turn me over to the Germans. To the military." Exhausted and desperate, he was at the end of his rope. "I still have my dog tags. I'll be treated as a prisoner of war," he said. "They'll give me medical treatment. It's the Geneva Convention."

No one in the apartment shared Roy's faith in the Germans or the Geneva Convention and, in any case, turning him over to the *boches* was simply out of the question. Monsieur Roy was strong and courageous, but in his present condition, he might compromise the *réseau*, the evasion line, everything. Instead, Georges raised another possibility. The group had contacts in a hospital close by, in Vincennes, with a doctor on the medical staff. The Germans occupied the hospital, but the staff was French and the doctor, Georges explained, could be trusted. It would be risky, certainly, but the doctor might do it. He would explore the situation.

The next day or the next—Roy had lost all sense of time—Georges walked into the bedroom where Roy was drowsing and announced that the arrangements had been made. The group's contacts at the hospital had been alerted. An ambulance was waiting on the street below. "You are expected," Georges said. "You will get treatment for the back." In his hand, he carried a small green booklet. "Your identity papers are also at last ready." He opened the booklet. "You are, as before, Louis Rouet, mason by trade, from Cherbourg, and a deaf-mute." He smiled weakly, and then, squatting beside the bed, his lips almost touching Roy's ear, he whispered, *"Mon ami,* you must be extremely careful in this. You will not be registered at the hospital. The doctor will find you. In the meantime, trust no one, speak to no one. The *boches* are everywhere in the hospital." Turning to face his friend, clutching the papers tightly in his hand, Roy did his best to nod.

Georges rose slowly and motioned the other men into the room, and together they lifted Roy onto a stretcher. A dry dusty heat billowed up the darkened stairwell as the men began the laborious descent down five flights of steps. The ride was a short one, and when the ambulance pulled to a halt, the men leapt out and slipped the stretcher from the back. They whisked Roy through a narrow entranceway, along a crowded corridor, and down two flights of stairs. In a nearly deserted basement, Georges turned into another corridor and began checking the room numbers. *"Ici,"* he whispered over his shoulder, *"ici,"* and pushed the door open with his back.

A single bed stood in the middle of the room, with a washstand and basin just beside it. Curtains covered a small eye-level window on the chalk-white wall, and streaks of brilliant sunlight framed the dark edges of the casement like strips of satin. Roy slipped off the stretcher and climbed into the bed. Perhaps it was adrenaline, perhaps the fear, but for the moment his back did not hurt.

"Remain calm, *mon ami*," Georges said as he turned toward the door, his voice echoing slightly in the austere room. "You will see us again soon." Roy waved and Georges opened the door and they were gone.

Roy lay back in the bed and closed his eyes. He had never felt so alone. Then, stripping off his shirt and pants, he hung them carefully in the tiny closet by the door. His dog tags, he realized, were still in his pants pocket, and he decided to leave them there. If caught, he would need them. He lay back in the bed and tried to sleep. He wished he had brought the crosswords with him but, of course, that would have been foolish. With his eyes closed he began to hum softly to himself, all the songs he could recall, one after the other.

He wondered where May was at this moment, wondered whether she was listening to the radio, to the dance program on WPHL. Judging from the fading light around the curtained window, he guessed it was early evening outside. It would be six hours earlier in Philadelphia. Was it a Sunday? It must be August already, he thought. He tried to calculate the number of days he had been in Paris, but it was no use. Beyond the door, he heard footsteps and female voices, the clattering of instruments, and carts moving along the corridor, but no one stopped in the room. The hours crawled by. At last he slept.

He did not know what woke him, but when his eyes sprang open in the weak morning light, the dark figure of a man was gliding into the room. He wore no smock, no stethoscope dangled from his neck. He did not speak, but he did not seem surprised to find Roy in the room. Closing the door behind him, he turned to switch on the overhead light. In his hand he carried a chart and with barely a glance at Roy he advanced on the bed. Pulling the sheets aside, he raised Roy's cotton T-shirt and, pushing down Roy's shorts, began probing his abdomen. He asked no questions, made no comments.

Uncertain what to do—he was not even sure this was the doctor sent by Georges—Roy gestured toward his back, grunting, rubbing his hand along his spine. The man ignored him and continued to press along his side. Then, without a word, he pulled the sheet back up, turned, and left the room. Within minutes he was back again with a stretcher cart and, still avoiding Roy's eyes, motioned for him to climb on. They were met at the door by an orderly who wheeled him down the corridor, through a pair of swinging doors, and into what appeared to be an operating room.

Two nurses busied themselves in the room, obviously preparing for some sort of procedure. Roy could hear water running and the metallic tinkle of implements. Turning his head to the side, Roy caught sight of the doctor at a nearby counter. He stood above a tray of assorted surgical instruments, and in his slender fingers he held a long colorless tube. At its tip, several small blades gleamed in the dim overhead light, and as Roy watched, his eyes riveted on those razor-sharp blades, he remembered. He remembered the lurid VD films they watched all through training, the rotting genitalia, the ghastly treatments, and suddenly the word "catheter" roared in his head like a thunderclap.

Roy snapped upright on the table, gesturing wildly toward his back. As a deaf-mute he could not speak, he could only desperately try to show the doctor that it was his back that hurt him, not his balls. He couldn't even mouth the words. His mind was racing. What were the words in French? How often had he heard Colette and Georges and all the others refer to his back? The doctor nodded impatiently, as if he understood, but, undeterred, he proceeded to prepare the catheter. Oh, God, Roy thought.

A nurse took up position beside the doctor. Ignoring Roy's awkward efforts to pound his back, they turned him onto his side. He watched as the doctor prepared a syringe, held it up to the light, then flicked the needle with his fingernail. A jet of colorless liquid shot into the motionless air, and Roy groaned. Suddenly he felt a sharp sting at the base of his spine, then another, and slowly a warm numbing sensation spread over him. He sank back. The doctor placed the syringe on a tray beside the operating table and picked up the catheter. He was not even wearing gloves.

When Roy woke, he found himself back in his room. The doctor and nurses were gone. A small plate of food had appeared while he was sleeping, and for the first time in days, he had an appetite. His head was clear, too, and he realized that aside from a dull throbbing in his groin, he was free of pain. In the late afternoon, the doctor returned. He examined Roy, pressing, probing, again without uttering a word. As he prepared to leave, he hesitated before opening the door. "Kidney stones," he said in English, and pointed to his lower back. "You will be recovered." Then he turned and was gone.

His friends from the apartment visited him regularly in the days that followed. They brought baskets of food, some fruit and a little cheese, even a bottle of wine, and they laughed and talked so loudly in the near-empty room that Roy wondered if the war had ended and he had missed it. The doctor did not return but neither did the pain, and with each passing day, his spirits rose. He rested, strolled around the room, gazed out the tiny window into a cluttered courtyard, and thought about home. His own personal liberation had come.

He was sleeping one afternoon—it was several days after the operation—when the door opened and a young woman dressed in a nurse's uniform peeked into the room. She carried a clipboard, and seeing Roy in the bed, she frowned. Puzzled, she leaned backward and checked the number on the door again. Then she stepped into the room. Standing at the foot of the bed, she ran her finger down a list on the clipboard. The patient was obviously not registered, not on her list. Speaking rapidly, she asked him a question and waited. Roy grinned dumbly, pointed to his ears and moved his lips noiselessly. She spoke again, her voice tinged with suspicion.

"Qui êtes-vous?"

Roy shrugged his shoulders as he had seen Colette and Georges do so many times.

"Il n'y a personne dans cette chambre," the nurse continued. "Vous n'êtes pas sur le liste?"

Roy repeated his pantomime. "Muet," she muttered to herself, as if she at last understood, "sourd-muet." But deaf-mute or no deaf-mute, this man was not supposed to be in this basement room. While Roy smiled sheepishly, unsure what to do next, the woman turned abruptly and left.

In the days of his recuperation—it must have been five, as he tried to calculate—not a soul from the hospital had entered the room. Every day he heard voices, in German and French, and once a German soldier, an enlisted man, had blundered into the room seeking a light for his cigarette, but no one from the staff had appeared to check on him. No chart hung on the hook at the foot of the bed. So this intruder meant trouble. She would report him to the hospital authorities, and they would consult their records and find nothing. Then they would descend upon him. It was time to go.

Roy sprang out of bed and scrambled into his clothes. He checked the identity papers he had been given and shoved them back into his jacket. He took the dog tags from his pants pocket and slipped them around his neck, patting them flat beneath his T-shirt. If the hospital authorities came, he would maintain the Louis Rouet story as long as possible. But who was he kidding? Without Georges or Robert he would never be able to pull this charade off. Finally he would be forced to produce the dog tags, giving himself up as an American officer. It was his only choice.

Maybe he should make a run for it now, slip out of the hospital, try to locate Georges or Robert. He would recognize the apartment building, he told himself, if he could find his way to the Avenue Michel Bizot. But he had no idea where he was. He could not even ask directions.

As he stood facing the closet, running through possible scenarios, he heard footsteps in the corridor. Faint at first, they grew louder and louder, resounding in the near-empty corridor until they stopped just outside the room. Voices, low and indistinct, murmured beyond the door, and as it swung slowly open, Roy turned, bracing for the inevitable.

"*Tiens*, Robert," Georges practially shouted, pounding Roy on the shoulder, "our friend is up! He is dressed for an outing!"

"We gotta get out of here," Roy said, tugging them toward the door.

"*Un moment, un moment*," Georges said, the smile vanishing from his face. "Calm yourself." Then Roy explained about the nurse.

"Outside we have bicycles," Robert said. "Are you able to ride?"

Roy nodded.

"*Bon*, you will ride along with Georges. We will rendezvous later at the apartment. It is not so far."

"Let's get going," Roy said.

Georges peeked out the door and motioned for them to follow. For the moment the corridor was empty. The men crept up the stairs, crossed a courtyard cluttered with garbage bins and bicycle stands, and stepped through a massive archway into the street.

All along the sidewalk, dozens of bicycles were tethered to the trunks of the overhanging trees and stacked against the grime-streaked walls of the buildings. As Georges searched among them, Robert darted into the traffic, dodging the bicycles that swept down the narrow street. Roy watched him disappear under the awning of a crowded café on the other side. He did not look back.

It had rained during the night and the paving stones were slick and the air fresh. When Georges emerged from the thicket of handlebars and wheels with two battered black bicycles, Roy felt a surge of pure excitement. He was out and he was free of pain. He climbed shakily onto his bike and followed his friend out into the stream of traffic.

Later, in the Avenue Michel Bizot, the mood was festive. Taking Roy to the hospital had been an act of desperation, and his friends were giddy with relief. Germans had been everywhere, roaming the halls, eating in the canteen, chatting with the nurses, and still they had pulled it off—the surgery, the recovery, the escape, everything. It called for a celebration, for champagne. Perhaps they would "liberate" a *poulet* from the rooftop. Someone made clucking noises, scratched at the linoleum floor, and everyone laughed.

That night Roy discovered another cause for their celebration. There was good news from Normandy, Georges told him. Roy could hear it himself when the power came on. The electricity supply in the building had grown even more erratic—now they could count on no more than thirty minutes in the evening but when at last the lights flickered on, the men gathered around the radio in the living room, listening through the static and jamming to the war news from London. After weeks of stalemate in Normandy, there was movement now near Caen and St. Lô. The long-awaited Allied breakout seemed imminent.

A map was spread on the floor, and the men bent over it, dropping flecks of cigarette ash onto its folds as they talked and pointed. When the Allies broke out of Normandy, the Germans would fall back toward the Seine. But the river could not be defended, Georges argued, running his finger along a sinuous blue line that meandered from Paris to the sea. There were too many bends, too many crossing points. Once the Wehrmacht began retreating, the rout would be on, and the hour of liberation would be at hand.

Stooping over to study the map, Roy tried to follow the conversation. He sipped the champagne and watched his friends as they jabbed at the map and talked. Sometimes it seemed as if he could understand them by an act of will, by sheer concentration, and he would stare at Georges and the others, following their lips, their gestures, until one of them would glance up at him and say something to him in French, even ask a question, then resume the conversation without waiting for his reply. They were happy and excited, and on this night, warm with wine, surrounded by his friends in the secure apartment, Roy slept his first untroubled sleep since leaving Jouy.

The next morning he rose early and, well rested and almost free of pain, he felt an almost irresistible urge to be outside. After the long days and nights of confinement in the school at Jouy, at the apartment, and in the hospital, he was bored and restless. He had been thrilled to be outside on the day of his escape from the hospital, to be on the busy Parisian streets, coasting along in the August sunlight, thrilled to know that he could ride a bike, walk, even run a bit with only a few twinges of soreness at the base of his back.

Left alone in the apartment, Roy prowled the familiar rooms with growing agitation. He peered through the living room shutters at the apartment houses just across the way, each with its matte-colored plaster façade, its sloping mansard roof and tiny dormered windows, mirror images of his own hiding place. Above them, squalls of pigeons swept across a skyline of weathered chimneys and graceful spires and cupolas, green with oxidation and age. During the late-morning hours, he searched the sky for contrails, wondering if the Eighth would be up today, if the 457th was flying. He wondered, as he did every day, where Joe and the others were. Maybe they were concealed somewhere in the French countryside or maybe they were somewhere close by, hiding in a Paris attic, waiting for the liberation, just as he was.

In the evening Georges and the others returned and they listened to the radio broadcast from London and pored over the large Michelin roadmap, unfolded now on the kitchen table. The Americans were clearly on the move, breaking out of the Cotentin Peninsula, and there was heavy fighting beyond Caen, but Roy was not as confident as his friends. It had been two months and the Allies were still slogging their way out of the hedgerows of Normandy. It might be weeks more before they reached Paris, weeks he would spend waiting, cooped up in the apartment.

After another day of watching Roy pace gloomily from room to room, Georges made a suggestion. They would make an outing. Their first foray would be a short one, to the park nearby, in the Bois de Vincennes. There was a pleasant lake and the *parc zoologique*. They would go as a group, with Roy safely insulated from passersby. Under no circumstances was he to speak, and he was to remain with the group, at its center, at all times.

Georges anticipated no controls at the park or along the way, though the Germans sometimes conducted spot-checks for papers at public places. If they were stopped, Roy would simply have to present his papers. If he remained calm, all would go well. His *carte d'identité* was an excellent forgery, as good as Georges had ever seen, and Robert had even secured for him a *carte d'alimentation* and a few accompanying ration tickets, of which he was particularly proud.

When the time came, Roy could hardly restrain himself. It was all he could do not to bound down the steps and race on ahead. They walked a short block, dodging the stalls of the street vendors, and turned into the Avenue Daumesnil. The boulevard sloped gently downhill, passing beneath an iron railroad trestle whose bolted stanchions were papered with weathered flyers and peeling propaganda posters. The day was warm and a soft breeze swept down the street, rustling the leaves of the towering trees, and the group ambled along with the crowd toward the park.

The sidewalks teemed with people. Some stood waiting patiently outside the crowded shops, queuing up for this week's dwindling ration of bread or cheese or coffee. Without electricity, the small stores gave off a gloomy aspect, even on this bright August day, and many merchants had pulled carts out onto the broad sidewalk, taking up stations beneath the awnings of their shops or in the sun-dappled shade of the plane trees. Nearly empty bins of clothing and racks of wooden-soled shoes stood outside the darkened storefront windows, and craftsmen, their tools spread on tables carried from their dreary shops, worked in their shirtsleeves in the sunlight. In a cobblestone side street a row of women, their hair wet and dripping, sat in chairs on the sidewalk while the *coiffeuse* clipped and trimmed and pedestrians passed without so much as a glance.

Between the cafés and shops, placards had been plastered to the walls, offering a different glimpse of Paris. In stark black letters they advertised musical revues at the Folies-Bergères, the Casino de Paris, Moulin Rouge and dozens of other nightspots. A Danish circus was scheduled to open later in the month at the Palais Royale, and Robert said that the cinemas, open only during daylight hours, were overflowing, their screens kept operational by bicycle-powered generators. The racetracks at Longchamp and Auteuil were still drawing their regular weekend crowds, he added, and the Deligny swimming pool and the beach near the Pont d'Iéna were packed every day.

Just inside the park, Georges led them to a crowded café where they sat in canvas chairs at a long metal table beneath a canopy of chestnut trees. The fashionable restaurants in the center of the city, those frequented by the Germans and the collaborators, always had wine, Robert explained, but the small neighborhood cafés and bistros served alcohol only on certain days. On this afternoon the sign proclaiming *Jour sans alcool* was absent, and while waiters in black jackets and starched white aprons bustled among the tables, tiny trays of drinks balanced effortlessly on their upturned palms, Robert ordered wine.

In the lush, sunlit park that stretched out before them, lovers sauntered arm-in-arm along the wide gravel paths and rowed in weathered blue boats on the glittering pond. Sunbathers sprawled along the grassy bank, while children ran and shouted, scuffling along the dusty paths or pushing sailboats on the rippled surface of the water. In the languid August afternoon, the group picnicked beneath the trees, visited the zoo nearby, and had something that tasted remarkably like coffee at a small bistro Yvette knew. The war, Roy thought, seemed a thousand miles away.

Buoyed by their success, Georges was ready to venture farther afield. The next day they would show Roy the sights of Paris. He would see Notre Dame, the Eiffel Tower, the Latin Quarter, everything. Maybe they would even stroll by Gestapo headquarters near the Bois de Boulogne, in the Avenue Foch—"Avenue Boche, we call it," Georges laughed. It would be an outing to remember, to tell Mrs. Roy about when the war was over. Roy was elated.

The excursion was carefully planned and the procedure was the same as the day before. Surrounded by his friends, Roy would walk arm-in-arm with Yvette, who would laugh and talk in her vivacious way. He would be carefully screened from passersby and would remain silent. After some discussion, they decided to take the metro to the center of the city. There would be Germans everywhere, of course, soldiers mostly, but the metro could be particularly dangerous. The Gestapo sometimes conducted spot-checks of papers at the exits, but Roy's papers were in good order, and, they all agreed, it was worth the risk.

Early the next morning, the group set out for the metro station Daumesnil. There were no checks along the way or on the metro, and the short ride in the crowded carriage passed uneventfully. Emerging at the grandiose Hôtel de Ville, they strolled along the rue de Rivoli, past the gray stone and wrought iron of the Louvre, past the Jardin des Tuileries, and then across the vast expanse of the Place de la Concorde to the gardens and cafés of the Champs-Elysées. At noon they watched the daily German military parade proceed down the great boulevard from the Arc de Triomphe, a ritual, Georges said, that had begun in the dreary summer of 1940, and one conspicuously ignored by the Parisians who read newspapers or chatted or sipped their ersatz coffee in the crowded sidewalk cafés.

Some twenty thousand German troops were stationed in Paris, Georges said, and they were everywhere. They browsed the bookstalls along the Seine, dined in the stylish restaurants, and gawked like tourists at the sights. They rode the metro in carriages specially reserved for them and attended their own movie theaters, the Soldaten-Kinos, sprinkled around the city. Their sentry boxes, painted in black-and-white chevrons, stood guard at the major intersections, and their signs, like semaphores raised on a mast, directed traffic to "die Nor-mandie Front," the Luftwaffe-Lazarette, and dozens of other military destinations. Stark, black-lettered placards bearing impossibly long Teutonic words clung to the façades of the city's buildings—Platz-Kommandantur, Frontbuchhandlung, Soldatenheim—and gigantic Nazi battle flags fluttered from the elegant hotels and graceful arcades along the rue de Rivoli.

Although German motorcycles with sidecars roared through the streets and occasionally an open staff car would whip by, German military vehicles, Roy noticed, were not much in evidence on the streets. Mottled with camouflage paint and covered with branches, they remained parked beneath the trees at the sides of the wide boulevards, waiting for darkness to move out for the front. They could no longer travel during the day, Georges told him, because of roving Allied dive-bombers. The narrow roads to Normandy, he had heard, were littered with overturned trucks and burned-out armored cars, even tanks.

At first Roy found it unnerving to see the Germans up close, to rub shoulders with them in the streets and on the metro platforms, but his anxiety quickly faded. Although the *feldgrau* uniforms had been every-where and Georges had pointed out the plainclothesmen on the metro platforms and the Gestapo's black Citroëns along the curbsides, they had encountered no controls, no spot-checks during their outing. It was a strange experience, hiding amid the Germans in this strange and beautiful city, but at the end of the day, as the group settled back in the apartment to listen to the war news, Roy felt satisfied and confident. He was learning the ropes, learning how to behave and what to expect. Anyway, the Allies would be here soon. Maybe he could wait it out.

CHAPTER 8

Captain Jacques

August 1944

The labored footsteps resounded in the stairwell, rising flight after flight, drawing nearer and nearer until they stopped and someone tapped lightly on the door. The men at the kitchen table stiffened, looking at one another in alarm. No one was expected. Rising quietly from his chair, Georges motioned Roy back into the hallway, and the men checked their weapons.

From his post, Roy could hear a voice in the corridor, low but insistent, and Georges, poised just inside the foyer, answering. Georges glanced at the other men, who had taken up positions in the living room. They were ready, their revolvers drawn. Then slowly Georges unlatched the door. He moved aside, and a short, stocky man stepped into the apartment.

The man wore a rumpled coat and a tie pulled slightly askew, and his round face was beaded in sweat. It was hot in the room, and he was winded from the five flights of stairs. The stranger spoke first, addressing Georges in a matter-of-fact, confident manner, and although Roy could not understand, he could discern the words *"américain"* and "Robert." When Georges replied, there was no mistaking the edge of suspicion in his voice. His comments were terse, tinged with a harshness Roy had never heard from him before. Then the others joined in, firing question after question, and the man answered them calmly, his hand resting on the back of a living room chair for support.

The conversation continued for some time, adjourning at last to the kitchen, where Georges and the stranger sat at the table and the others stood around them, watching. As they talked, Roy slipped into the doorway, half hidden behind the others, and listened. Throughout the interrogation the man remained unruffled, his voice never rising. He spoke with remarkable patience, and he would not be rushed. Finally, the questioning flagged, and while Georges shifted uneasily in his chair, Roy heard the stranger say distinctly, "Why not ask your American friend?" Georges exchanged glances with the others, and Roy, without waiting to be summoned, stepped into the room.

The man looked up at him without surprise.

"*Bonjour,* monsieur," he said, a smile spreading across his face. "*C'est un grand,*" he added, gesturing toward Roy. "He is a big one." The stranger was of middle age and balding and there was something about his face that seemed, even under Georges's relentless grilling, pleasant, even jovial.

"I have come for you," he said. "I am the contact from Robert."

Roy only nodded, uncertain how he should react.

"It is wise that you are careful," the stranger continued in English. "I understand this. Since a long time I have helped many of your *compatriotes*. The arrangements are made." Roy looked at Georges in confusion.

"What arrangements?" Roy asked. There had been no discussion of moving him for some time, not since before the hospital. Recently not even Robert had mentioned this possibility. During his last visit to the apartment he gave no indication that anything was in the works.

In a combination of French and English the man described how it would work. Roy would come with him. He would be taken to a safe house in the third arrondissement, in the center of the city, near the river. There he would be provided with money and other necessities for the journey. At the proper time he would be picked up by another contact. The contact would be a British agent, an officer in the Intelligence Service who had handled the escape of many Allied aviators, arranging for them to cross the Pyrenees into Spain. Some, he understood, were now even flying out of one of several secure landing strips in the vicinity of Paris, all arranged by the British War Office.

"I will not press you," the man said. "It is your decision. If you have doubts, do not do it. But time is of the essence, monsieur. There are many others awaiting evacuation. If you decide to go, I will come for you tomorrow. But you must give me your answer now."

Roy understood the risks, especially of a long trip to the south. The warnings of Colette and Monsieur Florin—the high mountains, the many German controls, the potentially treacherous guides—still rang in his ears. But a quick flight out of France, that was something else. The British *did* make these landings all over France, dropping off agents, scooping up others in fields like those he had seen at Vimbré. It *was* possible. To be back in England again, at the base—and soon—to be in touch with May, with home! He had never really allowed himself to contemplate this in any concrete way, but now this short plump man was offering him a ticket home.

He did not hesitate. "I'll be ready," he said. "Just name the time."

"*Bon,*" the stranger replied. "I will call for you tomorrow, *après-midi.*" He glanced at the little group of men in the room. Their faces were grim. "Do not worry." He smiled. "It will go well." He bowed slightly and was gone.

Throughout the long windless afternoon Georges and the others dissected the situation. Their gestures were animated, and their words came rapid-fire. Roy paced around the periphery of the conversation, pausing beside the table to listen, and although he could not follow its ebb and flow, he was certain that his friends were against his leaving.

Toward evening, Georges said that they had sent for Robert. What did Robert know about their visitor? The man seemed to be in order—they were saying nothing against him—but they did not know him. This in itself was not so surprising, given the organization of the resistance. Still, everyone was uneasy. Why, Georges asked, take any unnecessary chances with the Allies so close to Paris? If Roy stayed in the Avenue Michel Bizot, they could vouch for his safety. It would not be long. Every day the Allies drew nearer.

Roy knew what they said was true. Again he would be going into the unknown, placing himself in the hands of strangers. But he had been lucky so far. His instincts had been true, with André, with Colette, with Robert and Georges. Now, with a ticket home almost in his hand, why should he wait?

It was late when Robert arrived, and the conversation resumed in the candlelit kitchen. Yes, Robert assured them, he knew the man and trusted him. His name was Georges Prévost and he was an official in the Prefecture of Police. He had good connections in the resistance and had helped many people, *résistants*, French escapees from the German camps, even Jews. He had moved many Allied aviators through Paris on their way to Spain, even providing false papers, which he secured through his position in the police. He could be trusted.

Georges was not convinced. All through the following morning, he pleaded with Roy not to go. According to the BBC, the Allies had broken out of Normandy. They were advancing rapidly toward Paris, and the Germans were in disarray. Surely the sensible thing to do was wait. Roy listened, but he would not budge.

When Prévost arrived late in the afternoon, the atmosphere in the apartment was tense. He exchanged a few words with Georges and Robert, smiling and nodding, but he was anxious to get under way. He gave Roy a quick briefing on their movements, going over a few instructions, making sure he understood. Roy nodded. Then it was time to go. As Prévost moved toward the door, Roy paused for a last moment, looking around the living room where he had passed so many days. He extended his hand to Georges. In it was a small slip of paper with May's address in Philadelphia.

"Good luck, *mon ami*," Georges said to him, gripping him by the shoulders. "Perhaps we will meet again."

"Yes," Roy said. He clasped Georges's hand. "After the war."

"And," Georges said, "in a free Paris."

Then Prévost opened the door and nodded to Roy, and they stepped out into the landing.

Robert decided to accompany them as far as the metro stop. It was not far and they walked up the avenue beneath the plane trees toward the Place Daumesnil. The tables and wicker chairs of a café stretched out to the very entrance of the metro, and the men paused beside them while Prévost rooted in his pocket for the tickets. "*Au revoir,*" he heard Robert whisper, "*et bon courage.*" Then his friend turned and melted into the passing crowd. For an instant Roy watched his black beret bob in the current of passersby, swept along around the vast circular plaza, and with a pang he realized that the last living soul he knew in Paris was gone.

In the crowded metro carriage, Prévost sat across from him, hidden behind a newspaper. Roy did as he was told. Pressing his face against the cool window of the train, he appeared to doze. They would exit at Les Halles, Prévost had told him before leaving the apartment, the fourth stop. Roy should be alert. The stations flashed by in short bursts of yellow light, and at each stop more passengers crowded in, standing belly to belly in the narrow aisles. As the train slowed for its fourth stop, Prévost rose, tucked his paper under his arm, and edged toward the door. Roy waited until the train had squealed to a halt and then, staying always several meters behind, followed him through a progression of dingy white-tiled passageways that smelled of urine and mold, through the barriers, and up the stairs into the light.

Emerging on the fringes of the vast market, they found themselves surrounded by swarms of men in faded overalls and chest-high aprons smeared with blood. The aproned men pushed two-wheeled carts laden with slaughtered livestock, salted fish, and baskets of vegetables through a maze of open-air stalls into a series of cavernous sheds. Everywhere the ripe odor of raw meat and rotten produce permeated the still August air.

Following his instructions, Roy trailed a half-block behind as Prévost strode briskly through the shabby alleyways of Les Halles. Prévost did not look back or slacken his pace, and Roy had to watch closely just to keep him in view. They had not gone far when Prévost turned onto a wide thoroughfare. He paused at a busy intersection for a break in the bicycle traffic, then scurried across. Roy had to wait, but Prévost pressed on, weaving his way through the throng on the opposite sidewalk. Toward the middle of the block, he paused to light a cigarette. Roy saw him strike a match and cup a hand in front of his lips. He tilted his head upward, exhaling the smoke, but as he did, the passing crowd seemed to swallow him up. Roy strained to catch a glimpse of him, but the man was gone without a trace, evaporated on the busy sidewalk.

There was no letup in the torrent of bicycles sweeping past. Almost in desperation Roy began walking rapidly along the sidewalk, paralleling Prévost's path. He scanned the crowd on the opposite side of the street but could see nothing. At the end of the short block, he was able to scramble across and make his way back to the spot where he had last seen his contact. Along the way he searched the faces of the passersby and peered in the windows of the seedy bistros and the nearly deserted shops, but there was no sign of Prévost.

Toward the middle of the block, Roy stopped in front of the only door that did not open into a shop. He stepped back and looked up. Squeezed into a jumble of shabby storefronts, the building looked like an apartment house. Its faded plaster façade rose above the sidewalk in tiers of shuttered windows and wrought iron balconies. To the side of the door a small blue plaque read 20 Boulevard Sébastopol. Could this be it? He took a deep breath and leaned against the door.

Stepping into a deep, dimly lit foyer, he hesitated for a moment as his eyes adjusted to the sudden darkness. To his right a bank of badly tarnished brass mailboxes angled unevenly across the wall. He squinted, searching for Prévost's name, but it was not there. Through the glass panels of the inner doors in front of him he could see a flight of narrow winding stairs ascending into the gloom. He pushed tentatively against the door, and it gave way. He stepped inside. To his left the walls of the musty staircase coiled tightly upward, the only light provided by a pair of recessed windows at each curve of the stairs.

"Monsieur," a voice whispered. "Monsieur." The words seemed to tiptoe down the carpeted stairs. He began to climb. At the first-floor landing, Georges Prévost, beaming as pleasantly as ever, was waiting for him. Without speaking, he motioned Roy to follow.

The apartment was on the top floor, five flights up, beneath a slanting skylight of dingy frosted glass. When Prévost opened the door a stout but handsome woman ushered them quickly inside, leading them into a living room bathed in warm evening twilight.

"*Soyez à l'aise,*" she said, smiling at Roy.

Prévost dropped heavily into a chair. "You must make yourself comfortable," he said, motioning Roy to a small sofa. "*Asseyez-vous.*"

Roy looked around him. The apartment's rooms were more spacious and more comfortably furnished than those in the Avenue Michel Bizot and through the open windows he could see the sun slip behind the dark silhouette of the buildings across the broad street.

"The flat belongs to my sister Geneviève," Prévost said, indicating the woman who had returned from an adjoining room with a bottle of wine and glasses, "and my *beau-frère,* Jean. My brother-in-law. You will meet him later. They are both active in the evasion line. Many of your comrades, sixty, maybe more, have passed through this apartment, *n'est pas,* Geneviève?"

"*Oui*"—the woman nodded in agreement—"*une soixantaine.*"

"When do you think I will be moved?" Roy asked.

"It is not possible to say with certainty, monsieur," Prévost answered, mopping his brow. "You will sleep here tonight. Tomorrow Captain Jacques will call for you."

"Captain Jacques?"

"*Oui,* he is your contact. He has made the arrangements."

"He's the British agent?" Roy asked.

"He is working for the British, yes," Prévost answered. "Their top officer in Paris."

"Good," Roy said, as much to himself as to his hosts, "good." It was then that he realized that he was nervous.

Later in the evening, Jean Rocher, Prévost's brother-in-law, arrived and they sat down to a dinner of soup and bread. Madame Geneviève carved a single pear and a bottle of wine was poured and afterward there was a desultory discussion of the war. The 9:15 broadcast from London was hard to decipher through the high whining static—there must be thunderstorms in the vicinity, Prévost speculated—but the news was good. Like Roy's friends in the Avenue Michel Bizot, Prévost and the Rochers believed that liberation was at hand. Only a matter of days. In the Prefecture of Police, Prévost reported, there was much talk of a rift within the resistance between the Gaullists and the Communists, and a vigorous political conversation ensued that Roy did not understand.

He could not focus on the war news anyway. His mind was far away, in Philadelphia, in the gabled row house on Seventy-seventh Avenue. It was August 9 or 10. He had been MIA for almost two months. He tried to remember when the baby was due. For some reason he always thought of the baby as a girl and when he wrote to May from the air base, he always referred to the baby as "she." Could it be that May had already delivered? If Captain Jacques could really get him out of here, get him back to England tomorrow or the next day, he would send a wire. Maybe they would even rotate him home. What was the policy on returned evaders, he wondered? He seemed to recall hearing that they were sent back to the States, then, after a furlough at home, reassigned to a new theater of operations. He had not paid much attention to that briefing. It hadn't seemed relevant at the time.

That night Roy could not sleep. After dinner Madame Geneviève showed him to a bedroom that overlooked the street. Listening to the cooing of the pigeons on the cornice just outside the window, he tried to imagine what tomorrow would bring. It would be a plane, of this he was sure. It *had* to be a plane. He tried to visualize himself strapped in the cramped rear compartment of a Lysander as it skimmed the treetops on the long nighttime flight back across France, the RAF pilot navigating by the seat of his pants.

He suddenly realized that he had no idea about the phase of the moon. Was it full now? If not, could they fly? He jumped out of bed. Pushing open the shutters of the tall French windows, he stepped out onto the balcony and stared up into a sky sprinkled with stars. In the distance he could hear the motorized murmur of a German convoy grinding toward the front, but below him the streets of Paris were still and dark. He could not find the moon, but the milky night sky convinced him that, yes, surely, it was full. That was why Captain Jacques had called for him now. He had waited for the full moon.

Tugging the shutters closed, Roy fumbled for a match on the bedside table and finally succeeded in lighting the nub of candle Madame Geneviève had left for him. Sitting up in bed, he pulled the folded pages of crosswords from his jacket pocket. As he had done so many times in Jouy and in the Avenue Michel Bizot, he would divert himself, wear himself out with the crosswords, with the lists of songs. He began with the Hit Parade for May 1944, humming to himself as he wrote. He worked methodically, moving backward to April, March, February, on and on until the candle flickered and died and the first pink tendrils of dawn crept through the slats of the shutters.

Roy was sound asleep when he heard a tapping on his door. "Monsieur," a woman's voice was saying. "Monsieur Roy, *levez-vous*." He had no idea where he was. He shook his head, trying to get his bearings. "You must rise," the voice repeated. "Captain Jacques is here." Swinging his legs over the edge of the bed, Roy sat up. He splashed water on his face from a basin at the foot of the bed, threw on his shirt, and straightened himself a bit. He was excited as he walked into the sunlit living room.

Prévost and Madame Geneviève were sitting over coffee at the dining room table, and just beside them a slender young man stood examining a print of a Paris street scene on the wall. At first he did not notice Roy enter and as he inclined his head ever so slightly to one side, then the other, it struck Roy that he was not looking at the print at all but examining his own reflection in the glass. When he saw Roy, he blushed slightly, the faintest shadow of a smile passing across his lips. His ginger-colored hair was carefully combed back in a wave from his forehead and his bulging blue eyes were as round and cold as marbles.

"Monsieur Roy," Prévost said, "please to meet Captain Jacques."

The man nodded toward Roy, even bowed slightly, but said nothing directly to him. Instead, he addressed a series of questions to Prévost. His manner was detached and businesslike, almost brusque. He was nothing like Captain Paul or the animated circle of friends in the Avenue Michel Bizot. At last he turned to Roy.

"You are to go tonight," he said in perfect BBC English. Reaching into a smart leather briefcase at his feet, he produced several packs of French cigarettes, a small bundle of French currency, and, lastly, a pair of rough hobnailed boots. Roy stared at the boots.

"I will need your military identification, your discs, please," Captain Jacques said as he handed the boots to Roy and placed the other items on the dining room table.

"What for?" Roy asked, startled.

"You will not need them on your journey," the man answered. "It is too dangerous." He seemed rushed.

"I don't get it," Roy said. He shot a troubled glance at Prévost. "I need to keep the dog tags." They were his lifeline, his proof, if captured, that he was military personnel.

"If you insist," the man continued, a note of impatience creeping into his voice. "Allow me to see them, please." He took Roy's dog tags, examined them quickly, and handed them back. He seemed satisfied.

"This afternoon I will send my assistant to pick you up. She is very experienced in these operations. A Belgian. Monsieur Prévost knows her. You will go with her to the rendezvous point. I believe you know the drill."

"Yes." Roy nodded. "I know what to do." He looked down uneasily at the boots in his hands. "Will I be flying out?"

"You will know in good time, monsieur," Captain Jacques replied, a hint of gold tooth showing between his lips. "All in good time. But do not worry. You will be back in England soon . . . *very* soon."

Captain Jacques addressed another question in French to Prévost, who consulted his watch and nodded, and then the young man was gone. As Roy listened to the footsteps recede down the staircase, a wave of uneasiness washed over him. For the first time since he had been in hiding with the resistance he had a bad feeling about a contact.

Throughout the long morning hours, Roy paced the apartment. He stood on the shallow balcony in the cool morning air and watched the traffic on the Boulevard Sébastopol, trying to collect his thoughts. He could not shake the feeling that something was wrong. There was something unsettling about Captain Jacques, about his manner, his clothes. Paul Guérin had exuded confidence and command. He inspired trust. But Captain Jacques seemed impatient, distracted. Then there was the matter of the boots and the money. Why would he need sturdy work boots if he were being evacuated by plane? Maybe he was bound for the Pyrenees after all.

Prévost tried to reassure him. Monsieur Roy's misgivings about the man were not unusual. He sometimes made an odd first impression. Prévost understood this, but Monsieur Roy should not be misled. He had worked with Captain Jacques for months, delivering dozens of Allied aviators to him, and all had gone smoothly. To Prévost, it sounded as if arrangements had been made for Roy to be evacuated by plane, though he could not be sure. He did not know the next step along the line. Certainly Captain Jacques had used the Pyrenees route often, personally conveying some of his charges there by train. Once he had even crossed over into Spain himself, testing the contacts on that side of the frontier. He was a bit eccentric, but experienced. He could be trusted.

For all his misgivings, Roy wanted to believe in Captain Jacques. To think that this very night he might be on his way back to England, that tomorrow he could be at the base, in touch with home, with May, was too much to resist. Everything would be okay, he told himself. After all, he trusted Robert and Robert trusted Prévost and Prévost trusted Captain Jacques. This was the way the resistance worked.

In the late morning Prévost left the apartment. He had some pressing business to attend to, he said, but he would return in the early afternoon. The contact was expected around four o'clock. Madame Geneviève was left to keep Roy company, but he was too anxious, too lost in his own thoughts, to talk, and after several futile efforts to strike up a conversation, she fell silent. The hours crawled by. Roy paced back and forth through the apartment, the ancient parquet floor groaning with every anxious step. He worried about Captain Jacques, about the contact, about the Pyrenees. He worried that the Belgian woman might arrive before Prévost returned. Would the exchange take place if Prévost weren't back? Did Madame Geneviève know her? Even if she did, he wanted Prévost to vouch for her, to give the operation his stamp of approval.

It was late afternoon when Prévost, sweating and panting heavily in the heat, labored into the apartment. He was not alone. Trailing him into the foyer were three men. Allied aviators, he explained as he slumped down into a living room chair, *tous Anglais*—all English. He had picked them up from a safe house in the eleventh arrondissement and would turn them over to Captain Jacques for evacuation. The men were wary and ill at ease, but Madame Geneviève produced glasses and a bottle of Calvados, and Prévost, chatting casually and smiling, moved from man to man, his pleasant face aglow with confidence and goodwill. Only last night he had done the same with Roy.

The afternoon sun still hovered high over the buildings to the west when the contact arrived at the apartment. She was a spare, shovel-faced woman with bowed narrow shoulders, and her short rust-tinted hair was streaked with strands of burnt orange. As she glanced at the men in the living room, her face was frozen in a serious expression, and her glasses, easily as thick as those worn by Captain Jacques, lent her a pinched, owlish look. With a quick glance, her dark eyes raked the men sprawled in the spacious living room. She did not speak or acknowledge them in any way but conferred briefly with Prévost.

"This is the assistant of Captain Jacques," he said to the men. "She will lead you to the rendezvous. She will take only one of you at present," he explained, and turning to Roy, said: "You will go now."

Roy stood up. He had been ready for hours, and yet now as the moment to go arrived, his legs seemed filled with lead.

"I'm afraid you must leave your identity discs here," Prévost added. "Captain Jacques has insisted. Otherwise it is too dangerous."

"But why?" Roy blurted out. "We've been over this."

The Belgian woman stared blankly at him.

"It is not the time for argument, monsieur," Prévost said. "Others are waiting their turn." Roy glanced back at the men lounging on the divan. With great reluctance he reached under his shirt and pulled loose the beaded silver chain. Staring down at the dog tags he had worn now for over three years, he rubbed their smooth reassuring surface between his thumb and forefinger one last time and handed them to Prévost. He did not like this.

The Belgian woman moved to the door, her fingers already grasping the brass handle. She was impatient to get under way. "Everything is arranged," Prévost said. Roy would walk with the woman to the metro at Châtelet. It was just a few blocks away, toward the Seine. They would ride a short distance, then she would deliver him to the next contact. "*Tout est prêt,*" Prévost repeated. "All is ready."

Roy barely had time to shake Prévost's hand and mutter a farewell before the woman pushed open the door and stepped onto the landing. Madame Geneviève watched in silence from the foyer. Reflexively Roy patted his chest to make sure his papers were still there, that the cigarettes and the French currency, the small colorful bills and lighter-than-air aluminum coins, were in his pocket. How many times had he done this over the past few hours of waiting? The Belgian woman was already disappearing down the musty staircase. Roy started down. From the open doorway Georges Prévost waved. *"Bonne chance,"* he whispered, but his words were drowned in a fit of coughing.

On the street, the Belgian woman guided Roy through the crowd, a large net handbag slung over her shoulder. She took his arm and leaned against him as if they were lovers, but she made no effort to speak. They strolled briskly along the Boulevard Sébastopol toward the Seine, crossed the rue de Rivoli, and found the entrance to the Châtelet metro station. As they waited on the platform for the train, he wondered where she was taking him. She might deliver him to another apartment in Paris or to a safe house on the outskirts. Or maybe she would turn him over to another contact who would get him to a landing field or a truck or a southbound train. He was still confused about the money and boots and cigarettes Captain Jacques had given him. Maybe he would have to remain in hiding for some time near the landing site and would need money. He did not want to contemplate a trip south, to the mountains.

There were no seats on the metro when it slid to a halt, but the waiting crowd squeezed in, packing the narrow aisle. The ride, just as Prévost had briefed him, was short, and Roy and the orange-haired woman stood pressed close against each other in the airless carriage. Moments later they exited at the Place de l'Opéra, climbing the steps to a spacious sunswept plaza. All around them German signposts sprouted in profusion, and ranks of camouflaged military vehicles were stacked like cordwood all around the plaza. Soldiers swarmed everywhere, darting among the parked trucks, bustling along the sidewalks, barking orders to one another.

The woman paused for a moment to get her bearings, then set off again, leading him into a small tree-lined street that emptied into the plaza. It was cool in the shadows of the elegant street, and they walked, still arm in arm, beneath colorful canvas awnings that unfurled over the sidewalk like circus tents. They strolled for several blocks past posh shops and bubbling cafés whose marble-topped tables and delicate cane chairs and potted geraniums stood in brilliant clusters all along the street. Far from the Place de l'Opéra the flood of *feldgrau* uniforms gradually ebbed, and Roy felt himself begin to relax. With every step, he could almost feel the war, like an outgoing tide, sliding away from him. It was then that it struck him that he was actually leaving Paris, that his strange odyssey through occupied France had entered its final phase. Even if it meant a hike over the

Pyrenees, he would make it. He was on his way home, if not tonight, then tomorrow or the next day.

Approaching a busy sidewalk café, the woman suddenly slowed. Releasing Roy's arm, she nudged him discreetly toward a table at the edge of the crowd. Two men sat at the small oval table, one apparently absorbed in a newspaper, the other gazing vacantly out at the passersby. For an instant, Roy hesitated, not knowing what to do. Was this the rendezvous point? Should he approach the table or simply stand along the row of flower boxes that marked the boundary of the café? Was one of these men his contact? He turned to his companion, but the orange-haired woman was nowhere in sight.

When he turned back toward the café, both men had risen from the table. They were burly but surprisingly nimble men, and they stepped toward him with the easy animal grace of athletes. One of the men nodded to Roy, a flicker of recognition in his eyes. Grabbing Roy's elbow and leaning close, he smiled reassuringly and in heavily accented English whispered above the clatter of crockery and café chatter, "Sorry, monsieur, but you are our prisoner." Roy froze. Had he heard correctly? Was this some sort of password, some sort of resistance lingo for the transfer? At the same instant, the other man edged closer, and Roy felt the cold barrel of a revolver pressed just beneath his ear. Instinctively he recoiled, but struggling was useless. With astonishing economy of effort the men pinned his arms tightly behind his back, and handcuffs bit into his wrists. They gripped him firmly between them, almost lifting him off the ground, and muscled him quickly through the crowd. At the curb a long black Citroën had appeared, its motor idling. From behind the wheel an enormous brick-faced man glanced back at them. He wore a dark, broad-brimmed hat and his small pig eyes watched as all three men clambered into the rear seat. Then he released the brake and accelerated out into the sparse traffic.

The car careened through a labyrinth of cobblestone streets, then turned onto a boulevard that ran beside a park. Wedged tightly between the two men, Roy tried to get his bearings. Through the window he recognized the Arc de Triomphe as the car swung around it and proceeded down a wide avenue flanked by towering trees and fashionable villas. No one in the car spoke, and in the prevailing silence Roy clung to the hope that somehow this was some sort of elaborate ruse that he did not understand and that he would still be delivered to a contact.

But when the car slowed in front of a block of elegant houses and turned through a narrow archway into a cobblestone courtyard at the rear of the building, the man sitting to his right turned to Roy, grinning. "Welcome to the Avenue Foch," he leered. "We hope you will be most comfortable during your stay here at Gestapo headquarters." The driver snorted knowingly and the door snapped open and Roy was dragged out of the car.

Uniformed guards stood at the back entrance as the two men pushed him through the doorway, through a series of corridors, and into a grand entrance hall. Inside everything was in motion. Clerks in civilian clothes scurried along the corridors carrying armloads of heavy files, phones rang frantically in unseen offices, and wisps of smoke streamed along the high, scrolled ceilings, collecting in the corners. From somewhere up above, a ghastly wailing echoed through the building, a high-pitched shrieking so saturated with pain and terror that the hairs on Roy's neck stood on end.

Without pausing the men shouldered him through the lavish foyer and up a sweeping marble staircase. Flight after flight they prodded him up the wide steps, dragging him whenever he stumbled, until somewhere in the upper floors the marble ended and the high-ceilinged hallways disappeared and they entered a narrow wooden staircase. When they reached the top-floor landing, the men left him under guard while they disappeared into an adjacent office.

As he waited beneath the low, sloping ceiling, Roy tried to take stock. His mind was reeling. The Belgian woman had betrayed him—that, at least, seemed clear. It was all a setup. She had led him right to the Germans, to the Gestapo. But she was Captain Jacques's assistant, a woman the captain trusted. Prévost had recognized her, vouched for her. Then maybe it was Captain Jacques himself. But Prévost was so sure of him. Yet, what in the end did he know about Prévost? Robert had been Prévost's only contact with the group in Vincennes. Maybe Prévost was a traitor. Maybe the whole evasion line was a Gestapo operation.

Roy glanced over at the thin, sallow-faced guard. The man sucked on a foul-smelling cigarette and muttered to himself, shifting his weight from foot to foot. He seemed uninterested in Roy. Snatches of German, French, even English, slipped from beneath the doors that receded down the brightly lit corridor. What would happen now? His friends in the Avenue Michel Bizot had talked in chilling detail about Gestapo tortures, about the chamber of horrors in the Avenue Foch.

The Nazis tore out fingernails and burned testicles. They dunked handcuffed prisoners into a bathtub of frigid water until their lungs almost burst, then revived them, only to do it again and again until the prisoner either talked or drowned.

What *do* I actually know, Roy asked himself. His friends in Paris had been careful to use only first names, probably false ones at that. Noms de guerre, they called them. He was not even sure that he had heard their real names. But he knew some things. He knew Colette and the Florins. He knew Paul Guérin, Jonckheere and Pivert. He knew Georges and Yvette and Robert and the apartment in Vincennes near the park. But he would keep his mouth shut. He was an American officer and he would demand to be treated as such. He would give name, rank, and serial number, nothing more. Then he remembered his dog tags.

He had not been waiting long when a nearby door opened, and his captors reappeared. They tugged him roughly along the corridor and into an office where a tall wiry man in a well-tailored suit sat behind a plain military desk. In his hands he held a bulging yellow file. When Roy entered the man closed the folder, placed it on the desk, and looked up at him with eyes as cold and clear as ice cubes. While the man stared, the two thugs emptied Roy's pockets onto the desk, then shoved him into a straight-backed chair and turned it toward the desk. They took up positions behind and on each side of him, just out of his line of sight.

With one hand the tall man sorted casually through Roy's things, pushing the cigarettes, the coins, the wadded French currency, the identity papers into a crumpled pile. "*Nichts,*" he muttered, "*nichts Besonderes.*" He hardly glanced at the papers. Then he leaned over and, arching his eyebrows, reached for something in the heap. "*Was haben wir denn hier?*" Pressing the paper flat on the desk, he studied it for a moment. Because his handcuffed arms were pinned behind him, Roy was forced to sit pitched toward the desk, as if leaning forward to hear. From his vantage point he could see the edge of a folded piece of paper in the man's hand. He had no idea what it was. Had the Belgian woman planted something on him?

The man glanced up at Roy with an inquisitive, almost scholarly expression and smiled. It was a smile of stunning cruelty. Then without warning he leapt to his feet, bellowing so loud Roy jumped. "*Schweinehund,*" he barked at the top of his lungs, his face turning bright crimson. *"Spion, Saboteur, Terrorist! Das sind Sie! Das wissen wir schon."* A shower of saliva spewed from his gaping mouth. "We know all about you," he sneered, stepping forward around the desk. "You are a spy and a terrorist. It will avail you nothing to lie." He glowered at Roy.

"I am an American airman," Roy responded with as much force as he could muster. "First Lieutenant Roy W. Allen, U.S. Army Air Corps, serial number 0753841 . . ." With no warning the man smashed his fist into the side of Roy's face. Knocked sideways, Roy tumbled from the chair, crashing head-first into the floor. Powerful hands gripped him from behind, yanking him back into place on the chair. They held him there as the tall man stepped forward again. His thin lips flattened into an ominous smile. In his hand he held a long dark object. For a moment he waved it in front of Roy's face. Gently he touched the tip of the hard rubber hose to Roy's cheek and nose, toying with the nostrils. His smile widened. Then he raised his arm and with a swift chopping motion, like the falling of an ax, slammed the truncheon into Roy's neck. Grunting with each blow, he pounded savagely at Roy's neck and shoulder and head. Roy's ears rang and a roaring filled his head. Phosphorescent coils of crimson, green, and gold swirled behind his eyes. The room, the desk, the lights fluttered, faded. Then the world went black.

Someone was shaking him, slapping him back to consciousness. Straining to focus he saw the tall Gestapo man step back toward the desk. He placed the truncheon beside the yellow file, fastidiously aligning the edges. Then he drew a handkerchief from the breast pocket of his jacket, fluffed it, and wiped his hands. He straightened his tie.

"You are a spy, monsieur, and you work with the terrorists," he said with mannered calm. "This we know with great certainty. These little charades are so futile, so boring. If you are a soldier, where is your uniform? If you are a soldier, where are your identity disks, your dog tags? You have papers. They identify you as Louis Rouet of Cherbourg, a mason and a deaf-mute. Now you tell us that you are Roy W. Allen. Neither, of course, is true."

Roy's tongue was thick and the warm taste of blood filled his mouth. His left arm was numb from his shoulder to his fingertips. A strange choking noise gurgled from his throat. He coughed, fighting to get his breath, to speak. He had hidden his uniform after he bailed out, he said, his voice almost a whisper. He had stolen clothes and bought the false identity card. He had found his way into Paris. Somewhere along the line he had lost his dog tags.

"Dog tags!" the man scoffed. "It would mean nothing if you had these dog tags. Such things are easier to come by in Paris than a French whore. No, you are a terrorist. And we know your friends, your *réseau*." Bending over the desk, he picked up a piece of paper and held it up for Roy to see. "*Wollen Sie uns das erklären?*" Roy squinted, trying to make out the blurred sheet of paper that fluttered before him. "Perhaps you would like to tell us about this," the man continued. He began to read aloud, his words enunciated in a thick German accent. "Number one, 'I'll Be Seeing You'; number two, 'Is You Is or Is You Ain't My Baby?'" He paused, looking up at Roy expectantly. "Number three, 'Roll Me Over in the Clover.'"

Despite the brutal throbbing in his head, it was all Roy could do to suppress a bitter smile. Jesus, he thought, the Hit Parade list, the crosswords. Through his swollen eyelids he could just make out the crosshatched squares, the scrawled lists. How would he explain?

"It's just a list of songs," he stammered. "Popular songs from the radio, from America." His gums ached and his teeth felt loose. "For a crossword puzzle." The explanation sounded feeble even to him.

"Just songs," his interrogator sniffed. "For whom are these messages intended? What do they mean?" He took a menacing step toward Roy.

"I am an American officer and I demand a military interrogation," Roy said as forcefully as he could. He could think of nothing else to say.

The man studied him for a moment, his balled fists only inches from Roy's face. "You will next quote to me the Geneva Convention, I suppose," he said wryly. "It is always the same. At first." He shook his head. "*Aber trotzdem.* We can be very persuasive when we apply ourselves. We will send you downstairs to think it over for a while. Perhaps later you will need a bath. We will help you. It is very refreshing." He smiled. "And remarkably good for the memory." The two guards stationed behind him jerked Roy to his feet. "One last word," the man said as Roy staggered toward the door. "The Geneva Convention means nothing here. You are either a *Terrorflieger*, an air gangster, or a saboteur, it makes no difference. Either way you are a dead man. *Morgen werden Sie sowieso erschossen werden.*"

With that Roy was shoved out the door. His two guards dragged him along the corridor toward the steps, never allowing him to regain his feet. In the stairwell trails of acrid smoke wafted all around them. As they passed an open door Roy caught a quick glimpse of flames flickering in a cluttered room and men hunched over a heaping pile of yellow folders, shoving great sheaves of paper into a shallow fireplace. The trash cans smoldered, spitting flame. They're burning documents, Roy realized. The Allies must be very close.

The men passed once again through the buzzing entrance hall and down a flight of winding stairs into a large basement. A heavy metal door clanged shut behind them and the air grew cool and the light faded into murky pools of darkness. Keys jangled. Metal hinges creaked. After the brightly illuminated upper floors, Roy's eyes at first could not focus, but gradually dark forms materialized, black silhouettes against the prevailing gray. The guards removed his handcuffs. They shoved him forward, and he tumbled into a large crowded cell. All around him hushed voices murmured in the darkness, and low doleful moans rose and fell in a desolate chorus. From somewhere in the gloom, children cried out for their mothers. Above it all, there rose a hideous whimpering so filled with horror, so shorn of all self-control, of all self-respect, that Roy's skin crawled.

He stood in a large cell, a sort of holding pen, with many inmates. Some huddled together in small clumps. Others sat, their legs pulled in against their chests, along the crumbling plaster walls. Just at Roy's knees, a man slumped on the floor, his face battered into a ghoulish pulp. He blubbered incoherently. Beside him another prisoner, his fingers no more than bloody stumps, sat in shocked silence, staring down at his trembling hands. Here and there dark forms curled on the damp floor, while others milled listlessly, picking their way across the crowded cell. Roy was surprised to see several GIs in the wretched crowd. Still in uniform, most were clearly airmen, but others were ground troops. Some, he thought, were British.

The inmates of the crowded cell did not converse with one another. They paced or sat or stood in silence. Yet, the whispering and wailing, the muttered prayers, and the sobbing of the children never subsided. Roy's head throbbed and his left eye was swelling shut. He leaned against the wall of the cell, trying to make sense of what had happened. "We know your friends," the Gestapo bastard upstairs had screamed. "Your *réseau*." Did the others know that he had been taken?

Would he see Robert or Georges in this hellhole tomorrow? If they took Robert, the trail would lead back to Bannost and then to Jouy, back to Colette. Maybe she was already sitting in a Nazi jail wondering, as he was, who had betrayed her.

Sleep was impossible. During the night another prisoner was hurled into the cell. His front teeth were broken off near the gum. Dried blood clogged his nose and whenever he tried to breathe, inhaling through his battered mouth, the cool air struck the exposed nerves of his shattered teeth like jolts of electric current and he screamed until he choked.

Roy was wide awake the next morning when the metal door clanked open and uniformed guards appeared at the entrance to the cell. "*Aufstehen*," they bellowed. "*Los, los, ihr Scheisskerle.*" Exhausted and frightened, the inmates did not stir. "*Raus*," the soldiers shouted, raking their rifle butts along the bars. "*Ihr drei dort*," their leader shouted, pointing at three of the men, "*und ihr beide*"—you two— "*und,*" staring straight at Roy, "*du! Alle sechs von euch, raus!*"

"*Mon Dieu,*" someone in the cell screamed. "*Mon Dieu! Ils vont nous fusiller!*"

"Shut your bleedin' trap," another barked in English.

The children, who during the night had at last collapsed into a restless sleep, began again their desperate wailing. "*Maman, Maman.*"

Roy staggered to his feet, and the guards herded the six men out of the cell. Handcuffed and prodded by the guards, they stumbled up the steps, through a heavy oak door, and filed into the back courtyard. Low clouds scudded over the treetops, and light rain was falling. Water stood in dark puddles on the uneven paving stones, running in black rivulets to a drain in the center of the courtyard. In the tepid light of dawn, it might have been blood.

"The freakin' buggers are going to shoot us," a British soldier swore as the guards pushed them into line along a high windowless wall. With their rifles at the ready, the guards stood evenly spaced, facing the prisoners. A firing squad. Roy closed his eyes. The Germans were yelling, bawling out orders. Their voices sounded remote. He let out a sigh. Slowly opening his eyes, he caught sight of a hulking black vehicle parked beyond the soldiers. He recognized the type—a special van, designed for transporting prisoners. His friends in Vincennes had pointed one out to him during one of their excursions. A Black Maria, they called it. As Roy watched, a soldier unlatched the rear gate of the van and the motor started up, belching blue diesel fumes into the morning rain. Then the guards stepped forward and began to hand-cuff the men against the wall.

Leading them single file across the courtyard, the guards directed the small group of prisoners toward the van. Roy stood in line, wait-ing as the guards prodded the men into the back. When his turn came, he hauled himself up and staggered into a narrow center aisle that separated two rows of windowless metal compartments barely large enough for one man. Pushed from behind, he squeezed into a com-partment, then the door slammed shut and a lock turned. A rectangu-lar slit of wire mesh at the top provided the only source of light and air, and in the low, cramped space he could neither sit nor stand. Forced into an awkward crouch, his knees slightly bent, he was already sweating when the van ground into gear and rumbled out into the early morning quiet of Paris.

The tires made a sluicing sound as the van sped along the wet streets, and whenever it slowed or stopped, Roy could hear the drum-ming of raindrops on the metal roof just above his head. The ride was not a long one—not more than thirty minutes—but with his hands cuffed behind him, he could not keep his balance and whenever the van swerved or braked he slammed into the sides of the cage. At last the van slowed, entered a series of tight turns, and eased to a halt. He heard the rear gate clap open and the guards enter. One by one the compartment doors were flung open and the men stumbled out.

Aching all over, Roy stretched as best he could and looked up at a gigantic building that loomed before him. Five stories of pale color-less plaster and frosted glass crowned by a slanting red-tiled roof, it might have been a school or a hospital but for the bars that darkened the narrow windows. Behind the idling van, the arched doors of an entrance gate were swinging shut, and beyond the high stone wall of the courtyard a row of cypresses wavered in the summer breeze. The rain had stopped and the sun had come up and steam rose from the pavement where the prison guards, dressed in immacu-late green uniforms and armed with light machine guns, assembled the men.

Pushing the prisoners along, the guards led them into the massive building. They passed into a vaulted hallway so empty and silent it reminded Roy of a monastery. After stepping through another iron gateway, they found themselves standing in a canyon of steep metal walls that towered four stories above them, merging into a high, arched ceiling. Each floor was nothing more than a shallow steel gangway etched into the pale green concrete walls. With their chest-high iron railings, the gangways were layered in tiers and looked like balconies punctuated at regular intervals by windowless metal doors. A narrow bridge at the center of each floor arced over the abyss below, linking the gangways along the opposite wall, and sentries patrolled the iron-barred balconies, their hobnail boots echoing with each step.

Pale light poured into the cavernous space from rows of high windows at the far ends of the building, creating elongated rectangles of gray on the brick floor far below. The men were marched into a warren of wooden cubicles where their handcuffs were removed and one by one they were stripped and body searched. The guards took their ties and belts and then, after much waiting, led them back into the gallery. From there they climbed several flights of stairs, then were prodded along the third-floor gangway until they were halted in front of a narrow steel door. Fumbling with a ring of heavy keys, the lead guard opened it and the men, six in all, squeezed into a close airless room.

The door slammed shut behind them. No more than four paces wide and eight paces deep, the cell contained a single metal-frame bed that folded down from the wall, a filthy straw pallet tossed into a back corner, a table with several small bowls, a chair attached to the wall by a chain, and a foul-smelling seatless toilet with a spigot above it. The single window was of frosted glass and sealed shut, and as the sun shone full on it, the dark lines of the bars could be seen as clearly as tire tracks in the snow. A single lightbulb hung suspended from the ceiling but could be turned on only from outside.

Without speaking, the men staked out their turf in the cell. They stole glances at one another, sizing one another up. No one showed much inclination to talk. All bore the signs of rough treatment— bruised, purple faces, cracked lips, an eye swollen shut. Dried blood was caked in the mangled ear of one man, trailing down into the stubble of his jaw before disappearing beneath a torn shirt collar. Roy recognized scraps of American flying clothes, odd streaks of olive drab mixed with bits and pieces of ill-fitting civilian apparel.

"Jesus H. Christ," one of the men finally muttered, poking with his foot at the soiled pallet in the corner. "This thing's alive." Straw, smelling of urine, spilled from the pallet. Another man squatted beside it. "Lice," he said. "The thing's crawlin' with lice. Fleas, too." Standing with his back against the door, Roy couldn't help but smile. The man's voice, his accent, rolled with the same slow southern drawl, the same flat elongated "i" he loved to hear when Joe spoke. Texas, maybe, or Oklahoma.

"Hey, you down there!"

The men looked around in confusion. None of them had spoken.

"You guys," the faint voice repeated, "who's down there?" It seemed to be coming from the water pipe that ran up through the front corner of the cell and into the ceiling. "You just come in today?" It was a low, insistent voice, clearly American.

At first no one responded. Then one of the men climbed onto the chair and, raising his head to the pipe, called out: "Yeah, today."

"Americans?" the voice asked.

The man looked around at Roy and the others and then replied, "Yeah, Americans. I think. Where the hell are we?"

"You're about eleven kilometers south of Paris," the answer came. "At Fresnes. It's a Gestapo prison." The men in the cell exchanged glances. "You'll see. They aren't through with you. They drag prisoners out for interrogation all the time," he said. "The s.o.b.s come to the cells in the morning and yell 'Tribunal!' and they haul your ass out, either back into Paris, to Gestapo headquarters, or downstairs here somewhere. Some nights you can hear the screaming down below."

The voice paused and the men stood in silence, absorbing this news. "There are two other blocks or divisions in this joint, buildings just like this one," the voice continued. "Must be three thousand prisoners, mostly French political types. Resistance fighters. This is the third block. There are a lot of American and British airmen here. Even women." He paused, but no one in the cell spoke.

"Any news? Any news about the war?" the voice from above asked.

Before anyone could respond, there was a stirring outside on the gangway, and the cell fell abruptly quiet. The clicking of hobnail boots echoed in the gallery, drawing closer. A round peephole in the door slid open with a snap. No one moved. *"Ruhe!"* a voice from beyond bellowed. Then the peephole slid shut and the sound of the boots resumed. They waited for several minutes, listening, then called out again into the pipe, but the voice from above did not return.

As the day wore on, the men paced and sat, arranging themselves in the cramped cell as best they could. They exchanged a few random remarks, occasional observations and general complaints about the accommodations. Sometimes they could hear muffled voices, so faint it was impossible even to determine the language, and a persistent metallic tapping, distant and indistinct, that rattled through the pipes.

"Morse," Roy said. "It's Morse code." The men listened expectantly, but the distant tapping was too feeble and finally stopped altogether.

"Whaddaya know," one of the men said, bending over the pallet and pushing it gingerly aside with his foot. "Look at this." Directly beneath the sealed window lay a book. Its spine had begun to unravel and its filthy blue cover was faded and badly frayed. The man lifted it, holding it at arm's length between his thumb and forefinger as if he was handling a dead rat. He dropped it onto the table. Fleas jumped in all directions. The men gathered round, leaning over to examine it. "It's in English," someone said. *Wild Justice*, the book's tattered title page read, written by George A. Birmingham and published by the American Library in Paris, 9, rue de Teheran. But it was not the text that drew their attention. The pages were worn thin and deeply stained, and all along the margins inmates had scrawled messages and addresses. Some were barely legible, engraved into the page with a fingernail or a wisp of straw from the pallet.

They read them, mumbling the names and addresses aloud. "T. Sgt. S. Joe Marshall 20932531. Captured June 22, '44 still here at Fresnes Prison July 25, '44 USAAF." "Sgt. J. Clarke, RAF in France 7 June '44 captured 19 July '44 still here 1/8/44." "Hey, here's a guy from Massachusetts," one of the men said, pointing to the name Edward Vallee. He had been brought into Fresnes on August 3. Roy's eyes were drawn to another name: "S. Sgt. John A. Watson of Blairsville, Pa.," no date. What was the date today, Roy wondered. August 12?

"Listen to this," one of the men said, laughing. Flipping through the book, he stopped at page 109 and read aloud: "If they took the bugs out of the soup—we would all starve to death and dry up and blow out of the window." And this, on page 139: "If you are a First Lieut. in the USAAF and the war lasts two years you will have saved approximately seven thousand five hundred dollars."

The men pored over the book, reading the inscriptions. Here and there words had been underlined, sometimes whole sentences. "Must be a code of some sort," one of the men ventured, but no one cared to pursue that. "I hope to God this guy isn't still here," someone said, pointing to an entry from the summer of 1943. After a time the men lost interest in the book and settled back once again against the plaster wall, each alone with his thoughts.

They had been in the cell for hours when a persistent metallic rasping rose from the gallery beyond the door. It progressed in stops and starts along the steel gangways of the vast building. Doors slammed open and shut, and the scraping, clattering sound continued, rattling on and on until it became mixed with voices, drawing steadily nearer. Finally it halted just outside their own cell and the peephole slid open. The key jangled in the heavy lock, and the door swung open.

An iron-wheeled food cart blocked the entrance, and a shabbily dressed man, a prisoner himself, stood behind a large tureen, a ladle in his hand. "*Amenez vos gamelles,*" he said, gesturing toward the table. "The mugs," Roy said, scrambling to his feet, "he wants us to bring him the mugs." One by one the men picked up the rough bowls that were stacked on the table, and the man ladled out a clear greasy broth. Bits of gristle and stumps of vegetable matter floated desolately in the luke-warm soup, but the men were famished. They ate without complaint.

As the afternoon wore on, the men began to talk, relating their stories one by one. They did not offer details. They were careful not to reveal anything about their units or their missions or the names of the people who had helped them in France. They talked about bailing out of burning planes, about landing in trees and wheat fields, hiding with the resistance in barns and bakeries, and about being smuggled into Paris.

"I was hidden in a private home behind a butcher shop in a village northwest of Paris," one of them said. He spoke with a British accent, not, Roy noticed, of the BBC variety. "I had been there for about a fortnight when a bloke offered to take me to Paris. The family I was staying with, the butcher and his wife, didn't want me to go, but after all that time cooped up in the back room of this little flat, I just had to have a go. Rode into Paris in the back of a lorry. Smelled like the devil's own self. The driver checked me into a hotel, the Hotel Piccadilly, somewhere near the Champs-Elysées. The place was full of fliers, mostly Yanks, some RAF chaps. Must have been a dozen or more of them, all waiting for the contact, fellow named Jacques, to pick them up. We were going over the Pyrenees to Spain."

Roy stirred in his corner.

"Jacques?"

"Short, slender sort of fellow. Captain Jacques, he called himself."

"Big bulging eyes?" another man interrupted.

"Matter of fact, yes. Looked like they might pop out of his head."

"Did a red-haired woman work with him?" the man asked.

"A Belgian woman."

"I know those two," another chimed in. "We called him Jean, though."

Roy listened in amazement. The circumstances varied—a trip over the Pyrenees or a flight back to England. Sometimes the Belgian woman was there, sometimes not; but Captain Jacques or Monsieur Jean or Jacques the Belgian appeared in them all. To some he posed as a French *résistant,* to others a British agent, but all the men in the cell had fallen into Jacques's hands. From their description of the locale and the contact, some, it was clear to Roy, had even stayed at Prévost's apartment near Les Halles. Prévost must be part of it, Roy thought. And maybe his friends from the Avenue Michel Bizot were sitting in a cell not far away, wondering if he, Roy, had betrayed them.

During the night the tapping began again. Roy lay curled in a ball on the cold floor. They had agreed to take turns on the metal-framed bed. In the chill dimness of the cell he could see that one of the men had crawled onto the pallet, taking his chances with the bedbugs rather than sleep on the damp floor. The sound of the tapping was faint at first, coming in short metallic bursts that rattled along the pipe from somewhere below. Roy, on the rough fringes of sleep, listened as it grew louder, more insistent. The man beside him was listening too, squatting beside the pipe, his back against the toilet.

"It's definitely Morse code," the man whispered. Roy sat up, straining to hear. He wished he could remember more from his radio classes in flight school but it was hopeless.

"The Americans are at Chartres," the man said during a pause in the tapping. "They'll be here soon. You think that's right?" Roy tried to visualize the briefing map at Glatton. Chartres was close by, he thought, somewhere to the northwest.

"Some guy thinks the Krauts are going to empty the prison before the Allies get here, though, take us all to a POW camp in Germany." He bent his head closer to the pipe. "Somebody else is saying they're going to kill us all, shoot us before we can be liberated." The man, his voice husky in the darkness, nudged Roy to see if he was still awake. "You think they might just pull out, leave us here in the cells? Why would they go to all the trouble to transport us out?"

Roy didn't answer.

"You don't think they'd shoot everybody in the prison, do you? Three thousand people? Allied military personnel? Prisoners of war?"

"Did the goons at the Avenue Foch believe you when you told them you were military personnel?" Roy asked.

"No," the man responded, "they didn't. Just yelled at me mostly, knocked me around a little. Called me a terrorist. I didn't understand much." He touched his cheek with his fingertips. "Said they were going to shoot me."

"Sounds familiar," Roy said

The man fell silent, and Roy nodded, unable to find anything more to say. He did not want to consider this possibility. The tapping continued at intervals throughout the night. In the darkness Roy slapped at the fleas, itching all over. He listened to the groans and troubled breathing of the others and the gentle tapping sound from the pipes until at last he drifted into a light, uneasy sleep.

Timid early morning light brightened the frosted windowpanes and the men were stirring when Roy woke to the grating sound of the food trolley edging its way along the gangway. The morning ration, consisting of a single mug of bitter ersatz coffee, did not revive him. His friend from the night before was reporting what he had learned from the pipes, when they heard the approach of hobnail boots. They halted just outside the cell and the peephole slid open. Keys scraped in the lock, and two armed guards appeared in the cell. The men froze where they were sitting. The guards looked from one prisoner to another. Finally, they grunted toward Roy. He was to follow.

Yanking him to his feet, the guards escorted him down the long walkway, past dozens of cell doors. Out of the corner of his eye he could see sentries pacing the narrow walkways across the chasm. They wore knee-high black boots, highly polished, and black helmets with swastikas painted on the sides. Occasionally, they would stop to peer through the peepholes, then resume their routine.

The guards led him to a stairwell at the end of the walkway, and as they began their descent, Roy tried to steady himself. Was he bound for Paris, he wondered, for the Avenue Foch?

Down and down they went, beyond the ground floor. They're taking me to the torture chamber, he thought. He tried to prepare for the worst. But when the guards thrust him into a brightly lit, cell-sized room, he found himself facing a man wearing, as best Roy could determine, the blue uniform of a Luftwaffe officer. The officer sat behind a large desk and hardly seemed to notice when Roy entered. A number of files were neatly stacked on the desk. One was open, and the officer appeared to be studying it. Finally looking up, he smiled and motioned Roy to a chair across from him.

"Cigarette?" he asked in slightly accented English, indicating a pack of Chesterfields between them on the desk.

"No, thanks."

The officer studied him for a moment. "You know," he began, "I have never understood why it should be that your president has dragged you into this war. Germany has no quarrel with the United States. Our objective is to save Europe and all of Western civilization from the barbarism of Bolshevism. It is such a pity that events have led us to this unhappy point, don't you agree?"

Roy stared at him, unable to think of a response. Should he talk? The officer's bearing was urbane, his tone disarmingly casual, almost friendly. There was nothing in his manner of the Gestapo's menacing hostility. At a loss, Roy blurted out his name, rank, and serial number.

"Yes, of course." The officer smiled. *"Allen, Allen, na ja. Wo ist denn die Akte?"* He shuffled through his files. "It is admirable of you to do your duty," he said, opening a blue folder. "But I am afraid it is a misguided effort. We know all that. Let's see," he read from the file. "First Lieutenant Roy W. Allen, airplane commander, you are flying with the 457th bomb group, 749th squadron. On June 14, you were in the deputy lead position on a mission to Paris when your aircraft, a Fortress, was shot down by flak—or was it fighters?—no decision has been reached on this in the official report, the *Abschussmeldung*. Both the flak battery and the fighter squadron are claiming you, of course. There is keen competition for this honor, you understand. But then on June 14 there were so many shot from the skies. Several from your group alone."

Roy tried to hide his amazement. At Gestapo headquarters he had been harangued and threatened as a spy, a saboteur, his identity as an Allied flyer disputed. Should he ask about the others in the crew?

"Your commanding officer, Colonel Luper, is a most impressive leader," the officer said. "His raids are always skillfully executed. When he leads a *Feindflug* it is quite effective. This I must concede." He exhaled smoke elegantly through his nostrils and sighed. "But, of course, we will get him, too."

Roy had heard that German intelligence was very good, that they had amassed an astonishing amount of information on the bomb groups, culled from newspapers in the States, spies in Britain, and captured airmen. They were meticulous in collecting tiny pieces of information that could then be used to impress the naïve and frightened.

When it became apparent that Roy would offer nothing more, the officer leaned back in his chair and pursed his lips in disappointment. *"Also dann,"* he said crisply, dismissing him, *"das wäre es."*

The guard appeared behind him. *"Aufstehen,"* he barked.

"Sir," Roy said, turning back to the officer, "may I ask you a question?"

"But of course."

"Will you tell me whether you are going to regard me as military personnel or as a saboteur?"

The officer rose from his chair and, stepping around the desk, looked Roy directly in the eye. His charming manner had vanished.

"Where is the escape hatch for the pilot on a B-17?" he asked. Roy described it in detail. For a moment the officer stared at him. "*Na ja, Lieutenant,*" he said at last, "I can do nothing for you until these papers clear Berlin. That will take time. Until then, you are our guest here. And," he added, "I am afraid you will find my Gestapo counterparts are not so patient."

One by one the other men were taken from the cell and interrogated, each returning relieved but astonished at what the Luftwaffe knew about them. Their mood was anxious but upbeat. The German military representative at Fresnes clearly understood that they were Allied airmen. He was in possession of the relevant files, the documentation. He had not challenged their identity. If they were not left for the Allies to liberate, they would be transferred to a stalag somewhere in Germany and treated as prisoners of war.

But their good mood did not last. Throughout the long dismal day and into the night disturbing rumors passed along the pipes and through the walls. The Germans were evacuating Paris, but before pulling out, the rumors insisted, they would shoot the inmates of Fresnes—the political prisoners *and* the Allied fliers. There would be no escape, no liberation, no transfer to POW camps.

The men talked deep into the night, discussing the possibilities. They had been given a small half-loaf of bread at five o'clock when the food cart made its last noisy round of the day, and Roy had saved his, waiting until he was ready to sleep before eating. As the men talked, he gnawed at the tough grainy bread. It was now August 14. He had been in France for exactly two months. It seemed like two years. What a colossal mistake it had been to leave Colette and Jouy. He tried to think of home and May and the baby, but his mind was flooded with images of the echoing vastness of Fresnes, the uniformed sentries, and the fleeting sensation of standing, his back against the wall in the courtyard of the Avenue Foch, knowing with certainty that he was going to die.

"I just don't believe they would do that," one of the men was saying, "even the Jerries."

"No, they couldn't shoot everybody. The political prisoners maybe, but not military personnel."

"Those Gestapo sons of bitches are capable of anything."

The men were still speculating, still listening to insistent tapping on the pipes, when Roy, hugging his knees and resting against the metal bed frame, slipped away into something like sleep.

The cell was still dark when he snapped awake. All through the immense gallery metal doors were slamming open and shut. Hurried footsteps clattered along the steel walkways, and men shouted out, their bellowing voices rising through the chasm like panicked passengers on a sinking ship. The building seemed to quake and rumble with sound. Outside in the courtyard far below, gunshots rang out. "Jesus," Roy gasped, jumping to his feet, "they're shooting the prisoners."

CHAPTER 9

The Train

August 15–20, 1944

Sporadic volleys of gunfire crackled through the courtyard, then died away, and the bellowing of the guards echoed throughout the building. From the gangways down below, steel doors slammed, and boots clattered on the metal floor. Men scurried by. Somewhere up above glass shattered. Prisoners were breaking their windows, trying to see what was going on in the courtyard below. Roy stood at the door, listening.

The shooting did not last long, but the clamor along the gangways continued, rising floor after floor. The frantic sounds seemed to come in waves, erupting in sudden clanging explosions of metal on metal, then subsiding as one stretch of cells after another was emptied. The men waited in silence. From time to time they tapped out a message on the pipe, but there was no answer. During one of the sudden lulls in the commotion, Roy thought he could hear a familiar sound. "Listen," someone whispered. From down below, between the shouts and the slamming doors, the unmistakable squeal of the food trolley could be heard. "Morning rations," someone said. "They're distributing the morning rations. Surely they aren't going to feed us and then shoot us." No, Roy thought, the prisoners, at least some of them, were being evacuated.

Pale light was beginning to seep through the frosted glass of the window when the food trolley finally reached their cell. The usual bedraggled inmate handed in a shrunken loaf of bread and ladled out the thin coffee. From behind him a tall, uniformed guard told them to be ready to leave immediately.

The men picked nervously at the food and waited. After the dull chill of the night, the air in the cell grew surprisingly hot. There was very little chatter. Roy watched black dots jumping from his arm to his thigh and back again. His crotch itched. Something moved in his hair, along his scalp. All around his waist, where his belt would have been if the guards had not taken it, a trail of red welts had risen. The fleas were everywhere, and as it grew light, he passed the time by catching them, crushing them between his forefinger and his thumbnail. They were hard as grains of sand.

It must have been almost noon when the guard returned and motioned them out. Prisoners from neighboring cells were already assembled along the narrow gangway, separated at intervals by armed guards. Roy and his cell mates fell into line. A pale, hard-faced corporal carrying a clipboard counted them, then counted them again. He grunted out an order, and the prisoners shuffled along the gangway, down flight after flight of the steel stairwell to the ground floor. From there they marched along a broad passageway, stepped through a grilled gate, and filed into a courtyard that separated two blocks of the prison.

After the dimness of the cell block, the harsh afternoon sky was stunningly bright, and the men blinked and squinted, stumbling forward into the glare. The courtyard was crowded with prisoners. Unshaven, bruised, and filthy, they made a motley crew. Some were decked out in fine French suits, soiled and torn after God knows how long in Fresnes or the Avenue Foch. Others wore shabby collarless shirts and faded vests or blue laborer's smocks or spattered peasants' overalls. All bore yellowing purple-green bruises or ugly gashes.

Armed guards, their machine pistols at the ready, ringed the courtyard, eyeing the swelling multitude of inmates. Another set of uniformed officials—Gestapo probably, Roy thought—assembled the prisoners, counted them, and then divided them into groups of fifty or so. At the open end of the courtyard a line of green-and-yellow buses—Paris municipal buses he had noticed parked around the city—idled noisily. While the new arrivals were being formed into groups, other prisoners, aligned into columns, were directed toward the buses. When the buses were packed and a contingent of guards had climbed aboard, they groaned away, and others took their place. All through the late morning buses came and went, spewing diesel into the already sticky air, and the prisoners milled about, waiting their turn.

The mood in the courtyard was a mixture of elation and defiance. Freed from the grimy cells and allowed for the first time in days or weeks or months to mingle with one another, to talk, the men were animated by an almost electric surge of excitement. Some—Americans mostly—were boisterous, singing, shouting at the guards, yelling out to friends or crewmates they recognized in the crowd. From the French prisoners assembled across the courtyard a rowdy chorus of "La Marseillaise" burst forth at intervals, punctuated by catcalls and taunts at the Germans. Just listening to them gave Roy a boost. An almost palpable sense that liberation might be at hand hung in the humid air, tempered by a vague disquiet that he couldn't shake.

He picked his way through the crowd, searching the faces. Maybe Joe or one of the other boys from the crew was here, maybe somebody from the 457th, somebody with news. But he saw no one he recognized, and it would do no good to ask. He knew that there were other Americans in the prison, but he was surprised to find himself surrounded by so many, and after two months in France, it was good to hear the familiar cadences of their voices. His group and the ones clustered close by seemed to be made up almost entirely of Allied airmen. There were over one hundred and fifty of them, a short man with a heavy beard and an even heavier Boston accent told him, officers and men from Britain, Canada, New Zealand, Australia, and the United States. All airmen. As far as he could tell, most were Americans. They would finally be treated as prisoners of war, the man seemed to think. They were being moved to a POW camp, probably one of the big stalags in Germany. Maybe the brass had even arranged some sort of prisoner exchange. The Allies were that close.

At last word was passed for the airmen to form up. There was a general commotion, a shuffling of feet as the men arranged themselves into something like a formation. "*Achtung, Achtung,*" a voice from the front of the group shouted, and the men quieted down. A trim SS officer stood ramrod straight and faced them. He said something in German. Then one of the prisoners stepped out of the crowd, a Dutch officer in the RAF, someone said. He would serve as interpreter.

It was a short speech, and from Roy's position in the crowd he could catch only bits and pieces of the translation. "What'd he say?" Roy asked, and the word was passed back. "We're being transferred, taken by bus to a train. It will take us on to our next destination."

"Where's that? Where are we going?" someone called out.

"Didn't say," the translator spoke up. "But the Herr Sturmbann-
führer warns us that if anyone tries to escape, that man will be shot on
the spot and a grenade will be tossed into the bus he came from."
There was an uneasy shifting of feet. "He's serious," the Dutchman
warned.

The men resumed their waiting. The buses continued to arrive,
load up, and depart. From out of the crowd another group of inmates
appeared, tugging several steaming tubs into the courtyard. The tubs
contained soup, supplied, someone said, by the French Red Cross.
The men lined up, and sweating inmates ladled it out in bowls. They
had no spoons, but it was a surprisingly thick bean soup, a distinct
improvement over their daily ration. Maybe this *was* some sort of Red
Cross operation, after all. The guy from Boston could be right. This
could be the prelude to some sort of prisoner exchange.

As he licked the last of the soup from the bowl, something in the
crowd across the courtyard caught his eye. It was the merest shadow
of a face among a group of prisoners jostling toward the line of waiting buses. He did not get a good look, just a glimpse, but something in
the shape of the man's downcast head, the flushed oval of his half-hidden
face seemed somehow familiar. Roy shifted to get a better look. For a
moment the man slipped from view, then the guards shoved the column of prisoners forward, and the familiar figure reappeared. He was
a short, round-shouldered man, and he shuffled along the wavering
fringes of the column. Suddenly the man looked up, glancing back
over his shoulder as if someone had called his name. The somber face
was florid and swollen, but there was no mistaking who it was. For an
instant the man's gaze fluttered vacantly across the milling crowd.
Then he froze, and his eyes widened. He stared directly at Roy. His
body seemed to slump, and an expression of sheer desolation crept
across his face. His lips moved. Roy could not make out the words,
but it didn't matter. He knew what Georges Prévost was trying to
tell him.

The column surged and the man stumbled forward, climbing
between the guards into the bus. Behind him another familiar figure
shuffled into view. It was Prévost's brother-in-law—Jean Rocher,
unkempt and disheveled in a tattered suit, trudging toward the front of
the line. Was Madame Geneviève here too, he wondered with a sudden
rawness in the pit of his stomach, somewhere in the women's wing of
Fresnes? So Captain Jacques had duped them all. He had infiltrated

their escape line, using it for weeks, maybe months, to deliver airmen to the Germans. Now, with the Wehrmacht on the run and the Allies at the gates of Paris, the escape line was no longer of any value. The Gestapo had closed it down, and Prévost, his sister, her husband, all unwitting players in Captain Jacques's setup, were caught in the trap.

Seventy airmen had passed through the apartment in the Boulevard Sébastopol, Madame Geneviève had told him. Roy wondered how many of them were standing now in the courtyard at Fresnes. And what about his friends in Vincennes? Were they here too? Had the whole escape line been rounded up? Maybe even Gittard and the others in Jouy? Maybe Colette and the Florins?

The bus carrying Prévost and Jean Rocher rumbled out of the courtyard, and as a new string of buses arrived, the guards assembled Roy's group and began shepherding the men toward the curb. The columns moved forward between a corridor of guards, and one by one the prisoners squeezed aboard. The buses were antique and small, with a platform at the rear and high windows all around. The windows were sealed shut, and inside the heat was oppressive. Roy pressed his face against the glass, but even that was warm on his cheek. The prisoners were jammed in tightly, and a crew of guards stood on the platform and at the exits. In their heavy wool uniforms, they were sweating too.

The caravan eased through the gates of Fresnes, passed along a narrow cypress-lined street, and snaked its way through the outskirts of Paris, scattering bicycles as it plowed ahead. The sun was high and haze hung in the tops of the trees. The day was August hot. All along the boulevards people strolled in the shade of the plane trees or sat at the sidewalk cafés. Some glanced up as the buses passed, their faces momentarily puzzled or, seeing the German guards, even sad. A few waved defiantly, but most quickly returned to their newspapers or resumed their conversations. They made no sign. It was, after all, a lovely summer afternoon in Paris.

Roy did not recognize any landmark along the route. The streets slid by in a dreamy procession of white apartment buildings, empty shops, and waterless fountains, until at length the buses jerked to a halt at the side entrance to a rambling railway station. The men stirred and peered out. The usual jumble of bicycles, baggage carts, horse-drawn wagons, and *velotaxis*—the rickshaws he had seen on that first day in Paris—cluttered the entrance, but Roy did not recognize the station. *"C'est la Gare de l'Est,"* one of the French prisoners in front of him said, and the message was whispered from row to row. "It is the station for trains to the east, to Germany." The man looked over his shoulder at Roy. "It means deportation for us."

Suprisingly, the buses did not stop for long. Within minutes, the caravan rumbled on, down a series of side streets that carried them far beyond the station, past the fences and pens of a sprawling stockyard. The line of buses slowed, passed through a control point, and turned into another, smaller depot. All around them rows of boxcars sat motionless in the afternoon haze, and heat shimmered off the steel rails and the metal rooftops of the rust-colored cars. "The Pantin freight station," one of the French prisoners said. "What are we doing here?"

The buses inched onto a long ramp, jouncing to a halt alongside a waiting train. The doors wheezed open and the men tumbled out into a scene of utter bedlam. Boxcar after boxcar stretched out into the distance, and the siding teemed with thousands of prisoners. Soldiers darted in and out among them, shouting, shoving, lashing out at them with their whips and the butts of their rifles, goading them into the sweltering boxcars. Some resisted, digging in their heels. They screamed and flailed, fighting against the torrent of prisoners sweeping them toward the already crowded cars. In an instant the soldiers were on top of them, beating them to the ground, while dogs, straining at their steel leashes, snapped and snarled and tore at the stragglers. Weaving their way through the tumult, a handful of French Red Cross workers struggled to distribute food parcels to the desperate prisoners. Everywhere frantic hands reached out for them, imploring, but there were far too few.

Just in front of Roy the soldiers struggled to contain a swarm of women being funneled into the last five boxcars of the train. Some were pregnant, some were old, some seemed hardly more than children. A few sobbed and screamed. Others swore and spat at the soldiers, but most stumbled into the filthy boxcars in stony silence. Roy searched the sea of faces for Madame Geneviève, for Colette, but in the frenzied scene it was no use.

The boxcars were tiny by American standards, ten feet wide and no more than twenty-five feet long. A faded wooden sign affixed to each car read "40 *hommes*/ 8 *chevaux*," room for forty men or eight horses, the man next to him said. As Roy watched, dozens upon dozens of women disappeared into each car until they stood shoulder to shoulder, packed together like matches in a box. When not a single woman more could be wedged into the windowless cars, the soldiers slid the heavy wooden doors shut and bolted them. Roy could hear the shrieking and the pounding of fists from inside.

His group was next. The guards assembled them into a rough sort of order. Though some of the men clustered around him whispered and swore in French, most seemed to be Allied airmen, and as the guards turned to them, motioning them toward three boxcars just forward of the women, a voice rang out above the melee: "We are Allied military personnel." A short, broad-shouldered man stood facing the SS *Oberleutnant* in charge. His accent was Australian. "And we demand to be treated as such." A look of utter contempt flashed across the lieutenant's face. Beneath the black visor of his hat, his eyes narrowed, and he slammed his elbow into the prisoner's face, knocking him off his feet. He bent over the man. The veins in his neck bulged and sweat dripped off his nose. "*Schweinehund,*" he shrieked. "*Sie sind Terrorflieger*—baby murderers!—*Sie sollen alle einfach erschossen werden, und zwar sofort!*" He pulled a Luger from its holster on his waist and waved it wildly in the air. For an instant Roy thought they might all be shot on the spot, but the SS man stepped back, regained his composure, and began motioning the prisoners forward.

The soldiers continued to shove the men along, herding them into three boxcars just in front of those carrying the women prisoners. Before climbing inside, each man was issued a hard half loaf of bread, *Knäckebrot,* the Krauts called it. Some got a small can of meat—horse, someone speculated—and a few managed to grab a Red Cross parcel. The *Knäckebrot* was hard as a lump of coal, and Roy stuffed it hurriedly into his pants pocket.

Swept along by the flow of prisoners, he stepped into the boxcar just in front of him. It was already crowded, the men packed in like cattle, and still more prisoners were forced inside. Most had not bathed in days, in weeks, and under the black metal roof, the motionless air simmered. The stink was overwhelming. The only air came from two rectangular slits on the sidewalls close to the ceiling. No more than eight inches high and two feet long, they were crosshatched with barbed wire. At the center of the car stood two five-gallon pails, one filled with water, the other empty.

The wooden door rolled shut and locked. Pressed against one another so tightly they could barely move, the men stood in the sudden darkness, sweating. The only sounds were of German soldiers shouting back and forth to one another, and the clatter of their hobnail boots along the uneven cobblestones of the platform. The August sun beat down on the boxcars.

Parched and dizzy with heat, Roy squirmed for a little space. His shirt was plastered to his back and chest, and sweat streamed down his sides. His crotch was soaked, and the cloying stink of it, the taste of it clung to him like a mask. The man behind him rested his head on Roy's back. His hair was long and matted with filth. Roy jostled his shoulders to shake him off. The man moaned and reluctantly raised his head. Within seconds, Roy felt it fall again onto his shoulder blade. Again he shook it off, but it did no good.

Hours dragged by, and still the train did not move. All around him, men gasped in the suffocating heat, gulping for air. There was no room to sit or squat. Whenever anyone tried to climb up to the vent, desperate for a breath of air, the guards roared, motioning them to keep clear. Close by a man collapsed. His knees buckled and he slumped but, pinned between his companions, he could not drop. He stood unconscious in the crowd, his eyes rolling deep into his head. After weeks in Fresnes, many were suffering from dysentery, and the awful animal sounds and smells of their tormented bowels filled the fetid car. The pail for waste quickly filled, and the train had not yet left the freight yard. Tempers flared. Men snapped at one another, shouting senselessly.

"Sweet Jesus, you're pissing all over me!"

"He's pissing . . ."

"I can't help it."

"He's pissing all over everything . . ."

"Get off me, goddamn it, get your arm off."

"Why don't we move?"

"They're gonna fry us in here."

"Where are they taking us?"

"It don't much matter to me where the bleedin' sods take us as long as we get a move on."

"*Ils ne peuvent pas trouver une locomotive,*" someone muttered.

"What'd he say?"

"The railway workers are on strike," another French voice answered. "The *boches* cannot find a locomotive." Roy remembered seeing them, the tiny clot of railway workers cordoned off by the Germans, watching sullenly as the boxcars were being loaded. Maybe they would sabotage the train. Maybe it would never leave the freight yard.

Gradually the slant of the sun through the vents changed, and the light softened. Roy slipped his hand into his pants pocket, fumbling for the *Knäckebrot*. He tried to nibble at it, but it was dry and tough and he had no stomach for it. His mouth had no spit, and his tongue stuck to his teeth. He had no idea where the water pail was or if there was any water left. Beside him, a man raised his hand to his cracked lips and licked his own sweat. As he did, Roy watched three white specs dart along the man's scalp. Lice. He closed his eyes, fighting back a wave of nausea.

It had been dark for hours when the cars gave a sudden lurch and the couplings slammed and the train began to ease down the siding, inching its way out of the Pantin freight yard. In the pitch-black car, the movement brought a hint of fresh air through the vents overhead, and after hours of standing motionless, even the steady swaying brought a slight sense of relief. The train clattered along, creeping through the suburbs of Paris.

The train had just begun to pick up speed when it ground suddenly to a stop, and the men pitched forward. Far ahead of them they could hear shouting. Small-arms fire crackled, and muzzle flashes lit up the blackness. Hurried footsteps crunched in the gravel beside the boxcar. Pulling himself up to the forward vent, a man at the front of the car peered out. They listened in the darkness. "There's been an escape," he called out over his shoulder. He could not see what the commotion was, but word passed through the car that somewhere up ahead, in one of the French cars, some of the prisoners had gotten away. The Germans were looking for them.

A shaft of light swept suddenly across the vent, and the man dropped to the floor. The German voices boomed again, closer now, and lights flashed up and down the siding, slashing through gaps in the slats. No one in the crowded car moved. Roy could hear the commands, the metallic clatter of rifle bolts. Then nothing. Searchlights continued to rake the darkness, but the shooting stopped, the shouting faded. An hour passed, maybe more. Finally the train jerked forward. Slowly it picked up speed.

Everyone tried to settle down, slumping, squatting in whatever space they could secure, but for hours the train stopped and started, stopped and started, and at each jolting halt, the exhausted men toppled into one another, and the waste pail, already brimming, sloshed over. Frayed nerves snapped. A scuffle broke out in the impossibly cramped space. Bitter words passed in French and English, and a futile, foolish wave of shoving rustled through the car.

Gradually the jostling stopped, and the angry voices quieted, and an uneasy stillness settled over the car. The train rocked along. Bodies shifted and shuffled in the darkness as the men arranged themselves as best they could. The train continued to make frequent stops, pulling to the side while faster trains with higher priority rumbled by. Then it would lumber forward again. At each station, the men nearest the vent would try to see where they were or what time it was. They called the names of the towns and sometimes the hour. They were heading east, traveling at a snail's pace.

It was just after dawn when the plane attacked. Above the steady clatter of the rails, a shrill whining sliced through the morning air. Asleep on his feet, Roy snapped wide awake. An instant later thunderous bursts of automatic-weapons fire erupted around the train. The German guns scattered along the train opened up, firing off frantic volleys. The car shuddered and rattled. "We're being strafed," Roy heard himself mutter. The men hunched their shoulders and dropped their heads, huddling together even more tightly. Some covered their ears. Mustangs, he thought, they're probably Mustangs. Everything that moved in France was subject to Allied attack, and trains, especially slow-moving freight trains, made nice fat targets. The fighter boys loved them.

As suddenly as it began, the strafing stopped. The plane seemed to have made only one pass, roaring off to more pressing business. There were no casualties in the car, no damage as far as Roy could tell, but the men were shaken. "Sittin' fuckin' ducks," one of the men mumbled. His voice betrayed no fear, no panic, not even bitterness. A mere statement of fact. Roy looked at him without speaking. He nodded in agreement. It was a strange sensation, trundling along in a German train, with friendly fighters—Mustangs, Lightnings, Thunderbolts— taking their best shots at you. During the night there had been talk about the possibility of strafing, but no one really believed that the train would be on the move in the daylight. The Germans would surely know better. All along the road that paralleled the tracks, the burnt-out wrecks of other trains, trucks, and automobiles lay strewn in the early morning sun. But even after the attack, the train did not stop. It crawled at the same glacial pace, plowing east along the winding valley of the Marne.

In the late morning there was a commotion toward the center of the car. Voices were raised, one booming above the others. Roy could not see his face, but the voice was American. It commanded attention. No one had any idea where they were going or how long they would be in the train, the man said, but if they were going to be in this hell-hole for a while, they'd better get organized. There was a murmured ripple of agreement. After some jostling and confusion, a headcount was begun. Roy didn't hear the final figure, but when the count passed him, it was already over eighty. It took some time, but at last a system was devised so that each man could rotate to a position at one end of the car to rest. There he could stretch or sit, maybe even sleep for a few minutes. They would have to find a way to empty the waste bucket, and the water was going to be strictly rationed.

It was still early and the sunlight sluicing through the vents was bright and moist when everything went suddenly black, and the clattering of the wheels echoed like nails dropped down a well. Roy felt a sudden pressure in his ears. The train plunged deeper into the void, slowed, and suddenly the brakes let out a high metallic squeal. The men heaved forward. For several moments the train sat motionless. Then the wheels began to turn again, and slowly, laboriously, the train backed up. Still deep in the tunnel's darkness, it stopped. Something was wrong up ahead. One of the French prisoners was sure that the tunnel's exit had been blown. The resistance was everywhere along the route, he called out, excitement bubbling in his voice. The word had been passed to the maquis. They would never let the train reach Germany. A flurry of hope skittered through the car.

The train was stopped dead on the tracks, but its engine continued to churn, spewing smoke into the tunnel, thicker and thicker, roiling along the low tunnel ceiling, curling around the stalled train. The scent of it began to seep through the vents and slats, slowly settling in the cars. From up ahead, deeper in the tunnel, Roy could hear screaming, high-pitched and keening, and within minutes dense oily smoke billowed into the boxcar. All around him in the suffocating blackness men gagged and coughed. Fists pounded on the wooden walls. A whiff of hysteria swept the car.

Roy ducked his head and closed his eyes. The cloying fumes coated his mouth and tongue, scorching his throat. He tried to drop to his knees, hoping to find a pocket of air, but in the thicket of bodies there was no room. Arms and legs flailed at him in the darkness. The gray-black smoke coiled around him, squeezing the last air out of his saturated lungs. With his left hand he stretched his sweat-drenched shirt until he could hold it over his nose and mouth. He took a cautious breath. Then another.

The minutes staggered by like hours, and he drifted in and out of consciousness.

Finally, from somewhere deep in the tunnel a whistle screamed. The train stirred. He could feel it backing out of the tunnel. It was a very long train, but his car was toward the rear, and within seconds, tepid light from the vents filtered through the lingering smoke. The air began to clear, and sweaty, soot-streaked faces materialized all around him. The train stopped. All along the side of the track he could hear hurried footsteps and the usual guttural cries. Boxcar doors were sliding open. Then, with a screech of the rollers, the heavy wooden door beside him disappeared and a wave of fresh air gushed into the car and the men tumbled out between the bellowing guards.

Staggering forward, following the men in front of him, Roy stumbled away from the track, down a steep embankment and into a field. Over his shoulder he could see the long train, still spitting steam, poised at the entrance to the tunnel. One by one the Germans were emptying the boxcars, leading batches of prisoners into the broad meadow beside and below the tracks. Several carloads of prisoners were herded together into groups of about two hundred. The pails were emptied. A few men were chosen for a work detail and sent to unload the guards' equipment and baggage from the passenger carriages. Several more were selected to serve as hostages. If anyone tried to escape, a young officer explained, the hostages would be summarily shot. He spit out these warnings in German and halting French, but everyone understood.

Roy dropped to the ground with a groan. The air was moist and sweet and the field was fragrant with summer grass. Through a line of willows at the far end of the field he could see the bend of a river. It was the Marne, someone said. He squinted into the sunlight. His eyes were sore from the smoke. No one knew how long they had been in the tunnel, but the sun was high overhead now, and some believed it was two hours, maybe three. Roy had no idea, but at last he could breathe and stretch and sit. They were able to eat their meager rations. A muddy stream ran through the field, and the Germans sent men from each group to fetch water with the pails. Discolored and gritty with sediment, it was as sweet as nectar. Roy gulped it down, careful not to lose a drop. He gnawed at his stub of bread and took a tentative bite from the mysterious meat.

Milling about in the field, the prisoners talked, and, despite warnings from the guards, yelled back and forth from group to group. Some of the French prisoners were convinced that the mouth of the tunnel was blocked, that the maquis were all around them, that they would not be able to continue. The track to Nancy was being destroyed and, anyway, the Germans would never be able to find another train. The news was passed that the Allies had made another successful landing, this time in the south of France, near Marseilles, and were rapidly pressing northward. After their ordeal in the tunnel, the mood was good.

Roy had finished eating and the work parties were returning when the Germans assembled the men, boxcar by boxcar, and formed them into ranks of five. There would be a slight detour, the officer in charge explained. They would march about six kilometers, to the bridge at Tiernay. There they would cross the river. He reminded the men of the hostages and warned them again that any attempt to escape would mean death for their comrades.

Glumly the men and women formed up and began trudging forward in staggered batches of seventy or so. The pace was slow as the soldiers led them along a dusty country road that wound around the base of the tunnel and through a cut in the low hills, passing through several hamlets. They were smaller than Jouy, but the tightly clustered houses, crumbling plaster walls, and dusty streets gave Roy a pang. It seemed like a year since he had hidden in the blissful security of the École des Filles.

As the column entered the hamlets, people rushed from their houses to watch the sad procession. They smiled and called out to the prisoners. Some made the "V for victory" sign, others taunted the guards. In one village some tossed potatoes, apples, and small loaves of bread to the passing column. Others darted out from their doorways, carrying cups of water or cider, even wine, anything they could offer, before the Germans shooed them away. Once, while the soldiers were trying to restore order, a few prisoners slipped out of line at an ancient water pump beside the road and gave the handle a few frantic pumps. Jets of water gushed onto the filthy men and into the crowded road before the nervous guards roared forward, shoving the men back into line, threatening to shoot the lot of them.

At last the column reached a small road bridge over the river. It was badly damaged, no longer able to carry heavy traffic, but Roy and the others filed across and began walking along the far bank. They marched down a sunken road beside the slow-moving stream where the riverbank grass was the color of emeralds and cattails rustled in the shallows. They were doubling back, Roy realized, heading for a spot just opposite the tunnel. As they walked in the bright sunlight, they could see why the train had stopped. Just beyond the mouth of the tunnel, the railroad bridge was a skeletal hulk of curling spans and shattered timbers, and the hills on both sides of the river were pocked with craters. Shells had fallen in a village close by, and heaps of rubble from the shattered houses had cascaded into the narrow streets. "Would you look at that," a man just in front of him exclaimed, pointing to a tree a good forty yards from the riverbank. Hanging in its boughs, high above the ground, was a small rowboat.

In a cleft between two hills, a train had been backed up to the river just across from the tunnel, waiting on the approach to the destroyed bridge. It looked no different from the one the men had just left—a long dreary chain of grimy boxcars waiting in the shadow of the hills. "They found a train," Roy groaned, "the sons of bitches found a train."

As the column drew nearer the siding, he could see French Red Cross workers mingling with the waiting crowd. Most were women, and they carried containers of coffee and milk and cups of a watery lemon drink that tasted sweetly of saccharin. A few distributed the familiar Red Cross parcels containing fruit and nuts, sometimes even chocolate. How did they know we would be here, Roy wondered. Surely the resistance was behind this. Maybe they were watching right now, planning their next move. The train had been traveling eastward. He wondered if this was the territory controlled by Captain Paul.

The Germans began counting heads again, herding the prisoners into the cars. The process was slow and orderly, unlike the pandemonium at the station in Paris. Roy was among the first of his group to climb in. If anything, the car seemed even cruder and more cramped than the one they had just left. It was a genuine cattle car, recently occupied, and the ripe odor of the animals still lingered in the air. Clumps of fresh dung clung to the rough planking of the floor, and the first men aboard tried to scrape it out the open door.

The car did not have barbed wire over the vents, but the guards quickly produced a bundle. They chose one of the prisoners to string it up. Pressed against the wall of the car, Roy watched as a soldier

Roy Allen in crew training.
Ardmore, Oklahoma, 1943.
Private collection, May Allen

Roy Allen and crew after crash-landing May 28, 1944. Their faces reflect the ordeal they've just been through. Roy's anger at Colonel Luper is evident. Standing LEFT TO RIGHT: Colonel Luper, Roy Allen (pilot), Verne Lewis (copilot), Larry Anderson (bombadier), R. Grimes (tail gunner), Joe Brusse (navigator), J. Vaughn (left-waist gunner), Ray Plum (engineer). Squatting, LEFT TO RIGHT: W. C. Goldsborough (ball turret gunner), L. Henson (right-waist gunner), E. L. Smith (radio operator). *Private collection, May Allen*

Roy makes a successful one-wheel crash-landing in *Renee III* on May 28, 1944. Since the fuel was stored in the wings, the most common outcome of such a landing was a fiery explosion. "Roy saved our lives that day," Joe Brusse, *Renee III*'s navigator, said some fifty years after the event. "It was an amazing piece of flying." *457th Bomb Group Web site*

The wreckage of Roy's B-17 in a field near Jouy. *Private collection, Colette Loze*

Jouy-le-Châtel. The school where Roy was hidden is in the center-right, just beneath the prominent water tower. In the top-center, at the X, is Vimbre, the farm of Monsieur Pivert. *Editions Aériennes "CIM," Combier Imp. Mâcon*

Pierre Mulsant, aka Paul
Guerin, photographed in his
British uniform, London,
1943. *Private collection,
M. Ballaguet 1944*

Colette Florin sitting on the divan in the studio where Roy slept. *Private colletion, Colette
Loze*

The Florins stand-
ing on the front
steps of the forest
house. Roy jumped
out of the window
just behind
Monsieur Florin.
*Private collection,
Colette Loze*

Roy and an unidentified Allied airman on the day of their departure for Paris from Jouy. *Private collection, Colette Loze*

The main gate on the tower of KZ Buchenwald as it looks today from Caracho Weg. The camp's slogan, "Jedem das Seine" (To Each His Due), is found on the entrance gate below the tower. *Jürgen Maria Pietsch/Fotograf, Im Alten Pfarrhaus, 04509 Sproda*

ABOVE: Inside a barracks in the Little Camp, sketched by Auguste Favier. No photographs were allowed inside the camp while it was in operation. These 1944 sketches by Favier were illegal and, had the SS discovered them, would have meant torture and death. *Imperial War Museum, London*

LEFT: Denis "Charles" Barrett, sketched in Buchenwald by Auguste Favier on September 8, 1944. *Imperial War Museum, London*

BELOW: Pierre Mulsant, sketched in Buchenwald by Auguste Favier on September 11, 1944. *Imperial War Museum, London*

ABOVE: Prisoners in the Little Camp at the time of liberation. *National Archives, Washington, D.C.*

BELOW: Roll call in the Appellplatz, 1944, sketched by Auguste Favier. The X's on the back of some prisoners indicate a problem prisoner and a risk to attempt escape. *Imperial War Museum, London*

Stalag Luft III, winter 1944–45. *Private collection, May Allen*

May Allen and Roy Jr., March 1945. *Private collection, May Allen*

handed a man nearby a hammer and several strands of wire. The man was tall and thin and he complained to himself in French, but he did as he was told. He twisted the barbed wire into place, attached it to the first vent, and began to make his way to the second. Prisoners were still climbing aboard, crowding into the car. The pails were being handed in, the manure shoveled out, and for a moment the guard disappeared from view, lost in the shuffle. As Roy maneuvered to get a better look, the tall Frenchman suddenly bent down, and with the prongs of the hammer pried at the edges of a broad slat in the flooring. He worked quickly, skillfully, and in an instant it was loose. The man rose in a flash, stepped over to the second vent, and resumed his work. Other prisoners quickly closed around him, standing on the loose patch of flooring. They, too, spoke in French. The guard saw nothing.

The evening sun was disappearing behind the hills when the train at last lurched forward. The packed cattle cars were even more crowded than before. It didn't seem possible, but when they tried to establish some sort of order in the car, more than ninety men were counted. Roy began to work his way along the wall toward the tall Frenchman. It was tough going and men complained as he sidled forward, shouldering inch by inch closer to the Frenchman and the prisoners clustered around him. They were speaking in whispers as Roy drew near. He listened, unable to understand what they were saying.

"Nice work," Roy said at last, looking down at the floor, toward the spot where the loose planks, hidden now by the bodies of the men, would be. The tall Frenchman regarded him warily. He said nothing. "I wouldn't mind going, if you're planning an *excursion*," Roy whispered. He pronounced the word in the French way, knowing it from his outings with Jonckheere, and he grinned as he spoke it. A smile broke across the Frenchman's face. His sunken cheeks were sweat-stained and his heavy arched eyebrows seemed clotted with soot. "*Nous devons fuir,*" he whispered, "*et bientôt.*" He stared into Roy's eyes, his face only inches away. "We are heading to the east, toward the German frontier. If we are going to escape, we must do it now, while we are still in France." He estimated that they were still several hours west of Nancy. "Soon it will be dark, and we must go in the night. *Cette nuit.*"

They would have to proceed with great caution. They couldn't tell everyone of their plans. There might be a German plant in the car. Some of the men would be afraid of reprisals and try to stop them.

They might even alert the Germans. Only a few could be trusted. Escape while the train was stopped was impossible. Guards occupied every other car in the long train, and at each stop, they jumped down and made a thorough inspection. They checked the bolted doors, searched the spaces between the cars, and crawled up underneath, probing for holes in the flooring. No, they would have to make their move while the train was in motion. At the right moment, the loose planking would be shoved aside and the men would drop, one by one, onto the rail bed beneath the moving train.

In Paris, Roy noticed, the Germans had strung a sheet of barbed wire from the last car of the train. He had seen them working at it in the sweltering heat, though at the time he did not understand what it meant. Now he did. With the barbed wire dragging behind, no one could drop onto the tracks, wait for the train to pass overhead, and then sprint away. No one knew whether this train was similarly outfitted, but they couldn't take the chance. Each man would have to slip through the floorboards onto the railroad bed, then roll out between the moving wheels. There were many hills in Lorraine, the tall man said, especially on the approach to Nancy, and they would wait until the train was beginning the slow haul up a steep grade. This was their best chance.

Roy looked around the crowded car. He recognized faces but knew no one. There were some who, he was sure, would want to go with them, but they were too far away, impossible to reach. Still, the word was passed to a handful of men standing close by, and gradually a group of ten or so was maneuvered into position around the loose planking. Most were French. He watched their faces in the gathering dusk as they whispered among themselves. They waited.

After dark the train made several stops, and each time the guards took up positions beside the car. Lights swept all along the train during these surprise stops, and once there was shooting from somewhere far up ahead. Maybe someone else was making a break for it. Or maybe the guards simply fired into the night to impress the prisoners, to remind them that they were there, watching.

The train began to climb, struggling up and down a steady succession of low hills. Now, Roy thought, now will be the time. He tried to focus his eyes. Murky shapes jostled in the darkness. At length, the grade turned steep, and the train began to labor up a long incline, plodding slower and slower until it seemed to crawl. *"Vas-y,"* the tall man whispered, and the men lifted the loose slats and Roy felt the first man drop. They listened. They heard nothing, no shooting, no shouts, only the steady clatter of the rails. The train rattled on, straining with the hill. The next man dropped. Then another, and one by one, the men disappeared through the floor. Roy's gut tightened as he edged toward the black space beneath him. The hole was no more than two feet by two feet, and through it he could see flickering traces of the railroad ties. The metal grinding of the wheels seemed deafening. He felt lightheaded. Like jumping from the plane, he told himself, just like jumping from the plane. He crouched and took a deep breath. He braced himself. Suddenly a dark figure shouldered past him, squirming into the hole. Roy toppled backward. He could just make out the shape of a man's head and shoulders, could see his arms clamped on the floorboards. The man's legs were through the hole, but he would not let go. He would not drop. For an eternity he jogged crazily along, half in, half out. "Go on, for Christ's sake, go on," Roy whispered, but the man was frozen.

The train seemed to level out. Then, with a screaming of the brakes, it shuddered to a stop. Quickly Roy helped the man scramble back into the car, hauling him up out of the hole. They fumbled with the slats, sliding them back into place, but it was too late. Guards were everywhere, running alongside the train. Shots rang out and beams of light flashed across the vents. Within minutes, they could hear someone crawling in the gravel beneath them. The door rolled open, and brilliant, blinding light flooded the car. In an instant, guards leaped in, shoving their way through the huddled prisoners. They tramped about, kicking over the pails, scattering the puny bundles of food. It did not take them long to discover the loose floorboards and the hole.

While the officer in charge waited outside, the soldiers began a count, pushing the men one by one to the end of the car away from the hole. As they counted, another group of soldiers worked with the loose slats, nailing them back into place. *"Es fehlen sechs Gefangene,"* one of the guards shouted out. The officer listened to the report, studied the manifest, then glanced up at the boxcar filled with men. In the spectral glare of the lights, his waxen face loomed white as a corpse. Six men from the car were missing, but the officer was surprisingly subdued. He tapped a wooden walking stick smartly against his leg and spoke softly to his subordinates, issuing an order. Then he glided out of the halo of light, disappearing like an apparition down the track.

The men remained huddled at one end of the car, while two guards took up positions at the other, their black Bren machine guns trained on them. The door was left open as the train clanged into motion, and cool night air swept into the car. For now nothing was going to happen. The men tried to find a position to sleep, slumping in heaps on the floor. Whispered conversations drifted through the car. The guards had asked no questions, had interrogated no one. They had not tried to determine how the escape was organized or who had gotten away. But this was not the end of it. There would be trouble in the morning, Roy knew. He struggled to find a little space. Drained, dead on his feet, he tried to sleep.

At first light the train drew to a halt in the middle of a broad field. *"Zwanzig Franzosen, fünfunddreissig Terrorflieger,"* a voice boomed out, *"Zusammen wollen wir fünfundfünfzig Gefangene haben."* Soldiers appeared at the open door, climbed into the car, and began to sort the prisoners by nationality. An officer stood outside, watching carefully. He wore a green major's uniform with a black collar and silver piping, and he carried a heavy cane. Pale morning sunlight glistened off the gray bristles of his short military sideburns. He made a brief speech, then stopped and waited.

"They want twenty Frenchmen and thirty-five airmen," one of the prisoners translated. It was the Dutch officer from the RAF who had translated in the courtyard at Fresnes. "I have been instructed to tell you," the Dutchman continued, "that in order to prevent further escapes and to punish this car, twenty Frenchmen and thirty-five airmen will be shot." An angry groan went up from the crowd. Some of the Frenchmen made scornful gestures, spitting at the guards.

"Raus, ihr Schweine," a soldier shrieked from outside the car. *"Raus mit euch! Los!"* No one inside moved. The soldiers began shoving men from both groups forward toward the door. Others reached in, grabbing the closest prisoners by the ankles, and dragged them out. Roy felt a rifle stock across his back. A hand pushed him from behind. He resisted, digging in his heels, but the hand pushed harder, and he tumbled out into a rocky patch of earth beside the train. The soldiers pulled more and more men from the car, forming them into three ranks just beside the track, fifty-five in all. A detachment of soldiers stood at the ready, facing them.

The morning was bright and clear, not a trace of clouds in the blue sky. Dew glistened on the weeds. Roy stood in the third rank, toward the middle of the group. The soldiers were mounting two machine guns on tripods. A sickening fear spread through him. He felt himself begin to shake, first a slight tremor in his hands, then his legs. He closed his eyes. He had made one mistake after another—leaving Colette, trusting Captain Jacques, going with the Belgian woman— and now he was going to die in a French field, shot down in cold blood on a beautiful cloudless day thousands of miles away from home, from May, from a baby he would never see.

In front of him one of the Frenchmen began to mumble a prayer. Another joined in. One man sobbed.

"Before they start to fire, let's rush 'em," someone whispered. "When they clear the bolts. They can't get us all."

"Erste Reihe, ein Schritt vorwärts," a voice roared out, and the soldiers pushed the first row of prisoners forward, stepping briskly to the side to clear the line of fire. The machine guns swung into position. They took aim. Roy wondered if he could move, could charge the guns. Beyond the line of soldiers, a farmhouse, a field, the low morning sun hung motionless on the horizon, as still and vivid as a painting, the last things he would ever see. The major stepped forward and raised his arm. He snapped out an order. Roy clenched his teeth.

But the soldiers did not pull back the bolts. Instead, they rose from behind their weapons, leaping to attention. Roy looked on, unable to understand what was happening. The major motioned for the Dutch prisoner to come forward. They conferred for several moments. Then, without a backward glance, the major strode away.

The Dutchman turned to the prisoners waiting in the ranks beside the train. "The major has decided not to shoot you after all," he said. He seemed to be struggling with his voice. "The Herr Major has made his point. He hopes the lesson has been learned. But the next attempt to escape will bring the most severe punishment. For now," the man went on, "he has ordered you to remove all your clothes, along with everyone still in the car, and hand them over to the guards. They will be returned to you when we reach Germany."

A wave of relief washed over the men. Roy felt his body go limp. *"Ausziehen,"* the soldiers shouted, *"schnell."* With their rifles they prodded the men beside the train. *"Deshabillez-vous!* You undress!" Dazed and trembling, the men began to strip. They wrapped their soiled clothes into bundles and left them in the gritty dust where they stood. Stark naked, they scrambled back into the car. The guards were already collecting the clothes of the other prisoners in the car, tossing the squalid bundles out into a pile beside the train. When they had finished and the naked prisoners were rammed shoulder to shoulder into the cramped car, the soldiers jumped down. Before sliding the door shut behind them, they kicked out the waste and water pails.

The train rolled forward, gradually picking up speed. The sun had risen in the cloudless sky, and in the steamy cattle car the men suffered in silence. Sweat poured from their pallid bodies, and the stench hung in the stillness, more unbearable than ever. They rode through the long hot afternoon in a cloud of misery. Roy was lucky. He found himself pressed against the wall of the car, and some air slipped through the uneven slats. He tried to remember the old neighborhood, the smell of the stable behind Beck's Produce on Cayuga, the crowded number-six trolley on Ogantz Avenue, sledding with May in Fisher's Park, anything to hold on to, anything that would blot out the sight of the black machine guns on their tripods and the soldiers crouching behind them. But the images were jumbled. The hours passed. He leaned against the wall, drifting into a shallow slumber, snapping awake whenever the car swung or slowed or stopped.

It was high afternoon when the train halted. Roy could hear the guards taking up their positions outside the car. Someone climbed up to peep out the narrow vent. From his position slumped against the wall Roy could see him clinging to the lip of the vent like a fly. It was forbidden to look out the vents. The guards had warned them repeatedly, but whenever the car stopped or pulled into a station, someone would climb up and steal a peek. Suddenly, a blast of gunfire ripped the car. Bullets thumped into the roof, ricocheted. The figure at the vent tumbled backward, yelping in pain. Outside the guards were shouting. Within seconds the door rolled open.

The guards were looking for the man at the vent. "He's hit," someone called out. "The kid needs help." Reluctantly the bodies parted, and a figure stumbled forward. His dirty face was thin and pale. He didn't look old enough to shave. "The boy's knuckles are torn up," one of the prisoners said. "He needs medical attention." The guards brushed past without a word. They pulled the naked boy from the car, hurling him to the ground. As he lay sprawled in the dust, they grabbed him beneath the arms, and then yanked him to his feet. An officer stepped forward, towering above him. The boy looked up, clutching his hand to his chest. Blood ran between his fingers and along his forearm.

"*Franzose?*" the *Oberleutnant* snarled. The boy was terrified. He could not answer.

"Engländer?"

"Français," the boy stammered at last. His eyes were wide and his hands were shaking. *"Je suis Français."*

The officer looked the boy over with a cold stare. He nodded to the two soldiers and said something. The men in the car watched through the open door.

The soldiers motioned the boy toward the slope beside the rail bed. The boy looked confused. With his hands raised, he took a tentative step, then another. Then he turned and glanced back at the soldiers. One nodded his head. "Go on," the gesture seemed to say. "Go on down the slope into the field." The boy hesitated, then turned back to the field. As he did, the soldier closest to him raised his rifle, and with a swift motion fired point-blank into the boy's back. The boy lurched forward. Another shot rang out. The boy seemed to rise on his tiptoes. He flung out his arms. Then his knees buckled and he tumbled down the slope, sliding to a stop in the dust and short ragged weeds below the track.

The officer strode calmly down to the body. He studied the boy for a moment, and then with the toe of his boot he flipped him over onto his stomach. Then he pulled his Luger from its holster, leaned down until the muzzle almost touched the back of the boy's head and pulled the trigger. The shot crackled, and the boy's head exploded.

The men in the train watched in stunned silence. No one moved. The officer gave the order for a burial detail, and two naked prisoners were hauled out of the open car. The soldiers thrust small shovels into their hands, and the men stumbled down the slope to the body. The soil was dry and hard, and they hacked away, scooping out a hole no more than spade deep. The guards were impatient, goading them along. The men placed the boy's body in the depression and covered it as best they could. Then the soldiers hustled them back into the car, closing the door behind them. They left no marker, no identification, nothing. The train churned again into motion. Staring through the narrow space between the slats, Roy watched as the shallow grave slid past. Jutting plaintively through the upturned, discolored earth rose two hands and a foot, white, imploring, silent.

Light turned to darkness, then to light again. Another day passed, then another. Roy was numb with weariness. Desperate for water, his lips were cracked, his stomach cramped. He had not eaten in two days. A man forward in the car went into shock. His eyes widened, then disappeared back into his head. His limbs stiffened. The men closest to him massaged his arms and legs, slapped his cheeks. They rubbed his forehead. In the stifling heat his skin was as cold as marble. Slowly he came around.

Roy was not awake when the train crossed into Germany. Someone said they were at Saarbrücken, but he did not see it. Through the cracks he caught glimpses of neatly cultivated fields and hillsides covered with vines. He saw a river, long black barges. Once inside Germany, the guards seemed to relax. They returned the prisoners' clothing. The pails reappeared. The train made more frequent stops, and the men were allowed out for short stretches. There was water, and at one stop even a bit of food.

The train was still progressing eastward. Some in the car were convinced that they were bound for Dulag Luft. Roy recognized the name. All fliers had been briefed about it. Dulag Luft was a big interrogation center for Allied airmen somewhere near Frankfurt. It was staffed by Luftwaffe professionals, not Gestapo thugs. They were expert interrogators, clever, tricky. They knew how to get guys to talk. Just a tidbit here, another there, nothing that seemed very important, but little by little they pieced things together. It was amazing how much they knew about Allied air units and personnel. After processing at Dulag Luft, the prisoners would be shipped off to different POW camps scattered around the Reich, officers to their stalags, enlisted men to theirs. Everyone was eager to be out of the train, and at Dulag Luft they would be out of Gestapo hands.

But the train did not stop in Frankfurt. It rumbled through the shattered station and block after blackened block of the devastated city with hardly a pause. They were swinging to the northeast— Hanau, Fulda, Gotha, Erfurt, men called out the names of the towns as they slid by. The French prisoners were bound for labor camps, everyone understood this, but what about the airmen? The Germans knew that they were military personnel. The interrogators at Fresnes had acknowledged as much. The men discussed the possibilities, but no one had an answer. A grim uneasiness descended on the car.

Early on the morning of the fifth day, the train slowed and eased into a station. Signs in stark black letters read Weimar. The name meant nothing to Roy. Near Leipzig, someone said, in Thuringia. The train stood motionless in the station, wheezing steam. It was an unusually long stop. At length they felt a jolt, and wheels stirred beneath them. Still, they did not move. Word filtered down the line that the last cars of the train—those occupied by the women—were being uncoupled. Another locomotive had pulled into the station and was taking them to a labor camp for women, the French prisoners agreed. Some of the women were allowed to move down the platform in search of their loved ones—husbands, brothers, fathers—held in some other part of the train. Roy could see them on the platform. He could hear their frantic cries as they ran from car to car. They were saying farewell.

Just before noon the train backed out of the station. It crept through the nearly empty rail yard, swinging at last onto a solitary spur that led away from the town. It began to climb. In the car men peered through the cracks and from the vents. They were passing through a dark forest, groaning up a steep hill. There was something about the single track, the slow, deliberate movement of the train that seemed to suggest that they were nearing their final destination. The train leveled, passing through the pillars of a gate, a high fence of electrified wire, guard towers. A hush fell over the car.

Inside the fence a crew of men in threadbare blue-and-white striped uniforms worked beside the track. "*On se trouve où?*" someone from the car called out. Roy strained to see through the slats. One man, a skeleton with a shovel in his gnarled fingers, stopped his work and looked up. His ragged clothes hung on him like a scarecrow. His face was sallow, his cheeks sunken. He stared without expression at the anxious faces in the vent. "*Wo sind wir, Kamerad?*" someone yelled from the car. "Where are we?" The man's thin lips parted. From his black toothless mouth he uttered a word Roy did not quite catch. "*Wo?*" the voice from the car repeated. "What is this place?" The car was slipping slowly past, the crew of shabby workers fading behind.

As he disappeared from view, the scarecrow spoke again, words called out over the steady clatter of the wheels and the electric hum of the fence. "Buchenwald," Roy heard him say. "*Konzentrationslager* Buchenwald."

PART IV

BUCHENWALD

CHAPTER 10

Jedem das Seine

August 20–September 9, 1944

From far behind them a whistle screamed. The train ground to a halt, and the men shifted uneasily. Above their groans and whispers, their awkward shuffling, Roy could hear shouting, the barking of dogs, hurried footsteps. With a crash, the door rolled open, and the men, squinting in the harsh afternoon light, spilled out onto the cobblestone platform. Armed guards swarmed around them, roaring. Some stood back, their weapons trained on the stunned prisoners; others rushed forward, swinging truncheons. Dogs, straining at their leashes, snapped and howled. Across the tracks, cordoned off by a wire fence, dozens of ghostly figures, specters in striped rags, were working around a series of high colorless sheds—a factory complex, parts of it still under construction. Some strained behind crude wheelbarrows filled with stone; others wielded picks or shovels. Their movements were agonizingly slow, as if laboring underwater. A few paused to stare.

The guards herded the prisoners into a street just beyond the platform, assembling them into ranks of ten abreast. Within minutes the formation began to move, marching slowly at first, then, at the prodding of the guards, at double time. Famished and weak, the men straggled along, stumbling as they tried to jog over the roughly paved road. Rounding a bend, they passed through a set of gates anchored in the center by a large Nazi eagle and entered a corridor of

253

well-maintained buildings. Here the surface of the road was paved and smooth. Geraniums sprouted from window boxes; curtains fluttered in the open windows. Men in SS green and black came and went, paying no attention to the parade of prisoners. A tall hand-carved signpost, so brightly colored it might have been a totem pole, depicted a scene of three prisoners rushing along the road. Beneath the painted figures, a sign in Teutonic script told them they were on something called Caracho Weg.

For three hundred yards the men struggled along the straight road. Trucks and a few staff cars rumbled by. On the left stood a motor pool, with a set of gas pumps and a bustling garage. Then the road swung into a graceful curve, past a grove of trees and the entrance to some sort of park. Roy thought he could make out a sign: *Zoologischer Garten.* A zoo? The column bunched and slowed. Across a wide plaza a massive gatehouse of dark wood and stone appeared, rising from the black pavement like a medieval fortress. At its center was a low portal, the entrance filled by a gate of crosshatched iron bars. The wings of the fortress were thick and forbidding, their windows covered with steel shutters. A high fence, its electrified wires held in place by concrete stanchions that curved inward at the top, extended out from the wings as far as the eye could see. A string of sturdy watchtowers, spaced at fifty-yard intervals, jutted high above the fence, and sunlight glinted off the searchlights and the muzzles of the machine guns housed there.

The lead elements of the column stopped in front of the gatehouse. Above the portal, a handful of SS officers lounged on a broad, banistered balcony, looking over the railing at the prisoners. Crowning the gatehouse, a clock tower rose above them, its eaves studded with searchlights and loudspeakers. It was exactly 12:30. From his position toward the rear of the column Roy watched a contingent of guards from the train conferring with their counterparts at the gate. The officer in charge was handing his prisoners over to the camp authorities. The men waited, sweating in the mounting heat. Finally, the formation stirred, inching forward. The camp guards were counting them, over a thousand men, as they stepped, five abreast, through the open gate. As Roy passed through the cordon of guards into the shadow of the portal, his eyes fastened on an inscription, forged in black iron, at the very center of the gate's grating. *Jedem das Seine,* the words read. He had no idea what they meant.

Reassembled, the men found themselves in a vast parade ground that sloped downward at a surprisingly steep pitch. Beyond it, row after row of long low buildings receded in arcs toward a line of distant watchtowers. A fringe of dark trees, black even in the murderous sunlight, hung on the horizon. Scattered across this desolate expanse, gaunt, disheveled figures hovered like phantoms. They stood or squatted between the grim wooden buildings or shuffled from place to place with no apparent purpose. Closer at hand, a crude platform stood like a monument in the midst of the parade ground. A gallows.

Escorted by guards, the column turned right and, following a roadway that paralleled the fence, marched toward a squat A-frame building. A massive soot-stained chimney rose from the building's tile roof, spitting coils of smoke into the sky and choking the humid air with a putrid stench. Just past the building, the column wheeled left down a broad street. A procession of larger buildings—a kitchen, a coal depot, and a laundry—slid by. In front of the laundry stood a solitary oak. Offering the only bit of greenery in sight, it seemed more like a monument than a living thing. On his right, beyond the electrified fence, Roy could make out what appeared to be another industrial site.

As the men walked down the hill, skeletal figures seemed to materialize from nowhere, lining the roughly paved street. Their faces were drawn and ashen, scarred with sores and blisters. Their emaciated limbs swam in the filthy threadbare uniforms. Most shambled along in stiff wooden clogs; others had bundled their feet in rags or newspaper tied with string. Round striped caps topped their heads, though some wore nothing, their skulls straining against the taut, closely cropped skin of their scalp. A few called out, asking in French for news of the war. Most simply stared in silence from the barren spaces between the clustered buildings. No trees dotted the roadway; no grass grew there. The very earth underfoot, rough and gray and flecked with black, seemed scorched, like a field of volcanic ash. In the ranks no one spoke.

The head of the column halted in front of a low stone-and-plaster building. A massive, four-story structure towered beside it. Roy could just make out a commotion far ahead. At the head of the column, thirty, maybe forty men were being shoved inside the building. The others waited. After a time, the guards ushered another group inside. Then another. No one emerged from the building.

The men watched and waited in the unrelenting sun as group after group of prisoners disappeared through the wide doors. The column grew shorter. From time to time they caught sight of naked men darting from a small building close by into another, shepherded by prisoner-guards in the striped uniforms, wearing black armbands on their sleeves. No one knew what it meant.

An hour dragged by. Then another. Four o'clock, four-thirty. The guards gave the men permission to sit in place while they waited. Those who had somehow managed to hold on to a bit of food ate it. Some produced cigarettes from their sweat-soaked shirts. A feeble vapor of blue smoke trailed along the column, as cigarettes were passed from man to man. While the men waited, the ranks inched slowly forward, and the ghostly figures from the parade ground and nearby barracks drifted steadily closer. Like predators at the edge of a forest clearing, they watched with ravenous eyes as the smoke from the cigarettes rose and the men gnawed at the wretched lumps of *Knäckebrot* and the spoiled potatoes hoarded from the trip. The guards shooed them away, but always they returned.

Rumors floated up and down the ranks. Some of the French prisoners knew this place. They had heard of it in resistance circles. It was a labor camp, one of the biggest, one of the worst. Political prisoners were sent here from all over Europe. No one returned. They would all be shot, probably in short order, or die at hard labor. Someone claimed that the Germans gassed prisoners. Roy had heard his friends in Paris speak of such places, labor camps in the Reich where *résistants* were sent, stories of torture and terrifying executions, but he had never heard of any gassing. He did not believe it.

The SS had arranged it so that the last ranks of the dwindling column were almost entirely Allied military personnel, and while the men waited, they counted off, each man giving name and rank. One hundred and sixty-eight men strong, they quickly determined that a broad-shouldered man with long sandy hair and what Roy took for an Australian accent was the ranking Allied officer. Roy recognized him as the man who had challenged the German guard at the station in Paris, demanding that the men be treated as Allied officers. His face still bore the ugly red gash he received as a response. The man's name was Phil Lamason; he was an RAF pilot from New Zealand, a squadron leader. As the men baked, he paced up and down beside them, talking. The Germans, no matter how they blustered, know who we are, Lamason said. The Gestapo officer in charge of the train had admitted as much, with his threats about *Terrorflieger,* and the camp officials knew it, too. So, while in this camp, the men would conduct themselves as soldiers. They would maintain their military discipline and bearing. At every opportunity he would press their case, insist that they be treated as prisoners of war, according to the Geneva Convention, and be removed from this place as soon as possible. They can't keep us here long, he said, but as long as the bastards do, the men should act as a military unit.

It was late afternoon when Roy approached the entrance to the building. Exhausted and nervous, he stepped with his group into a large brick-floored anteroom. A man in a striped uniform with a black armband spat out an order. "*Auskleiden,*" he said. He, too, was apparently a camp prisoner, though healthier and better fed than the wretches lining the street outside. Other similarly clad prisoners stepped forward to hand each man a coat hanger, a length of string, a small paper bag, and a label. The man in charge motioned for the men to strip. "*Taschen leer machen,*" he bellowed, reaching into his pockets and turning them inside out. The men were to place their clothes on the hanger and their valuables in the bag. To Roy's astonishment, some of the men still had money, watches, fountain pens, even a penknife or two. They were to tie the bag to the hanger, write their name on the label and attach it to the bag. The prisoner orderlies made a careful inventory, recording every penny, every centime, and every guilder by the prisoner's name in a large ledger. Roy had nothing; everything had disappeared at Fresnes. Still, when he had finished, he handed over his stained, foul-smelling bundle and was given a numbered metal disc as a receipt.

Naked now, clutching the metal discs in their hands, the men followed an orderly into an adjoining room. A dozen or so prisoners were waiting for them. They stood ankle deep in hair beneath a series of clippers that dangled from the ceiling on long electric cables. Along with the others, Roy was shoved forward. A prisoner grabbed him by the shoulders, turned him, and sat him down on a bench. With brutal efficiency he whipped the clippers roughly over Roy's head from back to front and back again. The clippers sliced into his ears. Tufts of filthy matted hair cascaded to the floor. Without pausing, the clippers swept downward. Roy felt them plow through the thick stubble of his face. They gouged under his arms, over his chest. "*Aufstehen,*" the prisoner said. He motioned for Roy to climb up on the bench, to turn around, to bend over. The clippers jabbed into his crotch, snagging, ripping free. They seemed to be tearing the hair out by the roots. The buzzing continued down his legs, across the tops of his feet. "*Fertig,*" the prisoner snapped, pushing Roy off the stool. *"Der Nächste,"* he called out, motioning toward the next man in line. The shearing had taken less than two minutes.

Nicked and bleeding, hairless as worms, the group moved quickly to the next station. A prisoner sat on a stool with a large bucket of evil-smelling liquid in front of him. In his hand he held a thick brush. Raise your arms, spread your legs, he gestured, and, one after another, the men reluctantly spread-eagled. Dipping the brush into the bucket, the prisoner slapped it along Roy's armpits, then sloshed the dripping swab into his crotch. With a last jab, he swiped the bristles along Roy's anus. A scalding flash shot through him. His eyes blurred. He jumped and wheeled around, letting out a yelp. Oblivious, the man with the brush was already busy with his next customer.

Prodded by an orderly, the men hurried along another corridor. *"Eine Dusche. Jetzt eine Dusche,"* another prisoner called out, trying to explain. He spoke an incomprehensible something, Polish maybe, or even Russian. He pressed a stub of rough soap into Roy's hands, and the men were pushed into a large white-tiled shower room. Pipes ran along the ceiling. Dozens of showerheads hung overhead. Doors closed behind them, and the men, their plucked bodies streaked with disinfectant, stood packed beneath the sprinklers. The cement floor was damp and sticky. For several minutes nothing happened. Roy burned from head to foot. He seemed to have razor slashes, each thin as a paper cut, under his arms, on his throat, his face. His balls stung. He ran his hand across his strange, smooth scalp. Here and there patches of stubble remained, missed by the barber's shears. He hardly recognized the feel of his own body. Staring up at the grid of black pipes just above him, he waited. Then, with a sudden rattle, a burst of steaming spray shot from the nozzles, flooding down.

Shocked by the sudden warmth, Roy hardly moved. Steam filled the room. He sighed, closing his eyes. He could not remember when he had last felt warm water. Gripping the soap, he tried to scrub. Hard as a pebble, it would not lather. He rubbed it across his face and chest, between his legs, trying to remove weeks of sweat and grime, to stop the stinging. The hot water poured down on his shaved head, coursing over his shoulders and down his back. The sensation was delicious. For a brief moment he was lost in mindless reverie. He could feel his cramped muscles trying to relax. Abruptly, the nozzles coughed, the spray seemed to stagger, then a jet of frigid water shot over him. He jumped away, but even the startling cold was welcome. Then the water stopped. Dripping wet, the men were ordered out of the shower room. At the doorway, an orderly handed each man a thin, threadbare towel, small as a handkerchief. Little more than a rag, Roy's was still wet from the previous user.

Next the prisoner orderlies rushed the dazed men outdoors, then into a large building, up a staircase, and into a large supply room. Here other prisoners stood behind a long wooden counter, piles of clothing stacked neatly in bins behind them. The men were lined up single file, then hurried down the counter. As they passed, the prisoners tossed items at them: a shirt or jacket, a pair of pants, a cap, some bearing the familiar vertical stripes of faded blue. They paid no attention to size or shape. Each man received whatever was at the top of the stack. The orderlies issued no underwear and no shoes, not even the crude wooden clogs worn by the prisoners.

At the end of the room, the men were herded together and ordered to dress. Roy looked down at the items in his hands. Tattered and frayed, they smelled strongly of disinfectant. The pants were a bit short, not quite reaching his ankles, and the waist, held by a fragile button, would hardly close. No belt was issued. The crotch and seat bore faded stains he did not want to think about. The coarse collarless shirt fit as tight as a hand-me-down glove. A crude patch over one elbow was already unraveling.

Harried by the orderlies, the men scrambled into their clothes. For several moments each of them was absorbed with his own garments, twisting, stretching, struggling to get comfortable in the ill-fitting assortment he had been given. Then, one by one, they looked up. Blinking, they stared at one another in stunned, uncomprehending silence. They stood in a small uneven circle, each man surrounded by the chalk-faced, hairless creatures who had stared at them from beyond the barbed wire, who had shambled across the parade ground, or haunted the empty spaces along the road, watching them eat. Then it sank in. "Oh, God," someone muttered, "oh, God."

"*Mützen auf,*" the orderly shouted, pointing them toward a door at the end of the room. "*Man muss die Mützen tragen,*" he said impatiently, as if speaking to children. He pointed to the cap Roy held in his hand. Roy patted it into place on his head. "*Mützen ab,*" the orderly bellowed, swiping the cap off again. He looked around at the new men. Did they get it? "*Mützen auf,*" he repeated, barking out the order, and the men slapped the caps back on. Satisfied with the lesson, the orderly opened the door, and the group stepped out of the building into the early evening twilight.

Others, dressed in the same shabby, ill-fitting uniforms, waited for them there, re-formed into ranks of five abreast. Orderlies wearing black armbands shouted out orders, and the column churned into motion. Barefoot, they labored up the rough street toward the parade ground and were again counted through the portal of the gatehouse.

The column halted at the entrance to a low wooden building close to the gatehouse, and the men were led in small groups into a large office. At one end of the room six prisoners in black berets and armbands sat behind tables covered with papers. Six lines of prisoners stood before them. Typewriters clattered. A hum of different languages filled the room. After some jostling, it became apparent that the new arrivals were expected to fall in, to take their place in the lines. This was the *Politische Abteilung*, the Political Department, someone explained. They would be processed, personal data taken, and registered officially as prisoners of the camp.

As Roy watched the lines creep forward, the men whispered back and forth. Virtually everyone in his group seemed to be a flier, and word passed along the line that each man should give only name, rank, and serial number, nothing more. They should demand to be treated as prisoners of war. Already Roy could see trouble at the head of the line. One man after another was pulled aside, harangued briefly by a burly prisoner who seemed to be in charge. Towering behind the six seated prisoners, he slammed his fist on the table and screamed at one of the men in line, an American Roy recognized from the train. The prisoner swaggered and bullied, but the American remained unmoved. The prisoner conferred with his colleagues sitting behind the table. Finally, he waved the flier aside. Then another, and another, over and over again down the line.

When Roy reached the front of his line, the weary prisoner seated behind the table, an older man with ink-stained fingers, a fountain pen, and a sheaf of printed forms, asked him something in French, then in German, and waited. Roy spat out his name, rank, and serial number. The prisoner hardly looked up. Switching to English, he asked question after question—parents, profession, age, and address. He spoke slowly, in heavily accented English, but he no longer expected answers and Roy gave none. When he reached the end of his questions, the man looked up and sighed. "Very well," he said, and scribbled something on the form: *Feindflieger.* Enemy flier. From a stack on his left, he produced a small white patch. "For your uniform," he said, handing it to Roy. It bore a number in bold black letters. 1st Lt. Allen, Roy W., USAAF, serial number 0753841, was now Buchenwald camp prisoner number 78357. He joined the others.

It was almost dark when the column re-formed on the road. A group of SS guards was waiting for them. Each carried a wooden club the size of a pickax. "*Schnell,*" they howled, rushing at the men. "*Los, ihr Schweine.*" The column staggered into motion, trotting raggedly toward the main gate. The guards swarmed all around them, laughing and screaming, swinging their clubs at stragglers. Their speech was slurred; they seemed drunk.

Beyond the portal, the column rejoined the French prisoners from the train, and together they marched across the empty parade ground. Heading down the slope, they plunged into the cluster of gloomy wooden barracks. From the shadowy doorways prisoners called to them in a multitude of languages, asking for news of the war. Would it be over soon? Where were the Allies? Was Paris still in German hands?

Finally, the column passed through several rows of larger two-story concrete barracks, slipped down a slight embankment, and halted in front of a wire fence. They were counted through a gate, trudged on through a thicket of dark stablelike structures, dilapidated wooden shacks, and coils of barbed wire laced with windblown trash and scattered straw. The posts holding the wire in place were not the solid concrete stanchions from the camp perimeter but crude wooden poles. Some tilted and pitched at odd angles; the wire sagged in spots. Rats scurried along the ravines.

Still descending, the road gave way to a rough dirt-and-gravel path. The men encountered another fence, another gate. They were counted through again, and led into an open compound. They were at the absolute bottom of the camp. Dark forms stood or sat or squatted everywhere in the moonlight. Some were trying to sleep, curled as tight as snails in the open. Some clutched blankets in their hands; others were covered with tattered sacks or bits of straw. A handful of large military tents, like circus big tops, rose from the rocky black clay. Men were pulling at the flaps, trying to get inside for the night. A small stone hut, no larger than a truck, stood in an open space between the tents. It was the only permanent structure in sight. A string of red lights dotted the black horizon.

The French prisoners from the train had already crowded into the tents, so the airmen, following a prisoner guard, picked their way gingerly through the throng. Snatches of French, Polish, Russian, Hungarian rose from the huddled figures all around them. The guard led them to a patch of rocky ground near the stone hut. Its surface seemed to consist of cobbles and shattered rock. Word passed down the line: they would sleep here. No blankets, no bedding. They were to make themselves as comfortable as possible.

While the men were settling in, trying to find space on the broken stones, a tub of soup arrived, hauled into the compound by a team of prisoners. Battered tin bowls and a few gnarled spoons materialized. They stood in line in the darkness. The soup was thin and tepid, and lumps of god-knows-what floated in it. But it was almost warm, and they gulped it down.

The night was mild. Above them stars glittered in a clear sky. Roy crouched on a patch of cobblestones, trying to pry several uneven ones loose, hoping to smooth out a place where he could sleep. Men from the train were all around him. Exhausted by their ordeal, some had already collapsed into sleep, stretched out like corpses in a morgue. Others whispered to one another: What was this place? What were they in for tomorrow? Roy lay back, unfurling his legs. His feet were bleeding and black with dust. Turning on his side, he slipped an arm under his head. Rocks jutted into his ribs. He closed his eyes. From across the crowded compound groans and cries drifted like dust. Shouts flared in the darkness, then subsided. Exhausted, he slept.

It was still dark when a commotion rustled through the compound, and Roy jerked awake. He was stiff and cold, wet with morning dew. All around the tents dark forms were moving, thousands of men shuffling, shambling, limping across the bleak terrain, forming at last into rough squares. Many appeared in the striped uniforms, or parts of it, but others wore every assortment of ragged clothing—military caps, berets, misshapen jackets, tattered trousers, woolen knickers, a baker's tunic, even a priest's cassock.

Guards in black berets swarmed around them, screaming. *"Appell, Appell!"* The guards wore black armbands, *"Lagerschutz,"* prison guard, printed in bold white letters across them. Prodded and harassed, the prisoners drifted into a large assembly area beside the tents and formed up in ranks of twenty. Roy and the other fliers remained motionless on the mound between the tents, not knowing what to do. No *Lagerschutz* came for them, no SS men. They watched the spectacle unfold below them.

The *Lagerschutz* were yelling incomprehensible instructions, motioning men into position. *"Rückwärts, ihr Vögel! Du, Drecksau, aufrechthalten! Achtung! Maul halten, du!"* Gradually, the open area filled. Over two thousand prisoners stood at something like attention. A group of SS men, some carrying a riding crop or whip or short rubber club, appeared on the path between the tents, sauntering toward the formation. As they approached, someone shouted: *"Mützen ab,"* and the ranks of silent men swiped the caps from their heads in unison. The SS halted in front of the formation and conferred with a prisoner who seemed in charge of the roll call. *"Mützen auf,"* the prisoner roared suddenly, and hundreds of arms swung upward, replacing the caps. Within seconds, the *Lagerschutz* fanned out through the formation. They seemed to be counting.

An hour passed, then another, and the count continued. The prisoners stood at rigid attention, waiting. Occasionally men shifted their weight or shook their heads. The sun rose over the enclosure. Morning shadows appeared. Down each rank, the counting continued, with painstaking thoroughness. As the *Lagerschutz* counted, the SS men swaggered through the formation, jabbing at men who slouched or had fallen to their knees in exhaustion. Roy watched as one of the SS with a club in his hand stopped suddenly and spun around. Diving into the ranks, he swooped down on a prisoner, roaring and flailing at him with the club. Between the shaved heads Roy watched the club rise and fall, and in the sudden silence heard the sickening thud, the pitiful groans.

Roy could see, at the fringes of the formation, several corpses laid out neatly side by side. Flies swarmed over them, crawling across their necks and feet, skittering over their lips and sunken, unblinking eyes. The *Lagerschutz* paused above them momentarily. They, too, were counted. The roll call went on and on. At one point a burst of shouting erupted from the front of the formation. Roy leaned forward trying to hear. "They've made a mistake," one of the men behind him said aloud. "The count doesn't tally. They're going to start over again."

Time crawled by. One prisoner in the ranks, a Frenchman Roy recognized from the train, soiled himself. Like so many, he suffered from dysentery. Crumpling slightly, he let out a series of low agonizing moans. The awful smell wafted through the ranks. Several SS quickly descended on him, joking and taunting, jabbing him in the gut. The man groaned piteously, his bowels emitting horrible sounds. But he did not fall out. He held his place, standing as erect as he could until the SS, smirking but disappointed, lost interest and drifted away.

Finally, the count was completed. An order boomed over the formation, and the gray-brown mass of men dissolved into chaos as the prisoners streamed away from the roll call area in every direction. Within minutes, a detail of prisoners tugging a large aluminum tub arrived. The tub, a fifty-liter vat, contained a dark pungent liquid, cold as a dead fish and identified by the prisoners who carried it as coffee. A number of crude bowls, *gamelles*, appeared. Every man was supposed to have one, but only a few could be rounded up.

The detail also handed out miniature loaves of bread, gray/black and tough as horsehide. Roy could see coils of sawdust in the moldy grain. Famished, he tore into it, trying to chew. A dry, rancid taste filled his mouth, and he gagged. All around him men were spitting it out. One man tossed his loaf away in disgust. Instantly several other prisoners who had hovered around the men dove for it, shoving each other aside to get at it. A young boy scooped it from the rocks and tried to gobble it down. Another prisoner tore at his fingers; another, draped over his back, clawed at the boy's face. While they scuffled, others closed in, watching the men eat.

As the morning wore on, other prisoners drifted by to stare at them. Were they really Americans? Really RAF? Some wanted to talk, testing their English. Poles with relatives in Chicago, Czechs who had visited Toronto or New York. They asked questions and offered advice, trying to give the newcomers the lay of the land. A few offered spoons, a cracked *gamelle*, even cigarettes, which, they explained, were like gold. They could be bartered.

At noon, the tub appeared again, this time containing soup. The thin broth was watery, laced with dehydrated vegetables, strands of grass, and, in Roy's bowl, several bugs that the man next to him, a navigator from Ohio, identified as maggots. The tub was carried from the prisoners' kitchen in the main camp, and by the time it reached them, the soup was cold. It didn't matter. When Roy's turn came, he drank it down from a communal bowl. Instantly he wished he hadn't.

Toward evening, Roy watched as the prisoners were summoned back to the roll call area in front of the tents for another *Appell*. Again the group of airmen was ignored. Maybe they enjoyed some special status and might be transferred out the next day, heading for a POW camp. It was growing dark when the ragged formation broke up, and the prisoners wandered back to their tents. Cones of white light, flashing from the guard towers, swept the distant perimeter. A breeze was blowing from the west, but it was still warm. Most important to Roy, and the others without shelter, it did not rain.

The next day, the men were plunged into a new routine. Before the first morning light, whistles blared throughout the camp, and Roy woke to find a tall florid-faced prisoner making his way toward the airmen. He wore a black beret and carried a club. Sputtering out orders, he arranged the men into a rough formation and the *Lagerschutz* began a count. The men stood in formation for over an hour as the guards counted their prisoners, then waited longer as an SS man began the process anew.

Roy had assumed that their stay in the open would be short, that they would be transferred out or housed in one of the barracks in the main camp. But days passed, each one a carbon copy of the other. Each morning they were roused before dawn, gulped the weak coffee, and assembled for roll call along with the other prisoners in the enclosure. Sometimes *Appell* went relatively quickly, an hour, maybe two. Other times it plodded on for hour after endless hour as the guards counted and then counted again. Three hours, four. All around them, prisoners fell out in the heat, consumed with dysentery or fever. Beaten senseless, they lay sprawled in the ranks. The dead from the previous night were dragged out for *Appell*, their shrunken bodies lining the open spaces between the tents. Later a crew of prisoners piled them onto a cart they pulled through the camp like oxen.

Around noon the wooden tub arrived, bringing soup and half loaves of black bread. Sometimes there would be a smear of margarine or honey or jam, just enough to taste. Sometimes the orderlies brought potatoes, though when they did, the soup ration was cut in half. Late in the afternoon, the men had a bowl of weak coffee or clove tea. Then came the evening *Appell*, a repeat of the morning roll call, which sometimes reached into the night.

One morning, just after *Appell*, the men were herded out of the enclosure, marched across the lower reaches of the main camp to what appeared to be a theater with a small stage and rows of wooden seats. There a man in a white smock, claiming to be a doctor, instructed them to strip and form a single file. They were to hold out their hands, palms up. "*Sind Sie krank? Are you ill?*" he asked as each man filed past. He did not wait for an answer. Shortly thereafter, the men were returned to the theater. They lined up to be photographed, each man holding a sign with his camp number under his chin. Real mug shots, front and profile.

Most days, though, they drifted back from morning *Appell* and took up positions on the rocks. Work details came and went, but the airmen were left alone. They rested, dozing, talking, getting acquainted. They compared their odd bits of clothing, exchanging shirts or jackets or pants, trying to find something that fit. No one had socks or shoes. No one had underwear. Some of the men fanned out, searching for bowls and blankets, cooking utensils, shoes. Some scrounged, gathering bits of wood, scraps of burlap, straw, hoping to barter, to bargain, to steal. Scrounging was the order of the day.

Some of the men knew several languages, and they mingled with the other prisoners, talking. Each day they reported back, sharing what they knew. "We are in something called the *Zeltenlager*, the tent camp," a fellow from Indiana told Roy. He had spent the afternoon with some Polish prisoners nearby. "There are maybe three thousand men in here. It's a kind of quarantine area. This tent camp is the worst part of the *kleine Lager*, the Little Camp. New arrivals are left out here in the open for about three weeks, then sent to a barracks up there," he said with a sweeping gesture toward the stablelike barracks just beyond the barbed wire. "After that, everyone is transferred to a block in the main compound and assigned to a work detail. The camp was built to hold about ten thousand prisoners. Over forty thousand are here now. Prisoners of all kinds—political opponents of the Nazis, criminals, Russian POWs by the thousand, homosexuals, Gypsies, Jehovah's Witnesses, and the like. Jews come and go, transported somewhere farther east, in Poland. More transports are arriving all the time.

"The whole camp is crawling with disease. Pneumonia, scarlet fever, diphtheria. Almost everyone has dysentery, and there's always the danger of typhus. Everything in this place is filthy, the ground, the water, the air, everything. A little cut on your foot or your finger, one you would never even notice on the outside, will bring on an infection." Roy looked down at his blackened, lacerated feet. "There's as good as no medical treatment here, not for the prisoners. There's an infirmary, I'm told, but you don't want to go there." He smiled grimly. "It's the quickest route to the crematorium." He pointed to the column of black smoke rising from somewhere up the hill in the main camp.

"A lot of the prisoner guards, the *Lagerschutz*, are common criminals, mostly Germans. Some are recruited from asylums for the criminally insane. Brutal sons of bitches. The big guy is in charge of us in the *Zeltlager*. He's been here for years, they tell me, since before the war. The SS allow lackeys like him to run the place. And don't count on any sort of solidarity among the prisoners. Some will help, but most are just too caught up in the business of surviving. There's no room left for sympathy. In Buchenwald it's every man for himself."

It was clear that the men needed to get organized. If they were going to make it, to be treated as POWs, they had to act as a group, a military unit. As the ranking officer, Lamason took charge. He began a new count, taking names, ranks, and nationalities. Eighty-one Americans were scattered across the rock pile; forty-seven British; twenty-nine Canadians; nine from Australia, and two from New Zealand. Keeping the national groups together as much as possible, he divided the 168 airmen into seventeen sections, with an officer in charge of each. This way the men would get to know each other, and the sections would have responsibilities—security, intelligence, supply. The men had staked out their patch of turf—the rock pile, they called it— and guarding the area was imperative. Many of the items they managed to gather had already disappeared, vanished during a single night. They needed to make contacts with other prisoners, to learn more about the camp and how it operated. They needed blankets, bowls, spoons, and shoes. They did not know how long they would be out in the open, but they had to be as prepared as possible.

Merle Larson, a captain from Texas, was the ranking American officer and set about compiling a list of the American prisoners. There were guys from everywhere, from Michigan, Missouri, Massachusetts, Ohio, Idaho, California, New York, fighter pilots, gunners, navigators, and bombardiers. There was even a glider pilot who had been captured on D-Day, escaped, and captured again in civilian clothes. Roy asked around, hoping to find someone from the 457th who could tell him anything about the Group or the crew, but he came up empty. Still, as the men milled about on the rock pile, the Americans sticking together, the English, the Canadians, he *did* hear that there was a guy from Philadelphia somewhere among them. Roy found him sitting on the rocks, dozing. He had managed to gouge out a spot for himself, a shallow cleft between two outcroppings. "You the guy from Philly?" Roy asked. The man glanced up as if he had been interrupted reading the paper on the Market Street El. "Who wants to know?" he answered. Roy heard Philly in every vowel. "Guy from Olney, Fifth and Cayuga," Roy answered. The man's face broke into a broad grin. "Marshall Street," he said, "between Butler Avenue and Pike Street. Near Erie Avenue." Roy laughed out loud. "I'll be damned."

The man's name was Warren Bauder. He had grown up not far from Olney and graduated from North East High, a rival school, two years after Roy. Neither had seen Philly for almost a year—they had come overseas about the same time—so they had no news to share, but it didn't matter. They reminisced about the city, the neighborhoods, the ball teams, the food. Mostly the food—cheesesteaks, scrapple, shoofly pie, the big bread pretzels with mustard. They compared corner candy stores, diners, parks, girls, summer outings "down the shore," the boardwalk in Atlantic City. And finally, they talked about flying, trading stories about flight school, instructors, and airfields.

Warren was a B-24 pilot from the Forty-fourth Bomb Group, flying out of Shipden in Norfolk. The Forty-fourth was a famous group. In August of 1943 it had flown the daring low-altitude raid on the Ploesti oil refineries in Romania. The Group had been sent to North Africa for that raid alone, then back to their base in England. But he didn't get to know the Group or the base very well. The crew had been at Shipden for less than a month, hadn't even had a liberty run into Norwich, when they were shot down.

His story had a familiar ring. It was May 11, just three months ago, and the target was Mulhouse in eastern France. It was their fourth mission, and it was supposed to be a milk run. But fighters jumped them before they reached the IP, and the plane went down west of Metz. The whole crew, all ten men, got out. Warren saw the chutes drifting away in the distance, but he found no one on the ground. Germans were everywhere, searching. A French farmer picked him up, hid him beneath a pile of leaves until nightfall, then smuggled him to his barn in a hay wagon. The farmer's family fed him, got civilian clothes for him, even a pair of shoes, though they were far too small. The next morning, armed with his cloth map, he headed west. He walked for days, dodging German patrols, hiding in barns and abandoned buildings. Several people helped him along the way, giving him food and shelter for a night. In the morning they gave him directions west. No one wanted him to stay. It was just too dangerous.

Then, at a farm just west of Orléans, he stumbled across a family with connections to the resistance. They took him into the city by bus, where a contact picked him up and continued on by horse-drawn carriage to a small village to the north. If stopped during the journey, Monsieur Warren was to be a deaf-mute. Roy smiled when he heard this. How many Allied airmen, he wondered, were stumbling around occupied France pretending to be deaf-mutes?

Warren stayed at a farmhouse outside the village for over three weeks. The family was very active in the resistance. They had good connections and took good care of him. But after twenty-five days hidden in an attic room, he grew antsy. The invasion had come, and he wanted to leave, to make it back to his unit. His French friends pleaded with him to be patient, to wait—liberation was at hand—but he insisted. Roy let out a heavy sigh.

With great reluctance, they made arrangements for him to be moved to Paris. The contact picked him up at a neighboring farm. She had red hair, and she was driving a car. "I should have known," he said. "The car was a dead giveaway. But I wanted to leave so badly." Two other airmen were hidden at the farm, and together they were driven into Paris, passing through several checkpoints without incident. The redheaded woman deposited them at a hotel, the Picadilly, just off the Champs-Elysées, where he stayed in a room with five other Americans. The place was crawling with Allied fliers—ten, fifteen guys—all waiting to be transported back to England. They would be flown out in a British plane, they were told, from a landing strip just outside the city.

The next morning—it was July 3—a well-dressed man called for him at the hotel. He spoke excellent English. He asked all sorts of questions about Warren's background in Philly, adding his own observations about the city, about Trenton, about the Jersey shore. He seemed to know the area well. Warren climbed with him into a waiting car. They drove up the Champs-Elysées, around the Arc de Triomphe, down a wide tree-lined boulevard, and straight through the gates of Gestapo headquarters. He was knocked around a bit in an upstairs room, then tossed into a big holding pen in the cellar, a nightmare with bleeding prisoners and terrified children screaming for their mothers. After that, he spent forty days at Fresnes, in a cell with three other men. Roy knew the rest.

Several days later, Roy and Warren were sitting on the rocks, talking. The afternoon ration had come, and they shared a *gamelle*, dipping the rock-hard bread into the soup. Roy was weary, and his chest ached. Earlier, after the morning *Appell*, a camp doctor—who the hell were these "doctors" everyone wanted to know—had passed through the area. Assisted by a team of orderlies, he had administered an "inoculation" to the men. The syringe held a sinister greenish liquid, and as Roy tried to shrink back, the doctor jabbed the needle directly into his chest. A vaccine against typhus, one of the orderlies claimed, but no one believed it. Rumors of SS medical experiments with human guinea pigs swirled around the rock pile, and for hours everyone sat uneasily on the rocks, waiting for some dreadful agony to begin.

At first it was just a distant rumble, but Roy recognized it immediately. So did Warren. The sound grew louder, heavier. They looked up, squinting. All over the rock pile men jumped to their feet, pointing. Off to the northeast, high over the horizon, streaks of silver flashed in the blue sky. Planes, dozens of them. Far away, they could hear the thud of bombs. They were bombing in the area, probably airfields, someone speculated. But the formation did not swing into a turn. Instead it followed a southwesterly course directly toward the camp. "Probably heading for Leipzig," Warren said. "That's probably the primary," someone added, "about fifty miles away." For an instant Roy thought about Leipzig, the flak and the fighters, and the wounded aircraft, *Renee III*, limping back to the field. It seemed like another lifetime.

A siren began a shrill earsplitting whine. Some prisoners in the tent camp scurried about, frantically seeking shelter. Others sat mute, unmoving. There was no place to take cover. The stream of glittering planes swept onward, clearly visible now. Fortresses. Roy started to count.

"That's a whole combat wing," he said. The planes were too high to make out the markings. Maybe the 457th was up there. Watching the stately formation sail unchallenged through the hazy German sky, a burst of pride—and envy—filled him. He could almost feel the controls in his hands and hear the crackle of the interphone as Joe and Larry called out from the nose. He longed to be there, to hold her steady through the flak, to feel the sudden buoyant lift when the bombs tumbled from the racks, and to watch, seconds later, as the silent explosions covered the target five miles below.

As the formation drew near, the lead elements began to uncover. "Look at that," Roy said. "They're on the bomb run."

"Target must be Weimar, then," Warren speculated. The lead element was almost directly overhead. The formation seemed to fill the sky. The howling of the siren was deafening. Then, as they looked on, spellbound, a streamer of white smoke flared from the lead aircraft, arcing slowly downward.

"Sweet Jesus," Warren shouted. "Target marker!"

All through the formation bomb bay doors were swinging open. Before Roy could utter another word, a progression of objects tumbled like pellets from the planes—clusters of incendiaries, "sticks" the airmen called them, and larger GPs, general purpose bombs. For an instant, the only sound was the rumbling drone of the engines. Then the sky itself seemed to let out a scream, piercing the air with a high whistling shriek. Roy hit the ground, burying his face in the loose rock as the first thunderous blasts erupted. The ground beneath him trembled, and booming detonations came in clusters, shuddering across him like waves. Roiling clouds of gray-black smoke, streaked with orange flame, erupted from somewhere beyond the Little Camp, billowing higher and higher.

The deep, bone-jarring concussions continued, on and on, until at last the final elements of the formation droned past, and the sky went blank. The detonations were muffled now—secondary explosions, not three hundred yards away. Roy could hear sporadic gunfire crackling from beyond the enclosure, shouting. Slowly he pushed himself up on his elbows. He glanced over at Warren. All around them men were sitting up, shielding their eyes, looking toward the dense pall of smoke. A shower of fluttering white suddenly appeared in the sky above the camp. Leaflets, thousands upon thousands, were fluttering down like doves. Roy watched as they drifted into the compound. Several men rushed for them.

For an instant Roy held one in his hands. It was singed, the print smeared, but two grainy photographs leapt out. Groups of German soldiers stared out at the camera beneath a heading in bold black print that read: "These are German prisoners of war in England. They are treated according to the rules of the Geneva Convention," or words to that effect. Roy read quickly before crumpling the leaflet and tossing it away.

As the formation swung away from the camp, disappearing over the horizon, another siren, the all-clear, sounded. Dazed, the men slumped on the rocks. Did the Allies know that they were here in this camp? Was it a warning to the Germans? Within minutes, rumors flitted like bats through the compound. The factory, the munitions plant, was destroyed. Many of the prisoners who worked there were dead, killed in the blast. Others had tried to take cover, but were mown down by the SS. The SS compound, beyond the main camp, had been hit. Over one hundred of the bastards were dead, including the commandant's wife and children.

Suddenly a contingent of SS appeared, red-faced and furious. Led by the Kapo who presided over the roll call every day, they made their way through the tent camp toward the rock pile. *"Alle Amerikaner, alle Engländer, raus, raus!"* They waved their Schmeissers in the air, screaming. *"Schnell machen, schnell!"* They motioned the men toward the gate. "This doesn't look good," Roy said. Warren shrugged his shoulders, nodding. "This is where we get it," one of the men behind them swore, "this is where we get it." All around the rock pile men shook hands, said good-bye and fell in line. The guards drove them quickly out of the barbed wire enclosure, up the incline, and into the main camp.

Everywhere there was pandemonium. A rambling expanse of buildings just beyond the wire—a weapons plant someone said—was burning out of control, and flames sprouted from several buildings inside the compound. Broken beams and shattered windows littered their path. Showers of sparks and chunks of burning cinder rained down like meteors in the compound. Prisoners and guards ran up and down between the barracks, screaming. In the giant *Appellplatz*, the roll-call square, dead and wounded lay scattered like confetti, men with shattered legs, missing arms, charred faces. The wounded screamed piteously. The iron gate to the camp stood wide open, and men streamed through the portal, rushing in and out, prisoners, *Lagerschutz*, and SS, all mixed together.

To the left of the gate, beyond the wire, the sprawling factory complex they had seen on their first day was consumed in flames. Blistering waves of heat rolled out from the gutted walls. Explosions rumbled through the ruins. Directly in front of them, fires raged through the Political Department, where they had been processed, and all along the Caracho Weg. The motor pool and several office buildings were burning out of control. Roy could see other smoke rising from beyond the trees, off to the right. The SS barracks, someone said, and the other industrial plant beside the railhead. It had taken many direct hits.

Dividing the men into small groups, the SS signaled that they wanted the men to fight the fire. Apparently they were to save what was possible from the burning buildings, to dismantle the wooden structures in the fire's path. They had no water, no hoses, no buckets.

Barefoot, the men were herded toward the inferno at the edge of the main camp. They tore away smoldering timber, clearing away flammable materials. Roy and Warren were shoved toward a low-lying structure, part of the factory complex. While smoke hissed from the eaves of the building, they carefully pushed open the door and stepped into the room. Trails of flame meandered through a chaos of desks and overturned chairs. Small fires flared like torches, ready to erupt into a general conflagration. The wooden floor beneath their bare feet simmered. Flailing at the flames, trying not to step into the sparks, not to blister their hands, they tried to smother the smaller fires with anything they could find, a scrap of towel, a jacket left on a chair, anything. It was no use.

Fleeing back into the road, they found themselves again in the midst of chaos. They joined another group of men from the rock pile who were taking down a small wooden structure, beam by beam, throwing the timber into the road behind them. They moved on to another, then another. Some carried wounded from the buildings. Another airman was ordered to defuse an unexploded incendiary. Others hauled food and clothing from a large storehouse, pilfering what they could. Gradually the fires in the main camp were brought under control, but the factory complex beyond the wire burned on and on. The water system for the camp had been hit, Roy heard. The Germans were helpless.

It was hours before the men, exhausted, smeared with soot and sweat, regrouped in the main roll-call square. Ambulance sirens still wailed, as they had for hours. Smoldering bodies, burned black as coal, were laid out like railroad ties all around them. Wounded men—prisoners and guards alike—lay everywhere, moaning in agony. Some were being carried away to the prisoners' infirmary on wooden planks, doors, anything that would serve as a stretcher, but most sprawled in the crumbling asphalt of the *Appellplatz*. Many of the corpses stretched out beside the formation were charred beyond recognition, but others were not burned or shattered. Their shabby prisoner's tunics, Roy noticed, were riddled with gaping, blood-soaked punctures—gunshot wounds. Others had been shot cleanly, in the neck or back of the head.

The nighttime sky over the camp was streaked with red when the men were at last returned to the rock pile. The fires in the factories still smoldered in the darkness, and an acrid stench hung over the camp. Along the way to the Little Camp, the SS guards snarled at them, swearing and spitting. Roy understood only one word—*Terrorflieger*, over and over—but that was enough. Everyone was jumpy, sure that there would be reprisals. Slowly, creeping gingerly on his bleeding feet, he found his way back to a spot among the rocks, where he tried to sleep.

The next morning, after roll call, the men were summoned again to the *Appellplatz* in the main camp. No one had really slept. In front of the gatehouse, a group of SS officers waited for them. The officer in charge strode up and down before the assembled men, bellowing. A translator in prisoner garb tried to keep up—the horrors of bombing, the criminality, the barbarism of the Allies. Finally, the officer paused. His expression softened. He looked out expectantly at the men. He seemed to be asking a question. The breathless translator explained: the Herr Sturmführer wanted to know if there were any carpenters, plumbers, or electricians among these *Luftgansters*. No one spoke up. The officer waited. After a long silence he stepped up to a man in the first rank. The man's face was smudged with black grime, his cotton shirt singed and torn. The major addressed him calmly, and the prisoner, standing just behind him, translated. Roy could not make out what was said, but he could hear the airman's response. Name, rank, serial number. Then the next man and the next, down the line. The officer exploded into another rage, swearing at the formation. Finally, he collected himself, and through the translator, said with disgust that he didn't realize there were so many *Taugenichts*—good-for-nothings—in the Allied military. The men were marched back to the rock pile.

In the days that followed the air raid, various rumors swept the tent camp. The commandant's wife and children had not been killed, they learned, but a bomb shelter holding the families of several SS officers had taken a direct hit. As many as one hundred SS were said to have been killed, dozens more wounded. Most of the casualties had been prisoners employed in the factory—maybe a thousand, someone estimated. Many had been shot by the SS as they fled from the plant. Hardly any bombs had dropped into the camp itself. Some incendiaries had fallen inside the wire, that was clear, but the devastation was mostly beyond, in the factory complex and the SS compound. It looked like an amazingly accurate job of bombing.

The giant factory adjacent to the railhead, the Gustloff Works, they learned, was a munitions plant, producing ordnance and delicate instruments for the rockets that were raining down on England. The structure was almost totally destroyed, the precision machines melted.

And the plant just outside the wire, the German Armaments Works, was also out of commission. It would take months for the Germans to rebuild them, if they could. Even the ancient oak Roy had seen near the camp laundry on that first day was hit and had to be cut down. The Germans called it the Goethe Oak. The eighteenth-century Weimar poet was said to have sat beneath it on summer days, and it was the only tree the SS left standing in the camp. A Polish prisoner gleefully told him that the SS believed that as long as the centuries-old tree existed, Germany would never fall. Now it was gone, and the prisoners, in spite of their losses, were jubilant.

Shortly after the raid, Lamason requested a meeting with the commandant, and it was granted. They met in a room in the gatehouse, since the commandant's office on Caracho Weg had been destroyed in the attack. Lamason renewed his protest over the airmen's presence in the camp, and the commandant, SS-Oberführer Pister, responded that their internment at Buchenwald was, in fact, an error. Their status was under review. Maybe there was pressure from the Allied governments, Roy thought. Maybe Berlin would act soon.

At about the same time the men also discovered that other Allied prisoners were being held in the camp. From an English prisoner who visited the group regularly, they learned that thirty-seven men from the British intelligence service, secret agents who had parachuted into France, were housed in an isolation barracks somewhere in the main camp. Block 17, he said. As an official translator, the English prisoner—Christopher Burney was his name—had permission to move about the camp, and he acted as a liaison, passing messages between the two groups. Several times he managed to smuggle the leader of the British agents into the tent camp to meet with Lamason. There was even talk of planning an escape.

Meanwhile, the men sank gradually into the brutal routine of the tent camp: the endless roll calls, the savage beatings, the starvation rations, the filth, the vermin, the disease. Over ten thousand prisoners were confined in the barbed wire enclosure, they learned, and every day, it seemed, new prisoners—Poles, Czechs, Hungarians, Jews— were tossed into the already horribly crowded tent camp. They wandered around the barren compound, trying to find a place to sit or sleep, a place to escape the surprisingly brutal sun. It was impossible to take more than a few steps without bumping into another dismal soul, and vicious fights broke out over scraps of food, draining away even more energy from the starving men.

The late August days were brilliant and hot, but at night, when the wind picked up, the men shivered in their thin cotton shirts—a chilling foretaste of winter on the exposed mountainside, the Ettersberg, where the camp had been scraped out of the surrounding forest. Every day the men scavenged for scraps of wood, planks, paper, bits of burlap, anything that would cover them or soften the hard ground beneath them. In time several blankets appeared, a few pairs of wooden clogs. So far they were lucky. It had not rained.

Everyone was hungry all the time; everyone was parched. After the first day in the camp, they found that they could cook the bread, roasting the shrunken loaves over tiny fires. It was still moldy, still tasted like sawdust, but it could be softened. Occasionally there was a slice of sausage, one day an apple. The only source of water, they discovered, was the faucet beside the latrine, which was turned on for just a few hours each day. It gave off a rank, organic odor. Whenever they could, they boiled it over the small fires, but still it stank. After a short time, the Kapo put an end to the fires. There would be no more boiling, no more campfires dotting the rock pile. As the days dragged by, most of the men—Roy included—found it impossible not to drink from the faucet. They splashed it on their faces, cupped their hands, and sipped it cautiously. Then, after the air raid, the SS could not fully restore the water system, and no water at all reached the Little Camp. Prisoners were detailed to collect water from the main camp, but there was never enough, and the familiar nauseating smell rose from tubs.

Roy was surprised to find that the SS rarely made an appearance inside the wire—usually only at *Appell*. Whenever one of them appeared, swaggering through the formation at roll call or making a surprise check of the latrine, the prisoners stiffened, trying to become invisible, waiting for the worst. The *Lagerschutz* were bad enough. They kept everyone nervous, looking over their shoulders. Every day the starving prisoners were badgered, humiliated, or beaten by the guards, subject to their slightest whims. Men died like flies. Their shrunken, naked bodies piled up, stacked in a room just beside the latrine, their camp numbers scrawled on a leg or arm in an ink of indelible purple.

A number of prisoners from the main camp slipped back and forth into the *kleine Lager*—the prisoner guards at the gate could be bribed with a cigarette, a slice of sausage—and brought stories of SS horrors in the main camp. "You have heard of the 'singing forest,'" a Czech asked Roy one afternoon as they rested on the cobblestones, "the 'rose garden'?" Roy shook his head. "Ah," the man laughed grimly, "you will see them soon enough. Men die by the thousands in this sewer," he said, "all in their different ways. Perhaps that is the true meaning of the camp's motto: *'Jedem das Seine,'* to each his due, his just reward. Such a perverse sense of humor these Germans have. Here men are starved to death or worked until they drop in the stone quarry or one of the subsidiary camps; they are drowned in the washrooms, buried alive, shot down like dogs, beaten, hanged on meat hooks in the cellar of the crematorium. On Sundays the SS hold public hangings in the *Appellplatz,* while the camp band—the SS have a prisoner band, even uniforms—plays merry tunes. The victims are led to the scaffold, lifted up, then dropped. They die very slowly."

The man stared down at Roy's arms. "It is fortunate that you have no tattoos. You don't, do you? On your chest? No? Good. And you?" he asked, glancing at Warren. "The commandant's wife is strangely attracted to them. The medical orderlies check the new arrivals for them. When an interesting one is found—a dragon breathing fire, a billowing flag, a ship with many sails—its owner is skinned alive. Some are on display at the Pathology Block; some are quite large, covering a man's whole back or chest; some—the most spectacular ones—have been made into lamp shades. They adorn the commandant's villa. There are even," he paused for effect, "shrunken heads. I know men who have seen them.

"Then there are the 'medical' experiments, of course, the mystery injections in the SS Institute of Hygiene. But even if you are not singled out in this manner, a trip to the infirmary will finish you off. In Buchenwald it is best not to get sick. Few survive a visit to the infirmary. At the prisoners' infirmary—the *Revier,* the Germans call it—they have almost no medicines and few instruments. It is always crowded, men more dead than alive. The beds, the bandages, the instruments drip with filth. Every kind of disease flourishes there. Just a short stay, and it is the crematorium for you. Poof, you go up the chimney." He laughed hysterically.

Roy took it all in, but agreed with Warren that it was pretty hard to believe—the shrunken heads, the lamp shades, the hangings. He wasn't that gullible. But what the man said about the infirmary was troubling. During the three-hour roll call that morning, Roy had felt a mounting pressure in his bowels, uncontrollable bubbles of gas. After days in the boxcar without food, the bitter coffee and the mysterious soup curdled in his gut. His rumbling intestines seemed to balloon, then cramp. The small latrine was only about fifty feet from where he and Warren slept, and during the night he had watched men filtering back and forth, hunched over, clutching their bloated stomachs. He knew the symptoms, the slumped walk, the soiled trousers, the smell. Everyone was coming down with the shits—no one wanted to call it dysentery. "The runs," he muttered as he staggered to his feet. Warren nodded. He had visited the latrine earlier. Roy snaked his way across the cobblestones toward the hut.

The *Abort*, as the prisoners called it, was nothing more than a large open pit, with water trickling through it. An A-frame roof hung over it, but there were no seats, no screens around it, only a raised concrete border and a wooden railing to hold on to. The floor was slippery with scum that sluiced between his toes as he edged carefully across it. The smell was overwhelming. There was no space. Men were already squatting shoulder-to-shoulder over the pit. In order to use it, they had to crouch over the concrete border, extending themselves out over the pit while holding on to the railing. Some wavered unsteadily on the edge. Weak and tormented, their bowels gripped by violent spasms, they seemed ready to topple in. Some had terrible appendages, hemorrhoids that hung like grapes, balls swollen as big as oranges from disease and beatings.

Dizzy, Roy perched over the precipice. His body heaved convulsively. Sweat rolled off his forehead, burning his eyes. He thought he might faint. Finally he pulled himself away from the pit. Stumbling, his fingers slid along the soggy floor. He regained his balance, wiped his hands on his pants leg. There was no way to clean himself. He staggered out, bracing himself against the stone wall of the hut. He was suddenly desperate for a drink of water. In spite of the smell, he kneeled beside a bucket of water, and took a gulp. He shuddered. Another prisoner nudged him aside and shouted at him in Polish. Roy staggered to his feet, turned away from the *Abort*, and wandered back again to the area of cobblestones. He made several more trips that day.

In the early morning, clouds began to build in the west, rolling across the slate-colored sky toward the camp. The first timid drops fell during the midday ration, slowly at first, then steadily, a lazy summer rain. It did not stop. By nightfall, as the drenched men stood at *Appell*, the black clay of the assembly area had turned to a thick noxious ooze. All through the night the rain fell, slackening at times, only to turn into a downpour the next minute. There was no escaping it. The tents were overflowing, filled with the sick and dying. The *Abort* was even worse. Gusts of rain swept through the open sides, soaking the slick cement floor.

The men hunkered down among the rocks. Roy pulled his shirt over his head. Water dripped from his nose and ears. It hung on his eyelids. Toward evening the wind turned raw, blustering across the barren compound. Cold rain fell through the clammy night and through *Appell* the following morning, pelting down in endless sheets. A layer of gray seamless cloud hung just above the watchtowers, and the dark trees beyond the wire disappeared in the mist. Water streamed everywhere, running in widening rivulets between the rocks, collecting in the niches the men had hollowed out for themselves.

It rained for three days and nights. On the rock pile the shivering men, soaked from head to foot, huddled under their few blankets, their shirts, anything that might shield them from the relentless drenching. They stood for hours at roll call, their bare feet submerged in the muck. They waited in line for the cold soup and watery tea. They trudged through the mud to the *Abort*. And still it rained.

Roy lost track of the days. They fell away, one indistinguishable from the next in their ceaseless misery. Then, one sodden evening, the news came. They were moving, going to one of the barracks up the hill, in another sector of the Little Camp. Block 58. A steady drizzle was falling as the mud-spattered men gathered on the rock pile. In their hands they carried their bowls, their sopping blankets, their crude, handmade utensils. They followed a *Lagerschutz* over the broken cobblestones past the stone hut and the *Abort*, straggling through a gate in the barbed wire. A cluster of gloomy barnlike structures stretched out before them. Roy stumbled along, trying to focus his eyes. Warren patted him on the shoulder. Inside it would be dry; it would be warm. They had survived the rock pile. Roy nodded. A fit of coughing shook him. He shivered. For two days he had had a fever.

CHAPTER 11

Nacht und Nebel

September 12–October 4, 1944

They had been gone now for two days and two nights, and Pierre Mulsant was uneasy. They had marched smartly, in rows of four, maintaining even in their shabby prison garb an impressive military bearing. From behind the fence he had watched them stride up the hill between the barracks until they turned into the *Appellplatz* and disappeared. Sixteen of them from the group had been summoned, their names blared out over the battery of loudspeakers just after midday ration—"*Achtung! Achtung! Die folgenden Gefangenen vom Block 17 müssen sich sofort am Turm melden* . . . Benoist 13092, Garry 8051, Hubble 14930, Culioli 9548 . . ." and on down the list. Ordinarily an order to report to the main gate was a summons to unspeakable terrors—a round of grotesque tortures in the bunker or a transport to one of the camp's *Aussenlager*s, like Dora or Ohrdruf, from which no one ever returned. Yet hardly anyone in the group was particularly anxious about it that day. The sixteen men had expected the summons. The night before, Rothmann, the block secretary, had posted their names and camp numbers on the blackboard at the entrance to the barracks. They would report to the tower at the main gate next day, if their names were called out.

It was a routine matter, most of them believed, an identity check or an interrogation, perhaps in the Political Department. They had been in the camp for almost a month, and there had been no interrogations or assignments to a work detail, a *Kommando*. Except for the occasional blow from a *Lagerschutz* or the SS noncom who conducted their roll call in the block enclosure, there had been no beatings. They had not even been fingerprinted. Some among the group were convinced that this meant they were still in transit, that they would yet be transferred to a proper POW camp, their special military status recognized. A rumor had slowly gained ground among them that they would be exchanged for German spies held in Britain. The Gestapo had hinted at this when they first arrived in the camp, and the *Blockältester*, a hard-bitten Communist who had been in Nazi prisons and camps since 1933, agreed.

"See you again soon," Yeo-Thomas, the leader of the group, called to his friends as they formed up in the block enclosure, ready to march to the tower. "You will be able to tell us all about it when you get back."

"We won't be long," Pierre heard one of them reply. "Expect it is some damned formality."

But now, two days later, they had not returned, and the words uttered by Marcel Leccia when he saw his name on the block secretary's list reverberated in Pierre's head: "They're going to hang us all," the little Corsican had whispered, and despite the efforts of his comrades, he could not be consoled or brought from this view. Later that night he had gone to the *Blockältester*, Otto Storch. In his seven years in Buchenwald, Storch had seen every form of cruelty and death. He knew the camp, and he could find no words of optimism to offer. "It is a bad business," he had said, and his melancholy expression told the rest. When prisoners were called to the gate in this manner, they didn't usually come back. Leccia pressed his engagement ring into Storch's hands. "Please get this to my fiancée." The block chief had taken it.

Pierre touched his face tentatively with his fingertips. The bruises on his cheeks and eyebrows, almost a month old now, were faded yellow but still tender. His front teeth felt loose. He had not been called to the gate, nor had Charles, but they would be. Of this he was certain. Leccia was right. The whole group of thirty-seven, all agents of SOE or the Gaullist underground, would be executed as *parachutistes*.

Block 17, where they were housed, was an isolation barracks in the main camp, reserved for special prisoners and separated from the other blocks by a double barbed wire fence. Incongruously—Buchenwald, he discovered, was filled with improbable contrasts—a bedraggled flower bed, grim and unkempt, extended along a stretch of the wire. The broken stems of the flowers—at one time they must have been daisies—were stripped clean of their petals. The prisoners had eaten them or sprinkled them in their weak tea or tried to smoke them. By his reckoning today was September 12. The group of thirty-seven had been in the camp since August 16 or thereabouts—he could not be precise about the dates. They had departed from the Gare de l'Est on August 8, of that he was reasonably confident, and the trip, with stops at internment camps in Verdun and Saarbrücken, had taken eight nightmarish days.

A dull throbbing gripped his shoulders. The weather was changing, the damp air growing cooler every day. He pulled the frayed cotton shirt over his chest. He had trouble raising his arms. Both shoulders, he thought, might be separated, a painful reminder of his "special treatment" at the hands of the Gestapo. The ghoulish brutalities of that "treatment" had come in Paris, in the days following his arrest on July 13. During the interrogations in the rue de Saussaies, in the Avenue Foch, and Fresnes, he thought they would never end.

July 13 was his birthday, his thirtieth, and for days he had expected a signal from London to deploy the circuit for its final action. He had only recently toured the *réseaux*, checking on weapons and personnel in Rozay, Courpalay, Jouy, and a half dozen other villages. Mimi, his courier, was on the road, touching base with **MINISTER**'s teams in the northern sector. Things had developed more slowly there, but Désiré, who was in charge of the area, appeared on track and ready.

On that Thursday morning in July, Charles was transmitting from the little apartment behind the Boulangerie Ballaguet in Nangis. He was working on the morning sked, listening for his call sign on the scheduled frequency, when the message clattered through the headset. He wrote it down on the notepad, listened again as the message was repeated, then spread his code sheets on the rumpled bed and decoded it. It was not what he expected. A team of commandos—two or three men, it was not clear—had parachuted into the Forêt de Fontainebleau during the night and gotten into trouble. They had landed in the area near the Plaine de Chanfroy, south of Barbizon, on the western edge of the forest. German troops were in the area, thick as fleas, searching. The message contained coordinates. Could **MINISTER** do something?

Charles studied the decoded message. It was a peculiar request. Barbizon was some fifty kilometers to the west, at the edge of the circuit's sector. One of **MINISTER**'s teams operated in Fontainebleau, a small group of seven organized by Roger Veillard before his departure to England, but Charles did not know them. And there was something else, something more troubling. The signal did not seem to be from the codist who normally communicated with him from Home Station. The touch was unfamiliar. "Not my 'sister' at the other end," he told Madeleine Ballaguet when she brought in the morning coffee from the bakery as he was decoding. "I don't like it."

Neither did Pierre when Charles told him later that morning. The *parachutistes,* the message said, were from SAS—the Special Air Service—and he had never worked with its teams before. SAS, he knew, was an international unit, a brigade of troops whose small teams were dropped into France following the invasion to organize and conduct armed operations. Some of its men were French, some British, Dutch, and Belgian, even a few Poles. They wore uniforms, like regular military personnel, but they worked with maquis units, arming them, instructing them, and leading them into battle. In spite of the uniforms, the Germans treated them as terrorists to be summarily shot. Sometimes they cooperated with F-Section *réseaux,* helping to train recruits, but their mission was not to build and maintain underground networks, and they tended, Pierre believed, to be less security conscious than SOE circuits. Why, he wondered now, did they not use one of **MINISTER**'s grounds for the drop? Why Fontainebleau?

Consulting the worn Michelin map he carried with him, Pierre located the coordinates in the Chanfroy plain. The landing party seemed to be approximately thirty kilometers south of Melun, between the *forêt* and the marshes west of Arbonne. Several times he tried to reach the circuit's contacts in Fontainebleau by telephone, but without success. Anyway, the telephone was not secure, and he had only the vaguest notion of what sort of instructions he could give over the line. There was no alternative, he realized, but to make the trip himself. If all went well, he could reach the area in the early afternoon, and it would remain daylight until almost ten. For all his misgivings, or perhaps because of them, Charles insisted on coming along. Pierre would need help searching for the party, and a third man would be even better. Pierre did not argue.

Marcel Ballaguet would alert the *réseau.* The baker understood the drill. If they did not return within twelve hours, the circuit would disperse, the letter boxes would be changed, the arms caches moved immediately. There would be no time to waste. No one could be expected to hold out under interrogation indefinitely—twenty-four hours, maybe forty-eight, that was all. As he gathered his things, Pierre wished he could get word to Mimi. She would be returning to Nangis over the weekend, but there wasn't time to track her down.

They left Nangis in the late morning, driving west toward Melun in the *traction avant,* the rugged front-wheel drive he had used to travel the back roads and rutted tractor paths of the district. On the way they stopped at the farm of Bernard Bemberg. A cousin of Désiré, Bernard had worked with **MINISTER** on the reception committees, and he agreed to ride with them. It was a sultry day, with low clouds that trailed languidly across the sky from the west. Aircraft—Me109s and Ju 88s bound for the German aerodrome at Melun—soared overhead. Pierre had seen no Allied aircraft during the morning, but the Luftwaffe was up in force. Perhaps an alert had sounded and the bombers were on their way. He hoped so. There had been many raids on the aerodromes in recent weeks, and a diversion would be welcome today.

On the road, traffic was sparse, and they made good time. Entering the bleak industrial suburbs of Melun, they crossed the Seine at the Pont de Lattre. In the rue de Paris they made a stop at the garage that served as a letter box, alerting Raymond, the proprietor, of their mission. Then they stopped briefly at the home of Roger Veillard. The house in the Boulevard Henri Chapu, where they had stayed during their first weeks back in France, was deserted, the shutters drawn, and light, windblown debris lay scattered on the porch and steps. They had had no word of him since early June, when the BBC message— *"François bien arrivé"*—confirmed that he had made it safely to England. He was out of harm's way.

From Melun they followed the *route départementale* south, skirting the western fringes of the forest. They passed without incident through the market town of Chailly, where a convoy of German vehicles idled beneath the trees on the high street, and into Barbizon, down the famous *grande rue,* with its once luxurious hotels and fashionable restaurants, its shaded villas. Then, just outside the village of Arbonne-le-Forêt, as the car swung around a bend, a German control post blocked the narrow, tree-lined road. It looked to be a routine matter, the *Feldgendarmerie* halting traffic, lazily checking papers. Pierre had passed through such checkpoints dozens of times without a hint of trouble.

But today, the soldiers, waving their machine pistols, motioned for the three men to climb out of the motorcar. The *Feldwebel* in charge demanded to see their papers. Assuming the air of mild boredom he always adopted in these situations, Pierre slid out from behind the wheel. The *Feldwebel* took his wallet, snapped it open, and turned it inside out, examining the sheaf of identity and ration cards, the demobilization papers and the crumpled francs.

As the sergeant probed into a fold, his brow knitted. *"Hallo,"* he muttered. *"Was haben wir hier?"* In his fingers he held a small square of paper, hardly larger than a stamp. Unfolding it with great care, he spread it on the hood of the automobile. As he studied it, his eyes widened. He looked up at Pierre, and raised the paper, holding it up for him to see. Pierre froze. In the *Feldwebel*'s hand, pressed out now to its full size, was a deeply creased diagram, a set of instructions, printed in several languages, on how to assemble a sten gun. Pierre stared at it in disbelief. The ground seemed to open beneath his feet. How could he have left it there? How had he overlooked it?

The *Feldwebel* did not wait for a response. *"Terroristen!"* he snapped, and the other soldiers closed in quickly. They grabbed at Pierre, hurling him roughly across the hood of the car, pinning his arms against his back. Metal bit into his wrists. Behind him Charles or Bernard must have made a break for it. He heard scuffling. Shots rang out. Within seconds, all three men were handcuffed, and the soldiers stood facing them, obviously nervous. For a moment he thought the Germans might shoot them on the spot, lined up against the peeling white trunks of the plane trees that stretched along the roadside. But the sergeant spoke breathlessly into a field telephone, and soon a large military automobile, accompanied by a motorcycle with sidecar, appeared on the road and, after a hurried conversation among the soldiers, the three prisoners were bundled into the back.

They drove east into the forest, past the deep Gorges de Franchard, toward the prison at Fontainebleau. There they were questioned by the *Feldgendarmerie*, singly and together, and then, toward evening, they were turned over to three men in civilian clothes who had the look and smell of Gestapo. During the hours of interrogation that followed, the Gestapo thugs beat him, smashing his face and neck with a rubber truncheon, and when he collapsed, gasping for breath, onto the floor, they kicked his ribs and groin until he teetered on the fringes of consciousness. His comrades Charles and Bernard had betrayed him, they snarled at him. They wanted to know where the wireless sets and weapons were hidden. They were already on the trail of his contacts. They merely needed a few details. Surely there was no reason to endure such torment. Why make it hard on himself? Alternating with these appeals came the bullying threats. They would find his wife and parents. "And not all our colleagues are as sensitive as we are," they said.

Still, Pierre would not speak. For a day and a night he had remained silent, his nose clogged with blood, his eyes swollen almost shut. He did not believe that Charles had talked. Or Bernard, who, after all, could tell them relatively little. Forty-eight hours, he told himself over and over again. Hold on for forty-eight.

Next day, he was bustled into a black Citroën bound for Paris. As he climbed inside, his hands cuffed in front of him, he caught a quick glimpse of Charles huddled between two Gestapo thugs in the backseat. A trail of encrusted blood tracked from his ear across his cheek, and his blacked eyes stared past Pierre without expression. Bernard was no longer with them.

When the Citroën veered off the Champs-Elysées into the government quarter, turning onto the narrow rue de Saussaies, Pierre knew their destination. Squinting through the glare of the windshield, he watched the massive Ministre de l'Interieur loom into view. The Citroën slowed, passed through a side gate, and eased into a cobbled courtyard. Somewhere in this fortress was Gestapo headquarters. He had expected as much. Like the Avenue Foch, where the Gestapo's counterintelligence center was located, it was a house of horrors.

In an upper-floor room he was separated from Charles, beaten, harangued, and beaten again. While the chief interrogator, a tall skeletal man with broad shoulders and a face as sharp as an ice pick, asked him questions, two thugs smashed his face and fingers, his ribs and throat, even the bottoms of his feet. Whenever he blacked out, they poured water over his head, and he would sputter back to consciousness and the questions would begin again. "Where are the arms dumps? Where are the wireless sets, eh, '*Capitaine* Paul'?" When he still refused to talk, saying over and over again, "*Je n'sais rien . . .* I know nothing," they dragged him into another room, where his feet were bound together and his hands cuffed behind him.

"Now a new entertainment for you, monsieur." The interrogator smiled. He brushed a spec of lint from the tunic of his green uniform. "I hope it will amuse you." As he spoke, one of the men slipped a heavy chain through the cuffs, then ran it across a hook embedded in the low ceiling. His movements were slow and mechanical, allowing Pierre ample time to see what was in store for him. Grinning, the man gave the chain a short tug, testing, and Pierre's arms jerked awkwardly behind him. Then, at a signal from the chief interrogator, the two guards began to pull steadily at the chain. Link by link, the slack disappeared, and Pierre's arms rose stiffly behind him until at last his toes lifted from the floor and the full weight of his body fell on the joints of his shoulders. A crushing pain shot through him. Tears flooded his eyes. He gagged, choking back a scream. As he twisted, swinging just centimeters above the floor, the guards roared at him, slamming their truncheons into his kidneys and crotch. On and on it went, until he could bear it no longer. He could hear himself screaming as he passed out.

As soon as he regained consciousness, they hoisted him again and again until at last he was left blubbering on the floor. Dragged to a cell somewhere down below, he waited alone in the darkness. His arms dangled from his shoulders as if they had been ripped from their sockets. He drifted through the hours in a blur. After a time—it must have been near morning—footsteps resounded in the corridor, and a sliver of light appeared beneath the door.

"*Los, du französisch Schwein,*" one of the Gestapo guards bellowed, as he ripped open the door and kicked Pierre in the head. His partner appeared, and together they tugged Pierre back to the fifth floor, pushing him by the shoulders down a narrow corridor into a cramped bathroom. There they stripped him, peeling away the remnants of his blood-spattered clothes. On a bare, water-stained wall, a brown patch indicated where a water heater had been torn away, and a small basin stood beside a deep, claw-footed *baignoire*. He knew what was coming.

Cold water streamed from the open spigot, rising higher and higher until it reached the tub's round runoff drain, and the lead guard shut it off. With his hands bound behind him, Pierre dug his bare heels into the dingy floor, but he could do nothing. The two men dragged him forward, lifted him over the lip of the tub, and plunged him into the water. The shock of the cold stunned him, almost sucking the air out of his lungs. Powerful hands pushed him down, holding him beneath the surface. At first he squirmed and struggled, his shackled feet kicking against the bone-white tub. Through the frigid water he could see a dim watery halo from the overhead light fixture. He could hear the frenzied grunting of the men as their meaty fingers pressed into his neck and chest. Everything swirled and dissolved. Thrashing helplessly, he could stand it no longer, and with a desperate spasm, he inhaled. Water gushed into his nose, down his aching throat, flooding his lungs. His legs jerked wildly. He realized that he was going to die.

Then, with a sudden yank, they hauled him up. Water exploded from his mouth and nose. Gulping for air, he choked, coughing streams of water. As if from somewhere far away, the tall interrogator was laughing, speaking to him in French, asking questions he could no longer understand. Then, as Pierre fought for air, the hands grasped him and pushed him down again into the water. This time he did not struggle. He tried to hold his breath, but it was impossible. He felt himself slipping away, blacking out in the frigid water. Suddenly the hands pulled him up again. His eyes swam and his throat burned. He vomited water. Then, while he sputtered, they shoved him down again. And again and again.

Days passed, some without sleep, all without food, and he grew weaker. He had not eaten since he arrived at the rue de Saussaies, and on some days he was taken to the interrogation room, where the tall skeletal man would sit down to an elaborate luncheon, lingering over his *steak au poivre* without asking a single question. Then Pierre was returned to his room. Some days were filled with relentless questioning and threats. The beatings were less severe, less frequent, but he made more trips to the *baignoire* and he finally broke. Dragged back into an interrogation room, still naked and wet, he decided to talk. He had remained silent for far longer than forty-eight hours; he had bought time for the *réseau*, but he could hold out no longer. He had reached his limit. Struggling to regain his composure, he decided to give them a name.

"I am just a courier," he stammered, still trying to catch his breath, *"un agent de liaison."*

The tall man scoffed. *"Pas d'histoires!"*

"No," Pierre said. "No stories. I *can* give you a name, my contact. He knows much more than I do."

"Who is this contact?" The interrogator's voice was wary and he looked absently toward the window, but he was listening. Pierre hesitated, his head bowed in apparent shame. *"Allez,"* the tall man snapped. *"J'en ai marre!* I lose my patience with you."

His voice hardly more than a murmur, Pierre coughed out a name.

"And where do we find this man?"

Pierre glanced up, still naked, still shivering from the *baignoire*. He gave an address.

For a moment, the interrogator stared at him, his eyes mere slits. Then bending over his desk, he jotted it down and passed the slip of paper to an aide. "I hope that you will not disappoint me again," the tall man hissed at Pierre. Glancing at the paper, the aide read it aloud as he turned to leave the room: "Roger Veillard," he murmured, butchering the pronunciation. "Sixteen Boulevard Henri Chapu, Melun."

This bit of misleading information did not, of course, satisfy them for long, and the dagger-faced interrogator raged and bullied, but Pierre would say no more. So the days at the rue de Saussaies staggered by in a macabre sequence of interrogations and beatings, and the sleepless nights pulsated with heart-stopping shrieks from beyond his door. He tried to collect himself, to think out a story. At Beaulieu, his last training school in England, the instructors had discussed this situation. Maintain your denials for as long as possible, they said, but when your cover story has been blown, stick to the truth as closely as possible and give them leads that will send their investigation off on the wrong track. Inventing code names, mangling others, divulging obsolete addresses, parachute drops, and defunct arms depots, Pierre talked and talked, revealing nothing of value.

One morning he was roused from his cell, but instead of shoving him along the usual path to the interrogation room, the guards escorted him down in the lift. Emerging in the courtyard, they climbed into a black Citroën. Up the Champs-Elysées, they looped around the Etoile and the Arc de Triomphe, and delivered him to the Gestapo counterintelligence headquarters at 84 Avenue Foch. There, in an office on the first floor, he was interrogated by a polite man who sat behind a large typewriter and wore civilian clothes. The man—Pierre would later discover that his name was Ernest—offered him food and cigarettes and commiserated with him about the brutal methods used in the rue de Saussaies. "Here things are different," Ernest said as he watched Pierre devour the lamb and vegetables, the glass of wine. "Here, if you cooperate, you will be treated as an officer, a prisoner of war."

Opening a thick file on his desk, he thumbed through several pages. "I think you will find this interesting, Monsieur Mulsant, and informative. We know already a great deal about you and your operations." He read aloud from the documents. "**MINISTER** is your circuit, I believe, Capitaine Paul, alias Paulo, alias Paul Guérin. W/T operator for the circuit is Charles Meunier, in reality, Denis Barrett, an Englishman. Operates his wireless under the code name

INNKEEPER. Arms dumps at the farms of *les familles* Bemberg and Dubois, parachute grounds at Nangis and Bray-sur-Seine . . ." Sprinkled almost casually among these matter-of-fact statements were the usual questions—where were the other arms caches, the wireless sets? Who were the "terrorists" who held the arms? "You, Capitaine Mulsant, are doing your duty as an officer. We understand this. It speaks well of your sense of honor. But these weapons will be dispersed to unsound elements, to terrorists who will use them for their own criminal purposes. Unlike you, they do not have the best interests of their country at heart. They will not bring *gloire* to France. Think about this, I implore you."

The interrogations with Ernest went on for days. Often they were joined in the room by a colonel in a green Gestapo uniform who stood to one side, listening and observing Pierre. Sometimes he intervened in the questioning. Both he and Ernest took an almost childish delight in displaying cartons of cigarettes, boxes of chocolates, parachutes, and other items captured from SOE circuits in France. "Most of your reception committees are now operated by German personnel, you know," Ernest told Pierre. "Colonel Buckmaster and our other friends at Orchard Court are, as usual, in the dark, but we appreciate the goods F-Section so generously supplies."

During one of the sessions, the colonel showed Pierre an elaborate diagram of SOE's organization, with names attached. He talked in startling detail about SOE wireless procedures and about training schools in Scotland and elsewhere. He told anecdotes about instructors at Beaulieu and Ringway. Several times he spread a collection of passport photographs on the desk, some of whom Pierre recognized. "F-Section agents," the colonel announced proudly, rattling off their names and circuits. Did Pierre know this one, that one? "You should not be surprised, Capitaine Paul. After all, we have a man at Orchard Court who supplies us the names of all your agents."

This was pure nonsense, Pierre realized, a bluff, since no one at Orchard Court, except perhaps Buckmaster, would know the names of all F-Section's agents. Still, the extent of the Gestapo's knowledge of SOE was unsettling. "We know a great deal about your organization," the colonel boasted during a long session several days later. "Documents that your agents send to England are read by our people before SOE even sees them. Our man **CLAUDE** handles that. Did you ever meet him in London?" Pierre recognized the SOE code name. "He is an excellent man, you know," the colonel beamed. "From him we receive reports, documents, and the names of agents." Pierre smiled. For once, he had a surprise of his own. "Yes, I have met him," he said. "But then you must know that your man **CLAUDE** has been found out. As we speak, he is sitting in prison in London. I'm afraid you'll need a new informer."

At that, the colonel leapt to his feet. His eyes widened and his face flushed. He took a menacing step toward Pierre, who was sitting, as always, handcuffed to his chair. With the back of his hand, he slapped Pierre across his nose and cheek. *"Dreckschwein,"* he roared, stomping around the office, pounding the furniture and raging at both Ernest and Pierre. "Get him out of here," he screamed, and two guards hauled Pierre out of the office and back to his cell. The colonel's booming voice followed him up the stairs. A day later Pierre was transferred to Fresnes.

During the endless interrogations at the Avenue Foch, no one had mentioned Mimi or Désiré. Mimi knew more about the circuit than anyone except Pierre and Charles, and if the Gestapo had not nabbed her, she would hold things together until Désiré picked up the threads and continued their work. Everything they had struggled to achieve hung in the balance at this moment, with the Allies ready to break out. Someone would have informed London by now. Home Station would be scrambling to determine exactly what had happened and if **MINISTER** could be salvaged. He wondered if word had reached Raymonde in Troyes or at the château in Villefranche? The Ballaguets would have contacted her brother Robert, who would have made sure that she went into hiding. They had made contingency plans for such an eventuality.

From the beginning he understood that Fresnes was merely an interlude. Eventually the Gestapo would tire of his denials and false leads. Several times they returned him to Paris, to the Avenue Foch and the rue de Saussaies for tribunal—further interrogation and "special treatment"—but he had held to his story. They did not believe him, but it no longer mattered. In the end they would deport him to a camp in Germany or simply shoot him in the courtyard of Fresnes. Either way, he reckoned that it was only a matter of time.

Then, on a bright sunlit morning in August he was roused from his filthy mattress and hustled down the steel stairs into a courtyard. At first, when the cell door was flung open and he was prodded out onto the gangway, he thought that it was another tribunal. But in the courtyard he joined a group of prisoners, about three dozen battered men and several women, sweltering in the heat, slapping at the fleas. He recognized several familiar faces. Charles was there, bruised and disheveled but alive, and Émile Garry, who had brought Germain to him in Troyes just over a year before and who, along with Octave Simon, had introduced him to F-Section. Close by he recognized Robert Benoist, the famous motor-racing champion from before the war. Through contacts in Paris Pierre knew that Benoist operated an SOE circuit southwest of the city. Beyond him was another man he recognized from the Paris underground. Although the men and women shifting their weight from foot to foot did not converse with one another—armed SS guards stood all about them—most, if not all, Pierre realized, must be either F-Section operatives or Free French from the Gaullist underground.

Handcuffed in pairs, the group was directed to two waiting lorries. The heavily guarded convoy rumbled north into Paris, passing through the near empty streets that led to the Gare de l'Est. He was to be deported after all. The guards rushed the prisoners along a cordoned-off platform, manhandling them into what, from the outside, appeared to be an ordinary passenger carriage. But inside the men discovered two cramped compartments whose seats had been removed and whose windows and door were latticed with thick wire mesh. The compartments were of ordinary size, large enough to hold eight passengers comfortably, but the SS packed all three dozen men into them. The women were shoved into a compartment in between.

The journey east lasted eight grisly days. During the long sweltering afternoon of the first day, Allied fighters strafed the train. Squalls of machine-gun fire swept over them, and explosions rocked the train until it staggered to a sudden halt. In a panic, the SS guards leapt to the ground and ran, leaving their prisoners shackled and trapped in the train. If the carriage caught fire, they were done for, *fini*, but the attack ended in a matter of minutes and the planes were gone. Still, the train sat motionless on the track for hours, and the suffocating August heat bore down upon them.

At last, the guards returned, unlocked the compartment doors, and led the prisoners along the corridor toward the exit. Two lorries were coughing diesel alongside the track. They were being transferred, the men in one lorry, the women in the other, and, the guards made clear, if anyone attempted to escape, the entire group would be shot.

In the relative privacy of the lorry, the men, all together now for the first time, introduced themselves and began to get acquainted. The senior officer in the group was an Englishman named Dodkin—at least that's what he called himself. Charles had recognized him in the train and pointed him out to Pierre. In the early months of the war, they had served together as translators in an RAF unit in Reims. But the man's name was not Dodkin, Charles whispered, it was Yeo-Thomas. When Charles greeted him as they departed the train, the man warned Charles never to call him by that name. As far as the Germans—and the men in the group—knew, he was Squadron Leader Kenneth Dodkin, and that was how it was going to be.

Yeo-Thomas was a short stubborn man, tough and battle hardened, and he commanded instant respect. In the closeness of the lorry, he quickly took charge, and his first thoughts were of escape. Charles and his partner, Henry Peulevé, had already managed to loosen their handcuffs and slide them off. They were preparing to jump off the lorry when several prisoners warned them to stop. Hadn't they heard the guard? Did they want everyone in the lorry to be shot? Yeo-Thomas intervened. Maybe it *would* be possible, he argued, under the cover of darkness, to make a break for it, but they would have to plan. To attempt escape now, he had to concede, might be premature.

The lorries halted late at night at a camp near Verdun, where the guards shepherded the prisoners into a stable behind a military barracks. The men bedded down in several stalls on the right side of the long low building, while the women were to sleep on the left. The next morning, the SS rousted them out of the stable, briefly removed their handcuffs and allowed them a quick wash and a mug of cold ersatz coffee. Then they were loaded again into the dusty lorries, and the little caravan motored eastward, crossing the German frontier near Saarbrücken. In the late afternoon, they entered what appeared to be some sort of prison camp, a *Straflager*, the guards called it. As they jumped from the lorries, a pack of SS men descended on them, snarling and slamming them with the rubber coshes and wooden clubs they carried. Pierre had witnessed nothing like the frenzied savagery of it.

While the group was being registered, Pierre realized that the women had disappeared, carried away, he guessed, to another enclosure nearby and bound for a women's concentration camp in Germany. He never saw them again. The registration complete, the men were chained together in groups of three or four or five. Their ankles were shackled and linked to a metal ring that bound each group together, making it almost impossible to walk or even maintain their balance. As they staggered forward, the SS guards swarmed around them again. They chased the men round and round a small circular pool of green scummy water at the center of the compound, lashing out at the groups that inevitably tripped and fell. *"Steht auf, ihr franzö-sische Stinksaue,"* they bellowed. *"Lauft doch!"* It seemed to be a sort of rite of initiation, and the SS delighted in their sport, shouting and laughing hysterically as they pummeled the tangled men.

When the guards tired of this game, they led the men to a squat, windowless hut behind the camp kitchen where they removed the chains from their ankles and cuffed them together in pairs. Then all thirty-seven men were forced into the one-room hut. It was approximately three meters long, four meters wide, and perhaps three meters high. Light slanted into the space from a small, square aperture located high on the back wall, and a sliver of a bench, no more than ten centimeters wide, stretched along three sides of the room. It was impossible to sit. In a corner of the sweltering room, a rusting oil drum was to serve as the latrine for the three dozen men.

They remained packed in this sweatbox all day and night, and beneath the blistering tin roof the heat and stench grew more unbearable by the hour. In the days that followed, they were allowed out for only one hour each afternoon. Yeo-Thomas arranged a scheme whereby pairs of men could sit in shifts for several minutes, but the claustrophobic press of sweltering bodies made this almost impossible. By the third day, several in the group seemed on the verge of madness.

Pierre was not certain how long they remained in the camp at Saarbrücken—he thought it was three days, while Charles insisted that it was four and another comrade was convinced that it was five. But after several days of this misery, the SS guards flushed the men from the stink of their hut, ordered them into formation, and then, to the astonishment of all, handed them over to a detachment of the *Feldgendarmarie*. Still handcuffed in pairs, the men climbed into a waiting lorry that carried them through the camp's concentric rings of barbed wire, through the streets of the heavily bombed town, halting at the shattered remains of the train station. While the dozen or so armed soldiers from the *Feldgendarmerie* kept the crowds at a distance, the shabby prisoners were loaded onto a German troop train.

The *wagon* they entered was not a cattle car or a cramped prison van but a spacious baggage car where they could sit and even stretch out. A door was even left partially open as the train crawled out of the station, and cool air poured over them and the three armed guards in the car. Many of the prisoners even received small bundles that contained the handful of possessions, including currency, taken from them when they were arrested. Some were convinced that the worst was behind them, that the Germans were now transferring them to a proper POW camp where they would be interned with other military prisoners. Why else would the Gestapo release them to the military police? Why the better accommodations and the return of their personal belongings?

Others were not so sure. With darkness fast approaching and the guards obviously not expecting any trouble, this, they argued, would be their best—and perhaps only—opportunity for escape. Those who believed that they had seen the worst were deluding themselves. After the weeks of torture they had all endured, punctuated by the nightmare at Saarbrücken, could anyone in the car really trust the Gestapo? A bitter round of whispered bickering began. The idea of escape was fantastic, some insisted. It would not work, and then there would be reprisals. The guards had already warned them. They were on their way to an *Oflag*, a POW camp for officers, where they would be treated according to the Geneva Convention. Why do something so obviously foolish?

Finally, Yeo-Thomas, acting as senior officer, decided the matter. Now *was* the time to act. As soon as night fell, they would overwhelm the guards, either strangling them—that was preferable—or shooting them with their own carbines. Then, organized in teams of three or four, they would jump from the train and make their way back to France where the resistance would hide them. It was a desperate plan, Pierre thought grimly, but still worth a try. He had seen enough of German captivity, more than enough of the Gestapo, and most of the men felt the same way. They were ready to give it a go.

But, as Yeo-Thomas talked them through the plan, discussing timing and assigning each man a specific job, a handful of them balked. They would not go, they announced, and if anyone attempted to escape, they would alert the guards. More heated discussion followed, but the few refused to budge. For a moment Pierre thought Benoist might strangle each one of them, but, in the end, trembling with rage, Yeo-Thomas had to concede that under these circumstances, an escape attempt was impossible. There would be other opportunities, he said, glaring at the few resisters. After that, they rode on in troubled silence.

Just before nightfall the train halted, and the men were shuttled to yet another train, this time to a crude passenger car with no separate compartments but rows of empty wooden seats. Seeing this familiar third-class carriage seemed to brighten their spirits. It was another good omen, and everyone seemed livelier and more talkative. Even the guards seemed to relax. During the night, one of the men, fluent in German—Hessel was his name—managed to chat with the officer in charge. He asked the officer about their destination, and Pierre, shifting closer, listened in. "Oh, you are on your way to a camp, a *KZ*," the German responded cheerfully, "a *Konzentrationslager*." When Hessel's face darkened, the officer added: "But most certainly, you will be much happier there than in prison. There is a fine library with books in all languages, concerts on the square every night, a cinema, theater, and even a brothel. There is a finely equipped hospital and the food is very good; you get practically the same as the civilians."

"What is it called?" Hessel asked.

"Buchenwald." The officer smiled.

They arrived at Buchenwald in the dead of night. The camp was silent, and the rows of low buildings huddled like shadows in the gloom. Searchlights swept through the blackness beyond the fence, but the vast empty space just inside the main gate wavered in a ghostly bluish mist. An indefinable smell, pungent and sickly sweet, hovered in the night air. Through the eerie silence Pierre could hear the hum of the electrified fence and the sharp crackling of its circuits.

That first night they slept on the concrete floor in a deserted shower building, and sometime before daybreak began the ordeal of processing—the shearing and swabbing, the showers and the handing out of grotesque tatters of clothing, the wooden clogs. It was late in the afternoon when the group followed an escort of prisoner guards from the cavernous *Effektenkammer* to the Prisoner Records Office, the *Schreibstube*, where they were officially registered in the camp and assigned their new quarters. Along with the three hundred prisoners already housed there, they were to occupy a special quarantine block in the main camp, across the narrow street from the camp kitchen where teams of prisoners came to fetch the tubs of watery soup.

They were confined to the Block 17 enclosure, but a flood of hollow-eyed men shuffled by, coming to chat furtively through the fence in a dizzying array of languages. Some who sidled up to look at them were just curious; they wanted to see the English spies, the parachutists who had been caught by the Gestapo in France. Some wanted news. Some offered horror stories about the camp. Others were raving mad.

Among those haggard faces at the fence were two men whose advice Pierre and the others took seriously. On their first morning in the *Effektenkammer*, as they climbed into their prison clothes, joking with one another about their appearance, one of the inmates working there slipped up to them. "You have little to laugh about," he whispered in English. "This is one of the worst concentration camps in Germany. I just can't tell you how bad it is, but you'll find out for yourselves. The treatment is terrible and deaths can't be counted anymore. For heaven's sake, watch your step." The men stood in silence. "Don't let on that you are officers. And if any of you held any executive position in peacetime, keep it to yourselves. The internal administration of the camp is in the hands of Communists and they don't fancy either officers or capitalists." Later this man appeared at the fence of Block 17. He was known in the camp simply as Perkins, he told them, but his name was Maurice Pertschuk, and he was an F-Section operative who had been captured in April 1943. Somehow he had managed to conceal his true identity from the Gestapo for sixteen months and now worked in the *Effektenkammer*. He came often to the fence of Block 17.

Another frequent visitor was a prisoner who worked as an interpreter in the Disinfectant Building. His name was Christopher Burney, and he, too, was an F-Section agent. He had fallen into German hands in August 1942 and had spent a year and a half in solitary confinement at Fresnes before his deportation to Buchenwald. Burney was particularly helpful. Since as an interpreter he could move about the camp, he had access to information from many sources, and, like his friend Pertschuk, he had honed his survival skills. Their briefing on the situation was not encouraging.

"Every prisoner in the camp wears a colored cloth patch," Burney explained to Pierre and the others not long after their arrival, "a triangle, sewn onto the right trouser leg and left breast of his shirt or jacket. You'll see all the different colors." Pierre glanced down at the red triangle he had been given to sew onto his jacket. "The color identifies the category of prisoner. The purple triangles are religious prisoners—priests, Protestant ministers, conscientious objectors, Jehovah's

Witnesses, and the like. Not so many of those about. The pink tri-angles are for homosexuals. They are harassed by guards and prison-ers alike. Yellow is for the Jews. They are mostly German, and some have been here since before the war. Many are housed there, in Block 22," he said, pointing to a nearby barracks, "though more and more are arriving and are scattered across the *Lager*. The black triangles are what the Germans call '*Asozialen*,' antisocial types considered detri-mental to the war effort—drunks, pimps, vagrants, and petty thieves. You will find many of them about. The green badges are also for crim-inals—habitual, hardened criminals. They are very dangerous, the greens—murderers, rapists, thieves, and thugs of all sorts. Some have been taken directly from prisons for the criminally insane. Most of them are German, and at one time, before the war, they dominated the camp.

"You see, the SS run the camp by proxy, and from the very begin-ning the SS and the criminals understood each other perfectly. The SS entrusted the greens with all the important positions in the internal administration of the camp, from the *Lagerältesten*—he is the senior prisoner official for the whole camp—to all the *Blockältesten*, the chief prisoner official in each block, and their orderlies, the *Stubendienst*. The camp police—the *Lagerschutz*—and the Kapos, who run the vari-ous work details in and around the camp, were once all greens, and they used their positions to terrorize the other prisoners, beating them, robbing them of food, clothing, cigarettes, even money. Oh, yes, there is money in the camp—*Lagergeld*, which can be used at the prisoners' canteen, though there is rarely anything to buy.

"As the war dragged on into '42, all this changed. Now Buchenwald is above all about labor. All the camps in Germany—Buchenwald, Dachau, Sachsenhausen, and the others—are organized around labor. Labor in the factories, the forests, the mines, and quarries, all for the war effort. More than a dozen subsidiary factories are affiliated with Buchenwald alone. The German Armaments Works, the DAW just there, beyond the wire, is one. The Gustloff Works beside the train sta-tion is another. Dora is north of here and is spoken of only in whis-pers. No one knows exactly what the Nazis produce there. There are rumors that components of the new rocket bombs are made there, but we can't say for sure. No one ever returns from Dora.

"The red triangles, like yours," he said, nodding toward Pierre, "are for political prisoners. Most are Communists. The Communists, espe-cially the German Communists, are the dominant faction in the camp.

You will see them in positions of power everywhere. They dominate the prisoner administration, and they have created an underground resistance organization, the International Camp Committee, which is preparing for the day when they can rise up and seize the camp. Nothing happens in Buchenwald without them.

"The greens are savage brutes, of course, and they are also notoriously corrupt and inefficient. Before the war, this suited the SS quite nicely, but as the demands of the war mounted, the SS turned to the politicals, the reds. Like the greens, most of the reds are German, but, as Communists, they know much more than the greens about industrial production, the organization of labor, and the shop floor. They are also very well organized and disciplined, and although they can be a ruthless lot themselves, they are much better than the common thugs.

"There are other factions you must be aware of as well," Burney said, "national groupings that are designated by a black letter at the center of the triangle. From your patch I see that you, monsieur, are French," he said, gesturing toward the black "F" on Pierre's red badge, "and you," speaking to Charles, "must be English. Everyone wears such a patch. The Russian POWs have their own enclosure, but other Russians—the politicals—are scattered among the blocks. They are by far the most numerous, followed by the Poles and the French. You will find that deportees of the same nationality generally stick together. This is not simply a matter of linguistic convenience. It is for self-defense. Incidents between prisoners happen every day—beatings, robberies, even murders. The Kapos and the SS don't lift a finger. You will see this when roll call is over and the prisoners march away from the *Appellplatz*. When they reach the streets that run between the blocks, the columns dissolve, and gangs of thugs—Russians, Germans, Poles—set upon them. In Buchenwald you can trust no one, and you can expect help from no one."

"But why, for God's sake?" Charles asked. "What are they after?"

"They are trying to steal money—*Lagergeld*—which they hope to use in the prisoners' canteen or the camp cinema or the brothel. The brothel is located in the *Sonderblock* beside the cinema. The women are prisoners from KZ Ravensbruck, and only the Kapos and other privileged prisoners can afford a visit. Of course, everyone is always looking for food and cigarettes. They are the two most important currencies in Buchenwald and can be used for bribes or barter. Some prisoners actually receive packages from their home countries, the

Czechs and Danes, for example, or even Red Cross parcels, though this is rare. So, be careful. You will see all this and will learn the drill, but proceed with caution."

Burney's information and advice were valuable, especially in those first days of orientation in the camp. But even Burney, with all his sources, had been unable to find out anything about the sixteen who had been called to the gate two days ago. Pierre stood at the fence of the compound watching as prisoners straggled by on the muddy street outside. It was just after the midday ration, and they were carrying empty soup tubs back to the camp kitchen. Shrunken and colorless in their rags, they appeared as indistinct as shadows against the faded green of the building, but he could see the triangles, green and black and red, and the long white strips bearing their camp numbers.

From the alley between the kitchen and the rabbit hutches he heard the familiar thudding sounds of a struggle. Three prisoners were kicking one of their comrades, who lay sprawled face down in the muck. The victim's mud-spattered head gushed blood, and he made a muffled gurgling sound. The three men wearing green triangles—Poles, Pierre thought—ripped something from the man's hand, shoved his face into a filthy puddle, and darted off around the back of the laundry. After only a month in Buchenwald, Pierre hardly noticed.

The sun stood high above the camp, and elongated shadows cut across the fronts of the buildings. During the night, while rain thundered on the roof of the barracks, the crematorium had spewed its stench into the soggy blackness. No smoke belched from the chimney now, but a loathsome aftertaste lingered in the wet air. As he turned back toward the block, Pierre noticed several men from the group moving into the barracks. Rain or shine, they had only two hours, just after the midday soup, when they were allowed back inside, and everyone took advantage of this precious time. Pierre sauntered toward the barracks and stepped through the door.

He entered a small corridor, its floor caked with mud. To his left was the crude washroom with troughs and a circular basin, where each morning for several hectic moments the water was turned on and the four hundred men crowded around, trying to swipe some of yesterday's grime away. On the right, the smell of the lavatory and the urinals and the brimming latrine pans brushed against him like a curtain. Quietly he stepped past the *Blockältester*'s cubicle and turned left into the A wing of the building.

He found his comrades already lounging on the bunk beds that stretched in rows along walls and rose in three tiers to the ceiling. Two men slept to a bunk, sharing the thin palliasse of matted straw that passed for a mattress and the single threadbare blanket that did not cover even one of them. Several men were playing cards on the upper bunks. Cards were strictly forbidden in the camp, but Frank Pickersgill, one of the Canadian officers in the group, had managed to create four decks from strips of cardboard and stray drops of paint. The orange and blue containers for Osram lightbulbs, which he discovered stacked in the barracks trash, worked best.

Bridge was the game of choice, and whenever they could, the men climbed into the upper bunks to play. Several bunks away, another group was huddled around a small wooden chess set. An English agent, Desmond Hubble, had somehow managed to hang on to a portable set through all the stages of his imprisonment. It had been taken away from him when they arrived at Buchenwald, but after several days he had been allowed to reclaim it from the *Effektenkammer.* He had organized a tournament, and most of the men played. Sentries were always posted at the entry to their wing of the block, to alert them if the *Stubendienst* or *Blockältester* should appear.

Before he could reach his own bunk, where Charles lay draped across the palliasse, Pierre could see Yeo-Thomas motioning the men toward the back wall. He edged his way between the rows of bunks into the circle surrounding their senior officer. Since arriving at the camp, Yeo-Thomas had cemented his position as leader of the group. He focused on maintaining morale, demanding that the group keep as fit and clean as possible. Their roll call took place at 0600 in the Block 17 enclosure, and under his prompting, they did daily calisthenics just after morning *Appell.* After several days the men had been able to retrieve some of their belongings from the *Effektenkammer*—a pipe, Benoist's razor, several bars of primitive soap, and Hubble's chess set—and each morning he saw to it that they shared the soap and razor, washing and shaving in the circular metal basin in the block latrine. They would do all within their power to maintain some semblance of dignity and bearing, and they would not be beaten down.

He also remained obsessed with escape. As soon as they were settled in Block 17, he formed three escape committees and began exploring various schemes. He managed to establish a relationship of mutual respect with Storch, the *Blockältester*. Storch was a close-lipped and taciturn Communist from Eisenach. He had been imprisoned in KZ Buchenwald since it opened in 1937, and although he never openly acknowledged it, he was clearly involved in the underground Communist organization in the camp, the International Camp Committee (ILC). So, too, was his aide, block secretary Ottomar Rothmann. Both seemed impressed with the military discipline and the antifascist credentials of the group, and within days Storch took the extraordinary step of allowing Yeo-Thomas out of the block enclosure to explore the camp. Prisoners from Block 17 were never permitted out of their enclosure, and if Yeo-Thomas were caught, it would mean death for both him and the *Blockältester*.

With Burney as guide, he established contact with the wary German Communists of the ILC, who, he learned, had a wireless and caches of weapons hidden in the camp. He also sounded out the leadership of the eight hundred Soviet POWs quarantined in Block 13. He tried to convince both groups that the agents in Block 17 were ready to cooperate in any plans to liberate or escape from the camp. Both listened but remained cautious. "*Abwarten*"—wait and see—seemed to be their attitude. They would gather their own information about the parachutists in Block 17.

He also met with Pierre Julitte, a high-ranking leader in de Gaulle's underground organization whom he had known in London, and Dr. Alfred Balachowsky, a French biologist who worked in Block 50, the SS laboratory, and had many contacts in the camp. Balachowsky had been arrested for his work in SOE's **PROSPER** circuit, run by Émile Garry, and he was eager to help. He came often in the following weeks to Block 17. Burney also managed to slip Yeo-Thomas into the Little Camp, where he met with the leader of a large group of Allied aviators who had arrived in late August, hoping to enlist them in his escape plans.

Some of Yeo-Thomas's schemes, Pierre had to acknowledge, tended toward the fantastic, and the same small faction from the lorry continued to resist any idea of escape. The rumor that they would be exchanged for German spies held in England continued to gain ground. That was why they had been brought here and held in isolation. That was why their food seemed more plentiful, their clothes better than the other prisoners'. Some of the men were even recovering some of the weight lost during their time in Gestapo hands. Their fate was being negotiated by the Allies, and Yeo-Thomas's reckless plans would get them all killed. Pierre listened to these complaints about their senior officer with disgust. To him the man's irrepressible doggedness was a source of inspiration. They were still at war with the Germans, Yeo-Thomas insisted, and they should never lie down and behave like prisoners.

It also became apparent to Pierre that their senior officer was an influential man in resistance circles. He was one of the most experienced and skillful agents working for SOE. On his third mission to France in 1944, the Gestapo had snared him outside the Passy metro station in Paris. The Germans were convinced that a big fish had drifted into their net, but they could never quite determine his true identity. They beat him, doused him in the *baignoire,* hung him from the ceiling by his wrists, and left him to rot in a dark, rat-infested basement cell without light or food or company, and yet he never broke.

Now, in their section of the A wing, the men closed around him. He had something to report. "I'm afraid I have bad news," he began. "We have heard a report about our friends. A report from a reliable source. Yesterday, our source told us that all sixteen had been thrown into the bunker at the main gate." The bunker, Pierre had learned, formed the west wing of the main gate and consisted of narrow cells where prisoners were subjected to the most gruesome and sordid tortures Buchenwald had to offer. Men taken there were rarely ever seen again.

"Then, last night," Yeo-Thomas continued, "they were seen outside the bunker, exercising in the *Appellplatz,* roughed up but alive. It was a hopeful sign. But this morning, our source had new information. I am sorry to have to tell you, but our friends are dead." No one spoke. No one moved. All sixteen had been executed during the night, Yeo-Thomas told them, hung by rope from hooks in the basement of the crematorium. They died slowly, by strangulation, and their bodies were burned in the ovens in the room just above them. "This will almost certainly be our fate as well," he said, his eyes searching the gaunt faces gathered around him, "and because we shall have to die slowly it is all the more important that we die bravely."

Benoist, Garry, Geelen, Pickersgill, Hubble, and the others. All dead. During the long hours in the trains and lorries, in the stables at Verdun, in the steamy hut in Saarbrücken, and in Block 17 Pierre had gotten to know these men. They had exchanged life histories and shared their hopes for the time, surely coming soon, when the war would at last be over. Now they were gone, and he and the remaining twenty would not have long to wait before joining them.

From the outset he told himself that it must end this way. He knew, or at least sensed, that when his friends were called to the gate, they would not be coming back. And yet the news stunned him. He realized that despite his cold-eyed assessment of the situation, he had still managed to harbor illusions that somehow he would survive. Now, Yeo-Thomas's words shattered those illusions. Standing, with his hand resting on the metal frame of the bunk, he resolved that he would not wait passively to hear his name read out over the loud-speaker. He would do something. He needed a plan.

Before the *Stubendienst* drove the stunned men out of the barracks later that afternoon, Pierre sat for Auguste Favier. While Pierre slumped on a wooden crate between two of the bunks, the little artist stood above him, rough pencil and charcoal in hand. A prisoner from Block 34, Favier had been coming to visit the group for several days now, sketching portraits of the men. He worked quickly, using the backs of camp posters, cardboard boxes, stray sheets of paper, any-thing that would hold an image. Most of the men appreciated his work, hoping that the portraits would somehow find a way back to their families in England or France or Canada. "Make this a good one," Pierre remembered Robert Benoist saying to Favier two days ago. It was just before the group departed for the main gate. "This may be your last chance to capture my friendly kisser," he had said with a wry smile.

Pierre admired Favier. He took great risks slipping into Block 17 and even graver risks sketching the men and different scenes from around the camp. Favier also enjoyed Pierre's caustic observations about the camp, the Germans, and life in France. But today there was no biting wit, no laughter. When Favier finished, Pierre stood up and glanced at the sketch. A haggard, unfamiliar face stared back at him.

In the late afternoon, Pierre took up his position at the gate of Block 17, watching the ebb and flow of prisoners up and down the street. During the interminable hours standing at the fence of Block 17, he had gotten to know many prisoners, Poles, Czechs, and, of course, many French. Among them was a priest from Troyes named Curin, who sometimes came to the fence to talk. He had been arrested for distributing illegal ration cards. Père Curin, in turn, introduced him to another *résistant* from the Aube, a prisoner named Pierron, who seemed to know his way around the camp. Pierron had been a factory manager in Mussy-sur-Seine, a small town southeast of Troyes, and had become involved with the resistance in early 1943. He worked with reception committees for a local group and had hidden tons of weapons on the grounds of the factory. In November he had been arrested, tried in the rue Hennebeau in Troyes, then shipped to the camps at Châlons and Compiègne before being deported to Buchenwald. Pierre and Pierron hit it off immediately, and in their conversations Pierre told him, in very general terms, about his underground activities in France, while Pierron shared much of what he knew about Buchenwald and its administration. They had spoken on occasion since then.

He needed to see Pierron now. If anyone could help, he was the man. Several times in the past days, Storch had looked the other way while Pierre and other men from the group slipped out of the block enclosure. It had been a relatively fast evening *Appell*, and now he would have some time before the *Lagerältester*, making his rounds, would blow his whistle to signal all prisoners back to their barracks. He went to Storch. "I want to know nothing about it," the *Blockältester* growled in his gravelly voice. "I want to see nothing. You do not have my authorization," he repeated stiffly, turning to face away from the door. "*Mach keine Dummheiten, Kamerad*," he whispered over his shoulder. "Be careful." Pierre stepped quickly past the barracks chief's desk and down the steps into the enclosure. At the fence, the Viennese opera singer from the B wing whose job it was to control the gate turned his head, and Pierre disappeared into the narrow path that separated the blocks.

It was already twilight as Pierre made his way toward the column of barracks where most of the French prisoners were housed. The French Blocks where Pierron lived—14, 26, and 31—stood one behind the other, with the Czechs in Block 20 separating 14 and 26. Just behind this concentration of French barracks, in Block 37, were the Poles, who were renowned in the camp for their intelligence network. They always seemed to have important information, and perhaps he could coax something out of the contacts he had made among them.

He searched everywhere for Pierron, but he was nowhere to be found. No one seemed to know where he was. Perhaps he had been sent out in one of the *Aussenkommandos*, the work details, or had been beaten to death by another prisoner or was lying unconscious in the bunker, waiting for a trip to the crematorium. He tried to find Père Curin, but the priest had also disappeared. He had been transported, a prisoner finally whispered to Pierre, to a camp farther east, in Poland, a camp called Auschwitz.

Pierre hurried past the cinema, the brothel, and the wire fences of the Little Camp. He skirted the *Appellplatz*, sticking close to the buildings that faced it to avoid attention. It was growing dark when he caught sight of Pierron in a crowd outside the prisoners' canteen. They were waiting to buy a few cigarettes and the weak beer. Pierron was surprised to see him.

"We must talk," Pierre said. "I am to be executed without a trial. There can no longer be any doubt," he said, lowering his voice. "All of us in the group will be shot or hanged. Can you help me?"

Pierron pursed his cracked lips and stared at Pierre. For what seemed an eternity he did not speak. "*Allons,*" he said, "*promenons-nous.*"

The two men turned away from the canteen and trudged past the optical workshop, turning into the street beside the Pathology Department. Inside, Pierre knew, were the medical "specimens"—shrunken heads, heads sliced in two, preserved in formaldehyde, lungs and hearts, all on display in glass cases. Through the windows Pierre could see men in white smocks.

"I can think of only one course of action," Pierron said at last. "A switch of identities."

It was Pierre's turn to stare.

"Yes, yes," Pierron said, "an exchange of identities."

"But how?" Pierre asked. "Can such a thing be done?"

"*Mais absolument,*" Pierron replied, but he hardly sounded confident. "This is possible. You still have not been fingerprinted, no?" He thought for a moment. "We must find a prisoner who has either just died or is in his last hours and whose papers are not completed. Then your name and number would be recorded on the death certificate, and you would assume his identity."

Pierre nodded. A damp wind swept down the path between the buildings. It was turning colder, and it would rain again later.

"It will mean working with the *Arbeitsstatistik,* the Labor Bureau, in Block 5. The *Arbeitsstatistik,*" Pierron continued, "is the most important office in the camp. It is the bureau in charge of manpower. It is controlled by prisoners, almost all Communists, and they wield real power. They make all the work assignments for the camp. They have access to the prisoners' records—their occupation and other particulars—and they draw up the lists. When the SS want a work detail—fifty men to work on the road or empty the latrines or clear the swamps, the Labor Bureau selects who the fifty will be. The SS rarely pay much attention. The swine don't care who is selected as long as the bodies are there to do the work.

"These selections are a matter of life and death. If you are assigned to a work detail outside the camp, an *Aussenkommando*, you are a dead man. They smash rocks in the quarries and haul them away or break their backs clearing logs from the woods or digging from morning to night in the mines. Their life expectancy is short. Ordinarily, you want to stay inside the wire, and if possible, be assigned to some sort of indoor work, in the hospital or the *Effektenkammer*. The laundry is also good and the *Disinfektion*. But in your case, transfer to a work camp outside the *Lager* would be better. Less chance that you will be recognized or denounced."

"But how is this done? Do you know anyone who works there?"

"I myself know no one at the Labor Bureau. But I have a friend," Pierron said, turning his back into the stiff wind, "who has an important contact there. Many French work in the *Arbeitsstatistik*, and, in theory, they can shift men from one *Kommando* to another, though it is difficult to arrange and carries with it many dangers. That is especially so with you, a parachutist, a terrorist." He looked around as he spoke, his eyes sweeping the barracks.

"It is worth a try," Pierre said. "I see no alternative."

Pierron thought for a moment. "My friend's name is Roure, a deported journalist. Among his contacts at the *Arbeitsstatistik* is a French colonel who works there for many months now and is influential. This colonel selects the names for the *Kommandos*. He could arrange to change your number with that of one of the dead. Believe me, it is possible."

Pierre thought this over. It seemed a thin straw, but what choice did he have? "*D'accord,*" he nodded, "*d'accord.*"

"*Bon,*" Pierron said. "I will see my friend."

There was a nervous rustling around the blocks on both sides of them as prisoners scurried back to their barracks. The red lights on the distant fences glowed in the gathering darkness, and soon he would hear the shrill *Abpfeifen* of the senior camp chief. Anyone caught outside after *Lagerältester's* whistle would be shot or sent to the bunker. Pierre turned away and disappeared into the crowd, hurrying toward Block 17.

The following days were torment. Each morning and evening at *Appell*, the men, standing in ranks in the enclosure, waited to hear their names echo over the loudspeaker. During the restless hours in between, they tried to go about their usual routine in the block enclosure. They paid the same attention to their personal hygiene, to the calisthenics, and to their military discipline. They continued the chess tournament, and the bridge went on, though no one could summon much interest. Favier came and went, sketching more portraits. Pierre paced along the fence, waiting for word from Pierron, talking to other prisoners at the fence and gathering the latest news.

From a corner of the enclosure he could make out the empty spot where the Goethe Oak had been between the coal dump and the laundry. Weeks had passed since the air attack, and still the Germans had made no headway in rebuilding the DAW or the Gustloff Works. They seemed to have given up. That day had brought the only happiness he had experienced at Buchenwald. As the Fortresses rumbled overhead and the explosions began, the men of Block 17 had rushed out into the compound to cheer. While embers as big as cabbages rained into the compound and blast after blast shook the earth beneath them, they whooped and yelled and danced about like schoolboys.

Days passed with no word from Pierron, and Pierre grew nervous. It was no use trying to contact him. When his friend had news, he would come. The anxious days dragged by, and no one was called to the main gate. He was convinced that the ax would fall within days of the first executions, but a week slipped by, then another. Peulevé and many others in the group began to think that since only the sixteen had been executed, it was probable that those remaining were out of danger. If the Germans wanted to execute them all, they would have done so on September 11, in one action. Storch and Balachowsky and their other contacts in the camp concurred.

Meanwhile, autumn was approaching. The days were growing shorter, and raw winds whipped across the Ettersberg. Frost appeared on the hard ground in the enclosure.

Then one afternoon Pierron appeared.

"My friend, the journalist, has come to see me," he said. Pierre was able to leave the compound, and they walked shoulder to shoulder along the bowed line of barracks that led to the camp's main street. "The colonel will not do it." Pierron frowned. "He is frightened. There are many cowards among the French at the Labor Bureau. He is not the worst." He shrugged his shoulders. "It is your category, *mon ami.*

From their comrades in the Prisoner's Record Office, the *Schreibstube*, they learned that you are not only a political, you are *Nacht und Nebel*."

"What is that?"

"It means night and fog. Those who carry such a classification, I must tell you, are doomed." He paused, squinting toward the tower of the main gate, which had just come into view. "They are designated for extermination. No reprieve. They simply disappear, as the Germans say it, into night and fog."

The two men walked on in silence. Four bodies dangled on the gallows at the center of the *Appellplatz*. They had been there for two days, and the bloated faces were black as raisins.

"Then that is the end," Pierre said at last. His voice was hard, without inflection.

"Perhaps not," Pierron said. "There may be another way."

Pierre said nothing.

"I have contacted a man I know from Lorraine. He was arrested as a Communist in the Mosel area. From my position at the factory, I have helped many workers find jobs, especially after the *débâcle* of '40. I am on good terms with many Communists and socialists. I have been to see him, this Communist from Lorraine. I told him of your problem." From his threadbare jacket he produced the stub of a cigarette. With a deft motion of his fingers, he struck a match, cupped his hands against the breeze, drew slowly and exhaled the thin smoke from his nose. He handed the precious stub to Pierre. Pierre could feel the heat on his lips. He tasted the burnt paper.

"What did he say?" He handed the cigarette back to Pierron.

"His response was to be expected. '*Quelles sont les opinions politiques de Mulsant,*' he asked me. He wanted to know your politics."

"And how did you respond?"

" '*Comme toi,*' I lied. 'The same as yours.' "

"*Bien, bien.*" Pierre smiled. "Did he believe you?"

"The answer seemed to satisfy him. He did not inquire further. He will see his friend in the *Arbeitsstatistik*."

For a week Pierre waited. Several men from Block 17 had grown feverish and were transferred to the camp hospital. Among them was Yeo-Thomas. Pierre had heard the horror stories about the prisoners' hospital. Yeo-Thomas was a tough man, but Pierre feared they would never see their senior officer again. Surprisingly, the mood in the block was calm and resigned. Sitting on their bunks or sipping their watery gruel, the men seemed to draw back into themselves, marshalling whatever spiritual resources they possessed to get them through each day.

At night in the narrow bunk, huddling against Charles for warmth, Pierre's thoughts strayed to the château at Villefranche and Raymonde. From rumors that swept the camp he knew that the Allies had entered Paris. What was left of the Wehrmacht was retreating north into Belgium and east toward the Rhine. The liberation of all France was at hand, the end of the war in sight. If Raymonde had survived those first days after his arrest, if her brother had taken her into hiding in the south, she was safe. If she had remained in Troyes, even in a secure house, he could not calculate the risk. He had found no one in the camp who could tell him about the situation in Troyes, but surely it was by now in Allied hands. After all, de Gaulle was in Paris, taking mass at Notre Dame. There were no more German military parades down the Champs-Elysées, no more field gray uniforms along the boulevards and in the cafés. The Gestapo swine in the Avenue Foch and the rue de Saussaies had gone, scrambling away, he liked to think, like rats in the sewer.

Then, of course, there was Mimi. Perhaps the Ballaguets had managed to warn her. And even if they had not, she would have returned to Nangis and seen that something was wrong and disappeared. She was resilient and resourceful, and there was not a situation she could not charm her way out of; there was no man she could not mesmerize. Even now, shivering in the clammy barracks, to think of her and their nights in the room in Nangis brought a fleeting smile to his face.

He talked often with Charles about the circuit. On July 13, when they were captured, **MINISTER**'s teams were well armed and ready; they understood their objectives for the time when the Allies pushed out of Normandy. And, if the rumors swirling around the camp were true, if France had been virtually liberated, then the circuit's work was done. "They have performed their duties," Charles reassured him. "We have trained them well. And anyway, for them the danger is over."

Mostly, Charles liked to talk about home, about his wife, Rita. He worried that F-Section had contacted her. He hoped not. Why worry her when there was so little to tell? He wondered if his sister Joan knew. Perhaps she had heard something unofficial, a leak through channels. He could still remember the text of his last jaunty message to her just before their arrest. Home Station would make sure it reached her. "Am going strong. Plenty to do here. Am in the best of spirits and confident that we shall be together soon. Keep your chin up."

When Pierron came finally to Block 17, he had bad news. There would be no help for Mulsant. The French in the *Arbeitsstatistik* would do nothing. The journalist from Lorraine had sought out his Communist contacts there. He briefed them, and they explored the possibilities. It had taken them some time, but it was a difficult task. Mulsant's records in the *Schreibstube*, they told him, carried the term *DIKAL— Darf in kein anderes Lager*. "It means that you may not be transferred to another camp and you may not work outside the wire. The SS are taking a special interest in the parachutists in Block 17. The orders concerning you and your comrades come directly from SS headquarters in Berlin. It cannot be done."

Pierron began to speculate about other options, but each was even more farfetched than the last, and in the end Pierre stopped him.

"Thank you, my friend. You have done all you could. I understand."

"Do not give up hope, *mon ami*. I will explore these possibilities— the hospital, the TB ward, and Block 46, where they do the experiments."

Pierre patted his friend on the shoulder. Through Pierron's threadbare jacket he could feel the bones.

"You will hear from me," Pierron whispered as the two parted. Pierre nodded, watching his friend disappear in the crowd.

Charles stopped him as he was returning to the block for midday rations. Pierre had slipped away from Block 17 after morning *Appell*, hoping to find Balachowsky. Perhaps he could suggest something. It was a bright autumn afternoon. He had noticed for the first time slivers of brilliant color in the beech trees scattered among the firs beyond the wire. On days like this before the war he and his father had gone hunting, tracking deer and wild pig in the woods that bordered the château. He could almost smell the scent of the leather and the strong oil from the rifle.

"There is a new list," Charles said calmly when Pierre reached Block 17. "We are on it. We must have a haircut and a shave. Tomorrow

morning at 0600 we are to report to the tower for 'reassignment.'"
Pierre looked into Charles's eyes. He did not speak. He didn't need to.

The inevitable had come at last. At the entrance to the barracks
Pierre examined the list. Eleven names and numbers—Barrett, as
Charles called himself in the camp, Frager, Wilkinson, Lavallee, Mulsant—his finger moved on down the list. Tomorrow was October 5, a
Thursday. Pierre walked back through the barracks. The men were
gathered among the bunks to discuss the situation. They had sent a
runner to Balachowsky and decided to talk to Storch. Perhaps they
would be able to do something—anything to play for time.

Balachowsky arrived quickly. He was shocked by the order, having
assumed that after the hangings in September, the executions were
over for Block 17. He would contact Julitte and the Communists who
ran the prisoners' infirmary, promising to do everything he could. He
was not optimistic. "You'd best hurry," Wilkinson drawled as Balachowsky turned to go, "otherwise I'll need a shirt with a higher collar."
There was nervous laughter.

That afternoon Pierre went with Henri Frager and a small delegation
to the *Blockältester*'s room. Storch, of course, had already seen the order.
It had come to him directly from the *Rapportführer*, the SS roll call officer, and Rothmann had recorded it in the block's official log. They
talked over several possibilities. Storch revealed that he had hoped to
move them out of Block 17 in batches of three, transferring them to
other blocks, then to work details that would take them away from
Buchenwald. He hinted that the three men—Yeo-Thomas, Southgate,
and Peulevé—who had left for the prisoners' infirmary represented a
first step. But now there was no time. As a last resort, Frager asked, if
all else failed, could Storch provide them with poison. Better to die by
one's own hand as a final act of defiance than dangling from a meat
hook while the SS looked on, braying.

Storch said he would try, but he was not confident. Instead, he
advised them to slip away when the first morning orders were given,
to disappear during the confusion following roll call and hide. Men
had sometimes hidden for days in the camp while their comrades
sought ways to smuggle them out. Or they could resist, attack the
guards before their hands were tied and at least take some of their
executioners with them. The men rejected the idea of running away.
"If it must end, then I want to die like a soldier," Pierre said to the
block chief, "by firing squad." The others agreed. Helpless, Storch
merely nodded. *"Ich verstehe,"* he said, "I understand." As the men

filed out of the little office, Frager turned to him. "Give my love to my wife," he said, as he and Storch embraced. "It's a shame to die so close to the end, and like this, but this is what war is and anyone who fights has to reckon on his own death."

Later, after *Appell*, Pierre went with the others to have the stubble on his face and head shaved. There was little talk. Each man was making his own internal preparations. When they returned to the barracks, Pierron was waiting at the fence. Pierre showed him the blackboard and the list.

"*Tu as vu*," Pierre told him. "*C'est pour demain.*" Pierron stared.

"I would like to see a priest," Pierre said. "Do you know one?"

Pierron nodded. "There is an *aumônier*, a chaplain, yes. L'Abbé Lefèvre—or is it Lelièvre—I am not sure. He is from Marseille. I will take you to him."

Darkness was settling over the camp as they made their way through the maze of blocks to find the *aumônier*. The squalid barracks reeked with the usual odors, and the fading light was dim, but they found the priest. Religious observations of any kind were strictly forbidden in Buchenwald, punishable by death. Still, the priest did not hesitate. Pierre knelt, and standing before them beside a cluttered table, the abbé heard his whispered confession. With a thin crust of bread, he gave him communion. He gave him the last rites, and in the stillness, the priest's voice flowed over him, murmuring the soothing Latin phrases he knew so well from childhood. "*Misereatur vestri omnipotens Deus, et dimissis peccatis vestris, perducat vos ad vitam aeternam*"—"May Almighty God have mercy on you, forgive you your sins, and bring you to life everlasting." Pierron knelt beside him, and the abbé, a mere shadow now in the blue light, blessed them both.

Pierre did not sleep that night. In the darkness of Block 17, he could hear men muttering to themselves and praying, making their private farewells. The names of women and the pet names of children hung in the air all around him. His own thoughts drifted to Villefranche, to Raymonde and his parents. Close beside him on the bunk, Charles was restless, whispering to himself as he drifted in and out of sleep. They did not really talk. Lying back to back, the ratty blanket stretched tautly over them, they might have been on different planets. Yet he was glad Charles was there.

The sun had not yet risen when the barracks orderlies roused the men out of their bunks. The men formed up in the block enclosure. Their names were read aloud by the *Blockältester*. One man was missing—Peulevé, an F-Section man Pierre admired. He was in the infirmary.

Shivering in the cold mist, Pierre took a deep breath and steadied his hands. He raised his head, pulling himself to his full height. He stood at attention. He would be composed. Whatever the *salauds* did, he would die like a soldier. As they were marching out of the enclosure, the other prisoners of Block 17 were falling in for the morning roll call. The others from the group looked at the departing men. Only a handful of them remained now, and their time would be coming soon.

The little column moved briskly up the hill, past the walls of the crematorium, and skirted the crowded *Appellplatz*. The morning roll call for the main camp was still in progress, and row after row of gray-brown forms filled the gigantic space. Here and there, Pierre could see corpses, little more than piles of clothing, laid out neatly beside their block formation, ready for the count. At the tower, the men formed up in front of Signpost 3, as ordered, and waited.

From the *Appellplatz* Storch suddenly appeared. With him was Raoul Lubersac, a man Pierre recognized from the block. The *Block-ältester* handed round a cigarette. The men smoked and talked quietly. They were composed. Storch had not obtained the poison. But, he insisted, there was still time before the reporting officer arrived for them to dissolve into the bedlam following *Appell*. The men refused. They would not try to escape and they would offer no resistance. There would be reprisals, and the whole camp would pay, especially their comrades left behind in Block 17. They had no choice but to do their duty.

While they were talking, the reporting officer, SS Oberscharführer Hofschulte, approached them. A squad of armed SS accompanied him. Standing before them in the shadow of the tower, the *Oberschar-führer* read out their names and made a brief statement. The ten prisoners, Pierre understood, were now formally under arrest. Their hands were tied, and the guards led them through the main gate to an unmarked steel door just to the right, in the west wing of the tower. It was the entrance to the bunker.

The beatings did not last long, a few minutes. Then the SS departed, and the men were left alone in their individual cells. Standing in the center of the empty cell, Pierre could have touched both sides, but he did not want to. The walls were spattered with dried blood and traces of excrement. A dreadful, suffocating smell filled the air. He struggled against images of the crematorium and the meat hooks in the cellar. He prayed for strength.

Then he heard the shouting and the boots scuffling along the concrete floor in the narrow corridor. The doors were slammed open, and he was dragged from his cell, joining the others assembled again beside the main gate. A light rain was falling. The *Appellplatz* was empty. A prison van idled just beyond the gate, and the men climbed inside.

After several moments, the van lurched forward. They seemed to be traveling east, past the crematorium and the zoo. The van moved slowly, but it was a short trip. Then it halted and the doors opened. They were in a clearing somewhere in the ruins of the DAW factory. The SS guards directed the prisoners into a long open space. A large mound of earth rose at one end, with wooden posts aligned in front of it. A firing range.

The men were led, two by two, to a spot just in front of the posts. An SS major stepped forward and addressed them. His voice boomed out over the open space as he read each man's name from a sheet of paper. Then he spoke to each man again, reading out the sentence. No one buckled. No one cried out or begged for mercy. Pierre glanced at the brave men standing beside him. They had won the war. France was free. The Germans could snuff out his life, but they were beaten, and someday, on a morning not too far distant, they, too, would face the executioner.

Pierre stood erect between the SS guards. His feet were bound. His arms were tied behind the post. He looked out at the firing squad, a line of helmeted men with machine guns at their side no more than ten meters away. Then the officer, standing beside them, bellowed out an order. Slowly he raised his hand. The guards lifted their weapons and extended their arms. They took aim. The moment, no more than a second, seemed frozen. The officer's hand was dropping when Pierre's mouth flew open. *"Vive la France,"* he screamed. *"Vive la France!"* And then darkness.

CHAPTER 12

Alone in the Kingdom
of the Dead

October–November, 1944

When he heard the boots, Roy pressed himself down into the palliasse, trying to make himself inconspicuous. He could not yet see the Kapo, but he recognized the heavy tread of his thick-soled boots. A hush fell over the ward. The omnipresent wheezing and coughing subsided. Even the ward doctors, all prisoners themselves, stopped in their tracks and waited. Roy stared into the glazed eyes of the prisoner on the bunk just across from him. He was a new arrival in the infirmary. Boils covered his arms and legs, and pus oozed onto the thin-as-tissue blanket. He suffered from dysentery and God only knew what else. A puddle of viscous liquid, as thick and dark as motor oil, had formed on the floor beneath his palliasse. He would not make it. Roy listened as the Kapo skirted the little potbellied stove and passed slowly up and down between the narrow rows of cots and bunk beds, casting cursory glances at the patients.

When the Kapo drew nearer, Roy could see that he was the same German who came every morning, a tall florid-faced political prisoner who wore a white doctor's smock over his camp clothing. He was in charge of the prisoners' infirmary, although this daily inspection was the only time he appeared in the ward. For a few moments each morning he descended upon them with his orderlies and selected the men who would die that day. Dr. Langevin followed several paces behind them, his clogs scraping along the gritty floor.

"*Krematorium,*" the Kapo suddenly snapped, gesturing at a man hunched like a bent nail across a lower bunk. An anguished moan drifted into the stale air. Roy watched as two of the Kapo's orderlies seized the shrunken figure, pinning him against the palliasse. Another orderly stepped forward, an enormous syringe in his fingers, and jammed the long hypodermic into the man's chest. *Abspritzen,* the prisoners called it, a death shot. The victim would be dead within hours. It was one of several methods the Kapo used. Sometimes the German orderlies forced a deadly capsule down the throat of a gagging victim. On other occasions they would dunk a prisoner into a large vat of frigid water, leaving him to shiver for an hour or so. Then they would wrap him in a wet blanket or a clammy rubber sheet and deposit him back on his bunk. If the fever broke and he revived, then he would be tended to. He might even recover. But most of the victims were already suffering from pneumonia and died during the night or the next day.

Moving methodically through the ward, the Kapo reached Roy's bunk. For an instant his gray eyes peered directly at Roy in a cold appraising stare. Roy lay motionless, hoping to ignite not even a spark of interest. He did not want to appear too alert, catching the German's attention, but he couldn't appear too weak or listless either. Most of all, he didn't want the Kapo to recognize him as a man who had already been in the infirmary for three weeks. Such a prisoner would be worthless for the camp's labor system, and that would mean "*Krematorium.*" So every day for three weeks Dr. Langevin or the Polish medical student Roy knew only as Zbigniew moved him from bunk to bunk, shuffling him around the ward so the Kapo would not be able to place him.

Still staring down at Roy, the Kapo placed his hand on the badly nicked metal bed frame. His lips were thin and colorless and taut as piano wire. He tapped his chin with a forefinger. Finally, the Kapo opened his mouth, revealing a tongue as pale as a snake's belly, but he said nothing. He merely stifled a yawn. Then his gaze shifted to the creature on the upper bunk, and he passed on.

Twice more Roy heard the Kapo bark out "*Krematorium*" and listened to the short scuffling sounds of the orderlies subduing another prisoner. *Abspritzen.* Then, as the Kapo and his crew wheeled toward the door, their inspection over, a surge of relief swept over him. It was the same every morning when this moment of peril had passed for at least another day. Roy could now get on with the business of survival in the ward. But how long could this go on? On some pewter-gray October morning the Kapo would surely recognize him, ask for his name and number, and check the roster. No one was allowed to lie in the infirmary for three weeks.

When the thud of the Kapo's boots finally receded beyond the door, the ward erupted in great rasping explosions of phlegm and muted cries of despair. Two rows away a small group of Poles gathered around one of the condemned men, a countryman. Roy had witnessed this scene many times. He could not understand the words, but he didn't need to. The voices were always soft and soothing, offering what comfort they could. Often they prayed, and bits of Latin would mingle with the muttered Polish or Czech or French. Sometimes Dr. Langevin was able to provide a bit of paper, and the doomed man, his strength ebbing from him, would dictate a final letter to his family. These letters probably never passed beyond the main gate, Roy thought, but even if they went straight into the stove of some SS office, they seemed to offer a measure of solace in the last hours of agony.

Langevin meandered wearily through the ward, pausing to speak to one prisoner after another. He wore a stethoscope around his neck. In his breast pocket was a thermometer. These were his only medical instruments. Before the war he was a professor at the French Academy of Medicine in Paris, and even with his shaved head and shrunken body he carried himself with dignity. The prisoners' infirmary dispensed almost no medicines, not even aspirin. It had none. Paper bandages were sometimes available, but they merely stuck to the open sores and rotted. Sometimes the prisoners ate them. Most suffered from pneumonia, pleurisy, rheumatic or scarlet fever. Everyone had dysentery. Their only treatment was release from work, bed rest, and a slightly larger soup ration, sometimes augmented by warm tea. In some desperate cases, emergency surgeries were performed right there in the ward, using simple kitchen knives. There was no disinfectant or anesthetic, and the screams from the operating space at the far end of the ward rent the air for what seemed like hours.

Langevin tried to maintain a measure of hygiene in the ward, and certainly it was cleaner than Block 58, but it was an impossible task. Despite weekly fumigations, lice still infested the palliasses, and in the darkness mice scuttled across the floor and scratched behind the walls. Everything—the bunks, the floors, the instruments, the prisoners themselves—swam in a witch's brew of grime and human filth.

Miraculously, some patients recovered enough strength to be transferred back to their blocks. Roy had seen them stumble out, accompanied by a runner from the *Schreibstube*. Back in the main camp, assigned to a work detail, they would die within a week, maybe two. Those in the infirmary who showed no improvement after several days were declared unfit for work, and the Kapo, in his daily rounds, condemned them to the *Krematorium*.

Langevin paused beside Roy's bunk. From the very first, when Roy identified himself as an American, the doctor had taken a liking to him. They talked every day. *"Comment ça va?"* he asked, leaning down to speak.

"Can't complain," Roy responded.

"Et les jambes? How does it go with your legs today?" He was proud of his English.

"Okay," Roy answered, affecting a rugged smile, but after all this time, he still felt shaky. The pneumonia was behind him, but the pleurisy and its effects lingered. His breathing was labored, and his lungs ached. Sometimes he suffered from bouts of coughing that left him exhausted, wallowing in sweat. Lately his ankles had begun to swell. He could no longer bear to look at them. Each afternoon when Zbigniew came to move him to a new bunk, he leaned heavily on the bed frames and shuffled his feet along the floor like a man learning to skate. He still had no shoes, no socks.

As Langevin moved into the next aisle, Roy sank back into the bunk, closing his eyes. From nearby he could hear Zbigniew's high crackling voice, speaking to the doctor in his usual jumble of Polish and French. During his first days in the ward, when he was delirious with fever, thrashing in the narrow cot and raving like a lunatic, they had stayed with him and soothed him as best they could. They bathed him with cool water and fed him tea and somehow managed to keep him quiet when the Kapo arrived each morning. They had saved his life.

Roy learned this only later. He did not remember much about that first week in the ward. Only vaguely could he recall having been brought to the *Revier,* as the Germans called the prisoners' infirmary. He was already shivering with fever when the *Lagerschutz* herded the airmen—all 168 of them—from the rock pile into Block 58 in the Little Camp. That was in mid-September. At first he was relieved to be out of the tent camp, off the rock pile, and under a dry roof. But conditions in Block 58, he quickly discovered, were hardly conducive to recovery.

Like all barracks in the Little Camp, the long windowless block resembled a stable, with large barn doors that swung open at both ends, and, like all the others, it was teeming with prisoners. A notice board at the entry indicated that over eight hundred prisoners were already stuffed into the block when the airmen and others from the Paris transport arrived. Poles, Czechs, Hungarians, and French—the usual mix. Prisoners slept everywhere, jumbled on the floors or draped across the long trestle tables and scattered benches. There were no bunks. Instead, four tiers of crude wooden shelves extended along both walls. The shelves were divided into sections, like bins or cubbyholes. Each of the bins was about five feet wide and only two feet high, and from each of these cramped compartments, a row of shaved heads jutted out like eggs in a carton. Five men, emaciated and hollow eyed, were jammed shoulder to shoulder in each. They could not sit up or turn over.

A string of naked bulbs dangled from the high-pitched ceiling but when lit cast only a tepid, gauzy light. On Roy's first night in the block, as his eyes adjusted, other forms gradually took shape in the bluish gloom. Hundreds of boys—eight, nine years old, some a bit older—crouched on the floor and huddled beneath the tables. Here and there, some had wiggled into the compartments, but others, each as thin as a chicken bone, wandered listlessly about the block, searching for a spot to sleep. "*Zigeuner,*" the *Lagerschutz* groused, Gypsies. From the shadows their large black eyes peered warily at the men filing in out of the rain, and their shaved heads, grotesquely large for their emaciated bodies, wobbled eerily on their matchstick shoulders.

For several nights, while the rain pounded relentlessly on the roof, Roy and the other new arrivals slept on the floor, curling up wherever they could. Everything they touched was filthy. A crust of grime sheathed the floor, the tables, the benches, even the horse trough that served as the barracks washbasin, and the crude wooden bins, with their threadbare blankets and filthy palliasses, crawled with fleas and bedbugs. Pulling up his damp shirt on his first morning in Block 58, Roy discovered his waist and crotch dimpled with dozens of blood-red welts, each the size of a quarter. In almost no time, whole areas of his legs and groin turned a deep, purplish crimson as the bites congealed into larger, ragged splotches. The men grew frantic with itching. "You must resist the temptation to scratch," their *Blockältester* warned them. He was, Roy thought, a decent man, a longtime political prisoner who frequently offered advice about survival in the Little Camp. "You will only open up the skin and running sores will form and then will come the infection. In Buchenwald comrades die from such infections every day." Good advice, Roy conceded, but impossible to follow.

Once a week the *Blockältester* supervised a cleaning of the barracks. The men removed the scum as best they could, scrubbing the shelves and swabbing the floor with a harsh lime solution that reeked of chlorine. A delousing *Kommando,* made up of Czech prisoners, came twice a week to spray, but nothing could rid the palliasses and blankets and clothing of vermin. Night and day, standing outside the block or sitting at the crowded tables over their noontime rations, the men picked lice off each other's bodies. Like monkeys in the zoo, Warren observed.

Adding to their misery, the block contained no toilets. A low concrete wall loomed over an open pit just outside the barracks, and the men were forced to perch precariously on a wooden pole that extended over it. If they dozed or were just too weak to maintain their balance, they could easily topple in. Another latrine, Roy discovered, was two hundred yards away, in a long brick building just beyond Block 59. It served the entire Little Camp. Inside, the structure consisted of one enormous open room. Running down the center, a concrete trench extended the length of the building, over fifty yards. Dozens of men sat shoulder to shoulder on the concrete ledges that ran along both sides of the trench and leaned back against a common center backrest that prevented them from pitching head over heels into the filth. The long side walls of the building served as *pissoires,* drained by gutters that overflowed onto the stone floor. Despite the suffocating stench, many prisoners congregated in the *Abort* to talk or smoke or even to rest sitting atop the concrete trench.

Block 58 was one of five barracks in the quarantine section of the Little Camp. Ordinarily prisoners were held there for four weeks and then were transferred into the main camp for assignment to work details. Even now, some of the French and Polish prisoners in the block were sent out each day to work, returning in the evening white-faced and exhausted. After the air raid on August 24 devastated the factories at the camp, the SS could not keep the multitude of prisoners occupied, and with new transports arriving each week from all over occupied Europe, thousands of new prisoners swarmed into the *kleine Lager.*

Its muddy streets teemed with every variety of human misery and degradation, and each day Roy and Warren sat on the wooden tables in the Block 58 enclosure and watched the parade of shocked, weary prisoners shamble by. Their feet squeezed into the inflexible wooden clogs, the prisoners hobbled aimlessly about in the near constant drizzle. *"Le boulevard des invalides"* the French called it. Some men sat slumped and shivering at the edge of the street or huddled against the wire fence that separated them from the two-story barracks of the main camp. Some rushed toward the *Abort,* clutching their baggy, beltless trousers. Many could not make it and simply emptied their bowels or bladder wherever they stood. Others, their stomachs bloated from the starvation rations and convulsed by illness, fell to their knees to retch. Fellow prisoners stepped around them without so much as a glance.

Several days after the airmen settled into the Little Camp, a detachment of SS stormed Block 58 and drove the Gypsy children out. The boys darted crazily around the barracks, scrambling over the tables and benches, cowering in the dark recesses of the shelves. With brutal efficiency the SS swept through the barracks, flushing them from their hiding places, and shoved them toward the open doors. The boys kicked and flailed and reached out their bony arms toward the other prisoners, begging in their high children's voices for help. Powerless, the men stood by in shock, their ashen faces frozen in shame, as the children disappeared. In his bunk at night, Roy could still hear their screams.

Later he heard that the boys had been shot at the SS firing range, but the *Blockältester* denied this. They were simply being transferred to another block, he said, a special children's barracks in the main camp. It was possible, he added, that they might be destined for a transport east. "At any rate they will not be coming back to us in Block 58. Now there will be space for you."

With the children gone, the fliers were assigned four bins for sleeping. Lamason, their ranking officer, divided them into sections and assigned them spaces on the shelves. They slept four or five men to a shelf, with one blanket for every two men and a battered tin bowl for everyone who had not already scavenged one. Like the other prisoners, they slept with the bowl for a pillow. If left unattended, the orderlies warned, it would be stolen, and without a bowl, they would receive no soup or bread or the watery gruel the SS called coffee.

At first, Roy was happy to be off the floor, even in the cramped sleeping compartments, but he could not shake the chill that had dogged him since the rock pile. Every day, just after morning rations, the prisoners were driven out of the barracks and were forced to wander the streets of the Little Camp until evening roll call. Roy still had no shoes, and the clammy muck slathered his feet in a noxious black slime. The rain continued off and on for days. When it was not gushing through the sieve of low clouds, an oppressive mist lingered in the air. Roy's clothes refused to dry, and he was always cold. At night he couldn't stop shaking.

Warren, who shared a blanket with him in the cramped wooden compartment, pleaded with him to get help, to report to the prisoners' infirmary, but Roy had heard too many stories about the *Revier*. So for days, as his lungs burned and his fever rose, he resisted. Only when the pain left him so weak he could not drag himself out of the bin for morning rations did Warren go to the *Blockältester*. Lieutenant Allen needed help. Right away. The *Blockältester* summoned an orderly from the infirmary, who took one look at Roy and declared: "*Ins Revier.*"

The infirmary complex consisted of six low-slung wooden structures just beyond the brothel and cinema at the northwestern edge of the main camp. Some of the buildings stood in a grove of trees, lending the grounds an incongruous rustic aspect. From Block 58 it was not a long walk, but in the sea of mud Roy could barely manage. The two men assigned to deliver him deposited him outside the admissions building, and he took his place in the line of men waiting to be seen. Slowly the column inched forward. Leaning against the rain-streaked wall for support, he shivered uncontrollably. At the head of the column a prisoner orderly screened all would-be patients, returning some back to their blocks with a contemptuous scowl, selecting others for outpatient treatment, and sending still others, the more serious cases, to the wards. The orderly glanced at Roy and waved him inside with a grunt.

The admitting doctor instantly diagnosed pneumonia, a desperate case, and assigned him to the isolation ward. There were no empty bunks in the ward, so the doctor in charge there—Langevin—placed him on a cot near the potbellied stove in the center of the crowded room. In the sudden heat, wisps of steam rose from his wet clothes. His temperature soared, and his eyes lost their focus. A thunderous drumming pounded in his ears. Within hours he slipped into delirium.

For days he was out of his head, ranting and swearing. One night he screamed for orange juice over and over again, and once he tried to tackle the potbellied stove. When finally he came out of it, he remembered none of this.

Gradually he adjusted to the ward. The desolate faces around him changed, but the sobs and muttered prayers didn't. Each day he exchanged a few words with Langevin or Zbigniew, who liked to exercise their English, or one of the Czechs who told him stories about his homeland in Bohemia and asked all sorts of questions about America. Czechs seemed to be everywhere in the infirmary, and they talked constantly about politics—Czech politics as they would be after the war. Roy had only the vaguest notion of Czechoslovakia and certainly could not follow the arguments, but the conversations were animated and oddly entertaining.

One morning, just after the Kapo had passed through, Langevin told him he had a friend in the ward, an American from Block 58. He turned and pointed to a bunk not far away. The prisoner had arrived late in the night, suffering from scarlet fever and pneumonia. Peering through the tangle of bed frames and blankets, Roy recognized a familiar face. The man was semiconscious, his features distorted and streaked with bright slashes of red, but there was no mistake about it. "Warren," Roy called out, "Warren," and the man twisted about, searching for the voice. He seemed to raise his hand, then disappeared behind Langevin and the orderlies. Roy could hear him spluttering incoherently, and in time he fell silent. "He is asleep for now," Langevin explained as he stopped by Roy's bunk. "We will watch him in the night."

For days Warren burned with fever, squirming restlessly beneath the light blanket, muttering to himself, blurting out fragments of dreams. His already-short hair fell out in clumps, leaving livid splotches scattered in the stubble. Each morning Langevin moved him around the ward, as he did Roy, and finally his fever broke. He began to eat again, and, as a treat, the doctor slipped him a precious strip of bacon. He held it in his mouth for hours, savoring the salty taste.

Gradually Warren grew stronger, and whenever possible they talked. Speaking in whispers through chattering teeth, Warren brought Roy up to date about Block 58. Several of the men were sick and had been dispatched to the *Revier* or elsewhere for treatment. Levitt Beck, a P-51 pilot, was deathly ill and had been taken to the *Revier*. It didn't look good. Another, Phillip Hemmens, was dead. Roy vaguely remembered Hemmens from the train and their time on the rock pile, a wiry

Englishman who had broken his arm when his Lancaster went down over France. All things considered, he seemed in relatively good shape when the group arrived in Buchenwald, but during their ordeal on the rock pile and in the sodden days that followed, he had fallen ill. He had been sent to the *Revier* suffering from double pneumonia, rheumatic fever, and septicemia. He died in his sleep, the men learned, on September 27, and his body was burned in the *Krematorium*. They held a memorial service for him outside the barracks.

After two months in Buchenwald, the group was still being held as a unit in Block 58, and that, Warren and Roy agreed, augured well. The men had not been dispersed into the main camp or assigned to work details. On the other hand, there was always the possibility that one morning they would be summoned to the main gate and executed, like the English agents. Worst of all, it sometimes seemed that they had simply been forgotten by the SS and the Allies alike and would be left to rot in the filth of the Little Camp. They did not dwell on this in their conversations. Mostly they talked about food and home, about Philadelphia, anything to distract them from the circus of horrors around them.

But Warren's stay in the ward did not last long. One morning Roy awoke to find him gone, and another prisoner, gasping for breath, lying on his cot. Roy dragged himself past row after row of bunks, searching, but his friend was nowhere to be found. Later Langevin explained that Monsieur Bauder had been moved to another ward in the complex. He was on his way to recovery and would probably be returned to Block 58 soon.

Warren's transfer had been a blow, and in the bleak days that followed, Roy retreated more and more into himself. A curious numbness settled over him, dulling every sensation, even the pain in his chest. Now, as he did every night, Roy sipped the tepid soup and drank the watery tea in silence. Light sleet peppered the windowpanes, and the room turned cold. He watched the other men in their bunks. Some tossed fitfully. Some moaned. Others dozed, as motionless and silent as stones at the bottom of a lake. The viscous puddle beneath the bunk of the newcomer across from him had widened since morning. The man's mouth gaped wide open, displaying gossamer strings of spittle and a jumble of widely spaced teeth. Only an occasional flutter of his darkened eyelids gave any suggestion that he might still be alive.

The days were shorter now, and it was already dark when the Russian stretcher bearers arrived. The body-removal detail came only once each day, usually after the evening rations. They barged into the ward, stacking the bodies of all who had died since the previous night on stretchers made of wooden poles and chicken wire. Using an indelible pencil, they scrawled the patient's camp number on his leg in large orange figures that stood out like neon on the pale, dry-as-mortar skin. On the days when the little stove was stoked, the stench of the bodies lying untended in the bunks was unbearable, but today the room was cold as the grave.

After lights-out Roy lay in his bunk listening to the cacophony of languages and staring at the stains on the palliasse just above his head. Night was the worst time, worse even than the Kapo's morning inspection. He was no longer afraid of dying, he realized, not afraid of the pain. That was all beyond his control. His greatest fear was that he would simply disappear in this sewer without a trace. No one knew he was here. Not the Allies, not the Red Cross, not even the Luftwaffe. No one was looking for him. He was lost in the shuffle of war and when he died of disease or malnutrition or was shot or hanged, he would vanish up the crematorium chimney, no more than a wisp of smoke.

It was about four months now since May would have received the MIA telegram, four months with no word from him or information from the War Department. He tried to conjure up an image of her with a pleasantly swollen belly, ready to deliver at any time now, but it would not come. It seemed so long ago, so far away. Still, he composed letters to her in his head, sometimes mumbling them aloud amid the bedlam of the ward. Sometimes he sang softly, snatches of songs he had once known so well. No one paid any attention. Everyone talked to himself in the ward.

Sometimes a French phrase filtered through the damp air, reminding him of his friends in Jouy or the apartment in Avenue Michel Bizot. Paris had been liberated in late August, not long after Fresnes was evacuated—this he learned from the nightly Wehrmacht news bulletins that were broadcast over the loudspeakers—and by now most of France was free. Where were they all, he wondered—Jonckheere and Pivert, Georges and Robert—on this October night? Most of all, he prayed that Colette and the Florins had survived the last battles, and that they were sitting now at the forest house table in the yellow light of the kerosene lamp. They had their orders and had surely participated in the liberation—Captain Paul would have seen to that. It was a comforting thought, a buoy in this sea of trouble, and one he clung to with the desperation of a drowning man.

But what if they had been captured when he was, tracked down by the Gestapo because of some false step of his? Once again his mind raced through the labyrinth of contacts in Jouy, in Bannost, in Paris. For perhaps the thousandth time, he tried to reconstruct the meetings and conversations, the interrogations. He had given nothing away in the Avenue Foch or at Fresnes, but he could not shake the nagging fear that somehow his naïve attempt to escape had tripped a wire, setting off a chain reaction of Gestapo probes that led them back to Jouy, to the school and the forest house. He struggled with these torments every night.

Exhausted from the mere effort at recall, he turned on his side and pulled the thin blanket up over his head. He didn't want something seeping through from the palliasse above him, dripping onto his face in the night.

Just before dawn Roy could hear the whistles and the bellowing from the main camp. In the ward, prisoners stirred. He opened his eyes. Pale dusty light slanted into the room from a bank of windows on the opposite wall, falling across the bunks and floor. While he rubbed his face and squinted, he heard the slap of wooden clogs approaching quickly through the ward. That would be Zbigniew, ready to move him to another bunk before the Kapo arrived. Roy pushed himself up on his elbows in anticipation. But it was not Zbigniew or Langevin. The man squatting beside his bunk was an American, an airman he recognized from Block 58.

"Hey," the man whispered, "listen up. I've only got a minute. I'm not supposed to be here. Just came to the *Ambulanz*, the outpatient ward, and I'm on my way back to Block 58. Polish guy out front pointed me in here."

Lying on his back, Roy propped himself up on his elbows, his head suddenly clear.

"There's news," the man said. "Yesterday two men showed up at the main gate. One was a civilian from the big interrogation center at Dulag Luft. The other was a Luftwaffe officer. They were looking for us—for the Allied fliers. They assembled all the guys from Block 58 at the gate. Everybody was pretty spooked, especially after what happened to those British spies. But it looks like the brass in Berlin finally realized we were here and is ready to move us to a real POW camp."

Roy blinked, trying to comprehend. "You mean we're leaving this place?"

"It was all a mistake," the man continued, his voice heavy with sarcasm. "That's what the guy said. We never should have been in this hellhole. The Luftwaffe boys in Berlin sent our transfer papers to Paris, but the Gestapo had already moved us out. It's taken this long for the Luftwaffe to catch up with us. Anyway, in a few days we will be leaving under military guard, headed for a POW camp somewhere."

Roy was sitting now. He was dizzy, and his ankles were still swollen and ached with every move. The effort made him short of breath.

"The Dulag Luft man handed out personnel forms. Said they were from the Red Cross. The forms have all sorts of questions—things like hometown, military unit, length of service—that sort of thing. Even asks for military experience—what sort of aircraft you flew. A lot of the fellows don't want to fill them out."

Roy remembered the briefings about Dulag Luft and the warnings about phony Red Cross questionnaires the Germans used there.

"Lamason protested, but the Kraut insisted. Either fill them out fully or stay in Buchenwald. That's the choice."

"What's going to happen?"

"Lamason said he wasn't going to fill his out, but he would leave it up to each man."

"What about us?" Roy asked.

"The orders apply to all of us. There are ten or so guys here in the main infirmary or in one of the other medical blocks, but they'll round everybody up."

Roy was dumbfounded. Leaving Buchenwald, just like that? He could hardly believe it. Maybe it was a dream, or, more likely, some sort of German trick. Maybe this was what they had told the British agents—You are leaving Buchenwald for a POW camp; come to the main gate.

At a POW camp he would be able to write home. The Red Cross carried mail between the German POW camps and the States. He could get a letter off to May, tell her that he was alive and all in one piece. She could write to him, and he would learn about her and the baby. For weeks now he had hardly dared to think about them, to even conjure up a life beyond the squalor of the camp. But now, on the verge of liberation, murmurs of another life beckoned to him.

Roy was awake long before daylight. He had not really slept. In the evening, Zbigniew had moved him to the bunk, and he lay wide-awake inhaling the unmistakable stench of gangrene and listening to the groaning of the men all around him.

"There is someone here looking for you," he heard a voice whisper as Zbigniew drew up beside the bunk. The Pole leaned down. "A German from the *Schreibstube* is outside the door, inquiring after you," he whispered. "He checks to determine if you are still in this ward. He examines our records."

Roy's pulse quickened. "What does he want?"

"He would say nothing, except that he had first gone to the Block 58 where the other Allied aviators are."

Roy sat up as best he could. "What does it mean?"

Zbigniew hesitated. "It is perhaps prelude to your transfer," he said, shrugging his shoulders in the French fashion. "Perhaps you will be released or transferred back to the Block 58 or to another block in the main camp . . ." His voice trailed off.

"Or up the chimney," Roy finished the thought.

The Pole did not argue. He had seen too much to speculate.

Zbigniew hurried away, and Roy squirmed about in the bunk. "They're coming for me," Roy said to no one in particular. "They are really coming for me." His heart was pounding. Seconds later a German political prisoner appeared beside the bunk. Behind him stood Langevin.

"*Sie sind Häftling 78357, amerikanischer Kriegsgefangener?*"

Roy looked at Langevin for help. The doctor nodded yes, and the German rattled on. The guard glanced down at Roy again.

"*Der Häftling 78357 soll mitkommen,*" he said. When Roy still did not move, he turned to Langevin. "*Er soll mit den anderen alliierten Fliegern entlassen werden,*" he explained, pointing to Roy, "*und muss sich sofort am Turm melden.*"

"Well?" Roy asked, shifting his weight uneasily on the bunk. "What'd he say?"

"You are to go with him now," Langevin translated, "to the main gate." He paused. His thin face looked troubled. "He says that you are to be released with the other *aviateurs*, released from the camp. He refers to you as a prisoner of war. That is a good sign."

Roy sat up and swung his legs over the edge of the bunk. Gripping the metal frame to hoist himself out, he put weight first on one foot, then the other, and tried to stand. A terrific pain gripped his ankles, and his knees buckled. The German grabbed him before he fell and eased him back onto the palliasse.

"Was ist mit ihm los?" he asked, turning again to Langevin.

Before the doctor could answer, Roy pulled himself again into a sitting position, steadied himself, and tried to stand. He took a short shuffling step before collapsing back onto the bunk. His breathing was labored. Langevin reached for Roy's pant legs, delicately rolling up the cuffless trousers. Roy looked down. His ankles were swollen and stiff as marble pillars.

"Hydropisie," Langevin pronounced glumly. To the guard he said, *"Wassersucht."*

"What? What?" Roy gasped, turning from one man to the other.

"I am afraid that it is dropsy," Langevin sighed.

The German tried once again to lift Roy to his feet, but it was no go. *"Unmöglich,"* he grimaced to the doctor, "simply impossible."

Once again Roy struggled to extricate himself from the bunk, holding on to the bed frame. He wobbled like a man on stilts.

"Hier bleiben," the man from the *Schreibstube* said to him, and turning, walked on down the ward. He did not come back.

The next day no messenger from the *Schreibstube* came to the ward. No papers releasing Roy from the infirmary arrived, and on the following evening, October 18, Zbigniew stopped at his bunk to tell him that the Allied aviators were gone. They had been released from Block 58 and, he believed, had left the Little Camp. Where they went, he could not say.

In the days that followed, Roy tumbled down a rat hole of despair. For a brief moment, he had allowed himself to think beyond Buchenwald. Now he paid for it. In the months since he had jumped from the falling plane, he had never doubted that he would make it. Now, for the first time, he was truly shaken, and the soul-robbing hopelessness he saw all around him every day spread across him like an expanding glacier. A hollowness filled his chest, and his thoughts, mere fragments, swept by him as illusory and intangible as clouds. Only one thing was clear: the others were gone, and he was alone in the kingdom of the dead.

Transports were arriving almost daily now from the east, and the already crowded Little Camp was swamped. The *Revier* could not deal with the relentless tide of patients. Extra cots were added, and some of the new arrivals slept on the floor. Langevin was overwhelmed. Many of the sick went straight to Block 60, the "invalid block," where they were immediately *abgespritzt,* or simply allowed to die in the prevailing squalor. Still, Langevin continued to shift Roy from bunk to bunk, and some days Zbigniew hid him in the latrine while the Kapo made his inspection. But the stress was growing unbearable. He had been in the infirmary for nearly five weeks, and he was living on borrowed time. He could see the worry in Zbigniew's eyes.

Roy kept to himself. He could summon no interest in the new arrivals, and each new face, like each new day, seemed to dissolve into another and another, formless and without feature. He tried to recall the lyrics of the songs, the wordplay of the crosswords, anything to focus his mind. Sitting listlessly at the edge of his bunk, he brooded for hours. He could not hold a thought, and the days passed desolate and uneventful.

"You are an American, *nicht wahr?*" a voice murmured to him one frigid morning. Roy was lying on his back, his eyes open, half asleep. He was far from the tiny stove, and whenever he sighed, his breath materialized in the damp air. The voice seemed to drift toward him from far away, filtered through the torpor that had enveloped him for days. He turned and shook his head, trying to focus his eyes. A man sitting at the edge of the bunk just opposite stared expectantly at him. Like all the other prisoners, he was sallow-faced and thin, but he carried an aura of health about him. His manner was surprisingly robust and unusually open. "I have been in the ward for several days now," the man went on, "and every day I am hearing you speaking English to the doctor." He smiled and leaned so close Roy could smell the sourness of his breath. "I see also that you are moved from bunk to bunk. The doctor tells me that you are a pilot. Is this so?"

At first Roy would say nothing. Don't ask questions in Buchenwald, a German prisoner had warned him, and don't trust anyone who does. You will be suspected of being a *Spitzbube,* an SS informer. So Roy sat and listened, occasionally nodding his head but saying nothing. This did not seem to trouble the man at all. He chatted easily in a muddle of German and English, telling Roy all about himself and his family. His name was Günther, he said, and he had spent several years in America, in New York. He hoped to become a citizen, but when the war broke out, he was visiting family in Germany and the Nazis detained him. Later he was formally arrested. He was vague about the details. Politically unreliable, the Gestapo claimed, he was denounced as a defeatist and a traitor. They threw him into Buchenwald.

A red triangle was sewn on the surprisingly substantial coat he wore, and on his feet, Roy noticed, were thick wool socks. He slept with a rugged pair of thick-soled shoes beneath his head, a privileged prisoner to be sure. "I am working in the *Häftlingskantine*," Günther said, "the prisoners' canteen, in the *Hauptlager*." He smiled. "It is a much desired job—warm and dry, and there is food. Beer and cigarettes, yes, and all sorts of food are stored there, but the prisoners rarely see these things. They are hoarded by the Kapos and used to bribe the SS guards."

The man talked throughout the afternoon, and the next day, after Roy had been moved to another part of the ward, he dropped by Roy's bunk again. He seemed excited to know that the American was one of the Allied pilots in the camp—that much Roy did confirm—but he did not probe for information. He did not ask questions about Roy's military or personal life or about his experiences in the Little Camp. He seemed content just to speak English with someone, and to instruct Roy about survival in the camp.

"You are *verstört, mein Freund*. You suffer from the melancholia, that much I see immediately. Everyone in this *Schweinestall* feels as you do. Everyone. But you must overcome this or you will perish. Here your duty is to survive. *Durchhalten, darauf kommt es an*. Surviving from day to day, that is all that counts. Your wife, your home, your children—such nice memories will only get in the way. In Buchenwald you must check your humanity at the *Effektenkammer* with your other personal belongings. With luck, one day you will be able to reclaim it.

"My *Blockältester* gave me this hard advice when I first arrived at the camp. I was appalled, as you are, at what he said, and I would not accept it. But, as I have learned, it was wise counsel. You are here now, and this is all that matters. One is so degraded by this system that you must be hard or you will go mad. Lock your past in a safe place, and let the future take care of itself. Concentrate on today. You must hold on. Liberation will come, of that you can be certain. The Russians push now rapidly from the east, and the Anglo-Americans, too, are driving toward the Reich. When that day arrives, the camp underground will rise. The SS will try to massacre all the prisoners, but we will be ready. You must be, too."

Roy never argued with this, when day after day, Günther pressed his lesson. How could he? Through the long, desolate hours he watched men propped motionless in their bunks, staring empty-eyed at the floor or ceiling or the mattress just above them. Those who could walk drifted vacantly around the ward, deep in silent conversation with invisible partners. Sometimes a man would suddenly stop, stock-still, and erupt from this trance in a howling frenzy, clawing at the air with tremulous hands, before dropping to his bunk, exhausted.

Encouraged by Günther, Roy began to move around the ward, stepping tentatively through the crowd of prisoners strewn across the floor. The swelling in his ankles had subsided, and Langevin speculated that he would soon be reassigned. He *was* getting better, Roy realized. He could slide his bare feet along the grimy floor or take little mincing steps without Zbigniew's help. The doctor could not hide his relief. It was miraculous that Roy had survived this long in the ward, he admitted. He would never have believed it possible to conceal a man for such a time in the *Revier*.

"Today I must leave you," Günther declared one morning when Roy hobbled down to his bunk. "I will be returned to my block in the main camp. The order arrived last night." He smiled and patted Roy on the shoulder. "You will also soon be released from the *Revier*. When you are out, come to the *Häftlingskantine*. You will find it up the hill, to the right of the main gate, at the western edge of the *Appellplatz*. Ask for me, and I will see that you receive extra rations."

Roy was sorry to see Günther leave, but he did not have long to wait for his own release. A few days later, a runner from the *Schreibstube* strode into the ward just after evening rations, announcing that *Häftling* 78357 was to be transferred to Block 45 in the main camp. Roy pulled himself anxiously out of the bunk and looked up at Langevin. In his hands the doctor held a clipboard. "It is one of the two-story concrete barracks," he said as he wrote, "just across the wire from the Little Camp. It will be warmer than the smaller wooden blocks closer to the main gate. It is a block for political prisoners, a good block, I am told. You will find comrades there."

While the prisoner from the *Schreibstube* waited, Zbigniew produced what appeared to be the remnants of a burlap sack. These were cut into strips and wrapped carefully around Roy's feet and ankles, then covered with several layers of newspaper, and tied at the top with coarse string. Roy picked up his feet, testing, and found that with some effort he could stumble along. At the exit, he turned and looked back into the cluttered ward. Langevin and Zbigniew were already busy with other patients, and they did not see him go.

It was November, and the gritty black soil of the camp had begun to harden. Traces of afternoon snow lined the walkway and brushed the evergreens beside the *Revier* compound. Roy followed behind the runner as he trudged between the last rows of barracks in the main camp. Judging by the hazy sun that was setting behind the infirmary, they were walking east. After weeks of confinement in the *Revier,* the brisk air burned his skin, and he was winded after going only a few yards. The runner, who ignored him, did not walk fast, but Roy strained to keep pace.

Block 45 stood at the east end of a long arcing row of two-story barracks, just across a wide street from the *Effektenkammer* where he had received his camp clothes on that first day. Like the other barracks they passed, the entrance to Block 45 was at the center of the building, beneath two flights of concrete steps that formed a steep arch over the entry and led to another set of doors for the second floor. They passed beneath these, and the runner deposited him at the cubicle of the *Blockältester,* who coughed a few words in German and turned him over to the block secretary. Hardly bothering to look up, the *Blockschreiber* recorded his name and number in the block log and informed him that he had already been assigned to a work detail. Tomorrow after morning *Appell* he was to report to *Schild sechs,* signpost six, near the main gate for duty.

Roy followed an orderly up a flight of stairs and turned into a long room of bunk beds, stacked three high. The sleeping bay was almost warm and, in contrast to conditions in the Little Camp, an effort had been made to keep things reasonably clean and orderly. Most surprisingly, he discovered that he was not alone. As he trailed behind the orderly along the rows of bunks, he recognized a familiar form stretched out on a lower bunk. The man was startlingly thin, his face shrunken, his skin pasty and dry, but there was no doubt that it was Warren. They were overjoyed to see each other and embraced in the narrow space between the bunks. Warren looked him up and down and shook his head in wonder. "When I left you in the infirmary," Warren whispered, "I thought you were a goner."

There were others from the group, Warren told him, other airmen who had been too sick or too weak to leave with the main group on October 18. Five Americans, several Canadians, and an Australian, eight in all. Tom Malcolm, a navigator; Harry Hunter, a Thunderbolt pilot from Pittsburgh; Ed Vincent, a bombardier; and the others. Roy met them briefly that night. All were emaciated, their faces haggard, their clothes little more than tatters. He did not recognize a soul. They were exhausted from a day of hard labor in the cold, and after brief introductions, they were eager to crawl into their bunks.

Roy found his assigned place. Regardless of weather, Warren warned him, they were permitted to wear only a shirt while sleeping. The SS *Blockführer* sometimes appeared in the middle of the night to conduct spot-checks. Those found with anything more than a shirt on were dragged outside and chained to a post just beside the downstairs entrance. There they would stay for twenty-four to thirty-six hours, sometimes longer. "And in the morning," Warren added, "you've got to put your bunk in order. The Kapos conduct spot inspections during the day." Roy nodded, and in the familiar blue light, he stripped, placing his clothes neatly on a bench at the foot of the bunk. He tucked his tin bowl beneath his head and closed his eyes. He had no idea what tomorrow would bring.

In the darkness before dawn, the whistles sounded, echoing through the silent streets of the camp. Stiff and shivering, the men in Block 45 crawled from their bunks. They dressed hurriedly in the usual assortment of rags, rubbing their arms for warmth. They straightened their beds and then grabbed their bowls. A low grumbling rose from the sleeping bay. Tubs of soup and slabs of stone-hard bread appeared on the long tables in the center of the room, and the men filed silently by while the *Stubendienst* ladled out the lukewarm liquid from the greasy vats. They ate greedily, stored their bowls, and then slumped reluctantly toward the exit doors.

Stepping out onto the high concrete steps, Roy watched as men poured out of the other barracks into the frosty air, assembling by blocks along the camp's central street. The *Blockältester*s darted about, barking out orders, forming their charges into ranks of eight abreast. The men bent into the wind, stamping their feet to ward off the numbing cold, while the block secretary took a quick count. The dead were carried along. After much jostling, the miserable procession churned into motion, climbing the slope past rows of darkened barracks toward the *Appellplatz* and the main gate.

Roy followed along, marching as best he could over the crumbling pavement. Ahead of them, shafts of light from the guard towers and the main gate cut through the mist, forming a bubble of eerie brilliance over the *Appellplatz*. Thousands of men were already assembled there, and more continued to tramp into the square. Leading his men through the shuffling multitude, Roy's *Blockältester* directed them to their assigned position in the formation, reordering them into ranks of twenty. From the balcony of the gatehouse, below a bank of blinding floodlights, SS officers in their smart uniforms watched the assembling thousands, chatting, sometimes laughing and slapping their thighs in delight.

The roll call dragged on and on. The already biting wind picked up, hurling grit and ice crystals through the formation. In the phosphorescent glow, the men struggled to stand at attention, shivering in the ranks. Occasionally a prisoner's knees would buckle and he would slump forward, but the men next to him would quickly grab his arms, propping him up. Gradually the sky brightened and the floodlights were extinguished, leaving the buildings and grounds and the mass of huddled prisoners shrouded in a grim monochromatic gray.

When each block had completed its count, the barracks chiefs reported, one after another, to the SS *Rapportführer*. If anyone was missing or the block chief's tally did not mesh with the roll call officer's figures, the process halted and another count was made. Sometimes guards were sent to the barracks or to the infirmary, even the pathology department at the crematorium, searching for the missing prisoner. Meanwhile the entire formation waited. When his own barracks' turn came, Roy shifted in line just enough to give himself a view of the chief as he stepped forward and shouted out: "*Block 45 stillgestanden! Mützen ab!*" The shivering men of Block 45 whipped the caps from their heads and waited. Then, turning smartly back toward the roll call officer, the block chief bellowed: "*Block 45 mit 822 Häftlinge zum Appell angetreten. Keiner fehlt!*" Over eight hundred men in the block and all accounted for. On and on the count continued, until each of the nearly fifty blocks had reported.

When finally all sixty thousand prisoners were accounted for, the loudspeaker on the main gate blared a long list of announcements, which were laboriously translated into a dozen languages. At the conclusion of these *Bekanntmachungen*, the metallic voice boomed out the names and numbers of individual prisoners, ordering them to report to one of the signposts at the main gate immediately after roll call. Roy could feel a shudder ripple through the massive formation. Then the loudspeaker roared: "*Aussenkommandos antreten!*" and the labor details that would work beyond the wire began scrambling to their positions. As soon as they assembled, whistles blew, and the columns began marching, five abreast, out the main gate. During this spectacle, a small brass band stationed beside the gate suddenly burst forth, belting out bouncy marching songs. Made up of prisoners, the band wore brightly colored uniforms, like movie ushers in the big downtown theaters in Philly, and the already exhausted men of the work details sang as they passed through the gate.

After some confusion, Roy, too, found his *Kommando* at signpost six and fell in with the others. Their job was to clear away the debris in the ruins of the munitions factory just outside the wire. Throughout the day, with only a thirty-minute break at noon for tea and a lump of bread, he struggled to untangle the contorted steel beams and charred timbers of the demolished plant, separating and arranging them in tidy piles. By early afternoon the snow flurries gave way to sheets of freezing rain. Roy's fingers turned stiff and red, and his legs, trembling with strain, threatened to collapse under him at any minute. He was soaked to the bone.

Finally, in the gray pall of dusk, the Kapo's whistle sounded and the detail formed up again and marched back to the *Appellplatz* for evening roll call. There, beneath the blinding floodlights, the grueling process of the morning was repeated. After a day of backbreaking labor in the cold, standing for hours in the frigid downpour while the SS *Rapportführer* awaited the final count and bawled out the usual threats was even more draining than the morning *Appell*. Roy's legs quivered, and he teetered in the ranks, barely able to stay upright. Later, in Block 45, he was almost too weak to drink the tasteless grass soup and was asleep long before lights-out.

In the weeks that followed, this routine rarely varied. Roy worked outside every day, sorting through the rubble of the bombed-out DAW plant, moving stones, clearing debris. Aside from midday rations, the only break came from the increasingly frequent air-raid alerts. No bombs fell on Buchenwald, but the warning sirens howled almost every day and the men were expected to take cover wherever they could. On Sundays, there was entertainment. A camp orchestra performed classical pieces, a Russian choir sang, and once a Ukrainian played Slavic dances on his accordion. A few of the Poles and Russians even danced. Mostly, though, the men slumbered through the performances, glad to have an opportunity to rest during the day.

At Sunday roll call, the camp's brass band played waltzes as accompaniment to the weekly hangings. While "The Blue Danube" or a medley from *The Merry Widow* swept gaily through the square, a man, his hands tied behind his back and a block of wood wired between his teeth, stepped onto the platform of the gallows. While the thousands looked on, a noose was placed around his neck and the steps were kicked away and the man dangled beneath the cross beam, writhing as he slowly strangled to death. On other Sundays a prisoner was stripped, bent over and shackled to a wooden rack, and lashed with a whip until the flesh from his back and buttocks and legs was lacerated into bloody strips of meat that threatened to slip at any moment from the bone. Punishment, an SS officer brayed, for anyone attempting to escape. Meanwhile, the band played on, its cheerful airs fluttering above the horror like a butterfly over a corpse.

The weather grew steadily colder. Days passed in light snow and frozen drizzle, driven by the bitter wind that sliced across the mountaintop. For days at a time the sun disappeared altogether, and a damp mist shrouded the camp. Roy could never get dry, and gradually the burlap on his feet turned to sodden rags, and ominous dark patches began to appear on his toes. He was always cold, always hungry.

The meager rations seemed to shrink each day, and Roy felt himself growing weaker. Like all the men in Block 45, he was desperate for food. A potato peel, an extra nub of worm-eaten bread—any scrap would do. Eating the moldy *Knäckebrot* or standing in the cold at *Appell*, he found himself clutching a fragment of memory, an image that he had long forgotten. He was standing, a boy no more than ten, on a street corner in Philly. It was just before Christmas, and sleet was falling. He had no coat, just a thin cotton jacket, and was trying to warm his hands by a fire in an oil drum filled with splintered crates. Other men and boys were huddled around the flames and the flying sparks, rubbing their arms and stamping their feet against the cold. He had spent the afternoon, as he frequently did in those days, sorting through the scraps behind Beck's Produce, gnawing the wilted lettuce and spoiled beans, the rubbery carrots. Anything he could find. The men gathered around the barrel spoke in German and Hungarian— there were plenty in the neighborhood. They talked about finding work and where to get something to eat, good places where the garbage was bountiful and could be scavenged. Ever since Roy could remember, he had had to make do—*abkochen*, as the inmates of the camp called it— to look out for himself, to find ways over, under, and through the system just to survive. Buchenwald, he decided, was no different.

He recalled what Günther had told him before leaving the infirmary: If Roy was willing to come to the *Häftlingskantine*, the German would find extra rations for him. Roy had seen the prisoners' canteen many times while standing at roll call. To reach it, he would have to cross the *Appellplatz*, in full view of the main gate and guard towers, but he didn't care. He was desperate enough to give it a try.

He decided that in the time between evening *Appell* and lights-out he would make his way through the milling prisoners to the building he knew was the canteen. Exhausted and half frozen, he was gripped by a fatalism that was almost soothing. If the bastards shot him, they shot him. At least he would be doing something. He would not let them starve him to death. He would go to the canteen and he would ask for Günther.

The next day, a cold, unusually clear day, he carried out his plan. In the confusion following *Appell*, he slipped through the dissolving crowd, snaking his way toward the canteen. The building stood at the southwestern edge of camp and showed few signs of life as Roy approached. A handful of prisoners loitered around the entrance, and as Roy brushed past them, they stopped their conversation to stare. He tried the door, but it would not give and he could not see inside. There was no trace of light. Behind him the men were muttering, and Roy turned to face them. "Günther," he said slowly. "I'm looking for Günther." He knew no last name, no camp number. "Günther," he repeated slowly. "Günther . . . canteen." The men eyed him warily. "*Kamerad* Günther," Roy said, smiling broadly. "*Kamerad.*" The prisoners leaned together, conferring. "*Komm mit,*" one of the men whispered at last, and gestured for Roy to follow.

They walked along the building, turned a corner, and stopped at a side entrance. "*Hier warten,*" the man said, motioning for Roy to keep still. Then he knocked on the heavy wooden door and stepped back, waiting. He did not look at Roy. After a moment the door cracked open an inch or so and a voice inside asked something. The man answered and disappeared inside. Roy stood in the darkness and waited. He leaned against the wall and hunched his shoulders to coax a little warmth from his body. Stars were rising over the black trees, and searchlights from the guard towers had begun to rake the *Appellplatz*.

Within moments, he heard footsteps behind the door, and when it opened Günther peered out into the darkness and spotted Roy. "*Mein Gott,*" he exclaimed. "*Du bist's tatsächlich.* It is you. I knew you would come. *Das wusste ich schon.*" He grasped Roy by the arm and led him inside. In a darkened foyer, crowded with sacks of grain and lit only by candlelight, he blurted out a stream of questions—what block was Roy in, how long had he been in the main camp, what was his work detail? But time was pressing. The conversation would have to wait. The German vanished down the hall and after a few minutes returned carrying a five-gallon canister of soup. It was actually hot. *"Wir müssen uns eilen,"* he said, hurrying Roy toward the door. "Tonight we must rush, but if you have the nerve to come back tomorrow, I will have the nerve to give you more." Then, without another word, he pulled open the door, and Roy stepped out again into the starry darkness.

He had never envisioned such a bounty—a loaf of bread or a slab of sausage, maybe, but not a milk canister full of soup—and he realized with a jolt that he had no idea how he would get it back to Block 45. Somehow he would have to make it across the deserted *Appellplatz* and then down the slope through eight rows of barracks. He decided to take the most direct route, cutting diagonally across the broad square. Cones of moving light now swept over the vast space. Taking a deep breath, he set off. At first he tried to carry the canister, but after several paces his arms began to twitch, the canister bounced against his thighs, and the precious soup sloshed over the lip. He was afraid he would drop it all. For a few paces he tried dragging it, but the grating of the metal over the uneven pavement scratched and whined like bad brakes. He did not dare to pause or look up. The machine guns in the watchtowers were following his every step, he knew, and the SS guards on the balcony of the main gate stopped their conversation to stare.

Struggling to catch his breath, he slowed. Suddenly he was engulfed in a circle of dazzling light. His eyes squinted almost shut, and he could feel the blood pounding in his temples. Look busy, he told himself, look confident. Act like you know what you're doing, like you're here on orders from higher authorities with nothing to hide, nothing to explain. Act like carrying a canister of soup across the empty square in the dark is the most natural thing in the world. He gritted his teeth, squared his shoulders and stood as erect as he could. He would offer the bastards a big, broad target, and he would not hurry. He walked on, his ears alert for any sound. The cylinder of light followed him, burning a hole in his back, until he reached the camp's central street, which would take him away from the *Appellplatz* and the main gate.

Once he reached the first row of barracks, he turned into a narrow side street that ran between the blocks and heaved a sigh of relief. Here he was hidden from the searchlights, and his pace quickened. It was not the SS guards who threatened him now but his fellow prisoners. Dark figures milled about between the barracks, peering out at him, staring with hungry eyes at the canister. A few fell in several paces behind him, following along as he struggled with his load. He could hear the slapping of their clogs on the gravel and their muttered words. *"Was haben sie da, Freund,"* a voice called out, but Roy kept walking. "Is that soup you have?" Roy walked on. *"Lèche-cul! C'est un collu,"* a voice hissed, as he turned into another street. *"Ja,"* another spat at him. "A spy, *ein Arschlecker* of the SS." At any second, they would jump him, but he trudged on, exhausted but not daring to stop. He passed through the four rows of low wooden blocks, then the first of the brick-and-concrete two-story barracks, until at last Block 45 loomed up before him.

That night he shared the soup with the men in the surrounding bunks, about a dozen, airmen, Poles, Germans, whoever was close by. Their eyes were wide with wonder. How, they wanted to know, had he managed this? Where did it come from? The little group huddled around the canister, eagerly dipping their bowls into the warm soup. They ate quietly, absorbed in the sudden windfall. Beyond the charmed circle others stared at them from their bunks in silence. He wished he could get more for some of the others, but it was not possible. He would go back to the canteen tomorrow, Roy told the airmen, but he needed some help. He couldn't manage the large canister alone, and he couldn't guarantee that they would make it back. The men looked down at their hands, avoiding his eyes, and an embarrassed silence fell over them. No one volunteered. "Oh, hell," Warren finally spoke up. "Count me in."

The next day, just after evening roll call, Roy and Warren made their way to the prisoners' canteen, and Günther again ladled out a full canister of soup. He would do this every day, he said, if Roy and his comrade would come. They agreed and shook his hand. "You are brave men," Günther said as he held open the door. "Just hungry men," Roy said, and they began the agonizing trek across the *Appellplatz*. All was as it had been the night before—the dancing searchlights, the SS guards on the balcony of the gatehouse, the machine guns in the watchtowers. Despite the cold, both men were sweating, and neither spoke. They walked resolutely, their eyes locked on the first row of barracks and the central street that split them.

They repeated this ordeal each day for a week, altering their route through the rows of barracks to avoid attracting too much attention.

They were pushing their luck, and they knew it. One day, without warning, a guard might simply open fire. The SS sometimes shot prisoners for sport or just to break the boredom of their monotonous sentry duty. Or they could be set upon by starving prisoners. Still, they continued their trips to the *Häftlingskantine.*

Finally, there was trouble, but not from the SS. The *Blockältester,* a German political prisoner who had winked at Roy's visits to the canteen, ordered him to stop. The other prisoners in the block were grumbling, he said. They were envious, naturally, and suspicious. Some even claimed that the big American and his comrade must be SS spies, *Spitzbuben.* How else did he rate this special treatment? The chief did not believe this. He marveled at Roy's courage, at his audacity, but he wanted no trouble in the block.

Roy tried to plead his case, but it was a waste of breath, and the nights of extra soup came to a halt. Among the small group of airmen, spirits plummeted. Most were convinced that the main group had been slaughtered when they left on October 18, shot at one of the SS firing ranges. If they had reached a POW camp, they would have informed the Red Cross and the Luftwaffe authorities about those left behind and someone would have come looking for them. But here they sat over a month later, rotting in Buchenwald, forgotten.

From the Wehrmacht news bulletins read over the loudspeaker every day, it was clear that the Allied offensive in the west had ground to a halt in Holland. Patton was bogged down in Lorraine, and the high hopes of late summer, hopes for victory by Christmas, dissolved in their hands like melting snow. Everyone was tense. Tempers flared, and bitter words laced every conversation. Roy and Warren kept more and more to themselves, struggling to find the will to wake up in the morning. Gradually they forgot the war. The war was happening in another world, an irrelevant world beyond the wire. Instead, they talked about Philly, about food, about training, about their crews. They lived hour-to-hour, day-to-day.

Thick wet snow, the flakes as big as golf balls, fell regularly, and working ankle deep in the slush day after day left Roy with a constant throbbing in his feet. His toes burned, and he was convinced he had frostbite. His legs ached constantly, and his ankles had begun to swell again. Each day was an ordeal. Still, there were some surprising kindnesses. Once, during morning roll call as he swayed uncertainly in the ranks, he felt something being pushed into his hand from behind. A Russian prisoner he had seen around the block had slipped a pair of thick wool socks into his fingers. A Pole from the sleeping bay handed him a clove of garlic, a precious gift that was good for the blood and general health, he promised. Roy got to know a prisoner named Joe Chopp, a Belgian from Antwerp, who worked in the prisoners' kitchen close to Block 45. He took an instant liking to Roy and began smuggling small morsels of food for him from time to time—slices of sausage, a bit of jam, small loaves of bread, which Roy shared with Warren. Warren was amazed by the new contacts, the new friends Roy was always making. "Have you *ever* known a stranger?" he asked again and again. "*Abkochen,*" Roy answered, "just making do."

Thanksgiving was approaching. One of the men mentioned turkey and dressing and cranberry sauce and his family seated around the table at home, sending everyone's spirits into a nosedive. They were barely hanging on, worn down mentally and physically. One by one they would simply drift away, disappearing, like all the others in Buchenwald finally did, up the chimney.

Then, before dawn, on November 27, a hand shook Roy rudely awake. It was the German barracks orderly, the *Stubendienst.* "You are to report to the chief immediately," he said, then moved on. The barracks was ominously still as Roy dragged himself from the bunk and dressed in the bitter cold. Only the fliers were stirring, Roy noticed, climbing into their layered rags. The men looked uneasily at one another as they made their way to the *Blockältester*'s cubicle near the main entrance, but no one spoke. "I have news for you," the German growled in his broken English. His weathered face looked worried. "A runner from the *Schreibstube* has appeared this morning in the block with this order." He waved a sheet of onionskin paper before them. "After *Appell* the eleven Allied aviators are to be shaved. They are to go to the *Effektenkammer* for their clothing, then report to the main gate.

"It can mean anything," the chief said. "But I do not like it." He glanced around at the semicircle of men crowded into the shallow cubicle. "After you have been shaved and claimed your clothing, you must *veschwinden,* disappear. Hide until I can find out what is happening."

Morning *Appell* dragged by at its usual excruciating pace, but for Roy and the others it seemed to take days. "They're going to shoot us," one of the men said flatly as they walked toward the *Effektenkammer* after roll call. "But why go through the motions of having us claim our things from this place?" another said, pointing to the enormous *Effektenkammer* just across the street from Block 45. "Makes no sense if they're going to shoot us." Warren did not speak up, but Roy knew what he was thinking. "We're going to be transferred out," Warren had said many times. Through the ups and downs of the previous weeks, he held firmly to this view. On October 18, when the others had been taken, the Luftwaffe officer in charge had leaned down to him on his bunk and said: "*Machen Sie sich keine Sorgen, Leutnant* Bauder. Do not worry. I will come back for you." Warren believed him, and Roy wanted to.

Before entering the *Effektenkammer* the men were directed to an adjoining building where their heads were buzzed and their faces shaved. Then they were directed to the *Effektenkammer,* where they were taken to the long room on the second floor where prisoners stood behind the counter, waiting to distribute camp clothes to new arrivals. Alongside the high shelves of shirts and trousers and bins of wooden clogs, rows of bags hung on numbered racks that ran the length of the massive chamber. In his pocket, Roy clutched the small metal disc he had been given as a receipt on that first day in the camp. Hard to imagine, he thought, that he had actually managed to hold on to it. The number on the disc was worn smooth and hard to decipher, but when Roy handed it over, the clerk vanished among sacks.

When he reappeared, a bag, flecked with dust, was draped over his arm. Opening the sack, Roy found the same shabby clothes he had arrived in, the same clothes provided for him by Monsieur Florin in June. They had been disinfected but not cleaned. Only the shoes were missing, an item too valuable to have survived storage. The clerk handed him a form listing the contents of the sack—*Hemd, Hosen, Jacke* . . . , all with large check marks beside them. Roy was expected to sign.

The bag in hand, Roy moved on down the counter, stepped to the side, as the other men were doing, and undressed. The once-tight jacket, the shirt that in August bound his shoulders and arms, hung on him now like clothes on a hanger. The collar that would never close encircled his neck like a circus clown's. He could not only button it; he could place three fingers between the soiled collar and his neck. The trousers, which had been a reasonable fit, swallowed his waist and the cuffs brushed the floor. Of course, the belt was gone. One of the German clerks allowed him to rummage through the huge pile of shoes and clogs at the end of the counter, but after trying and discarding one pair after another, he gave up. All were achingly small, and he slumped on the floor and began retying the wrapping of paper and rags that swathed his swollen feet.

Afterward the men returned to Block 45. All were bewildered. Was this some sort of trick, another cruel game? It seemed incredible that they would be released, just like that, and yet it was just as maddening to think that they would be shaved and have their civilian clothes returned, only to be executed. But Buchenwald was all about madness, Roy thought. Anything seemed possible.

At Block 45 the chief was waiting for them in his cubicle. He had been to the *Schreibstube* and had spoken to the *Lagerältester*, the highest-ranking prisoner in the camp. Although no one could give any guarantees—this, of course, was out of the question in Buchenwald—all signs pointed to the *Entlassung*, the release, of the airmen. The men of the *Schreibstube* believed that a contingent of Luftwaffe personnel was already waiting at the main gate to take charge of the airmen. What was in store for them after the transfer, the *Blockältester* shrugged, was anybody's guess. He did not believe that the main party of airmen had been shot in October, but then again he had no firm information. And now, the paperwork had arrived from the *Schreibstube*, and the block secretary had already removed the men from his roster. They were to report immediately to the infirmary for a quick physical examination. The chief wished them well, then turned back to his writing.

Limping, Roy and the others followed a runner through the nearly deserted streets of the camp to the *Revier*. Everyone was in terrible shape, and everyone was nervous. A gruff hospital orderly led them into what might have been an examination room and told them to wait. Several minutes passed before an obese SS doctor brushed through the door. Impatient, repulsed by these verminous *Untermenschen*, these subhuman specimens, before him, he gave each prisoner a quick once-over, never touching them, never uttering a word. When it was Roy's turn, the doctor glared down at his feet. "Unwrap them," he ordered sharply. Slowly Roy unwound the strips of burlap, slipping off the paper and the damp socks that adhered to his misshapen feet like a layer of dead skin. Beneath the wrappings, his swollen ankles had turned a translucent blue, and his feet were hideously red. The long nails were discolored. Several were black.

"*Hier bleiben*," the doctor snapped at Roy. "You remain here."

Roy looked around at the others, his eyes wide and imploring. A wave of panic swept across him. The doctor was filling out a form, checking names off the list. Within minutes an orderly carrying the medical release form escorted the men from the *Revier*. All but Roy. He was to remain behind. He was not ready to be transferred, another orderly informed him. He would spend several more nights in the infirmary.

He was not in his old ward, and he did not see Langevin or Zbigniew. Even though the prisoner doctor in charge assured him that the camp authorities had officially released him—the paperwork had been processed—and he would be transferred as soon as he was physically able to leave, Roy was disconsolate. He sweated the agonizing days and nights away, more terrified than he had ever been. He was not required to work and his feet seemed improved, but the gnawing anxiety, the loneliness devoured him fiber by fiber.

Then, in the first week of December, he was summoned again before the same SS doctor, who examined him once more. *"Entlassen,"* he said after glancing distastefully at Roy's legs, and he signed the release form. That same morning a runner from the *Schreibstube* appeared to take him to the main gate. They climbed the slope, past Block 46, where the hideous medical experiments were conducted, past the special sealed blocks for the Gypsies and Russian POWs, and across the *Appellplatz* to the tower of the main gate. To their left, the crematorium spewed its putrid smoke, and fine flecks of ash mingled with the light-falling snow.

SS men were milling around the offices of the tower's east wing, and the iron gates of the low entrance stood open. The runner led Roy to a window beneath the tower. There an SS officer examined Roy's papers, asking questions, which the runner from the *Schreibstube* answered. Beyond the entrance Roy could see a solitary soldier, an *Obergefreiter*—a corporal—standing in the fresh snow. The soldier wore a steel helmet much too large for him and carried a carbine, but his uniform was not SS. The corporal craned his neck to see into the camp, but the SS moved quickly to block his view. When the paperwork was completed and the forms stamped, the soldier stepped forward to take charge of his prisoner, gaping at the skeleton that stumbled toward him.

The snow was falling more heavily, slanting from the soot-gray clouds, as Roy and the soldier passed down Caracho Weg, past the smashed camp headquarters and motor pool to the railway depot.

The sprawling Gustloff Works just beyond the tracks was little more than a shell, with shattered glass and pulverized concrete and steel shafts splayed wildly around the site. But the little depot was intact, and a locomotive wheezed steam as it waited at the landing. Attached to it was a single carriage. Looking back through the leafless trees Roy could see the tower of the main gate and hear the shrill whining of the whistles calling the work details to midday rations. *"Schnell machen,"* the soldier, limping and short of breath, grunted. "You are leaving now *Konzentrationslager* Buchenwald." He seemed as relieved as Roy.

PART V

PRISONERS
OF WAR

CHAPTER 13

Kriegie

December 1944–February 4, 1945

It had been snowing all night and day, and the ground was buried beneath a thick covering of alabaster white. For hours the train had crawled through the frozen landscape, stopping in small depots, slipping onto rural sidings to wait while faster traffic rumbled by. The devastated cities—Leipzig, Bautzen, Görlitz—lay far behind, giving way to forests and fields and villages huddled against the wind. Ribbons of brown smoke curled from stone chimneys, and horses, steam bursting from their black nostrils, toiled along the desolate roads, pulling wagons and carts in the driving snow.

There was no heat in the compartment, and fingers of ice had formed on the inside of the windowpane. Roy hunched his shoulders, tugging the collar of his jacket higher on his neck. Seated across from him, the soldier—a Luftwaffe corporal hardly more than a boy—was dozing again, clasping his carbine carelessly between his outstretched legs. His blue woolen cap was pushed back off his forehead, exposing his oily blond hair, and as the train trundled along, he snored easily. He must have been about eighteen, maybe a bit older, and patches of stubble had begun to sprout on the smooth skin of his untroubled face. Periodically his eyelids would flutter open, and he would shoot a startled glance at Roy, muttering a word or two beneath his breath before drifting off again.

Slumped on hard wooden benches, they were alone in the austere third-class carriage. Several hours out of Buchenwald, the soldier had removed Roy's handcuffs. He knew some English and, with no officers around and the SS far behind them, he chatted amiably. Before the war he had been an exchange student in Chicago, he said. He loved the city and hoped to visit it again when the war was over. He asked about the Cubs and knew the names of all the players—Billy Herman, Stan Hack, Gabby Hartnett, and so on down the lineup. His orders were to escort the prisoner to a POW camp about one hundred miles southeast of Berlin. "You are going to Sagan," he volunteered. "It is in Silesia, on the route to Breslau." Roy nodded, trying to visualize the giant briefing map at Glatton. Eastern Germany, he thought vaguely, near the old Czech frontier. "Stalag Luft III is your destination," the soldier continued, offering Roy a slice of sausage. "It is the largest *Kriegsgefangenenlager* in Germany, a giant camp that holds only Allied fliers."

They had left Buchenwald in the early morning, traveling through the long frozen day and windswept night. After dark both men had stretched out, trying to sleep. Whenever the train halted, the soldier would groan and sit up and peer out the frosted window. If the stop lasted for more than a few minutes, he would grab his rifle with a weary sigh and slap the steel helmet on his head. And if he could see the station sign, he would mutter the name of the town out loud, as if Roy would know where it was. Cold and stiff, unable to find a comfortable position on the unyielding wooden bench, Roy slept for only a few minutes at a time.

Not long after dawn, the train slowed, and the soldier slowly roused himself. Roy used his elbow to rub a bare spot in the icy window and peered out. They seemed to be stopping in a rail yard bordered by a dense pine forest. No station, no depot was in sight. "*Wir sind da.*" The soldier yawned, squinting through the window and stretching. "We are at Sagan." He had been here before. With a groan he gathered his helmet, slung the rifle over his shoulder, and nodded toward the door.

Stepping into the deep snow at the edge of the track, the soldier paused for a moment to get his bearings, then Roy followed him away from the train, down a road through a wide clearing in the trees. They walked single file, staying as best they could in the icy tire tracks that cut through the snow. Roy's feet were still wrapped in burlap and paper, and the gritty surface crunched beneath them as he tried to keep pace with the corporal. All around them a snowy silence prevailed. Within a few yards, Roy's feet were wet and frozen.

Soon the road led them into a wider field and clusters of low, weathered barracks loomed up out of the snowy mist in front of them. Arranged with military precision and enclosed by a maze of high barbed wire fences, the camp stretched across a vast clearing. Guard towers with searchlights and machine guns rose at regular intervals along the perimeter, separating what appeared to be different compounds. As they drew nearer, Roy could see that two parallel fences, about ten feet high, encircled each compound. The dozen or so yards between the fences bristled with coils of barbed wire. The soldier limped to a halt at a sentry box in front of the outer fence, presented papers, and then led Roy through a gate in the wire. There another guard took charge of Roy, escorted him through the compound, and deposited him at the entrance to an office building with gray-green siding. The guard pushed open the door, and Roy stepped inside.

Typewriters clattered and men in blue Luftwaffe uniforms moved busily from desk to desk. It was warm in the office, and Roy shivered at the sudden contrast. Stealing a glance around the room, he was relieved to see no sign of Gestapo or SS. The team of Luftwaffe orderlies who signed him in could not stop staring at the rags on his feet and muttered among themselves. With evident distaste, they searched him, picking at his shabby clothing, running their hands hesitantly beneath his scrawny arms and along his legs as if handling a corpse. That done, they assigned him a prison identification number and a set of tags. They took his fingerprints and photographed him. Then they turned him over to a major who interrogated him for almost an hour, asking, with clipped correctness and in impeccable English, the usual questions: name, rank, serial number, date and place of capture, his civilian occupation, his state of health. The major's behavior was calm and professional, his eyes betraying a flicker of interest only when Roy mentioned Buchenwald and the SS.

The interrogation over, Roy followed an orderly to a nearby building where he was placed in a large unheated shower room and ordered to strip. He had not seen his own naked body in months, and the pallor of his skin, the withered arms and legs, the shrunken chest and ribs came as a shock. It was the body of a stranger, a cadaver. *"Sie haben fünf Minuten Zeit,"* a sergeant explained, pressing a nub of soap into his hand. "Five minutes hot water." Roy stepped beneath a nozzle and looked up. Within seconds the pipes groaned, and a jet of steaming water burst over him. The spray was hot, and after months without a bath, without warmth, without a hint of physical pleasure, the sensation was glorious. Roy scrubbed himself, watching the grime slide off his skin in gritty swatches, forming a pool of filth that swirled beneath his disfigured feet. Then, without warning, the water turned cold and stopped. "You receive one hot bath per week," the German sergeant said as he stepped forward and handed Roy a towel.

Dressed again in his baggy French clothes, Roy followed another German officer through another wire fence into an even larger compound where men in bits and pieces of American uniforms milled about everywhere. Just inside the gate an American wearing captain's bars was waiting. He stepped forward, exchanged salutes with his German counterpart, and signaled for Roy to follow him. "Welcome to Stalag Luft III," the American said, looking Roy in the eye. "We were alerted that you'd be coming." As Roy trailed along behind the captain, he noticed that some of the men had stopped to stare at him. A few shouted out questions: "Where you from? What Group?" Roy lifted his hand to wave, but, paralyzed by his own weakness, he simply trudged on, unable to speak.

"We're in West Compound now," the captain said. "There are four others, sealed off from one another by the double fences you saw on your way in. Over ten thousand Allied prisoners, all fliers and almost all officers, are interned here at Luft III. Some prisoners, the RAF boys—they're in North and Center Compounds—have been here for two years or more. Some since 1940. Over two thousand men—all Americans—call this charming compound home. Colonel Alkire, Darr H. Alkire, is in charge. You'll learn more about the state of things after you're cleared by Intelligence."

"First, we have to establish that you are who and what you say you are," the captain said as they entered a long one-story building that appeared, to Roy's amazement, to be a library. In one room, he could see tables and chairs and racks of books. A handful of men were scattered among the crowded tables. Most were reading. Some dozed. Others appeared to be writing letters. For a moment Roy's mind cleared. Letters. Maybe he could write May. Even hear from her. Was that possible? "This building is called the theater," the captain said. "The boys put on shows here—plays, concerts, musicals, you name it. They're pretty good, too. It also houses the library and the newsroom." None of this seemed quite real.

In a deserted room down the hall, the captain pointed Roy to a chair. Two other officers, both lieutenants, sat at a long rectangular table. One offered him a cigarette—American, Roy noticed—but he waved it off. The lieutenants had paper and pencils in front of them, and as the captain began the questioning, they took notes. Facing them across the table, Roy gave name, rank, and serial number, uncertain whether he should reveal more. What if this was some sort of test? Should he talk or just clam up? When he hesitated, the captain leaned forward. "It's okay," he said. "Every incoming prisoner is examined by the Intelligence staff. It's your duty to answer the questions. You're not being singled out for special treatment. The Germans like to slip stooges into the camp. They're well trained and seem as American as apple pie. They know the streets and trolley lines of the major cities. They can give you the Big Ten football standings or World Series scores and tell you what Sinatra is singing these days. We have to be careful."

"I understand," Roy said. The captain began by asking questions about Philadelphia—high schools, neighborhoods, movie houses, parks. He asked where Roy trained, what unit he flew in, when he was shot down, and where he was captured. Who was the Group commander of the 457th? Who was his squadron leader? When Roy had answered, the captain wanted to know why he had not been taken to Dulag Luft for interrogation as all other downed fliers were. And why did he arrive alone instead of with a purge? "New arrivals usually come in groups of sixty, seventy, or more men at a time," one of the lieutenants chimed in, putting down his pencil for a moment. "A new shipment is called a purge," he explained, eyeing Roy suspiciously. "I've never seen a purge of only one man."

Roy could only shrug. He answered their questions as best he could, stumbling through his story in fits and starts—the resistance (he would still divulge no names), Capitaine Jacques and the orange-haired woman, Fresnes, the nightmarish train trip to Germany. All these things he could talk about, but some things, he discovered, simply would not come. He could not find the words to describe Buchenwald, to make sense of it or to make them understand. A series of jumbled images and disjointed incidents tumbled out, each seeming, even to him, more grotesque, more farfetched than the last. Why should they believe him?

When he finished, the officers exchanged glances. They asked no more questions. "You look pretty beat," the captain said, pushing his notes aside. "We'll arrange for you to get some hot chow at the cook-house and then escort you to your barracks. We have a tight military organization here and a strict chain of command. You're back in the U.S. Army now, Lieutenant. In West Compound there are seventeen barracks, and each barracks is divided into combines—groups of about twelve men who live together in a room. Each combine has a leader, and as soon as we verify your identity, your combine leader will brief you fully on how things work. We'll get you out of those clothes, too, and issue you a uniform, underwear, socks, even," he winced at Roy's feet, "try to find you some shoes. But for now," he smiled as he rose from the chair, "you need something to eat and some rest."

In the warmth of the cookhouse, the feast spread before him stupefied him. Canned turkey, potatoes, gravy, and hot barley soup steamed up from the table like a mirage, and the chocolate bar that garnished his tin plate was like a letter from home. He was given a cup and bowl, both made of ceramic, and a knife, fork, and spoon, each with a swastika engraved on the worn handle. "Hang on to these," one of the cooks warned him, "they're yours for the duration. If you lose them or break them, the goons won't replace them. So be careful."

Roy fell into a chair. The mere sight of the food was intoxicating. His mouth watered, and in spite of his resolve to do as the cooks urged him, to take things slow, he began wolfing down the chow, burning his lips and tongue in his eagerness. A banquet served at the posh Union League in Philly couldn't have been better. They poured coffee, or something that might have been coffee, into his cup and placed a small tin container of powdered milk and a packet of sugar down beside it. Astonishing.

After several frenzied mouthfuls, he suddenly stopped chewing. He stared down at his half-full plate, his fork poised in midair. In his gut he felt a sharp contraction. Beads of sweat formed on his forehead, and his shrunken stomach cramped, rebelling at the first taste of the gravy. A sudden spasm erupted in his bowels, then another. Dizzy, damp with sweat, he pushed back from the table. A surge of bile scorched his throat, and he realized he was going to vomit.

The men in the cookhouse helped clean him, washing his brow and finally helping him to his feet. They had seen this before, half-starved men, gulping down their first real meal in days or weeks, overwhelmed by the sight and smell of the food, forcing it on their ravaged systems. "Take it easy, pal," someone behind him said. "Just take it easy. There'll be more where this came from."

When he had recovered enough to walk, Roy trailed the captain along a mud-spattered path in the snow to another low prefab barracks. Like all the buildings in the compound, the barracks stood two feet off the ground, propped up by a series of brick supports. A small room near the entrance served as the night latrine, foul smelling but more hygienic than anything he had experienced in Buchenwald, and beyond that a kitchen with a curiously shaped stove, and a series of sleeping rooms on both sides of a central passageway.

"Here you are," the captain said, stopping in an open doorway. From beside him, Roy peered into a cluttered room outfitted with four triple-decker bunks arranged along the walls, a small cookstove, two tables, a wooden storage locker turned on its side, and several chairs and stools. A half-empty bucket of coal stood beside the stove, and on the locker, bowls, plates, cups, and an assortment of tin jugs and pitchers were neatly spread. A lanky first lieutenant stepped forward, and the captain turned to go. "I'm your combine leader," the lieutenant explained, "and these Kriegies," his hand moving in a sweeping motion, "will be your combine mates." Roy blinked. The lieutenant continued, "All POWs here are called 'Kriegies'—slang for *Kriegsgefangene,* prisoner of war in German." Several of the men sat on the crude stools, others were stretched out on their bunks. They nodded, staring at Roy's shabby French clothes and the wrappings on his feet. "Don't worry, everyone will warm up when you've been identified and cleared," the lieutenant said, patting Roy on the shoulder. "Shouldn't take long." Roy nodded. "This one is yours," the lieutenant said, pointing toward the low bunk on the back wall. "Looks like you could use some shut-eye."

Roy quickly slipped his cup and bowl and eating utensils beneath the large pillow at the head of his bed, a move that seemed to surprise the others. While they exchanged glances, he slumped down on the low bunk. The mattress and pillow were nothing more than rough, differently sized burlap palliasses filled with wood shavings, but they seemed clean, no mysterious stains or smells. In fact, the whole room, the whole combine, was clean and orderly. The floor was swept, the clothes hung on the unpainted wooden bunks. On the palliasse he found a woolen blanket of U.S. Army issue, and two thin German blankets laced with wooden fibers. He lay back on the bunk and closed his eyes. He could feel them watching him. Within seconds he fell asleep.

When he awoke, a dim light was burning in the room, and the men were preparing supper. Pleasant smells filled the room, and on the stool beside his bunk was a cup of powdered coffee. He swung his throbbing feet onto the floor, and looked out. Through the window he could see other men slogging through the snow in the early evening twilight. "The coffee's for you," one of men said. "Since you just arrived and are already down on the list to report to the hospital tomorrow, the goons let you sleep through *Appell*. That's roll call, in case you didn't know." Roy smiled grimly. "There's a morning and evening *Appell*," the man continued. "The goons do a lot of counting. You'll see."

"Thanks for the coffee," Roy said, feeling with his free hand to see if his bowl and cup were still under the pillow. His stomach was empty, and the cozy aroma of the cooking set it gurgling, but he was reluctant to eat. He was sipping the bitter coffee and watching the men carry plates and bowls to the table when the captain from Intelligence appeared in the doorway. With him was another lieutenant who hobbled into the room, a crutch under his arm. The captain nodded toward Roy. While the men of the combine paused to watch, the man limped forward and peered down at Roy. For an instant their eyes met, and a flash of recognition seemed to ignite between them. Roy had seen this man somewhere before, but couldn't place him.

At first the man simply stared, studying Roy's face but betraying no glimmer of recollection. Then, he turned to the captain. The guy on the bunk was, indeed, Roy Allen, pilot in the 457th Bomb Group, he said. Emaciated, about fifty pounds lighter maybe, but no question about it. For a moment Roy gaped at this man leaning against the bed frame. And then it came to him. Cotterell. Bob Cotterell, copilot on the . . . the Bill Dee crew. They had shared a hut at Glatton. Then sometime—it must have been just before D-Day—his crew had not come back from a mission. The personal effects man had come into the hut, folded up their mattresses, and cleared out their things. And yet here he was. Looking up at him, Roy's eyes suddenly flooded with tears. His chest heaved, and something inside—the tension, the fear, the loneliness—seemed to give way, to dissolve. The cup dropped from his hand, and he clutched Cotterell's arm. Someone patted him on the shoulder, his head sank, and he covered his eyes, unable to speak.

After a time the tension in the room lifted, and one by one the men in the combine introduced themselves to Roy. They offered him food and poured him tea, real tea with milk and even a bit of sugar. Roy managed to swallow a few bites. They respected his silence and did not press with questions. That could wait. Everyone gets to tell his story, one of the men said with a laugh, but just once. In Luft III the sort of "and there I was over Berlin with three engines burning" stories were a dime a dozen. Roy's story, they seemed to sense, would be different.

The next morning, Roy reported as ordered for sick call and marched along with several other men through a gate at the north end of the compound into the *Vorlager*. Before reaching the infirmary, he was diverted to another building and issued clothing—two shirts, two pairs of pants, two pairs of socks and underwear, a cap, a woolen jacket, and a sweater, all GI issue. The Red Cross had provided the clothes. Everything was too large and did not constitute a matched uniform, but it was clean, it was American, and, for the time being at least, it was free of lice and fleas. Slipping it on, Roy felt almost warm. He tossed his French clothes, still smelling of Buchenwald disinfectant, into a pile beside the counter. "Burn 'em," he said to the orderly in charge.

The infirmary for West Compound was called the *Revier* (Roy cringed when he heard that word again). It was crowded and its construction crude, but it bore little resemblance to the *Revier* at Buchenwald. Medicines, bandages, surgical instruments, most provided by the Red Cross, were not plentiful but at least some were available. The sick bay held over sixty beds, and patients were standing or sitting against the wall everywhere. It was austere but clean, and a team of doctors, German, English, and American, moved among the patients, asking questions, tending to the sick and injured. An American doctor, a major with a stethoscope around his neck, took Roy in hand, taking his temperature, weighing and measuring him, and listening to his lungs. "You're running a little fever," the major said. "Had this long?" Roy shrugged. The doctor could hear the lingering rattle of the pneumonia, and when Roy stepped onto the scale, the major, calculating kilos into pounds, informed him that he weighed one hundred ten pounds. He had lost one third of his body weight in Buchenwald.

The doctor examined Roy's feet, cleaned them, and swabbed them with a kind of salve, hoping to reduce the swelling. He wrapped fresh bandages around his feet and ankles and produced a pair of thick woolen socks. As he did, Roy recounted his medical problems in France, the excruciating pain in his back, the kidney stones, and the catheter procedure in Paris. Lately his back had been bothering him again. "Sounds like you're lucky to be here at all, Lieutenant," the doctor said.

Roy stayed in the *Revier* for several days, while the staff tracked his progress. It was his first real medical treatment since June 14. He tried the weak German soup in small doses, and the doctor gave him a special Red Cross "invalid food packet" that contained white bread and other easy-to-digest foods. Roy was ravenously hungry, but the major insisted that he eat lightly for three or four days, to allow his stomach to expand gradually. "Got to get that belly in shape for the holidays," the doctor told him. "The camp is planning a big bash for Christmas, Lieutenant, and you want to be ready to chow down."

One afternoon, as he sat at the edge of his bed, browsing through *The Overseas Kid,* an English language newspaper obviously printed by the Germans for propaganda, he watched as a man with a familiar gait passed near him. Roy folded the paper and looked hard. "Verne," he said to himself, and then louder: "Verne, Verne Lewis!" The man with broad slumping shoulders and thinning hair stopped and peered through the tangle of men. "Over here," Roy yelled, waving his arm. His copilot was alive! When Verne saw him, his mouth fell open and he called out: "You made it," his face relaxing into a grin, "you made it after all!"

Rushing over, Verne grabbed Roy by the shoulders, held him at arm's length, and looked him over from head to foot. Both men talked at once, words tumbling out, questions, recollections of that day in the burning plane. "I thought you were dead," Verne kept repeating. "We never saw a chute. And when you didn't turn up when we were captured, well . . ."

"Did you see other chutes?" Roy asked. "Did you see anybody on the ground?"

"When I got out of my seat," Verne said, "Joe and Plum were already at the forward escape hatch. Anderson had just jumped. Plum climbed down, ready to go, but at the last second, he wouldn't let go of the bar. His legs were dangling out of the hatch and Joe was yelling at him, telling to get out, but Plum wouldn't budge. Joe began prying his fingers loose, one by one. Papers—charts and things—were flying all over, and shell casings were rattling around underfoot. Finally, Joe got one of Plum's hands off and then the other and Plum disappeared. Joe looked up at me, but I don't know if he even saw me. One second later he was gone. Then I went out.

"I saw three chutes on the way down. Anderson, Plum, and Joe, I figured. I couldn't find any others, none from the back of the plane, not yours. We all came down almost together. I drifted a little farther away, but I saw Joe and Plum later, on the ground, after we were captured. I never saw Anderson again, and I didn't see the plane crash. Joe and I were together for a while after the Germans caught us, but we couldn't really talk and then we got separated. I didn't see him at Dulag Luft, and I don't know where he is now. I always think I'll see him here, but I haven't."

Roy asked about the men in the back of the plane. "Plum thought that they got out. He was pretty sure that they had already jumped before we got to the escape hatch. Probably went out the bomb bay and rear hatch." So, at least Joe, Verne and Plum had survived. If they were lucky, they were probably sitting in a stalag somewhere, maybe even at Luft III. And if Plum was right, then maybe Long, the new guy, had gone out the tail, Smittie, from the radio compartment, out the bomb bay. Henson was in the waist, and Goldsborough had been down in the ball turret. Goldsborough always worried about getting out of the ball. You could hardly blame him. Roy recalled the strewn wreckage of the plane in the field near Jouy. There had been a spare gunner, flying in the waist, that day, but he couldn't remember the name, if he ever knew it. No bodies had been found in the wreckage, Jonckheere had assured him. So maybe Plum was right. Maybe they had all gotten out. But Anderson . . . Anderson worried him.

When Verne had finished, Roy related his story. He skipped around and didn't say much about Buchenwald. "Have you heard from Helen?" he asked suddenly. No, Verne hadn't. He had been in the camp for five months and sent many letters but nothing from home had reached him yet. He was still hopeful.

In the late afternoon, after he had seen the doctor, Verne had to return to his barracks. He would not be back tomorrow but he would find Roy when he was released. Seeing Verne, with his slumped shoulders and weathered, open face, was an enormous relief. In the daily struggle to stay alive in Buchenwald, his world, like his body, had withered and his fears about the crew came only in spasms of disjointed memory. Now they came back, but with hope.

Released from the infirmary several days later, Roy was walking through the gate into West Compound when he heard someone call out his name. It was a familiar voice. The sky was clear and bright, and the reflection of the sun off the glazed snow was blinding. "Hey, Roy," the voice repeated. Shielding his eyes against the glare, Roy could see the silhouette of a figure striding toward him with arms out-stretched. Warren! "You, you!" Roy yelled, shuffling toward his friend. The two men hugged and pounded each other on the back. "I saw you coming in alone the other day and was yelling at you. A bunch of us were cheering, but you just kept on walking. Guess you didn't hear me. Next morning after *Appell* I asked about you and found out where you were. You've been transferred to my barracks, 157, at the end of the row there." He pointed toward a long low green structure just to the left, close to the *Vorlager* gate and across several parallel fences from another complex of barracks.

"That's North Compound over there beyond the wire," Warren told him as they walked toward the edge of West Compound's barracks. "Back in March seventy or so guys, mostly English, tunneled out. Dug all the way into those woods out there," he said, pointing toward the distant tree line. "Most of them were captured within days. Fifty of them were shot—executed—by the SS."

"The SS!" Roy said, stopping in his tracks. "I thought this was a POW camp."

"It is," Warren said. "The Luftwaffe runs the camp, and as far as I can see, it operates pretty much by the book, by the Geneva Conven-tion. Not at all like Buchenwald. But the SS handles escapees."

"What about our group?" Roy asked as they stepped onto the low steps to the barracks doors. "Are the guys who left Buchenwald before us here?"

"The main party is here, I'm told, scattered across the other com-pounds . . . North, South, East, and Center. I haven't seen any of them here in West." Warren looked at Roy. "When we left you at Buchen-wald," he said, his voice husky, "I didn't think you'd make it."

"Neither did I," Roy said. "Neither did I."

That night Roy settled into his new combine. The barracks was a car-bon copy, both inside and out, of his first. The crowded rooms, the crude wooden furniture, the frost-covered windows all looked familiar. Warren had prepared a little celebration in the room. Some food was left over from the Thanksgiving feast, and everyone in the combine joined in. Roy's stomach was still sour, and he picked cautiously at the food, while the guys briefed him about the camp and peppered him with questions about Buchenwald. Most had never heard of a concentration camp or, if they had, thought of it as a labor camp, if they gave it any thought at all. Since arriving in the barracks about ten days earlier, Warren had not spoken much about his ordeal in Buchenwald, and the men listened, spellbound.

That night, after lights-out at 2400, wind whistled through the barracks, seeping through the cracks in the walls and the broken windowpanes, which had been covered inexpertly by stray scraps of planking. Some of the men, Roy noticed, had managed to sew their two German blankets into a sort of sleeping bag and crawled inside, pulling the heavier GI blanket over them. Others had found sheets of newspaper and arranged them carefully in layers between the blankets. Roy sank down in the palliasse, tucking all three covers in around him. He pulled his woolen cap down over his ears and curled into a ball. Like the others, he slept in his clothes.

The next morning he began to learn the ropes. At 0700 he followed Warren and the others out of the barracks to the parade ground at the south end of the compound. Seventeen barracks, together holding over two thousand men, took their assigned position in the formation. Overseen by Luftwaffe officers, American commanders called the men to attention, conducted the count, and waited until the numbers were confirmed, barracks by barracks, by German guards. Then Colonel Alkire, the senior American officer of West Compound, reported to his German counterpart at the head of the formation, and, after a few brief announcements, the men were dismissed. The *Appell* was dreary and miserable but mercifully short, an hour, maybe a bit longer, and, most important to Roy, it was conducted without the brutal cruelties of the *Appellplatz* in Buchenwald. There were no harangues, no threats or beatings, no public hangings.

After morning *Appell* the men were free until evening roll call, and filling the empty hours was a challenge. No one was forced to work, and the men were free to roam the compound. "All Kriegies will tell you," one of his combine mates advised him, "that the key to holding body and soul together is to keep busy. The goons don't bother us too much, except for the ferrets. Those are the guys in the blue overalls and cloth caps you see skulking around the compound. They *are* trouble, always snooping, burrowing under the barracks, searching for tunnels, eavesdropping on conversations, listening for radios—that sort of thing. The ferrets are damn smart, and they all speak English, so you have to be careful what you say.

"There are activities to keep you diverted. We have 'Sagan U,' sometimes called 'Kriegie Kollege,' where you can take college-level courses from guys in the camp. The classes meet in the library, and the library itself isn't half bad—about seventeen hundred volumes. Detective stories, adventure, history, reference books—you name it. We have two Kriegie newspapers, a theater group—the Sagan Players—a choral group, and an orchestra called the Flying Syncopators. They've got trombones, clarinets, trumpets—the works. The YMCA supplies them. In October they put on a swell show, a musical revue with fancy bandstands and suits and lots of amateur talent. Right now they're rehearsing every day for a big Christmas party," he said. "If you play an instrument or sing or act, go over to the theater and see what's up.

"When the weather is better, a lot of the guys play sports—softball, touch football, boxing, volleyball. The barracks have teams and take it pretty seriously. The *Kriegie Klarion*—that's one of the papers—reports the scores and the standings in season. Now, in the cold weather, the guys have rigged up a hockey rink on the concrete fire pool there between the washhouse and the shower room. The YMCA provided the skates. For daily exercise everybody walks the perimeter track. Takes about twenty minutes to make a lap around the compound; ten laps amount to a little more than seven miles. It's a good exercise, and, if you want a little privacy, you know, just to get away from everything for a while, it can't be beat." Looking out the window, Roy could see men, singly and in small groups, trudging along a wide icy path that had been worn in the snow. It ran several yards inside a single strand of metal wire that stretched around the circumference of the compound. The wire was fastened to short stakes about knee high and about thirty feet inside the inner fence. "That's the warning wire," the man explained. "If you cross over that, no matter what the reason, the guards will shoot to kill."

All this was useful information, but most of all Roy wanted to know about the mail. He had had to wait almost six months to write home and didn't want to delay for another day. Following Warren's directions, he found his way to the mailroom, housed in Barracks 163, just beyond the theater. In the cramped office, the mail officer handed him three slips of paper, forms that folded in the center, with *"Kriegs-gefangenpost"* in stark black letters across the top. Roy had to ask what the printed parts of the form meant: *Absender, Gefangenennummer, Empfangsort,* and on down the page. The mail officer went over the form line by line—sender, prisoner number, destination . . . "You'll get used to it," he said, "and the mail *does* get through. Sometimes it takes four or five weeks for a letter to reach the States. Sometimes it takes two months or more. You can never tell. Some Kriegies get packages from home—you know, food, some clothing. So, when you write home, ask the folks to send you a package. They can be lifesavers." He rattled off a list of desired items—nuts, raisins, tooth powder, and gloves, among others. "Guys have waited six months for a package, so don't get discouraged." Roy frowned at the thought. Surely he wouldn't still be in Stalag Luft III six months from now. "As an officer, you are allowed three letters and four postcards each month," the mail officer said. "No limit on how many you can receive."

Rushing from the mailroom, the forms tucked carefully into his jacket pocket, Roy found a spot in the library, and for the first time since leaving Glatton he wrote home to May. The form was so small, the paper so thin and flimsy, it seemed impossible that such a note could possibly survive a trip from Silesia to Philadelphia. For months he had composed letters in his head, talking to May through the long days and nights at Fresnes and Buchenwald, but now, the blank sheet stared up at him and he found himself stymied.

"I'm late as usual," he began at last, hoping to keep it light and jaunty. "But this is the first opportunity I've had to write. I'm O.K. and in the same camp with Verne. He thought I was dead. How is 'my family' doing without the paternal instinct? . . . I still think it's a girl . . ."

He had barely begun and was already running out of space. Still, he couldn't resist asking about Colette and his friends in the Avenue Michel Bizot. "Have you received any mail from people in France yet?" he asked. He had left his address with Colette and with Robert in Paris, and maybe, after liberation, they had written. At the very bottom, recalling the mail officer's advice, he jotted a final practical note: "Consult the Red Cross and send me a package. Some chocolate if possible. Say 'Hello' to everyone. Don't worry, Love Roy."

Back in the barracks, Roy found the combine preparing midday rations. Pots, pitchers, plates, and skillets, all made of tin, were spread on the tables. Each combine, Roy already knew, had a cook and an assistant cook—"a *sous-chef*," he had heard one of the men joke. Both jobs changed on a weekly basis, so that everyone in the combine would be in charge of planning and cooking all the meals for a week. The rest of the men rotated as KPs, helping to prepare the meal and cleaning up afterward. The men did most of the combine's cooking in the cramped barracks kitchen down the hall. Working on a tight schedule, each combine had exactly twenty minutes on the stove to prepare meals.

"The Germans provide us with some food," one of the guys said. "Goon bread, as heavy and black as anthracite, potatoes almost every day, sometimes jam or margarine or cheese, always in small quantities, and a daily ration of soup. Not bad, if you like worms. On occasion we get some sort of meat—we're afraid to guess what it might be—and on very rare occasions in summer fresh vegetables. You won't see any now though. There's always the *Blutwurst*, congealed blood and onion. Only the desperate can stomach it. All of this in quantities just enough to sustain life. The Germans, at least the civilians, I'm told, aren't much better off.

"It's the Red Cross parcels that keep us going," he went on. "They're sent from Geneva and stored in the *Vorlager*. It's a box about three inches deep and a foot square and contains just enough food to keep a man alive for a week: a one-pound can of Klim—that's the brand name of the powdered milk—a can of margarine, a six-ounce can of instant coffee, a can of Spam, as well as a box of prunes, a ten-ounce jar of jelly or jam, an eight-ounce packet of sugar, a tin of liver paste, a K-ration biscuit, and, the highlight, a D-ration chocolate bar. Some, not all, contain three packs of cigarettes. Great for trading at the Foodaco."

Roy had already heard about Foodaco. It was a trading post located in the cookhouse and run by the Kriegies. The store operated on a point system. If you had more powdered coffee or cigarettes than you wanted, you could trade them at Foodaco and use the points to buy Spam or tea or whatever. Prices fluctuated depending on demand. The value of a chocolate bar, the cook told him, had soared from forty points just a few months ago to two hundred now.

"We get one Red Cross parcel for every two men in a combine, and I see to it that the parcels go into the combine's common larder. Used to be, a man got a whole parcel each week, but in September that was cut in half as a way of making the food go farther. Now sometimes it's only a quarter parcel per man. With all the Allied bombing and strafing, you can never tell when or if the shipments from Geneva will get through."

He pointed to the table and the miniature stove in the corner. "Everything we use for cooking—the plates, the jugs, the frying pans, are made out of the tin from the parcels. I don't know what we'd do without the Klim cans. The goons don't supply us with a damn thing. There are Kriegies around the compound who have developed into expert tinsmiths. Give them a few Klim cans and they can make anything."

Night and day Roy could hear trains moving in the darkness from the railroad yard close by. Sagan, he was told, was on the main rail line to the eastern front, and trains carrying troops and supplies lumbered constantly just beyond the trees. Snow fell and then thawed, exposing patches of frozen mud and stunted tufts of colorless weeds. A vista of barren ugliness stretched in every direction beneath the broad winter sky. His feet were steadily improving—supply found a pair of size thirteen shoes, but even they were too small. At the *Revier* he received new wrappings, burlap and oilcloth to keep out the moisture. He saw Cotterell and Verne and other men he had known in the 457th or in training, and every day he and Warren walked the perimeter track, trying to build up their stamina.

After the filth of Buchenwald, Roy was determined to keep himself as clean as possible and to wash out his clothes at least once a week. Of the fathomless degradations at Buchenwald, the worst, for him, was wallowing day after day in a pit of excrement and muck, his body crawling with lice and covered with welts from the swarming fleas. Growing up, he had washed one of his two shirts every night, and at the two-room apartment on Third Street, between Widner and Linton, the landlady raised his mother's rent a dollar per month because he took so many showers.

The washhouse, where laundry could be done, was a small rectangular building just across from the compound's showers, and he decided to inspect it. Inside, the washroom was dank and glacial. Beneath a prominent sign that read *"Kein Trinkwasser"*—"water not for drinking"—faucets sprouted from pipes that dropped from the ceiling, and several large basins with homemade scrubbing boards waded in frozen pools of moisture. There was no hot water. Same with the unheated shower room across the way. Neither had many customers. The hot water, he soon discovered, was turned on only for short periods each week, but just when, he never knew. Two weeks after landing in Luft III, he still had not dared a shower and soon gave up on washing his clothes, too.

He did wander by the theater while the orchestra was rehearsing, and after pausing at the door, decided to go in. In the large room where church services were held on Sundays, brass instruments gleamed, even in the dim light, and music flowed as lush and smooth as satin. Listening to the familiar songs was like a ticket home. For the first time since leaving Jouy, the melodies drifted back to him, and the lyrics, beyond recall in Buchenwald as if they had gone into hiding, once again resonated through his head. He decided to try out for the show.

On Sunday he went to church in the theater. Almost everybody attended one of the services, and he tagged along. Later he followed the crowd to the library, where the compound's two weekly newspapers were posted on the bulletin board just after church. The *Kriegie Klarion* and the *Stalag Stump* consisted of several mimeographed pages, looking more like a bulletin or an information sheet than a newspaper. They carried news from home garnered from recently arrived Kriegies, rumors, cartoons, opinion pieces, events in the camp, drawings—mostly of women and airplanes—and Kriegie poetry, most of it comical.

A week before Christmas the news from the front was not good. Four times a day loudspeakers mounted on several buildings around the camp blared the official German news broadcasts, and, even allowing for the usual Nazi propaganda, it was obvious that something bad was going on in the west. According to the official German communiqués, translated by one of the guys in the barracks, the Wehrmacht had launched a massive offensive in Belgium, in the Ardennes, and the Allies appeared to be falling back across a wide front. More important, from a radio hidden somewhere in the compound, news from the BBC broadcast was spread from barracks to barracks by runners who memorized the reports and then passed them on to a reader in each barracks who then repeated them to each combine.

The BBC tried to downplay the seriousness of the situation, but there was no denying that this German offensive had caught the Allies by surprise and some real damage was being done. Some longtime Kriegies clung to the hope that the war would be over by Christmas, but that would obviously not be the case. For some this would be their second Christmas in Stalag Luft III. For many of the British in North and Central Compounds, it would be their fifth. It looked like Roy was going to be a guest of the Germans for quite a while. Some of the men were saying April or May. A sense of gloom settled over the camp.

"Believe me it's quite a relief to be able to sit down and write," Roy's second letter began. "Send me some pictures when you can." Perhaps May could put together a special parcel of things he would need. "Include chocolate," he suggested, and "dried fruit, powdered milk, candy, soups, rice, macaroni, sugar, peanuts, dried beans, and gloves, scarf, wool socks, and sweater. Write as much as you can," he wrote. "So will I. Merry Christmas and Happy Birthday, honey. Love, Roy."

Light snow fell in the days before Christmas, punctuated by nights of bright, cloudless skies. Biting winds raged across the camp, and an implacable numbing cold descended upon them. The coldest December in Europe in the twentieth century, the BBC reported. Shivering, even in the barracks, Roy wove his thin German blankets into a sleeping bag, stuffing it with whatever he could find—strips of German newspaper, bits of cardboard, scraps of cloth—anything that would give some insulation. At night the men sat moodily in the drafty room in their overcoats and jackets. They played cards or talked about the war or tried to sleep. Their fuel supply had dwindled to nothing, and the little stove in the corner sat stone cold. Sometimes while they chatted, they could hear soft scraping noises from the crawl space under the floor. The ferrets were out, creeping along beneath them, listening.

Despite the cold and the dreary war news, the camp bustled with preparations for the holidays. Each combine had been holding back food for weeks, hoarding for a grand holiday feast. Then, just before Christmas, special Red Cross parcels arrived. These contained canned turkey, fruitcake, canned fruit, chocolate, sugar, and even Christmas decorations, which quickly found their way onto the barren walls. The extra rations would run throughout the holiday season, Colonel Alkire announced, from Christmas Eve through New Year's Day.

Special religious services would be held on Christmas Day, and rehearsals for the gala Christmas show picked up steam. "Holiday Harmonies" it was called, and Roy was chosen to sing in the chorus and even do a solo in two of the skits. His voice was surprisingly strong, and he enjoyed the afternoon rehearsals. He could sing as loud as he wanted, and he was happy for the diversion. Even the Germans did their bit. They supplied colorful paper hats and noisemakers for the celebration, and the *Kommandant* declared that on Christmas Day the men would be allowed to move freely around the compound until late at night. He would even permit the Kriegies to talk to their brothers in the adjoining compounds—through the fences, of course.

The cooks in all the combines began their serious preparations on the morning of Christmas Eve. By afternoon the aroma of mince pies, cookies, fruitcakes, and candies drifted through the rooms, and an air of mounting anticipation mixed with the light-falling snow. Then, at the close of evening *Appell*, as the men stood on the packed ice of the parade ground, the steam of their collective breath rising like smoke from a Pennsylvania steel mill, Roy heard a peculiar ringing sound. Far down the formation Kriegies were laughing and cheering. Everyone shuffled to get a view of the commotion. "Hey, look," someone shouted, "Santa Claus is coming to town!" Between the heads of the rank in front of him, Roy caught a glimpse of a figure decked out in red and white, a bedroll stuffed under his shirt. He was riding in a wagon, pulled by two other Kriegies dressed like reindeer. They slid jerkily across the parade ground, sleigh bells jingling, and as they passed each formation, Santa tossed a bundle into the cheering crowd. "Mail," someone yelled, and the formation dissolved in cheerful disorder.

The next morning after *Appell*, virtually the entire compound turned out for a special Christmas service in the theater, and then retired to their barracks for a breakfast of oatmeal, toast and jam, and sweets of various sorts. A few even had powdered eggs—an item universally reviled by the men while at their bases in England or Italy, now a delicacy sometimes found in the English Red Cross parcels and bartered at the Foodaco. After lunch, most of the men hurried to the eastern edge of the compound where hundreds of Kriegies from North and South Compounds were beginning to line the fences, calling out to one another. Roy followed along.

For a time he could make out nothing from the shouts of the men. The thin, eager faces seemed all alike. He moved on, skirting the rear of the crowd. Then, from the throng of prisoners across the way, he thought he heard someone calling his name. He scanned the swarm of men hugging the fence. "Hey, Roy, Roy Allen." Gaunt unshaven faces bobbed in a froth of olive drab. "Over here," the voice shouted again, and, turning, Roy saw a hand frantically signaling in the crowd. He couldn't believe his eyes. It was Joe, Joe Brusse, his navigator! Making their way through the press of bodies, they edged down the fence to a point where they could hear each other. "I saw you when you came in all by yourself," Joe shouted. "I yelled, but I reckon you couldn't hear me. You didn't look like much, but I would recognize that ol' sorry face anywhere."

Roy laughed. He didn't know where to begin. "Verne's here," he blurted out, "in West Compound."

Joe grinned in his shy Texas way. "So's Luper," he said. "I don't know what compound he's in, but the SOB is somewhere in Luft III. Hear he got shot down sometime in September."

"Luper, Je-sus!" Roy had not thought of the CO of the 457th in months, and he didn't particularly want to now either.

"Any news from Frances?" Roy yelled, cupping his hands around his mouth in the churning wind. Joe's wife, Frances, and May were good friends. They would keep in touch.

"Yep, heard from her once since I've been here." Joe paused, broke into a broad smile, and then added: "You're a daddy, you old rascal."

Roy stopped dead cold. "What'd you say?"

"May delivered in mid-September. You got a baby boy, Lieutenant Allen. Roy Junior, May calls him. She's fine. So's the baby."

Roy stared through the rows of barbed wire. The roaring voices around him seemed to fall silent, and all motion stopped, as frozen as the distant snow-daubed trees. For months he had prayed for this moment, and now it had arrived, and he could find no words.

"She's okay, you're sure she's okay?"

"Absolutely," Joe yelled, beaming.

Roy paused, trying to absorb the news. Wind-driven ice crystals pelted his face, and he looked down, rubbing his eyes. "How long you been here?" he finally called out.

"Got here middle of July, I guess it was."

"Did you see anybody else when you jumped? Any chutes?"

"Yeah," Joe yelled, "Verne and Plum—I had to pry that boy out—and Anderson jumped. Didn't see anybody from the back of the plane, but Frances wrote me that Smittie and Goldsborough and Henson evaded capture and somehow made it back to England. She got it from Smittie's family. He's been back in the States since September, the lucky stiff." He paused. "Anderson didn't make it. His chute opened. I saw it. But the Germans were firing at us from the ground. We came down in an oat field right beside a flak battery, and they shot at us all the way. I hit in the stubble and rolled, unhooked the chute, but they were on me in no time. They were the same guys who were trying to pick me off on the way down, and I thought I was going to get it, but they hauled me up and took me to a house near the flak battery. Messed up my leg pretty bad. I saw Plum there and Verne and several other guys, but no Anderson. When they took me into a room for questioning, they asked all about the crew, and showed me some dog tags and a crash bracelet—they were Anderson's. Said they had a body they wanted me to identify. I didn't know what to do. I didn't think I was supposed to give them any information, you know, just name, rank, and serial number. So I wouldn't look at the body. I can't say for sure that it was Anderson, but I'm pretty sure it was. Now I wish I had identified him. Plum and Verne thought the Krauts shot him on the way down, in his chute.

"After that we were taken into Paris—about two hundred of us—and marched from one railway station to another. They had people lining the streets all along the way, men and women, spitting on us and screaming at us. It looked to me like one of those orchestrated demonstrations, but it was pretty dicey there for a while. We got shuffled around several camps inside France and Germany, and I got separated from Plum, who was probably sent to a camp for enlisted personnel, and from Verne. I spent several days at Chartres in solitary and then went on to Dulag Luft, north of Frankfurt—everybody goes there, I guess, for interrogation. Roy, the interrogator there produced a file on me. That fellow knew about my training, my family, schooling, everything. He even asked me how Frances was doing!"

Roy shouted back the general outlines of his story, but he found it hard to concentrate. May had had the baby, and everybody was okay! The little boy, Roy Jr., would be three months old now. He couldn't fathom it.

Finally, as the afternoon light waned, the guards began moving the prisoners back away from the fences. Joe waved good-bye. Roy was ecstatic. That night, in the crowded theater, he sang with abandon. In the chorus he crooned the Christmas carols in a lush Bing Crosby baritone and belted out his solos in the skits. He had a great time. Later he attended the midnight service, taking communion with other Kriegies and, to his astonishment, a number of German guards who appeared in the theater without their weapons. Later in the combine, the boys asked him to sing "White Christmas," and no one talked much after that.

The next day, he wrote home. "Hey! What's the idea making me lose all my bets? Santa Claus was real good to me and told me it was a boy. Gee, it's good to stop 'sweatin'! Send me some pictures—you be there too . . . So, it's a boy—and I thought we had intuition. Is he a good kind of a baby? Oh well, I guess I can wait. I was talking to Verne and Joe yesterday and Joe told me about the baby!

"We had the usual festivities here and I took part in a Jack Benny show. What talent! I was Phil Harris and 'Bong' Sinatry, guest singer. I trembled through 'Beautiful Dreamer' then stuttered through 'White Christmas' after the show. I'm meeting somebody I know every day, either from my Group, college, Cadets, Philadelphia, and elsewhere." All things considered, it had been a Christmas to remember.

In early January, after a brief thaw, the weather turned bitterly cold and stormy. Arctic winds hammered at the barracks, and the men spent days in bed, trying to stay warm. Roy found it impossible to sleep. He would drift off for a few minutes, then wake up shaking. Food was running short. Due to the bombing of the train lines and truck routes, the Germans were having trouble making food deliveries. Bread became scarce, potatoes too. The anticipated Red Cross parcels failed to arrive, and the camp went back on half rations. After the short-lived excitement of Christmas, the mood in the compound turned grim.

The news from the BBC, on the other hand, offered some encouragement. The Battle of the Bulge, as the Allies were calling it, was apparently over. The German offensive had failed, and now British and American troops stood poised on the threshold of Germany proper. News from the eastern front was even bleaker for Hitler. The Red Army's offensive had resumed, Warsaw had fallen, and armored spearheads had reached Budapest and Krakow. Every day now German aircraft from the nearby aerodrome roared over the camp toward the east, flying one sortie after another, as the front drew nearer.

On January 17, a shipment of Red Cross parcels finally arrived from Geneva, and Colonel Alkire ordered the men back on full rations. With the Russians closing in, the Germans were planning to evacuate the prisoners westward, Alkire believed, deeper into the Reich. Since the German rail system was in such disarray, that would probably mean a forced march, and the men would need all their strength. A long winter trek would demand stamina and tough feet, and a few days later the general issued an order for all men to begin walking the perimeter track four times a day. Rosters and schedules would be established, the walking closely supervised.

Nervous energy gripped the camp. The men speculated endlessly about German intentions. Some in Roy's combine agreed with the colonel about the evacuation. Others thought that the Germans would simply pull out of the camp, leaving the prisoners for the Russians to deal with. Why drag us along, they asked. Why, indeed, others responded—the goons were just as likely to shoot them all, leaving nobody behind for the Russians to find. Roy hardly listened. He had heard it all before.

Every morning he walked the perimeter, and every afternoon he visited the library to examine the situation map on the bulletin board and hear the latest from the newsroom. The speed of the Russian advance was breathtaking. On January 24, the Red Army was closing in on Posen and Breslau, about eighty miles north and south of the camp. The next day Russian troops were reported to be in Steinau, on the Oder River, fifty miles away, and on the twenty-sixth a Russian spearhead was rumored to be only twenty-eight miles from Sagan, advancing from the northeast. The German military communiqués continued to speak confidently of strategic withdrawals, but to Roy it looked like a rout. Every day trains carrying troops and heavy weapons clattered past, chugging away from the front. More telling, Roy thought, columns of German civilians began appearing outside the wire, trudging westward on the frozen roads.

Within the camp, tension mounted by the hour. Be ready to move out at a moment's notice, Colonel Alkire had warned them, and in the barracks the men worked feverishly, putting their things in order, mending clothes, and devising ways of carrying their meager supplies. Woolen shirts were transformed into knapsacks by sewing or tying up the front and bottom and using the sleeves as straps, socks were turned into crude gloves, and blanket rolls, hardly different from those carried by Civil War soldiers, began appearing in the rooms. Some combines worked on sleds, overturning benches and fashioning crude runners out of bed slats. Stools were turned into sleds for individuals, and some ingenious men even tried to craft skis out of stray planks.

In each combine, men sorted through the food parcels, selecting the items that could be carried in their makeshift packs. For days Roy had eaten as much as he could, trying to build up his strength. He was nervous about the prospect of a long march in the snow, but he was getting stronger. He could feel it on his trips around the perimeter. His feet and ankles were recovering their flexibility, and even with the diminished rations, he was gradually putting on weight. To carry his supplies, he improvised a sort of musette bag, which he could sling over his shoulder, and filled it with the small cans of prunes, cheese, sugar, cans of Spam and corned beef, and as many D-bars as he could scrounge. Like the other men in the combine, he practiced wrapping his meager clothing into a blanket roll. He still had no shoes, but he had fresh wrappings for his feet.

During the afternoon of January 27, West Compound played South in a hockey game on the frozen fire pool, and the guards allowed some men from both compounds to attend. Throughout the day the temperature dropped, the clouds turned dark, and there was a scent of snow in the air. At the hockey game and in the barracks, the tension seemed to ease. The Germans, most now concluded, had waited too long to evacuate the camp. They didn't have enough rolling stock available to transport over twelve thousand POWs away from Sagan, and with the Russians breathing down their necks, they could never organize a forced march of so many men.

In the early dusk, Roy stood at the window of his cluttered room. All through *Appell* and supper he could hear the muffled thumping of artillery from the direction of Sagan. Now, above the black trees, flashes of iridescent red and orange flickered in the eastern sky, reflecting off the low clouds. Occasionally he could discern the faint rattle of machine guns and the popping of small-arms fire. The Russians were very near. As he watched, the twilight faded imperceptibly into darkness, and snow began to fall. He checked his equipment, stacked handily along the wall, and lay back on his bunk, listening to the muted din of the artillery barrage. He had written to May that afternoon but had not taken the letter to the mailroom. He wondered if the mail would continue when the Russians took the camp.

He was dozing when a commotion from outside the barracks jarred him awake. He could hear men running past the window, doors slamming, shouts. Within seconds, the door at the end of the passageway banged open and a voice roared out: "Get ready on the double! This is it! The goons have ordered us to be ready to move out within an hour. They're evacuating the camp! Get your gear together and fall out in front of the barracks."

For a moment the combine went silent. The men gaped at one

another, eyes wide. Then, as if a switch had been thrown, a bolt of excitement bristled through the barracks. Frantic shouts rang out; men pushed and shoved their way down the passageway. In the rooms, furniture toppled, plates and pitchers clattered, and cans crashed onto the floor as Kriegies scurried to put their packs in order. Roy jumped to his feet. He quickly stowed his spare clothing in his blanket roll, making sure that his extra bindings, the oilcloth, and socks were securely packed. He adjusted the burlap wrappings on his feet, and then checked the rations in his musette bag. Together the men in the combine sorted through the food in the common larder, distributed different items to be shared on the march, and then made their way down the littered passageway to the door.

It was snowing heavily now, and a stiff wind was rising in the east. Clumps of men stood in rough formation in front of every barracks, packs and other equipment piled at their feet. The barracks leader called the men to attention, took a count, and then they waited. An hour passed, then another. The men hunkered down, shivering, their backs turned to the wind. The snow was already several inches deep, and the searchlight beams sweeping across the compound seemed alive with falling snow.

At around 2300 Roy could see movement from South Compound. Long files of men, hunched over as they marched through the wind-driven snow, were leaving the camp, trudging westward into the darkness. They made slow progress, and it was over an hour before the last of them drifted past. Then, barracks by barracks, the men of West Compound began to move toward the *Vorlager*. As they passed through the gate, the goons counted them and handed each man a Red Cross parcel. It was after midnight, and the wind was howling.

On the road outside the camp, the roughly two thousand men of West Compound were formed into ranks of five. Glancing back from his position near the front, Roy could not see the end of the column. Over one German hundred soldiers were spread along the formation, some accompanied by the burly German shepherds that usually patrolled the fences. The excited dogs strained at their leashes, barking and snarling at the Kriegies. Most of the soldiers were on foot, tramping along in the deepening drifts at the side of the road. They carried heavy packs and rifles, and most, Roy noticed, were older men, many over sixty, he guessed. Other soldiers rode on horse-drawn wagons with machine guns mounted on the back. From time to time, a staff car skittered through the column, trying to keep the formation tight, hurrying the stragglers.

At first the pace of the march was surprisingly fast, and in spite of the worsening storm, the men felt exhilarated to be out of the camp. They were caught in a blizzard, the mercury dropping to zero, but they were moving, and, Roy thought, the Russians would surely overtake them soon. After an hour or so, the column halted for a ten-minute rest. Roy sat in the road, his blanket roll still on his back, and fished a chocolate bar from his musette bag. So far his feet were holding up. He was cold, but, with all the walking, it was bearable. Some men sprawled in the snow, but most stood in place, talking. Behind them the sky glimmered deep red, and some thought the Germans were burning the camp.

After the break, the march resumed, and as the hours passed the mood in the column began to change. The temperature was falling, and the snow swirled in gusts that took the breath away. The wet packs grew heavy, and men began tossing the heavier items into the snow. Cans, books, bits of clothing, sheets of paper now littered the road. Stragglers from South Compound were falling back in the column, and the formation of five men abreast dissolved. Men followed each other single file, heads bowed, shoulders hunched against the wind. Roy squinted into the snow, which no longer drifted down but flew horizontally, peppering his face like buckshot. Snow clotted his brows and lashes, and his eyes, tearing in the bitter wind, locked onto the heels of the man directly in front of him. He began to lose feeling in his feet, and his legs threatened to cramp.

Hour after hour, they plodded on, halting only for short rests. During the breaks, exhausted men dropped their packs and collapsed in place. Others tumbled into the snowdrifts at the side of the road, lying motionless until the whistle blew again. Roy looked forward to the ten-minute breaks, even in the open, but at each stop the cold crept deeper into his bones, and he hated to climb back up on his swollen feet. For energy, he chewed cubes of sugar and sucked handfuls of snow to wash them down. At first the men grumbled, swearing at the snow, at the Germans, the army, the war, but as time crawled by, they fell silent, too exhausted to be bitter, too dazed to speak.

At first light, low clouds drifted across the sky like ice floes, and the snow continued to fall—eight inches and still coming down. Even on the heavily trodden road, it was ankle deep. As the column slowed at the edge of a village, Roy saw a sign that read Freiwaldau, and another, facing down the road they had come from, read: Sagan 29 Kilometers. They had walked eighteen miles through the storm, and the time, a man next to him muttered, was 0800. Eight hours on the road.

As the men poured into the narrow streets of the village, the ragged procession bunched and then halted. Shivering and stamping their feet to keep warm, the men stood and waited. Word spread that there would be shelter here and a rest, and after some confusion, the guards began herding the lead elements of the formation toward a set of buildings that appeared to be some sort of prison complex. "It's a concentration camp," one of the men whispered, but everyone seemed too cold and tired to care.

Following along, Roy entered a dank abandoned building that was divided into a series of long narrow cells. The unheated cells were no more than fifteen feet across and about thirty feet deep, but the guards squeezed seventy or so men into each. Roy staked out a tiny space and slumped down on the floor. From all sides, weary Kriegies pressed against him, squirming to make room in the cramped space. He fumbled in his musette bag, extracting a D-bar and a can of prunes. The chocolate bar was frozen solid, and the prunes clung to one another as if huddling against the cold. He ate quickly between chattering teeth, then leaned back, wedged into place by the other Kriegies, and tried to sleep.

He was too tired and too cold to sleep, and after an hour or so the guards rousted the men out of the building into the street. Hordes of Kriegies now swamped the village, and more and more men were arriving as the column from North Compound reached Freiwaldau. There was not enough shelter for all, so the men rotated into the prison buildings in roughly two-hour shifts. The others slumped against leeward walls or under wagons or wandered aimlessly through the streets, seeking shelter anywhere they could find it.

During the night Roy had become separated from the men in his combine, and in the falling snow he picked his way through the crowd, searching for them. Maybe he could find Warren or Verne, maybe even Joe. But he found no one he knew, and in the feeble afternoon light, he curled beneath the tin overhang of a garden shed with several other men and tried to rest. His feet were wet and sore, but he dared not try to change the socks or wrap new burlap around them. One of the men complained of blisters, and when he pulled off his soaked shoe, a dark stain covered the heel of his sock, spreading along the bottom of his foot. He didn't know how much farther he could make it.

Just after nightfall whistles blew, and the guards shouted for the formation to regroup. For over an hour, they tried to conduct a count, but under the circumstances, Roy thought, it must have been impossible. Finally, the throng of shabby men shuffled out of Freiwaldau. The snow tapered off, but the wind still moaned through the snow-covered trees, and it was getting colder.

"*Verdammt noch mal,*" one of the guards groaned as he staggered along beside Roy. "*Minus vierzig Grad* . . . Below zero." He was a short, squat man, at least sixty years old, and he was breathing heavily. "*Verschissenes Wetter, was?*" he added, straining to adjust his pack. "Shit weather, yes?"

Roy nodded. "Where are we going?" he asked.

"*Keine Ahnung.*" The man coughed, his words erupting in bursts of steam. "No idea. No one knows, not even the Herr Hauptmann, I think."

Within a few steps, the soldier began to fall behind, muttering bitterly to himself. He was no longer guarding the men in the column but limped along in the deep snow on the shoulder of the road, his rifle slung over his shoulder, his eyes down. Soon Roy lost sight of him completely.

For hours the men groped their way along the icy road, passing darkened villages and silent, lifeless farms. Sometime after midnight, the snow stopped and the clouds parted, revealing patches of black sky and fields of brilliant stars. The cold was intense, and weak, bone-weary men began to fall out, staggering to the side of the road, dropping into the snowbanks. They had been warned when they left the camp that the Germans would shoot any stragglers, but the guards simply stepped around them as if they were invisible. Once shots rang out from somewhere along the line, and someone said the goons were shooting the dropouts, but a short time later a horse-drawn wagon loaded with exhausted Kriegies plodded by. Those who could not go on should move to the side and wait, the guards said. Another wagon would pick them up.

As the night wore on, civilians joined the column. Some were on foot; some rode in heavily laden horse-drawn wagons. Many were women with young children, joined by elderly couples, and slave laborers who whispered in Polish or Russian. At first the soldiers tried to keep them separate from the Kriegies, but that proved impossible. The column from West Compound alone stretched out for over five miles, someone said, and the guards found it difficult to maintain control. Most didn't even try.

One by one, then in small groups, Kriegies began drifting away from the column, slipping into barns, churches, taverns, even private homes along the road. At a sharp bend in the road, Roy and several other men bolted into a clump of trees and then into a nearby barn. Huddled together on the dirt floor of an empty stall, they managed to light a small straw fire, heated some powdered coffee and bouillon cubes, and stretched out on the frozen earth. It was too cold to sleep, but Roy massaged his feet and legs, wrapping them in his blankets, and leaned back against the rough wooden side of the stall to rest.

It was not yet light when the men stirred and filtered back into the passing column. Heavy snow was falling again. Through the long bitter morning the Kriegies struggled on at a snail's pace, and in the afternoon things got worse. The narrow road began to climb, meandering through an area of rough rolling hills that made each torturous footstep an act of fortitude. Roy strained to drag himself up each rise and then somehow maintain his balance on the icy downward slope. His blanket roll, sopping wet and heavy as a railroad tie, bit into his shoulders, and he began dumping the few cans left in his musette bag. Up and down the line, men were crying out for help, sobbing, pleading for a rest.

At last, the column entered a sizable town, straggling down a wide boulevard bordered by empty hotels and restaurants and brightly painted row houses. With its cupolas and spires blanketed by snow, the town—Bad Muskau, someone called it—had the air of a deserted winter resort. The men halted in a large square. Most were at the end of their rope. Some swayed back and forth in place, glassy eyed, asleep on their feet; others crumpled in the street moaning or staggered around in the confusion like lunatics. The guards, stationed along the unshoveled sidewalks, tried to maintain order, but with each passing minute the Kriegies became more desperate.

The commander was trying to arrange shelter for them, an ancient guard standing near Roy said. There would be a rest here, he assured them, rest and food. They must be patient. The guard looked on the edge of collapse himself. Finally, the formation lurched into motion. Toward the front of the column, several hundred Kriegies peeled off, following the guards into a large Lutheran church. The remainder continued on, crossing an icy bridge into an industrial area on the outskirts of the town. There the guards directed groups of men into a variety of abandoned buildings—warehouses, garages, a paper mill, and a large multistoried pottery plant.

The pottery plant, where Roy found himself, was still in operation, and in its basement enormous kilns, like bellows, exhaled drafts of dry heat that rose through circular holes in the floor. A luxurious warmth filled the building, and bright lights burned overhead. The exhausted men settled down wherever they could find a spot. Roy dragged himself up a flight of stairs, found a gap on the already cluttered floor, and fell back on his blanket roll, too spent to move. He had not slept in two days.

When he awoke, no one was stirring except the Polish slave laborers who worked in the plant and did their best to step around the sleeping men. He had no idea how long he had been out. His whole body was sore, and his stomach ached with hunger, but the sleep was like ambrosia. Roy sat up. All around him men were sprawled on the crowded concrete floor, contorted into odd shapes amid their small heaps of gear.

Drawing up his knees, he carefully removed the wrappings from his feet, peeled away the wet socks, and stared down at the raw flesh. Black patches of frostbite tinged his arches and toes, and his ankles were swollen. If the march went on for much longer, he would never make it. Unrolling his blanket pack, he found the extra burlap, oilcloth, and socks only slightly damp. He laid them out beside him to dry. He devoured his last box of prunes and a handful of soggy crackers from his musette bag, and then laid back down to conserve his energy. He needed to be ready when the march resumed.

While he rested, a rumor rose from floor to floor that they would be staying in the factory for the rest of the day—maybe even that night. At first he did not believe it, but the hours passed and the guards did not come, and gradually he relaxed. He spread his blanket roll on the dusty floor, stretched out, and napped through much of the day.

Later he found the building's one available toilet, where the line was already long, and the lone water tap, where he drew fresh water. He made bouillon and powdered coffee, warming them over one of the heating vents, and he finished off the last of his Spam. He was almost at the end of his Red Cross rations. His clothes dried. He even

381

managed to wash himself at the tap. He bartered for a stick of margarine and rubbed his feet with it, a good treatment for frostbite, his *Blockältester* in Buchenwald had told him. That night he slept for hours.

The next day, the guards surged through the building, rousting the men out. It was early afternoon before the loose formation assembled and set off again. They were headed to a place called Spremberg, Colonel Alkire told them, eighteen kilometers away. The day was windless and surprisingly mild, and the snow on the road began to melt, turning to slush beneath their feet. "About ten miles," Roy said to no one in particular. "I can make that." But after only an hour on the road, his toes were burning and his energy was melting away like the snow. Forty-eight hours of rest, and he had no strength. His breathing was labored, his muscles cramped, and the slush seeped through his leggings, soaking his feet. After sundown, the air turned cold and the melted snow froze, turning the road into a ragged sheet of ice. Men slipped and staggered, lost their footing, and crashed onto the ice. They lay on their backs, starring vacantly at the sky, unable to move. Somehow Roy labored on.

He slept that night in a barn near a village, along with a hundred or so other Kriegies. His musette bag was almost empty, and he husbanded his remaining food with care, gnawing at the precious D-bars like a mouse. The next morning, while waiting for the order to move out, he traded a bar of soap to a farmer for three gnarled uncooked potatoes and a half loaf of black bread. He ate one of the potatoes raw, slathering it with what was left of the margarine. The bread he stuffed into his musette bag for the march.

Late in the afternoon the men moved out again. They were only about eight kilometers from Spremberg, a woman who worked on the farm told them, about five miles, but the going was slow, and it was after dark before they stopped on the outskirts of the town. The march had taken four hours in a slashing intermittent rain that threatened at any moment to turn to snow. They were quartered at last in a cavernous warehouse beside a double set of railroad tracks, and the Germans served hot barley soup and distributed bread. It was the first food they had issued since the march began. Roy could hardly stand in line for the rations, but the soup was hot and delicious, the best he had tasted in months, or maybe he was just delirious from fatigue and hunger.

That night, as he lay on the muddy concrete floor, his shrunken belly full, air-raid sirens wailed. "Perfect," the man curled beside him grumbled. "Here we sit just behind the front in a storage area at the edge of a town right on a railway line. Just perfect." Roy shook his head in agreement, but said nothing. He was too tired to care. It was, by his count, February 1. They had been on the road for five days, and they had walked over sixty miles. His feet wouldn't carry him much farther, but he didn't care about that either. He was almost asleep when the all clear sounded. The RAF—or maybe it was the Russians— had droned on by, on the way to another target.

The next morning, they walked through Spremberg, which appeared to be a large garrison town. Soldiers were everywhere. The column followed the railroad tracks to the station and into a large marshaling yard. There they halted. Troop trains and long supply trains stood along an intricate grid of tracks, loading and unloading. Antiaircraft batteries dotted the grounds. Tightening the formation, the guards pushed the Kriegies forward, across several tracks, toward a long string of boxcars. The column inched ahead. As Roy approached the head of the column, he could at last see clearly what was happening. There, directly in front of him, was a waiting train. Men from the column were climbing into boxcars, while the Germans watched and counted. His heart shrank. They were 40-and-8ers, like the ones that had delivered him to Buchenwald.

"Where are we going?" he asked one of the guards as his turn came to squeeze aboard. *"Ein anderes Lager in Deutschland,"* he said simply. "Another camp. You will not like it."

CHAPTER 14

Liberation

For three days and nights the train plodded through the thawing German countryside. At first its course meandered to the southeast, but on the second day, the train looped suddenly westward, passing Dresden and Meissen, before plunging to the southwest. Their destination, a guard told them, was Nuremberg.

Almost sixty men were crammed into Roy's boxcar, and the weary Kriegies stood hour after hour in the gnawing cold, breathing the stink of the open pails. Before the train departed Spremberg, the Germans issued Red Cross parcels, three parcels for four men, and occasionally during the infrequent stops, the guards provided bread and *Blutwurst* and coffee heated by the train's engine. All along the way the stations were swamped with civilians and soldiers and black-uniformed SS. In the larger, bomb-shattered towns civilians glared at the prisoners from the platforms, but in the smaller depots, where the men were allowed out of the cars to stretch, they crowded around, bartering for soap and cigarettes from the Red Cross parcels.

At three o'clock on the fourth day, the train slid into the Nuremberg *Hauptbahnhof,* and the men were rousted from their boxcars. The afternoon sky was overcast and a cold drizzle was falling as the guards assembled the Kriegies along the tracks and began herding them westward. They marched through narrow city streets congested with rubble, and then along muddy roads that led them, after three hours, to a dismal clump of colorless buildings on the outskirts of the city.

Stalag XIII-D stood beside a cemetery on a gentle rise not far beyond the freight yard. The camp looked familiar—the guard towers, the dogs, the double rows of barbed wire fences, the pine forest just beyond. Inside the gates the same wood-frame barracks, cruder even than those of Stalag Luft III, stood in slump-shouldered formation in a quagmire of mud. Dilapidated and dingy, they had recently housed Italian POWs, who were moved to make room for the new arrivals from Sagan. The walls, the floors, and bed frames, even the windows, were caked with grime, and the foul-smelling palliasses crawled with lice. Fleas were everywhere. After the relative cleanliness and order of Stalag Luft III, the filth was a shock.

The men moved into the blocks, got organized, and began an energetic cleanup. The barracks had no enclosed rooms but sections marked off by partitions that jutted out from the walls. A wide aisle extended down the center of the building, with sets of triple-decker bunks for each combine's two dozen men on the right, and each combine's table, benches, and, in some cases, stove on the left. Some bunks had no slats, some no palliasses, and many men slept on the floor or on the tables across the center aisle.

The barracks were cold and damp; the roofs and windows leaked. The Germans issued two ratty blankets to each man but provided no coal or wood for the stoves. Roy had managed to keep an extra woolen shirt, a sweater, and two pairs of socks from the trek, and in the clammy barracks he layered up against the chill. Like most Kriegies, he slept in his clothes. Within days, men began ripping scraps of lumber from the drab, weather-beaten buildings to stoke the fires. The guards threatened them, but no one paid much attention.

Red Cross parcels arrived only once in February and again in March, and the men were forced to rely on the starvation rations provided by the Germans. The camp's food supply dwindled, and the men, already fragile from their ordeal in the snow, grew steadily weaker. They ate the meager ration of black bread and dehydrated potatoes. They drank the thin tasteless coffee and the soup, one variety called "green death," the other "gray death." After a time Roy even devoured the blood sausage whenever he could find it.

His feet were in bad shape, some toes almost black with frostbite, but except for roll call, he could keep off them. During the soggy days of February, he rested in the barracks and on rare warm days in March, he found a spot to sit in the late winter sun. There was little in the way of medical treatment, no well-stocked *Revier* as at Stalag Luft III, so he rubbed his ration of margarine on his feet and tried to keep them dry.

Because of the pain in his feet and ankles Roy stayed close to the barracks. He ventured to the washhouse only once for a brief shower, and he could not find Warren or Verne or Joe. Not all the Kriegies of Luft III had been delivered to Nuremberg, he discovered. Some had been taken north; others were sent to a camp outside Munich. Maybe they were there. Still, over fifteen thousand Allied POWs, most of them Americans, were housed in the camp. There was, Roy discovered, no library, no theater, no mail office, no sports facilities or choral groups, no Kriegie newspapers. There was no perimeter track for exercise, only the muddy camp streets.

On his first night in the camp, air-raid sirens howled across the city and freight yards and camp. It was after lights-out, but the men, locked in their barracks, rushed to the shuttered windows to get a glimpse. Guards appeared outside the barracks, quickly checking the locks, then raced for their foxholes. In the distance towering columns of light rose into the sky, as gigantic spotlights searched the low overcast for the Lancasters and Sterlings. The rumbling of engines grew louder as the formation approached, then suddenly from all around them volleys of thunderous anti-aircraft fire erupted. The deadly .88s hammered at the sky with deafening salvos, and bombs whistled down, dropping into the freight yard close by. The barracks shook and the sky turned bright with flame. Men pounded on the walls and doors, frantic to get out, to take cover, but without success. Crouching beneath the bunks, under the tables and benches, they had to wait it out.

Throughout February and March, American planes seemed to be overhead almost every day. Fighters, in flights of two or three or sometimes singly, roared in over the freight yard, strafing and dive-bombing. There seemed to be no pattern, no predictability to the attacks, and every day the men watched the sky. Sometimes the heavies came. On February 21 and again the next day hundreds of glittering Fortresses and Liberators appeared on the horizon, stretching across the sky like a veil of steel mesh. For more than an hour the vast formations droned over the city, and an endless torrent of bombs cascaded down. From the perimeter fence Roy could see sheets of flame in the distance, sweeping through the freight yard below, and locomotives and box-cars jumbled across the tracks like so many children's toys. Beyond the railyard, smoke roiled high above the medieval spires of Nuremberg, engulfing the ancient city.

The men worried about bombs drifting off target, especially during the RAF's nighttime raids, and began digging their own slit trenches just beyond the barracks. Fearing attempts to escape, the guards at first tried to confine the Kriegies to their barracks during the nighttime raids, but as the attacks intensified, they gave up. At the sound of the first alarm, day or night, the men would make a mad dash for the shallow trenches. Some were covered by strips of corrugated tin, others with shutters or lumber from the barracks. Most remained open, and the men hunkered down with nothing but doubled-up blankets or greatcoats spread over them to shield them from falling bomb fragments or spent flak.

Sometimes a speedy, low-flying Mosquito would slip undetected over the freight yard and release a single four-thousand-pound bomb—a cookie, the RAF boys called it. There would be no warning until a tremendous earth-shaking explosion would rend the night and the sirens, too late, would begin their howling. More terrifying were the big nighttime raids, with streams of Lancasters and Sterlings thundering overhead, dropping their bombs through the clouds.

The most terrifying of these RAF assaults came on March 16. Roy was hanging his extra shirt on a line in the sleeping bay when the sirens blared out the first warning alert, and he began hurrying to the trenches. An hour or so later, crouching in the trench, he could hear the deep rumble of approaching planes. Looking up into the moonless sky, he could see nothing. Suddenly, the flak batteries all around camp let loose, pumping shell after shell into the darkness above. Roy ducked. Then, peeking over the lip of his trench, he watched as pathfinder aircraft dropped yellow flares across the city to light a path toward the target for the following formation. Then a cluster of red, green, and white flares, burning as big and bright as Christmas trees, drifted lazily down to mark the aiming point, the bull's eye of the target.

Within seconds the first bombs fell. The earth trembled as booming concussions shook the camp, rattling the windows and shaking the flimsy walls of the barracks. Overhead the sky exploded in a kaleidoscope of brilliant color. Burning planes, caught in the dazzling white shafts of the searchlights, streaked across the sky, exploding finally in a shower of fiery orange. From time to time a parachute would drift eerily through a hail of yellow tracers, falling into the inferno below, where the red and green flares still glowed among the flames. The fires raged out of control through the night and into the following day. Dense black smoke hung over the city like a pall, and in the camp the air was thick with floating ash and the scent of creosote. That night the Lancasters returned.

The bombing and strafing continued, gathering intensity as the month progressed. Between the big raids flocks of P-38s and P-47s swept low over the camp, roaming at will across the surrounding countryside, and almost every night the sirens howled and the men dragged themselves to the trenches. The only good news arrived by radio. The daily German military broadcasts—*Aus Dem Führerhaupt-quartier*—blared over the camp's loudspeaker system, bringing veiled acknowledgment of the Wehrmacht's rapidly collapsing strategic position. The clandestine radio from Luft III had survived the march, and the BBC confirmed that the Allies had broken through in both the east and the west. The Russians were preparing for a final push across the River Oder just east of Berlin, and the Anglo-American armies had taken the Ruhr pocket and were pressing into central Germany. In late March rumors began to swirl that there would be another evacuation.

Roy still held out hope that the Americans would reach Nuremberg before the camp could be evacuated. He was anxious to get away from the nerve-jangling air raids, but he did not relish the prospect of another forced march. Then, on the afternoon of April 3, the German command announced that the prisoners should be prepared to leave Stalag XIII-D the next morning, and at 1130 on April 4, over fifteen thousand men began marching out of Stalag XIII-D under a steady drizzle. There was none of the frantic rushing about that had characterized their sudden departure from Sagan. The mood was calm, the evacuation orderly.

After almost two months in the camp, Roy's feet were much improved. He was still weak from the meager rations, but the snow had disappeared and the weather was springtime cool. A Red Cross delivery in late March had given him a small supply of food and other items for barter, and he would rely again on a blanket roll to carry his load. He took his position in the formation, and walking three abreast the men followed a narrow country road away from Nuremberg. The Germans gave no hint of their destination, but with Patton's Third

Army streaking across Germany to the north of them, the only direction they could go, Roy thought, was south.

For days the inmates of Buchenwald had lived in a mounting fever of anxiety. In late March the Americans had encircled the Ruhr, and began driving eastward. Kassel and Fulda had fallen by the end of the month. The U.S. Third Army was moving directly toward Weimar, and the final act of KZ Buchenwald was drawing near.

The camp underground suspected that SS Commandant Hermann Pister was under orders from Berlin to evacuate the prisoners rather than leave them for the Americans. Already thousands of prisoners had left the camp, transported to the camps at Dachau and Flossenbürg in Bavaria and the ghetto at Theresienstadt in Bohemia. Evacuation, the prisoners understood, meant certain death, either en route or upon arrival. On April 3 the commandant gathered camp leaders together in the theater and promised them that, contrary to his orders, he planned to turn the camp and its prisoners over to the Americans. Their cooperation was essential. The end of the war was at hand, he seemed to be saying, and he wanted them to know that he had resisted pressure from SS *Reichsführer* Heinrich Himmler to eliminate them. Few of his listeners believed him. Pister, they were convinced, was considering only two choices: attempt to evacuate the camp or liquidate the prisoners. The commandant was merely trying to lull them into compliance.

For months the Communist-dominated underground had been preparing for this situation. Small arms had been smuggled into the camp, especially in the chaos during and immediately after the August 24 bombing. Pistols, rifles, grenades, even *Panzerfäuste*, the shoulder-launched antitank rockets, had been distributed and hidden around the camp. Considerable mistrust still existed between the Communists and the non-Communists in the camp underground, but they agreed on a broad plan of action. It called for an uprising to prevent either a mass evacuation or the liquidation of the camp. Commando units—*Stosstruppen*—were selected and given specific objectives to seize when the signal was given. The key, everyone agreed, was choosing the right moment to strike. If they acted precipitously—that is, with the Americans too far away—the three thousand heavily armed SS troops would crush them with little trouble. If, on the other hand, they waited too long, Pister might execute Himmler's orders.

On the afternoon of April 4, the commandant showed his hand. With no warning, the voice of the *Rapportführer* rang out over the camp's loudspeaker system, reverberating in every block. All Jews, the voice demanded, were to report immediately to the *Appellplatz*. Until the fall of 1944 Buchenwald held relatively few Jews. But in January as the Russians drew near the giant death camps in Poland, the SS scrambled to evacuate their remaining prisoners, and transport after transport brought Jews from Auschwitz, Monowitz, and Gross-Rosen to Buchenwald. By the end of January the already desperately over-crowded camp held over ninety thousand prisoners, and in the first week of April transports were still arriving. Over twenty thousand Jews were imprisoned in Buchenwald, mostly new arrivals from Poland and Hungary who were dumped into the already teeming Little Camp.

The loudspeaker crackled again, repeating the order, but there was no movement toward the *Appellplatz*. Inside the barracks, the *Block-ältesters* made no attempt to round up the Jews, and the Jews worked feverishly to cut away the yellow star from their clothing. Many slipped away, hoping to dissolve into the camp. In the evening Pister called for the senior prisoner officer, the *Lagerältester*, and appealed to him. The Jews must come to the main gate, he warned. No harm would come to them. They were to be transferred to Theresienstadt, where they would be turned over to the International Red Cross.

The next morning the entire camp assembled for roll call. While the formation took shape, the SS set up machine guns all across the *Appellplatz*. The prisoners shot anxious sidelong glances all around them, waiting. Then as they stood in place, groups of SS dove into the ranks, screaming for the Jews and grabbing for anyone they took to be Jewish. Some prisoners suddenly broke from the formation and scrambled down the camp's main street toward the Little Camp. Guards raced after them, and gunfire echoed through the camp. Some of the escaping Jews were gunned down in the streets; others were cornered between the barracks and beaten to death. Meanwhile, squads of heavily armed SS rampaged through the camp, searching every building and shed. Those who were found were marched off to the grounds of the shattered German Armaments Works, the collec-tion site for the transport but also the scene of many executions. In the afternoon, the commandant announced that a transport of ten thousand prisoners would leave Buchenwald on the following day.

Leaders of the camp underground conferred that night. Rumors were circulating that the SS possessed a list of forty-seven antifascists, all important figures of the underground, and Pister was planning to arrest them all. The forty-seven were to go instantly into hiding. Some, especially among the French Communists, wanted to launch the insurrection against the SS immediately, to prevent the arrests and the transport, but this was rejected as premature. With the Americans still over fifty kilometers to the west, an armed uprising would only result in a bloodbath. Instead, they opted for the only feasible course of action—frustrate the SS as much as possible, delay as long as possible, sacrifice as few as possible to save as many as possible.

On April 6 the mutiny began. The morning broke with an air-raid alarm, delaying the roll call until after 1100. When at last the *Lagerältester*'s whistle shrilled out the call for *Appell*, the doors of the barracks remained closed. An eerie silence descended over the camp. Finally the loudspeaker spewed out: *"Blockältester, herhören. Das ganze Lager auf dem Appellplatz aufmarschieren lassen!"* The *Blockältesters* were to order their men, the whole camp, to march to the roll call square. Still no one appeared in the streets. Nothing stirred. Inside the barracks, the prisoners waited nervously for an SS assault, but none came. Later in the day, the SS organized another transport, hounding prisoners not only from the barracks and tents of the Little Camp but from the blocks of the *Hauptlager* as well.

After April 6, the commandant made no more attempts to hold *Appell*, and without roll call an accurate count could not be rendered and names could not be checked against rosters. Adding to the confusion, more transports were *arriving* from Buchenwald's many subsidiary camps, now caught in the path of the advancing Americans. Over ten thousand starving prisoners from Ohrdruf and Nordhausen staggered into the camp on April 6 and 7. Hundreds had died in the evacuations, and many stragglers were shot by the SS. Shriveled bodies littered the road from the station to the main gate. SS control of the camp was dissolving, and in the mounting chaos, prisoners slipped from block to block, hiding. Some took to the animal pens below the Little Camp, others hid in the latrines, in the guinea pig barracks, or beneath the *Revier*.

During the night of April 8 the prisoners' clandestine radio broadcast a message to the approaching Americans: "Concentration Camp Buchenwald calling! SOS. We ask for help. They are going to evacuate us.

The SS will exterminate us." The Third Army returned the signal. Help was on the way. On that same night, the non-Communist resistance took action on its own. They smuggled one of their leaders, Eugen Kogon, out of the camp on a special mission. Kogon was an Austrian attorney who had been a prisoner in Buchenwald since it opened in 1937. He understood how the SS leadership functioned and he knew the personalities of its ranking men. From Weimar he posted a letter to Commandant Pister. Pretending to be a British commando recently dropped into the area, he warned the commandant that the Allies knew the situation in Buchenwald and that he would be held personally responsible if the camp's inmates were evacuated or slaughtered. The war was over, and this was Pister's last chance for any leniency. The letter was signed Major James Mcleod of the British War Office.

Meanwhile, the evacuations continued. Between April 7 and 10 over twenty-five thousand prisoners were herded out of Buchenwald, bound, either on foot or by rail, for camps in the south. Thousands of hardened criminals, with their green and black triangles, were transported on April 9, and the next day thousands of Russian POWs marched out of the main gate, planning to overpower their guards at the first opportunity.

That night the black horizon erupted in flame as the RAF blasted targets in the Magdeburg-Halle-Leipzig area, and the camp secret radio reported that Erfurt, Eisenach, Langensalza, and Gotha had fallen. On the afternoon of April 10 the prisoners watched from the heights of the camp as German troops streamed across the open plain below them, retreating from the onrushing Americans. Liberation was at hand.

That night, with artillery fire resounding through the plain below and small arms crackling nearby, the SS hanged sixteen men in the basement of the crematorium, and two dozen more were beaten to death in the bunker. When their work was done, they scrubbed the blood-spattered walls of the cells and tried to pry the stubby iron hooks from the crematorium walls. The stains would not dissolve, and only a fraction of the stubby black hooks could be removed before the panicky SS rushed away.

By daybreak on April 11, an air of unbearable tension prevailed in the camp. At around 0930, with the battle closing around them, SS *Blockführers* entered the barracks. It appeared to be the final showdown. But on this day they were not interested in beating the prisoners or dragging them into the streets or shooting them; they were searching for clothes, civilian clothes, to slip on beneath their uniforms as they fled. An hour later, Pister summoned the *Lagerältester* to the gatehouse. "I hereby turn the camp over to you," he announced to the senior prisoner official. "Give me your word of honor that you will not let this fact be known until the Americans are here, to prevent a panic in the camp. From my side nothing will happen to you."

At 1145 an earsplitting siren wailed over the camp. A new alarm, only recently installed, gave the warning: "Enemy tanks approaching." Within minutes, an SS voice boomed over the loudspeakers: "All SS men leave the camp immediately." For the prisoners, the moment of greatest strain had arrived. All morning a rumor had swept through the blocks that the commandant had ordered aircraft from a nearby Luftwaffe base to bomb the camp as soon as the SS had departed. Huddled in their barracks, they waited. But no German aircraft appeared, only an American reconnaissance plane that slowly circled the camp.

For another hour or so, SS guards still manned the watchtowers surrounding the camp, but as the crackle of gunfire and the clattering of tanks grew ever closer, the guards abandoned their posts and scurried to the south toward the SS barracks. Warily the prisoners began to emerge from their blocks. Below them they could see American tanks driving toward the rock quarry to their left and another group emerging from the tree line, smashing into the stables and pigsties at the northwest corner of the camp. The tanks followed an easterly course in pursuit of the retreating German troops and showed little inclination to detour up the hill to the camp.

At 1445, the camp underground sprang into action. With weapons distributed, they charged toward the guard towers, disarmed the handful of terrified SS they found on the grounds, and advanced on the main gate. They rampaged through the abandoned offices of the gatehouse and swarmed through the deserted bunker, flinging open the metal doors of the cells. At 1530, the *Lagerältester* hoisted a white flag above the tower, and the iron gates of Buchenwald swung open. The underground's commando units, the *Stosstruppen*, stormed the SS weapons magazine, and then, well-armed and in good order, they marched off in pursuit of the SS. Speaking for the first time over the camp's loudspeaker system, Hans Eiden, the *Lagerältester*, made a simple announcement: "The SS have left the camp. It is in our hands." Shortly thereafter, two American tanks, their hatches open, rattled up to the main gate and halted. KZ Buchenwald was liberated.

Among the twenty-one thousand emaciated prisoners discovered by the Americans after April 11 were two men with connections to the British War Office. Christopher Burney and Alfred Balachowsky were leaders in the non-Communist underground organization in Buchenwald, and both had stories to tell. For months, SOE's F-Section had been desperately trying to determine the fate of dozens of its agents who had been arrested in France during 1944. Some had simply disappeared, others, F-Section's chief Maurice Buckmaster knew, had fallen into the hands of the Gestapo.

Burney and Balachowsky had worked for SOE in France, and upon liberation, they made reports for Orchard Court. Both possessed first-hand knowledge of the thirty-seven agents who had arrived in Buchenwald in August 1944 on the transport from Paris. They both gave the same grisly account of the executions of September 11 and October 5, describing with great bitterness their inability to save the men. But, they revealed, five of the group had been saved and, as far as they knew, were still alive. One of them was the group's leader, Yeo-Thomas. Burney and Balachowsky had been instrumental in rescuing the man they knew as Kenneth Dodkin, as well as Stephane Hessel and Henry Peulevé. Balachowsky worked in Block 50, the SS Institute of Hygiene, and after the September 11 executions he had approached Eugen Kogon for help. Kogon also worked in Block 50, where the typhus serums were developed, and was secretary to the SS physician in charge, Dr. Erwin Ding.

After the shock of the first unexpected executions on September 5, Balachowsky and Kogon moved into action. Kogon managed to convince Ding that with the war going badly, the doctor might still save himself and his family if he cooperated in a plan to rescue the agents. Kogon's plan was to slip the remaining twenty-one prisoners out of Block 17 individually and in small groups, inject them with a serum that would produce the symptoms of typhus, and then transfer them over time to the guinea pig block, where their identities could be switched with prisoners who had succumbed to typhus. After considering it, Ding agreed but would help only three men. More would be too dangerous. The three were to be selected by Dodkin (Yeo-Thomas), and, he insisted, one of the three had to be Yeo-Thomas himself. Yeo-Thomas resisted this idea, arguing that as ranking officer, he should be the last of the group to be rescued, but Ding would not budge. He would need someone of Yeo-Thomas's seniority to vouch for him when the Allies arrived.

Yeo-Thomas chose Stephane Hessel and Henry Peuleré. The three men were injected with a serum that gave them the symptoms of typhus, and one at a time they were taken from Block 17 to the basement of Block 46, the guinea pig block. While they waited anxiously for three French patients in the typhus ward to die, the second set of executions took place on October 5, and the men were thrown into despair. Finally, in early November Hessel and Peuleré, with their new identities, were assigned to an *Aussenkommando* near Jena, where they would work in an aircraft factory. About a week later Yeo-Thomas followed, assigned to the small sub-camp at Gleina, where Kogon had contacts.

Later the communist underground, which had refused to help with Yeo-Thomas or the others in Block 17 (they were combatants and not political prisoners like themselves, the International Camp Committee explained), agreed to assist two of the remaining members of the group—Pierre Culioli and Bernard Guillot, who were issued false papers and dispatched to work camps. Maurice Southgate, an SOE agent from the group of thirty-seven, managed to survive within the camp itself. Maurice Pertschuck—Perkins—who had often aided the group, was not so fortunate. The SS hanged him on March 29, 1945, two weeks before Buchenwald was liberated.

At his interrogation, Balachowsky also handed over to Allied intelligence a small strip of frayed white cloth with black numerals. 13474. It was the camp number of Pierre Mulsant, ripped from his uniform after his execution. Mulsant and Denis Barrett (Charles), he confirmed, had been executed at Buchenwald on October 5 with the second set of SOE victims. Buckmaster had known about Mulsant's disappearance since July, when word reached Orchard Court that Pierre and Charles disappeared after a rendezvous in the forest of Fontainebleau. He dispatched Benjamin Cowburn (Germain), who had worked with Pierre, Charles, and Mimi in Troyes during 1943, to determine the state of the **MINISTER** circuit and see if it could be salvaged.

Cowburn parachuted into France near Bray-sur-Aube on the night of July 30, 1944. In Mclun, he located Raoul Courman, the W/T operator Charles had trained, who, he believed, could lead him to Charles's sets and perhaps his silk code sheets. He also wanted to find Mimi. His first priority, however, was "to try and save Guérin [Mulsant] and [Charles]."

He made his way toward Paris, fighting a flood of Germans retreating from the front. "All along the roads," he reported, "the fleeing Germans were stealing bicycles and anything which would roll, and taking pot shots at . . . civilians." He first went to Fresnes, where *résistants* were usually held, but he could not contact the French jailer whose name he had obtained from contacts in Paris. "We got hold of a male nurse at the prison gates who told us that all political prisoners had been taken away to Compiègne and Germany, except for those who had been turned loose or shot." There the trail went cold.

In September, after the liberation of France, **MINISTER**'s surviving operatives were brought to London for debriefing—Désiré (de Ganay), Mulsant's leader in the northern sector of **MINISTER**'s operational area, the courier Mimi, and Roger Veillard, who was parachuted back into Seine-et-Marne in mid-August to resume his resistance activities in **MINISTER**'s area.

Désiré reported that he had driven to Nangis on July 15, where he found Mimi worried because Pierre, Charles, and Bernard Bemberg had not turned up after going to contact a party of SAS parachutists in the forest near Fountainebleau two days before. He wasted no time. He dispersed the group in Nangis, sending the Ballaguets and others into hiding. He took Mimi and Raoul to a safe house just west of Meaux. Then he returned to the south to see what could be done with the circuit. Nangis, he discovered, was crawling with Gestapo and Milice. They were searching houses all over the town and had already discovered several of the circuit's weapons caches. At the farm of André Dubois, the Gestapo discovered weapons and ammunition and shot Dubois on the spot.

Returning to Meaux he felt helpless. More and more of **MINISTER**'s supplies were being discovered in the south, and he had no weapons caches and no Lysander was available. After a time and with the American offensive going well, he went back to Nangis, trying to find out what was left of the circuit. He discovered that about 150 well-armed but poorly trained men were waiting for him. He established contact with local organizations in the area, all sorely in need of supplies, and tried to organize a resistance unit in a large circle around Nangis. The Gestapo had fled, but there were still many German troops in the area and effective operations proved difficult.

Complicating matters further for Désiré, Roger Veillard had returned to France on August 17 and had taken up activities just to the east of Nangis, around Provins. He found the **MINISTER** circuit in shambles, and he did not get along with Désiré. As a result, Désiré, who saw himself as the circuit leader, ignored his commands, and Veillard's contact with the former **MINISTER** circuit diminished.

Several days after Désiré filed his report for F-Section in November 1944, Mimi weighed in. She was furious at headquarters. The arrest of Pierre and Charles was, in her view, "due entirely to the sending of SAS parties in uniform. They were dropped in an area closely patrolled by SS troops who became immediately aware of their arrival and went to investigate. The SAS had already withdrawn . . . to a safe area, but Pierre and Charles were not aware of this and went to contact them and were immediately arrested." There was no direct news about what had happened to them, but Mimi had heard a rumor in Fontainebleau that they had been transported to Germany.

After their arrest she had done her best to keep the **MINISTER** circuit running until the Americans overran the area and she was sent back to Britain. With her she brought a detailed report on the resistance organization and its activities in the area of Jouy, written by the local chief of the gendarmerie, Rémy Jonckheere.

After reading through Mimi's report, Désiré attached a footnote of his own: "I would like to add my word to Mimi's . . . on the marvelous pre-D-Day work done by the Nangis party, which I knew well, and put down in writing all my admiration for Guerin's (Pierre's) organization and work, which was remarkable, and also Mimi's pluck and organization, and for Stephane's (Charles's) tiring work."

Dr. Lecocq told her father first, and her father told her. In the afternoon the doctor had received a telephone call from Paris. At first he did not understand the voice at the other end of the line. It was after all a trunk call, and there was much static on the line. Then he determined that the man at the other end was speaking English. It was difficult to understand, but finally he realized who was speaking and what he was trying to say. "Colette Florin," the man kept repeating, "Colette Florin." It was, of course, Mademoiselle Florin's American, the soldier he had treated in the school during July of last year, before the liberation.

"*Il est vivant*," her father shouted, his voice brimming with joy as he bounded into the forest house. "Monsieur Roy is alive; he is well!"

Seated at the table with her mother, Colette sprang to her feet. Her lips moved but made no sound. "He is in Paris," her father said. "I know no details, but he asks us to meet him tomorrow." Colette's knees almost gave way beneath her.

For months she had tried to get word of him. She thought daily of him and worried. She prayed that he had escaped across the Alps, making it, as he always said he would, back to England. After the liberation she traveled into Paris to make inquiries. She had learned that the serial numbers of prisoners held in Germany were posted regularly at the *état-major*, army headquarters in Paris. On her first trip to explore the list, she met a French officer whose wife had only recently been listed on the board. She was apparently alive in Germany. The officer explained how the system worked, and Colette, armed with Roy's serial number, began to check. Weeks after Roy had left Jouy, she had spotted a curious bit of writing high up on the wallpaper in the studio where Roy slept. Standing on a chair, she read off numbers . . . 0753841, Roy's serial number. At first she had been astonished that he had been so cavalier as to leave this number in her apartment, but had to laugh. So typical of Roy, she thought.

She made many trips to the *état-major* in the following months— October, November, December—and on into the new year. Then one day, as her finger moved down the long list, she stopped and squinted. If it was not a misprint, some administrative error, it was Roy's serial number. She double-checked, reading the numbers aloud to herself as she stood in the crowded place. It was the number. He had been caught after all. There was no other information available, but at least when this report was filed with the Red Cross in January 1945, he had been alive, probably in a stalag somewhere in Germany. She tried to obtain additional information, new leads, but time after time came away with nothing.

Roy had suggested that they meet at the American Officer's Club on the Place Saint Augustin, near the Gare Saint Lazare. Her parents insisted that they come along. Colette hoped to convince Roy to return with them to Jouy, to see his old friends from the resistance, Monsieur Jonckheere and Mayor Pivert. Perhaps he might stay for a while, make a short holiday. The Florins did not have a motorcar, but Monsieur Quignot, a farmer in the neighborhood, volunteered to take them. Not only did he own an automobile, more miraculously, he had petrol.

Roy. She could hardly believe it. There was so much to tell him. He would want to know how Messieurs Jonckheere and Pivert had led an uprising of the *réseau* around Jouy. Germans had been everywhere in the village and on the roads, sweeping to the northeast away from the Americans. One of **MINISTER**'s lieutenants appeared in the village to tell the *réseau* that the paratrooper landing planned by Paul Guérin would not take place and Jonckheere was free to take independent action. On August 25, as the spearheads of the American army approached, Jonckheere mobilized his teams, distributed rifles, grenades, mines, and antitank weapons, and assigned the men to take up blocking positions on the five roads leading into the village. During the night of August 26, the Germans tried to break through. Some Wehrmacht soldiers had taken up a position in the old château on the road to Petit Paris, and a firefight broke out. A local *résistant* had been killed. For several days sporadic fighting went on in the woods around the village. The little group was proud. They had taken seventy-five prisoners, a number of horses, carts, and even a few motorcars.

Pivert bicycled to the Florins' house in the woods to tell them that the liberation was at hand. Rushing into the village, they found American troops passing through Jouy in an endless stream of trucks, armored cars, and tanks. The people of the village lined the narrow streets, threw flowers, and cheered. Perched on top of one of the passing tanks, laughing and waving to the crowd, was a familiar figure. It was, Colette realized, none other than Mimi.

The American Officer's Club was in the eighth arrondissement, and Monsieur Quignot parked his motorcar in a near empty street behind the Madeleine. Colette was nervous. On the ride from Jouy she had been unable to keep up the conversation, and now as they strolled along the sidewalk, searching for the address, her anticipation and anxiety mounted. *"C'est ici,"* her father said, stopping beneath the awning of an ornate cream-colored hotel. They climbed a trio of short steps and entered a well-lit, congested lobby. American officers in their smart dress uniforms were everywhere, standing at the front desk, hovering over the crowded sofas, lounging in the overstuffed chairs.

Then from across the lobby she saw him. He wore a uniform that hung off his shoulders and seemed to billow around his narrow waist. He was thin. The same rough good looks were there, the blue eyes, the broad smile as he caught sight of her, but his face seemed chiseled and taut. Walking with a slight limp, he made his away across the lobby and stopped in front of her. For a moment they stared at one another. Then, without a word, he bent down, drew her to him, and kissed her. It was a long passionate kiss, and from all around the lobby men laughed, and whistled, calling out *"Oh là là!"* Colette dropped her head in dazzled embarrassment. Roy beamed.

"Let's get out of here," he said, laughing his old familiar laugh and patting Monsieur Florin on the back.

Monsieur Quignot knew a restaurant in the area. At a table against the window, they drew up chairs. They ordered wine. At first they all talked at once, laughing and toasting one another. Madame Florin asked Roy about his health; her husband asked about his capture, his captivity; and Colette told him about Jonckheere and Pivert and the woman Mimi at the liberation of Jouy. Roy answered their questions in general terms, not elaborating, providing few details. He seemed embarrassed by his appearance, Colette thought, and although he smiled and laughed and listened to their stories, his eyes were remote, as if he were somewhere else.

Roy wanted to know about Paul Guérin, about his role in the liberation, but they could tell him little. Captain Paul had not been seen in Jouy since July, when he visited Roy in the schoolhouse. Some in the region said he had been captured by the Gestapo, but no one was sure. Maybe he had had to disappear, go underground, and would surface again. This happened frequently in resistance circles. They knew only that in February, long after the liberation of France, Madeleine Ballaguet had received a letter from a woman in the south. She introduced herself as Madame L. Mulsant, the mother of Pierre Mulsant, whom they knew as Paul Guérin.

"I know that my son stayed with you for a long time," she wrote. "I was very touched that you have very good memories of my son and that you gave my daughter-in-law Raymonde a portrait of my son that you had made. It is a consolation and comfort . . . to know that . . . without even worrying about the price . . . he did his duty and that he was respected by those who were around him in these dangerous times. I thank you, Madame, for the services you rendered him. Sadly we have still not a single piece of news of Pierre, and we know absolutely nothing of where they took him. We maintain our confidence and hope that very soon he will come back to us and we will be able to live again in peace."

If anyone could beat the Gestapo, Monsieur Florin said, it was *Capitaine* Paul, and they all agreed. He would turn up. Monsieur Florin asked about Buchenwald, where, he understood, there were many French, but Roy said little. Instead, he told them about *Capitaine* Jacques, about Fresnes, about Stalag Luft III and the snow. He told them about the camp at Nuremberg and the ten-day march that took him to a new camp at Moosburg, about twenty-five kilometers northeast of Munich. On that trek he had slept in haylofts and churches and private houses, anywhere he could find to bed down. The guards found it difficult to maintain order, and groups of prisoners drifted away from the column, stopping at farmhouses to trade cigarettes or soap for something to eat. Some slipped into the pine forests and disappeared. Others dropped back in the formation, which stretched for miles, and stopped for a day or so in a village to rest.

They rarely saw soldiers along their route, and the Germans they did encounter, mostly women and children and old men, were open and friendly. Mostly, they seemed relieved that the end of the war was drawing near. One morning an elderly woman invited him inside and fed him eggs and toast; in another village, a young woman with two small children allowed him to sleep in a vacant room above the kitchen. Her husband was fighting somewhere against the Russians, in the north she thought, but she had had no word from him in weeks. She showed Roy a picture of a Wehrmacht corporal. On his chest, beneath a battle ribbon, was an iron cross.

In most towns, Roy wandered through the streets, bartering and scrounging. When he was hungry, he would go to a front door and knock, hoping to make a trade. If no one answered, he would try the lock and slip inside. He always headed straight for the cellar, where potatoes and other vegetables were stored. Once, he told them, as he hurried from a cellar, stuffing potatoes into his pants, he was met at the door by one of the guards and a gigantic dog. *"Was machen Sie da?"* the soldier shouted, pointing his rifle at Roy's gut. Still holding a potato in each hand, Roy shrugged. "What does it look like I'm doing," he said. "I'm stealing potatoes." For a moment the soldier just stared. The dog let out a low growl. *"Also los, los,"* the soldier said impatiently, motioning Roy back into the street. Roy waddled away, his pants legs bulging with potatoes.

On April 14, he walked through the gates of Stalag VII-A, on the outskirts of Moosburg, about thirty miles northeast of Munich. Elements of the formation had been straggling in for days. He had covered almost one hundred miles in ten days. At Moosburg the over-crowded barracks were splitting at the seams, and he slept on the ground in a large tent with hundreds of other Kriegies, waiting for the Americans to arrive. Two weeks later, on April 29, Patton's Third Army liberated the fifteen thousand POWs at the camp. On that same day, Adolf Hitler committed suicide in his bunker in Berlin.

Roy remained in the camp for over a week, waiting for his evacuation to a POE, port of embarkation, enjoying the luxuries of eating American rations, shaving, and wandering, a free man, through the streets of Moosburg. Hundreds of C-47 transport planes—gooney birds, the men called them—from all over Europe would be landing soon to ferry the men to a POW processing point in France. On May 8, while he waited, the camp loudspeakers crackled with radio broadcasts of the German surrender at Reims and the jubilant celebrations in the streets of London and Paris and New York. The next day, he climbed into an army truck and along with thousands of other POWs was driven in a long convoy to a Luftwaffe base near Landshut. There he boarded a C-47 bound for Camp Lucky Strike, near Le Havre.

Camp Lucky Strike, he discovered, was a gigantic tent camp built around an old French aerodrome that had been taken over and expanded by the Germans. Over twelve thousand large, pyramid-shaped tents stretched out as far as the eye could see. Theaters, hospitals, a PX, even gift shops filled with goods he had not seen in over a year were scattered among the relentless rows of olive drab tents. Someone said the camp held over one hundred thousand POWs, all classified now as RAMPs—Returned Allied Military Personnel. They were processing for the trip back to the United States and home.

For two days Roy marched through line after line, signed forms, and waited. He was deloused, fed breakfast, lunch, and dinner, assigned to a tent with a wooden floor, and given a clean bed with a pillow and fresh sheets. He shaved and showered and was issued a fresh uniform, including shoes that fit. At an orientation for the new arrivals, he figured that he would rank high on the list for rotation back to the States according to an elaborate point system adopted by the army. He was lucky. Some of the guys around him were going to be stuck here for a while.

But as he moved from line to line, all he could think of was Colette. He needed to get to a telephone, either on the base or in the town just adjoining it, and find her. During all the months since his capture he had agonized about her, worried that somehow, because of him, the

Gestapo had found her out. It was a fear he could not shake. Finally, he engineered access to a phone at the camp hospital, and placed a call to Jouy. He was confined to the base, but somehow he would find a way. "*Abkochen,*" he mumbled to himself, "*abkochen.*" After evening mess, he donned his new dress uniform, walked calmly away from his company area, and slipped through the gate. He hitched a ride into Paris with another officer who had both a jeep and a forty-eight-hour pass and who told him about the officer's club at the Plaza Athenée. In the morning he would call Jouy again to arrange the meeting. He had no papers, certainly no pass, but he didn't care. He had done it. He would see Colette.

Now, sitting across from her in the smoky restaurant, he studied her face. It was the face he remembered through the days and nights of Fresnes and Buchenwald and Sagan. She was safe. She had survived. She implored him to come with her to Jouy, to spend a night or two there, to see his old friends, but he refused. He had gone AWOL to get to Paris, he told her, and there would be trouble if the army discovered his absence. He could not go back with her to the village, and they both knew it.

They parted in the early evening in a street near the Gare St. Lazare. He stood at the side of Monsieur Quignot's automobile as Colette and the others climbed in for the trip to Jouy. There were no words to say. Reaching through the open window, he pressed his hand against her face. Then the engine coughed and throttled up. He stepped back and watched the car pull away from the curb. He watched it rumble down the narrow cobblestone street, staring until it disappeared in the Paris darkness. Later that night he made his way back to Camp Lucky Strike. The next morning he began the processing for his return to Philadelphia—and to May.

POSTSCRIPT

Roy Allen returned to the United States in June 1945 to discover that his mother had passed away only days before. After a brief period of recuperation, he was discharged and returned home to Philadelphia. He went on to a successful career in business in Philadelphia and, along with May, raised four children. They visited Jouy several times over the years, and Colette visited them in the United States. Roy Allen died in 1991 at age seventy-three. May Allen still resides in the Philadelphia area. She and Colette have maintained an enduring friendship since the end of the war, writing and speaking on the phone regularly.

Georges Banlier, who hid Roy Allen in Paris, and his friend **Robert Leduc**, who shepherded Roy into Paris and made the contacts with Georges Prévost, survived the war. In 1946 Colette, having gotten Leduc's name from Roy, wrote to him about Roy's time in Paris. Leduc responded immediately. "I was wondering if I would ever get news of Roy Allen," to whom he had written. "I had become a little more friends with this tall and likeable fellow than with the other airmen, and I would be pleased to hear what happened to him after he was taken by the Gestapo. . . . In early August Prévost came to pick up Roy at Georges Banlier's house and we accompanied him to the metro Daumesnil where we said good-bye. I have never seen Roy since.

Prévost told us he gave him up to the usual person he had given other airmen before. . . . Later I heard that all those persons [other airmen given to Prévost] were deported to Germany, the false 'intelligence service' fellow, whom I saw a few minutes while I was [once at Prévost's aparment] was in fact a Gestapo agent and all the airmen Prévost had given him before were also deported."

Denis John Barrett (Honoré, Charles) received the following posthumous evaluation from F-Section: "A grand officer. The ideal W/T operator. Technically perfect. Security first class. Willing to undergo any hardship for the safety of his mission. Unselfish, courageous, outstandingly efficient. A very honest and reliable man, with imagination and guts. One of the best men we ever put into the field."

Warren Bauder survived the trek from Sagan to Nuremberg and then on to Moosburg. He lost contact with Roy on the march from Stalag Luft III and caught only a glimpse of him until the men reached Moosburg. He maintained contact with Roy over the years after the war and lives today in southern California.

Joe Brusse survived the ordeals of Stalag Luft III, Nuremberg, and Moosburg and lives in retirement today in College Station, Texas. For many years he was an aeronautical engineer at the Texas Experimental Engineering Station.

Captain Jacques was a Belgian citizen named Jacques Désoubier, alias Jean Monnet. He was an undercover agent for the Gestapo and was responsible for the arrests of dozens of Allied airmen and SOE agents. He was captured in 1945 just after the war, tried, and executed in 1949. "Heil Hitler" were his last words. His lover, the orange-haired "Madame Orsini," was never tried.

Dr. Erwin Ding was captured by American forces and, although armed with a letter of endorsement from Yeo-Thomas, he committed suicide before his trial.

Colette Florin married Roger Loze, a local forester who had been a leader of the Gaullist resistance in Jouy. Her son Jean-Jacques was captain of a French nuclear submarine before his retirement from the navy. Colette lives today in Jouy-le-Châtel, several blocks from the former École des Filles where she hid Roy Allen.

Yvonne Fontaine (Mimi) survived the war and was recognized in both Britain and France for her work in the resistance. She moved to the south of France where she died in 1996.

Rémy Jonckheere survived the war and remained chief of the gendarmerie in Jouy until 1947. He occupied a similar position in Drancy until his death in 1956 at age fifty-two. For his work in the resistance he was awarded the Médaille Militaire, Croix de Guerre 1939–1945, the Médaille des Volontaires, and Mérite Franco-Britannique.

Colonel James Luper, group commander of the 457th BG, was shot down on October 7, 1944, and was imprisoned in Stalag Luft III. He distinguished himself by his leadership and courage on the "Blizzard March." He died in a plane crash after the war.

For his actions in the war against Nazi Germany, **Pierre Mulsant** was awarded the Military Cross, Chevalier de la Légion d'Honneur, and Croix de Guerre avec Palme. A street in Troyes bears his name. Perhaps the greatest tribute paid to him came from F-Section of SOE after the war: "An absolutely first-rate officer, very brave, very intelligent, and of the best type. His death is a tragedy for France, for he represented the finest type of officer."

SS Sturmführer **Hermann Pister**, commandant of Buchenwald, was captured by American forces shortly after leaving the camp. He was tried for war crimes and condemned to death, but died before the sentence could be executed. Although the military tribunal, which met at Dachau in 1949, sentenced twenty-two of the major SS figures at Buchenwald to death, fewer than half were actually executed. By the mid-1950s German courts had commuted those sentences and freed the prisoners. The remainder were released at the same time.

Georges Prévost and his brother-in-law, **Jean Rocher**, who hid Roy Allen in Paris on the Boulevard Sébastapol, were captured by the Gestapo on August 11, 1944, just after Roy left. They were deported on the same train as Roy and died in Buchenwald. Prévost's sister

Geneviève and his fiancée were also deported by the Nazis and although both survived the camps, they returned to France broken physically and emotionally.

F. F. E. Yeo-Thomas survived his long ordeal in German captivity and was returned to Allied control in 1945. After the war he testified at the trials of the Buchenwald SS and devoted much of his energy to winning recognition for the men who served in or aided SOE in France.

NOTES

Chapter 1: Operation *Amoureuse*

This chapter is based on interviews with Colette Florin Loze, conducted between 1992 and 2001 in Jouy. The events described of the 1940 debacle are taken from her diary of that year. Written in the form of letters to a Canadian friend in 1940, Colette recounted her experiences during the Battle of France. The letters were never sent. They were hidden until after liberation beneath the parquet floor of a neighbor's house. For vivid descriptions of France in May and June, see Herbert R. Lottman, *The Fall of Paris, June 1940* and Noel Barber, *The Week France Fell*. The operational log of 161 Squadron of the RAF, which flew the mission to Jouy on November 6–7, 1943, reports that Flying Officer Bathgate's Lysander took off at 2135. "Checkpoints along route were easily found in spite of poor visibility. Made area at 2305; picked up three passengers and several packages." Public Records Office (PRO), Kew, England. Air 27/1068. Hugh Verity flew many such missions and his *We Landed by Moonlight*, which lists in its log the landing at "Lulli," is an insider's view of Lysander operations in France.

Chapter 2: "Specially Employed"

The extensive personnel files of Pierre Mulsant, Denis Barrett, and Yvonne Fontaine constitute the documentary base for this chapter. Those files contain the history of their training in the various SOE schools, including the evaluations of their officers. The activities of the **TINKER** circuit are derived from the detailed interrogation reports of Pierre Mulsant, November 24, 1943; Denis Barrett, November 20, 1943; and Yvonne Fontaine, November 26, 1943. The reports not only give a detailed account of the circuit's activities but the views of the three on a wide variety of subjects—the Gaullist resistance groups, the mood in

409

France, weapons, personalities, etc., from their time in Troyes. SOE's operational history of the **TINKER** circuit, giving dates for its activities, was also useful. Benjamin Cowburn, nom de guerre Germain, was the leader of **TINKER**, and his *No Cloak, No Dagger* offers an excellent account of the circuit's activities by one of SOE's most successful agents. M. R. D. Foot's *SOE in France* is the standard work on the subject; it places **TINKER** in its broader operational context. Another passenger being smuggled out of France on that Hudson flight of November 17–18, 1943, was François Mitterand, the future president of France.

Chapter 3:   Milk Run
Interviews with Joe Brusse, Gordon Long, Leonard Wright, and May Allen. Gordon Long was a spare gunner who flew with the crew only on the June 14 mission. The Mission Reports of the 457th BG (H) are found in Record Group (RG) 30, National Archives. In a letter to Roland Byers, a historian of the 457th, Roy related his version of the Luper incident following the Dessau mission. Roy Allen to Roland Byers, June 5, 1989, May Allen Collection. Joe Brusse filled in the missing details. Byers's book, *Flak Dodger*, contains a useful description of the June 14 mission. An excellent addition, offering more detailed accounts of all the 457th's missions, is *Fait Accompli: A Historical Account of the 457th Bomb Group (H)*, compiled by Homer Briggs and James L. Bass and edited by John F. Welch. Flight training and life around a wartime training base are given evocative treatment by Samuel H. Hynes's *Flights of Passage* (naval aviation) and Eugene Fletcher's *The Lucky Bastard Club* (Army Air Corps).

Chapter 4:   *Un Aviateur Américain*
Interviews with May Allen and Colette Florin and Florin's written narrative of some of these events represent the documentary core of this chapter. The story of André Knisy is found in Lucien Cariat's article, "L'Épicerie-Buvette de Bannost: une épine dans le flanc allemand en juin 1944," in the *Parisien libéré*, September 8, 1974. Conditions in wartime France are treated in Ian Ousby, *Occupation: The Ordeal of France 1940–1944*, and Pierre Burrin, *France under the Germans*. The standard work on Vichy remains Robert O. Paxton, *Vichy France*.

Chapter 5:   MINISTER
SOE interrogation reports for Roger Veillard (July 2, 1944) and Jean Louis de Ganay (Désiré) offer many details of **MINISTER**'s activities. The personnel file of Yvonne Fontaine (Mimi) is also useful. Veillard wrote two letters to Madeleine Ballaguet (February 5 and 15, 1989), offering more observations and details, and Roger and André Hardy produced a narrative of resistance activities around Nangis in 1944, especially Pierre's. Marcel Ballaguet's "Resumé succinct de mes États de Service dans la Résistance," outlines his work both before and after Pierre's arrival in Nangis. These documents are found in the Ballaguet Collection. A brief published history of resistance in Nangis is found in René-Charles Planck, *La Seine-et-Marne, 1939–1945*, Volume Three, *De la résistance à la victoire*, pp. 176–181. Planck's second volume, *La Seine-et-Marne, 1939–1945: La vie quotidienne sous l'occupation, Dammarie-les-Lys*, 1985, is also very useful for everyday life in the region. See Maurice Buckmaster's *Specially Employed*; M. R. D. Foot, *SOE in France* and *SOE: The Special Operations Executive 1940–1946* for procedures and equipment. A good description of the various

tools of the trade—the S-Phone, Eureka, the Lysander—are found in Pierre Lorain, *Clandestine Operations: The Arms and Techniques of the Resistance 1941–1949*.

Chapter 6:   *Une Chaîne d'Évasion*
Interviews with Colette Florin and her written narrative. In a letter to Colette on January 5, 1946, Robert Leduc tells how he picked Roy up in Bannost and escorted him into Paris. Evasion lines are examined in Sherri Green Ottis, *Silent Heroes: Downed Airmen and the French Underground* and M. R. D. Foot and J. M. Langley, *MI9: Escape and Evasion 1930–1945*; Ian Dear, *Escape and Evasion: Prisoner of War Breakouts and the Routes to Safety in World War Two*.

Chapter 7:   Paris
In 1989 Roy Allen gave an interview for the Holocaust Oral History Archive at Gratz College, and in it he discusses his trip into Paris and his stay there. Robert Leduc's letter to Colette in January 1946 describes Roy's days in the apartment of Georges Banlier in Vincennes, his rendezvous with Georges Prévost, and Prévost's account of turning Roy over "to the usual person." The MIS-X Files, French Resistance, 1945–46 in the National Archives, Record Group 338, are useful here, especially the entries for Georges Michel Prévost and Georges Banlier. Interviews with May Allen filled in the gaps. For life in occupied Paris in the summer of 1944 see David Pryce-Jones, *Paris in the Third Reich: A History of the German Occupation, 1940–1944* and Gilles Perrault and Pierre Azema, *Paris under the Occupation*.

Chapter 8:   Captain Jacques
Captain Jacques was, in fact, Jacques Désoubier, a Belgian double agent who had infiltrated several escape lines and done tremendous damage to SOE circuits as well. See the Désoubier file in the RG 332, National Archives. Robert Leduc's letter to Colette also recounts his delivery of Roy to Prévost and the latter's arrest on August 11. See also Airy Neaves, *Saturdays at MI9*; Sherri Green Ottis, *Silent Heroes*; and Foot and Langley, *MI9*.

Chapter 9:   The Train
Conditions in the train are described in detail by all the men whose depositions were presented at the Buchenwald war crimes trial and listed in the bibliography under National Archives. See also the firsthand accounts collected in Arthur G. Kennis and Stanley Booker, *168 Jump into Hell*. Very useful is Colin Burgess's book *Destination Buchenwald*. Larry Collins, *Is Paris Burning?* offers a vivid description of the trip as well.

Chapter 10:   *Jedem das Seine*
Interviews with Ed Carter-Edwards, a Canadian airman in the group of 168, and Warren Bauder, and Roy Allen's interview with Gratz; Stanley Booker's unpublished manuscript in the archives of the Gedenkstätte Buchenwald is an excellent account of the airmen in Buchenwald, and the depositions of the Allied airmen for the Buchenwald trial as well as the essays in Kennis and Booker, *168 Jump into Hell*, provide powerful testimony of their travail in the camp. See, in particular, the pieces by Jim Hastin, A. G. Kennis, Ray Perry, and

Stanley Booker. There are several excellent books on Buchenwald and its history. *The Theory and Practice of Hell* by Eugon Kogon, a prisoner in the camp from 1937 until 1945, is a work based on the Buchenwald Report compiled by camp prisoners shortly after liberation. The report contains dozens of essays dealing with every aspect of prisoner life. A manuscript copy of the report can be found at the Gedenkstätte Buchenwald. David Hackett has made a translation of that report and an insightful introductory essay in *The Buchenwald Report*. See also, Burgess, *Destination Buchenwald*.

Chapter 11: *Nacht und Nebel*
This account has been pieced together from the comments of Auguste Favier, who sketched the men and remarked on "the caustic commentary of Captain Mulsant"; the recollections of Pierre Pierron, Pierre's good friend in the camp, in the Archives départementales de l'Aube, Troyes; the reports of Alfred Balachowsky, who spoke to men who witnessed the execution of Pierre and Charles; the report on the executions by Otto Storch, *Blockältester* of Block 17; the interrogation report of Maurice Southgate, an SOE survivor of the camp, and his testimony at the Buchenwald trial. Additional details were added by Ottomar Rothmann, the *Blockschreiber* of Block 17, in our interview of June 2001. Christopher Burney's memoir and analysis of Buchenwald, *The Dungeon Democracy*, gives an intelligent and powerful account of the camp and his role in the opposition. His speech to his men is derived from his account. Bruce Marshall's *The White Rabbit* and Mark Seaman's more recent and more expansive *Bravest of the Brave* both tell the riveting story of Yeo-Thomas. I also used Yeo-Thomas's own memoirs in the Imperial War Museum for additional details.

Chapter 12: Alone in the Kingdom of the Dead
Interviews with Warren Bauder and Ed Carter-Edwards, and the Gratz interview with Roy Allen. Documents from the Thüringisches Hauptstaatsarchiv in Weimar, where the papers for Buchenwald are housed, indicate that Roy was formally "released" on November 29, along with the other remaining Allied airmen. Frau Sabine Stein, archivist at the Gedenkstätte Buchenwald, and Ottomar Rothmann, who was responsible for all paperwork relating to prisoners in Block 17, confirmed that a prisoner might be formally released from his block, but sent to the infirmary for several days before his actual release. Roy Allen's letter to Ed Carter-Edwards, May 8, 1981, relates the soup episode. Also Roy's application for ex-POW compensation from the Veterans Administration, August 17, 1952, outlines his treatment at Buchenwald, the twelve-hour work days, his living conditions, and his medical problems. The details of the transfer of the main party of Allied fliers are found in the depositions of the American airmen, the essays in Kennis and Booker, *168 Jump into Hell*, and in Burgess, *Destination Buchenwald*.

Chapter 13: Kriegie
The letters from Roy Allen to May Allen from Stalag Luft III, December 1944, did not reach May until the war was over and Roy was back at home. It is a reflection of Roy's disorientation that he dated the two letters November 7, when he was still in Buchenwald, and not December 7. Interviews with Warren Bauder, Joe Brusse, and Robert Cotterell. Cotterell's book, *POW*, deals with his

encounter with Roy. Roy also described his experiences at Sagan in 1981 letters to the Veteran's Administration and discussed their common experiences with Warren Bauder in an exchange of letters in 1981. There are many firsthand accounts of life in Stalag Luft III, and I have drawn on three in particular. Because the authors were Kriegies in West Compound, these were the most useful: Bob Neary, *Stalag Luft III*; William P. Maher, *Fated to Survive: Memoirs of a B-17 Flying Fortress Pilot/Prisoner of War*; and Cotterell, *POW*. Also, Eugene E. Halmos, Jr., *The Wrong Side of the Fence: A United States Army Air Corps POW in World War II*. Neary, Maher, and Halmos based their accounts on diary entries. I have also drawn on other firsthand accounts of the camp, the most helpful being David Westheimer's *Sitting It Out*.

Chapter 14:   Liberation

Interviews with Colette Loze, May Allen, Joe Brusse, and Warren Bauder constitute the core documentation of this chapter. Roy's Gratz College interview also sheds light on events. For the SOE segment of the chapter I relied on the interrogation reports of Yvonne Fontaine (Mimi), Jean Louis de Ganay (Désiré), and Roger Veillard (SOE archive in the Foreign Office) and the reports of Henri Peulevé, Bernard Guillot, Maurice Southgate, Alfred Balachowsky, and Benjamin Cowburn, Public Record Office, HS6, Security Reports, including interrogation of returning agents. Christopher Burney's *Dungeon Democracy* highlights the noncommunist resistance in Buchenwald. See also David Hackett, *The Buchenwald Report*; Jon Bridgman, *The End of the Holocaust: The Liberation of the Camps*; and Robert Abzug, *Inside the Vicious Heart*.

BIBLIOGRAPHY

Archival Sources

UNITED STATES

National Archives, Washington, D.C.

RG 153, War Crimes Trials

Testimony of U.S. airmen held in Buchenwald:

2nd Lt. Stratton M. Appleman
2nd Lt. Robert H. Brown
2nd Lt. Fredrick W. Carr
2nd Lt. Donat F. Dauteuil
1st Lt. Ralph H. Dearey
S/Sgt. William L. Edge
2nd Lt.William L. Granberry
1st Lt. James D. Hastin
Sgt. William L. Lee
1st Lt. Joseph F. Moser
2nd Lt. Joseph W. Pedersen
1st Lt. Michael Petrich
S/Sgt. Thomas G. Richey
S/Sgt. George W. Scott
1st Lt. Ira E. Vance, Jr.
Sgt. James F. Zeiser

Testimony relating to Buchenwald:

Flight Commander Forest Frederick Edward Yeo-Thomas
Squadron Leader Maurice Southgate, testimony relating to Buchenwald
Josef Mueller (accused) testimony about execution of SOE prisoners at
   Buchenwald

Report of Squadron Leader R. J. Lamason, R.N.Z.A.F., to Delegate of the Protecting Power, Stalag Luft III, November 6–7, 1944

RG 18 Mission Reports, Eighth Air Force
457th Bomb Group—Mission Reports

RG 290 Records of the Escape and Evasion Section (MIS-X)
290/55/27/1: List of French Citizens Who Assisted American Airmen
Histories and Related Records Pertaining to French Evasion Organization and Networks 1945–46. 290/56/1/1
Files on Georges Prévost
Georges Banlier

Office of Air Force History, Bolling Air Force Base, Washington, D.C.
Diary of Stalag Luft III

Simon Gratz College, Holocaust Survivor Collection, Philadelphia
Tape and Transcript of Roy W. Allen interview

Air Force Museum, Wright-Patterson AFB, Dayton, Ohio
Stalag Luft III materials

U.S. Air Force Academy Library, Colorado Springs, Colorado
Stalag Luft III Collection

FRANCE
Archives Départementales de l'Aube, Troyes
Serie: NA 10000. Documents relatifs à la seconde guerre mondiale/Série nouvelles acquisitions. Materials relating to Pierre Mulsant
N.Acq. 10.227 Témoignage de Monsieur Pierron

Archives Départementales de Seine-et-Marne, Melun
Materials relating to Pierre Mulsant, Roger Veillard

Musée de la Résistance et de la Déportation, Besançon
Buchenwald Photographic Collection: Buchenwald Album

Bibliothèque de Documentation internationale contemporaine, Nanterre
Files on resistance organizations in Seine-et-Marne and l'Aube

GREAT BRITAIN
SOE Advisor in the Foreign Office (London)
Interrogation and personnel file of Pierre Mulsant
Interrogation and personnel file of Denis Barrett
Interrogation and personnel file of Yvonne Fontaine
Interrogation and personnel file of Bernard de Ganay
Interrogation and personnel file of Roger Veillard

· Bibliography ·

Public Record Office (Kew)
AIR 27/1068 Operations Record Book of 161 Squadron, November 1943
AIR 27/956 Operations Record Book of 161 Squadron, March 1944
HS6 SOE HS/
    6/437–440 Security Reports, including Interrogations of Returning
       Agents
    Report from Captain Peulevé 23.4.45
    Report by Lt. Bernard Guillot, 12.4.1945
    Further Details given by Lt. Guillot, 15.4.45
    Report of Prof. Balachowsky on Events in Buchenwald, 23.4.45
    Report S/LDM. M. Southgate, no date
    372
    6/585–587
    6/467

Imperial War Museum (London)
    Papers of F. F. E. Yeo-Thomas
    Papers of Denis John Barrett

GERMANY
Archiv der Gedenkstätte Buchenwald, Buchenwald
    Manuscript by Stanley Booker, 52-M-253a
    Bericht von Alfred Balachowsky, 15.5.45
    Bericht über die Ermordung der 32.französischen, englischen,
       kanadischen und belgischen Kameraden, Otto Storch, 31/274
    Bericht über Block 17 des KZ Buchenwald, Paris, 15.5.45. BWA
       Fallschirmjäger (Block 17), 50–2-15/2

Thüringisches Hauptstaatsarchiv, Weimar
    KZ-und Haftanstalten: Buchenwald (KZ-Hafta)
    NS4 Buchenwald

Private Collections
    Papers of M. Ballaguet: Letters, photographs et al. of the Anciens du
       Réseau Guérin-Buckmaster, in the possession of Mme. Ballaguet
    Papers of May Allen: Photographs, letters, and military records of Roy
       Allen
    Papers of Colette (Florin) Loze
       Letter from Robert Leduc, January 5, 1946
       Diary 1940
       Personal Narrative

Interviews
    May Allen
    Vera Atkins
    Madeleine Ballaguet
    Warren Bauder

Joe Brusse
Ed Carter-Edwards
Robert Cotterell
Colette Florin (Loze)
Gordon Long
Ottomar Rothmann
Leonard Wright

Memoirs and Firsthand Accounts

Robert H. Abzug, *Inside the Vicious Heart: Americans and the Liberation of the Nazi Concentration Camps*, New York, 1985.

Bruno Apitz, *Nacht unter Wölfen*, Halle, 1958.

Walter Bartel, ed., *Buchenwald: Mahnung und Verpflichtung*, Berlin, 1960.

Aimé Bonifas, *Détenu 20801 dans les bagnes Nazis*, n.p., 1945.

Jon Bridgman, *The End of the Holocaust: The Liberation of the Camps*, Portland, Ore., 1990.

The Buchenwald Report, translated by David Hackett, Boulder, Colo., 1995.

M. J. Buckmaster, *Specially Employed*, London, 1952.

——, *They Fought Alone*, London, 1958.

Christopher Burney, *The Dungeon Democracy*, London, 1945.

——, *Solitary Confinement*, London, 1952.

Peter Churchill, *Of Their Own Choice*, London, 1954.

Marcel Conversy, *Quinze mois à Buchenwald*, Geneva, 1945.

Robert Cotterell, *POW*, Philadelphia, 2000.

Benjamin Cowburn, *No Cloak, No Dagger*, London, 1960.

Eugene E. Halmos, Jr., *The Wrong Side of the Fence: A United States Army Air Corps POW in World War II*, Shippensburg, Pa., 1996.

Pierre Julitte, *Block 26: Sabotage at Buchenwald*, New York, 1971.

Arthur G. Kinnis and Stanley Booker, *168 Jump into Hell: A True Story of Betrayed Allied Airmen*, Victoria, B.C., n.d.

Rolf Kralovitz, *ZehnNullNeunzig in Buchenwald: ein jüdischer Häftling erzählt*, Cologne, 1996.

Pierre Lalande, *Special Agent: The Wartime Memoirs of Guido Zembsch-Schreve*, London, 1996.

William P. Maher, *Fated to Survive: Memoirs of a B-17 Flying Fortress Pilot/ Prisoner of War*, Spartanburg, N.C., 1992.

Frédéric Manhes, *Buchenwald: L'organisation et les actions clandestines des déportés français, 1944–1945*, Paris, 1953.

Rene G. Marnot, *Dix-huit mois au Cagne de Buchenwald: Dessins de Jaquemin*, Paris, 1945.

Bob Neary, *Stalag Luft III: Sagan . . . Nuernberg . . . Moosburg—A Collection of German Prison Camp Sketches with Descriptive Text Based on Personal Experiences*, North Wales, Pa., 1946.

Airey Neave, *Saturday at MI.9*, London, 1969.

Frank Pickersgill, *The Making of a Secret Agent*, Nova Scotia, 1983.

Jacques R. E. Poirier, *The Giraffe Has a Long Neck*, London, 1995.

Walter Poller, *Arztschreiber in Buchenwald: Bericht des Häftling 996 aus Block 36*, Offenbach, Germany, 1960.

Jean Puissant, *La Colline sans oiseaux: 14 mois à Buchenwald*, Paris, 1945.

André Rougeyron, *Agents for Escape: Inside the French Resistance*, Baton Rouge, 1996.

Delmar T. Spivey, *POW Odyssey: Recollections of Center Compound Stalag Luft III and the Secret German Peace Mission in World War II*, Attleboro, Mass., 1984.

Jerrard Tickell, *Moon Squadron*, New York, 1958.

Leslie J. Tyler, *Wild Blue Yonder: An Adventure of Hitler's Hostages*, Grawn, Mich., 1992.

Hugh Verity, *We Landed by Moonlight: Secret RAF Landings in France, 1940–1944*, revised edition, Trowbridge, England, 1995.

Philippe de Vomecourt, *An Army of Amateurs*, New York, 1961.

David Westheimer, *Sitting It Out: A World War II POW Memoir*, Houston, 1992.

Ernst Wiechert, *Der Totenwald: Ein Bericht—Tagebuchnotizen und Briefe*, Munich, 1957.

Selected Secondary Sources

Noel Barber, *The Week France Fell*, New York, 1976.

Colin Burgess, *Destination Buchenwald*, Kenthurst, Australia, 1995.

Roland Byers, *Flak Dodger: A Story of the 457th Bomb Group During World War II*, Moscow, Idaho, 1985.

Larry Collins, *Fall from Grace*, New York, 1986.

Larry Collins and Dominique Lapierre, *Is Paris Burning?*, New York, 1965.

E. H. Cookeridge, *Set Europe Ablaze*, New York, 1967.

Ian Dear, *Escape and Evasion: Prisoner of War Breakouts and the Routes to Safety in World War II*, London, 1997.

Arthur A. Durand, *Stalag Luft III*, New York, 1988.

Fait Accompli: A Historical Account of the 457th Bomb Group [H], compiled by Homer Briggs and James L. Bass, edited by John F. Welch.

M. R. D. Foot, *SOE in France*, London, 1966.

———, *MI9: Escape and Evasion, 1939–1945*, Boston, 1980.

———, *SOE: 1940–1946*, London, 1984.

Eugen Kogon, *The Theory and Practice of Hell*, New York, 1980.

Rita Kramer, *Flames in the Field: The Story of Four SOE Agents in Occupied France*, London, 1995.

Herbert R. Lottman, *The Fall of Paris: June 1940*, New York, 1992.

Bruce Marshall, *The White Rabbit*, London, 1952.

Mark Seaman, *Bravest of the Brave: The True Story of Wing Commander "Tommy" Yeo-Thomas—SOE Secret Agent—Codename "The White Rabbit,"* London, 1997.

AUTHOR'S NOTE

In the Shadows of War is a work of historical nonfiction. It is based on extensive interviews, diaries, letters, debriefing reports, courtroom testimony, military records, and government documents in Britain, France, Germany, and the United States. I have also drawn on many memoirs and firsthand accounts by survivors of the events depicted here. In researching the book, I have used the critical investigative methods employed by professional historians, but in telling the story, I have relied on literary devices more commonly associated with fiction. The events and people depicted here are real, and I have tried to portray them as faithfully as possible. In presenting some scenes, I have reconstructed conversations, but the ideas and sentiments and in some cases the exact wording are those of the individuals themselves, drawn from interviews, letters, interrogation reports, and other sources.

In reconstructing Pierre Mulsant's time in Buchenwald, for example, I was able to piece together firsthand accounts from postwar reports by Alfred Balachowsky, Auguste Favier, Pierre Pierron, Otto Storch, and Maurice Southgate, all of whom knew and interacted with Mulsant in the camp. Similarly, in recounting Roy's experiences on the train from Paris and his experiences in Buchenwald I drew on interviews with Warren Bauder and Ed Carter-Edwards and on the testimony of fifteen American airmen who were deposed in 1945 for the

421

war crimes trials of the SS camp leaders. These were supplemented by the firsthand accounts of over two dozen other Allied fliers imprisoned at Buchenwald collected in a privately published volume edited by Arthur G. Kinnis and Stanley Booker, who were themselves prisoners at Buchenwald.

I have also tried to re-create the interrelated experiences of Roy, Colette, and Pierre, as they understood them at the time, knowing only what they knew, without the intrusive—and distancing—presence of an omniscient narrator. The goal is to allow readers not only to observe and analyze the Second World War and the "ordinary" people who experienced it, but to put readers in the action, to allow them to see it, smell it, and feel it; in short, to make those ghastly, exhilarating, horrific, and inspiring times come alive in all their human complexity.

ACKNOWLEDGMENTS

The research and writing of this book have extended over a decade, and many people have contributed to the project, either directly or indirectly. Joe Brusse, Leonard Wright, and Gordon Long shared their memories of the Roy Allen crew, and especially their fateful June 14 mission to France. Joe Brusse, Roy's closest friend on the crew, was especially helpful, offering documents, recollections, and constructive criticism. I understand why Roy had such faith in his unflappable navigator. Coupled with the records of 457th Bomb Group (H) and the German captivity reports in the National Archives, they allowed me to reconstruct the crew's training and combat experiences.

Warren Bauder's memories of his time with Roy at Buchenwald and later at Stalag Luft III were invaluable. Warren kindly talked to me over the years, taking time to answer detailed questions about unpleasant experiences, and I am deeply grateful. Ed Carter-Edwards, a Canadian Royal Air Force veteran and Buchenwald survivor who was in the last batch of Allied airmen to leave Buchenwald, was always ready to help in any way, providing memories, documents, and addresses of other Buchenwald survivors from the group of imprisoned Allied fliers.

In France, Madeleine Ballaguet was able to offer letters and several firsthand accounts by members of the **MINISTER** circuit from her collection of documents as well as her own vivid observations of the personal and professional interactions of **MINISTER**'s leading figures. She and her husband hid Pierre, Charles, and Mimi in Nangis, and she knew them well. The staff of the Archives Départementales de l'Aube in Troyes provided me with many important materials, including the report of Pierre Pierron, who met Pierre Mulsant in Buchenwald, tried to save his life, and finally took him to a priest on the last night of Mulsant's life.

In England, M. R. D. Foot patiently guided me through the labyrinthian practices of SOE, making a heroic—and, I hope, successful—effort to save me from numerous errors. Duncan Stuart, SOE Advisor in the Foreign and Commonwealth Office, granted me access to the highly revealing personnel files and debriefing reports of Pierre Mulsant, Denis Barrett (Charles), Yvonne Fontaine (Mimi), Roger Veillard, and Jean-Louis de Ganay (Désiré). Mark Seaman of the Imperial War Museum, and the author of an excellent book on Yeo-Thomas, offered sound counsel on SOE documents and personnel.

In Germany, Sabine Stein of the Gedenkstätte Buchenwald provided documents and her considerable knowledge of the camp and its structures, and Dieter Mareck of the Thüringisches Hauptstaatsarchiv in Weimar extended himself above and beyond the call of duty. At a time when the archive had officially closed the Buchenwald files for restoration, not to be reopened for three years, Herr Mareck allowed me access to crucial camp documents. I am also indebted to Ottomar Rothmann, the secretary (*Blockschreiber*) of Block 17 in Buchenwald. Speaking from his own experience (he was a prisoner in Buchenwald for over three years), he explained camp policies and procedures, especially as they pertained to Block 17, where Pierre and Charles were held. He remembered the thirty-seven SOE men well.

In the United States, the staff of the Gratz College Holocaust Oral History Archive found the tape and transcript of Roy Allen's 1989 interview, allowing me to hear the voice of a man I had never met but had learned so much about. The staffs of the National Archives, the Office of Air Force History at Bolling Air Force Base in Washington, the U.S. Air Force Academy Collections Division, and the U.S. Air Force Museum archives in Dayton, Ohio, were also unflinchingly helpful. Professor Terry Issacs of Levelland, Texas, kindly shared addresses and notes from his early research on the Buchenwald airmen. Finally, Bruce Kuklick and Elizabeth Block, good friends and tough critics, read an early version of the manuscript, as did Jean Stromberg, all offering sound advice.

But the real pillars of this project are, of course, Colette Florin Loze and May Allen. Colette not only granted me numerous interviews over the years but access to family pictures, her own narrative of events, and her diary of 1940. Without her detailed recollections of Roy's time in Jouy, this book could never have been written. During the ten years I've been privileged to know her, she has always been helpful, divulging information cautiously, little by little, in bits and pieces, leaving me to connect the dots. As I told her on one occasion, I know why the Germans never caught her. Among her many contributions to the book, she showed me around Jouy and Chenoise, taking me to all the important sites of the story. She also introduced me to Madeleine Ballaguet.

May Allen shared her experiences and recollections of her husband with me, providing letters, telegrams, photographs, and military records. It was May who led me to Colette and to Joe Brusse and Warren Bauder. More than anyone, she brought Roy to life for me. After his return to the United States in 1945 Roy talked to May in detail about his experiences in Europe. He did not tell "war stories," but recounted incidents and people with considerable care. Sometimes, in the retelling of these incidents over the years, especially to outsiders, he abbreviated, using a sort of shorthand. Dates and names, especially of other inmates at Buchenwald, sometimes varied and had to be verified, but the central thrust of his recollections remained unswerving and, insofar as I have been able to check the details against official records or other eyewitness accounts, remarkably accurate. May's unflagging enthusiasm for the project, her extraordinary memory, and her patience with my many questions and requests have been exceptional. My respect for her and my gratitude for her tireless support are boundless.

George Allen, Roy's third son, first brought his father's remarkable odyssey through wartime Europe to my attention shortly after Roy's death in 1991. His enduring love for his dad and his determination to see Roy's story told have been an inspiration to me throughout the years of work on this book.

Finally, I wish to thank my wife, Kristen Childers, whose expertise in French history, knowledge of the country, and ease with the language opened new vistas to me. She has enriched this book—and my life—beyond compare.

INDEX

427

About the Author

Thomas Childers is the Sheldon and Lucy Hackney Professor of History at the University of Pennsylvania. He is the author and editor of four books about National Socialism and World War II. An internationally recognized expert on World War II and the Third Reich, he has consulted for and appeared on numerous television programs in the United States and Europe. He has held visiting professorships at Trinity Hall, Cambridge, Smith College, and Swarthmore College, and he has lectured in London, Oxford, Berlin, Munich, and other universities in the United States and Europe. He lives outside Philadelphia in Media, Pennsylvania.